1997

University of St. Francis
G   378.1 B558
Teaching well and liking it :

3 0301 00073144 4

W9-DAL-909

Teaching Well and Liking It

Teaching Well and Liking It

Motivating Faculty to Teach Effectively

EDITED BY JAMES L. BESS

LIBRARY
College of St. Francis
JOLIET, ILLINOIS

THE JOHNS HOPKINS UNIVERSITY PRESS
Baltimore and London

© 1997 The Johns Hopkins University Press
Chapter 13 © 1993, 1997 Stephen A. Stumpf and Violina P. Rindova
Chapter 19 © 1997 Martin Trow
All rights reserved. Published 1997
Printed in the United States of America on acid-free recycled paper
06 05 04 03 02 01 00 99 98 97   5 4 3 2 1

The Johns Hopkins University Press
2715 North Charles Street
Baltimore, Maryland 21218-4319
The Johns Hopkins Press Ltd., London

Library of Congress Cataloging-in-Publication Data will be found at
the end of this book.
A catalog record for this book is available from the British Library.

ISBN 0-8018-5364-8

378.1
B558

Contents

158,274

Introduction

The effectiveness of any system of higher education is contingent in some considerable measure on the quality of the teaching enterprise. What is learned, how much is learned, and progress in the psychosocial maturation of the learner depend importantly on the willingness of faculty to devote long hours to preparation and execution of the tasks of teaching. The sources of the motivation for this task and the conditions that inhibit or suppress it are the subject of this book. The collection of papers addresses the issues both theoretically and practically, drawing on the variety of academic and hands-on experiences of authors from many fields.

Challenging work opportunities and viable careers are not only necessary for economic well-being in societies, they also provide in organizational settings significant sources of personal identity and satisfaction. These latter are, in turn, some of the motivational ingredients needed for effective performance. Strong motivation is almost invariably a key to commitment, sustained effort, and creativity.

These observations about work and motivation in organizations in general apply as well to colleges and universities. The occupation of college professor is widely viewed as providing prodigious opportunities for identity formation and performance satisfaction and is high in public prestige. It is little wonder, then, that many are attracted to it. Nevertheless, the general public (including prospective faculty members) and the academic world are remarkably naive about the tasks that faculty members must perform in their work and about the nature of the occupational life they typically follow. The work is exceedingly difficult and requires a dedication to tasks that is initiated and must be sustained by strong motivation. (An underlying premise of the book, largely unstated throughout the chapters, is that "motivation" is a legitimate [read "real"] psychological construct, that something meaningful can be said about it [it doesn't "deconstruct" to meaninglessness], and that saying some things may lead to better understanding and perhaps even to action that will affect people's lives—particularly faculty and their student charges.)

In tasks requiring successive, unique qualitative judgments, as in teaching and research, unmotivated persons perform less well over the long run than do motivated ones. Thus, it is important to identify both enhancers and depressors of motivation. Workers can be motivated for good and bad reasons. They can be induced to work hard, or they can be constrained to do so. Administrators in colleges and universities worry about how to induce faculty to devote energy and attention to teaching, how to keep them committed to it, and how to recommit those who have drifted from it. Students and their parents dearly wish that faculty would become more dedicated to their teaching responsibilities. And faculty themselves experience guilt and disappointment at their own perceived failure to find sufficient satisfactions in their teaching to spur them on to high-quality work.

There are extraordinary satisfactions to be obtained in professorial activity but also many frustrations. Most faculty in American higher education suffer from role strain and role overload. They are required or elect to perform a great many tasks in a limited time frame, a fair number of which they do not like or are relatively unprepared to do (Bess, 1982). It is well known, for example, that faculty are poorly trained to perform as teachers. And although most faculty are somewhat better prepared to do research, there are frequently many frustrations in that work, stemming from inadequate funding, poor research facilities, insufficient or conflicting colleague interaction, and administrators who impose evaluation criteria that are unrealistic. The result is a degree of organizationally ineffective role performance as well as faculty who are not fulfilled in their work.

Despite these many difficulties and frustrations in teaching and research, however, most faculty claim to enjoy the professoriate; they say now that they would not have chosen another profession and would not now choose to give it up if given the opportunity. Although the proportion of time spent on teaching versus other roles varies across different types of institutions, even in universities, teaching is usually not considered a second-order priority among the tasks of a faculty member (Boyer, 1989,

1990). Research literature shows that even if given the opportunity, university faculty would reduce their weekly hours devoted to teaching by less than 10 percent. Teaching addresses some critical human developmental needs not only of the student but also of the faculty member. The rewards of self-demonstrated knowledge and competency, of facilitating the growth and development of others, and of warmth and intimacy have been well documented. Teaching forges new visions for teachers and students, opens vistas for further explorations, and empowers naive selves to greater imagination and self-initiated action. Good teaching is an aesthetic experience, enjoyable in the unselfconscious act of creation as well as in the cognitive hindsight of achievement.

Unfortunately, the personal, psychological salience of the joys, excitements, and life-fulfilling rewards of teaching is often subdued. The extraordinary potential of teaching and the evidence of its realization are suppressed through custom, norms, and formal role expectations, and, to some extent, because of an innate insensitivity (or lack of sensitivity training of faculty) to the classroom and other cues that give pleasure in teaching.

Interestingly, so too are the negative aspects of teaching unremarked. In part, this is due to the psychological necessity for workers in general to deny having made poor career decisions. With relatively few opportunities to move out of the academic world, faculty are constrained to believe and report that their interests are best served by staying within it. Or, if they admit openly to their frustrations, they are seen by others either as unable to overcome the adversity in their work lives or as psychologically maladjusted. The alleged lack of sufficient rewards from teaching to offset the emotional drain of preparation and performance results in a disinclination to discuss teaching, which in turn makes for an unreceptive audience for the too rarely expressed exaltations of success and pleasure, further inhibiting the airing of feelings and ideas. In short, teaching is an infrequent topic of conversation among faculty except for curricular and formal evaluation purposes.

Teaching well—and liking it—is very hard to come by. Like sports (and even chess, as Csikszentmihalyi notes), it requires extremely high energy, focus, and *total* commitment. Teaching is not a part-time job. It is also risky (or should be). It necessitates (in a Western sense) a continual testing of self as presumed expert—a perpetual and insistent questioning of one's basic understanding of society and of one's assumptions about and understanding and mastery of one's own field and of the field of education. It demands competency in the intricacies of teaching methods.

There are many obstacles to effectiveness in teaching, beginning with the diversity of student backgrounds, talents, and interests, through the ineffability of goals, the subtlety and ambiguity of signs of success, and often innate faculty indispositions to seek satisfactions in teaching (Bess, 1977).

Rather than view these positive and negative conditions as manipulable variables to improve teaching directly, this book considers them as having important relevance to issues of improving the antecedent prerequisite—the *motivation* to teach. The authors of the chapters in this book provide fresh insights into these issues. The chapters examine both the elements that suppress motivation and those that enhance it. The sources of the insights and solutions are a diverse set of academic literatures too rarely invoked in consideration of teaching motivation but replete with potentially highly relevant material.

The book is organized around themes that represent three related but separate realms of influence on faculty teaching behavior (cf. Bess, 1977, 1992; Katzell & Thompson, 1990b; Kanfer, 1990). Moving from inside to outside, the realms include (1) self- or personally driven conditions, (2) local organizational conditions, and (3) systemwide conditions.

These multiple approaches presume that there are many ways to inquire into the reasons for faculty motivation to teach and that there are, of necessity, many, sometimes redundant, modes of influence (cf. von Bertalanffy, 1950; Katzell & Thompson, 1990a). The authors of the chapters in this volume were selected because of their special expertise in a widely diverse set of subdisciplines. Hence, their perspectives bring to bear a broad group of theories on the complications of motivating faculty to teach. It is this multidisciplinary lens that sharpens the focus on a highly diffuse subject matter. But as the phenomena are complex, so also are the projected solutions. Parsimonious explanations at the practical level are difficult to develop.

The organization of the book is as follows. First, a three-chapter overview of the subject considers both theoretical perspectives available from the psychological literature on motivation and extant practical knowledge in the field of faculty in higher education. In the first paper, to prepare us for the theoretical underpinnings of the papers that follow, Charles Walker and Cynthia Symons provide an overview of theories of motivation which may have applicability to faculty as teachers. Wilbert McKeachie, in the second chapter, then takes us on an encapsulated tour of the accumulated wisdom as well as the myths about faculty motivation to teach drawn from the research and other literature. Many of these theories and the alleged wisdom, however, are grounded in some tenuous assumptions about "human nature" that may undermine their validity. In

Chapter 3, consequently, Judith Glazer, using a feminist perspective on motivation theories, reveals some potentially damaging biases in traditional theories and suggests how some feminist theory has previously unrecognized relevance to the teaching enterprise.

This first part is followed by chapters exploring the application of two different sets of motivation theories—Part Two comprising theories of internal (or intrinsic) motivation, and Part Three composed of theories falling into the external category. Deci, Kasser, and Ryan, in Chapter 4, introduce their theory of "self-determination" as a means of understanding how faculty behave. Self-determination proposes that individuals have certain innate needs that can be satisfied through growth opportunities, such as those that may be present through teaching. Relatedly, Csikszentmihalyi, in the following chapter, focuses on how experiencing pleasure in the here and now—enjoying the "flow"—leads to sustained motivation.

The authors in Part Three tend to see motivation as stemming largely from individual awareness of incentives and disincentives available in the environment. In a refreshing return to some older theories, Walter Nord, in Chapter 6, reintroduces us to behavior modification as an explanation of faculty motivation to teach. Following this, Rick Mowday and Sang Nam imaginatively apply contemporary expectancy theory to faculty in their teaching roles, while in Chapter 8, Latham, Daghighi, and Locke share their insights about how the creative setting of goals can enhance the motivation to teach.

The chapters in Part Four cover a diverse variety of conditions in the typical academic worker's environment to reveal the impact of those conditions on faculty motivation. The chapters deal with cultural and structural conditions in the typical academic organization and with the ways in which leadership can utilize them in service of greater motivation. The last two chapters in this section are concerned with the impact of information about students on faculty motivation.

In Chapter 9, Jan Beyer applies her own and others' theories of organizational culture to the college or university, showing how academic norms evolve and may be conducive to or may inhibit teaching motivation. In Chapter 10, Tim Hall and Max Bazerman reveal how organizational structures can themselves constrain faculty from dedicating themselves to teaching, even in the presence of personal motivation to do so. Since structures respond (or should respond) to the technological imperatives of the work, it is critical that attention be paid to the rapid new technological developments in the delivery of teaching services. Because these new modes of teaching also contain subtle and potentially insidious "demotivators," it is important to anticipate how they will affect the motivation to teach. Addressing this question in Chapter 11, Diane Dunlap cautions that many faculty will need to be reoriented to seek quite different personal satisfactions from teaching in the light of these technological advances.

Culture, structure, and technology constitute "levers" for action by skilled leaders. All three can be imaginatively manipulated in the service of improving teaching, as Jerry Hunt and Arja Ropo illustrate in their description in Chapter 12 of the introduction of a new curriculum at one university.

Chapters 13 and 14 reveal some of the sources of faculty motivation stemming from student feedback of one kind or another. Daryl Smith notes that the current and anticipated increases in the diversity of students present both a challenge and an opportunity for faculty to become more involved in teaching. In the final chapter in this section, Stumpf and Rindova show how limited are our present means of assessing student learning, not only in validly measuring that learning but in providing feedback to faculty that can be motivating for them.

The chapters in Part Five expand the range of potential influences on faculty motivation to teach. Stetar and Finkelstein begin the section by pointing out what kinds of individuals are induced to select the academic profession and how their backgrounds may influence their susceptibility to be motivated by the conditions they find in their work settings. Blackburn's chapter considers the question of whether the phases in the typical career paths of faculty can explain changes in their motivation to teach. They cannot, says Blackburn. Dot Finnegan, in Chapter 17, continues to explore the faculty career by looking at how the academic labor market operates to inhibit cross-institutional movement that might improve faculty motivation to teach. In the final two chapters in this section, the locus of attention moves outside the college or university boundaries. Jack Schuster explores the question in Chapter 18 of whether there is a role for public policy in support of better teaching motivation—just as public policy can and does affect the motivation to conduct research. To help us avoid too parochial a perspective on faculty motivation to teach, Martin Trow concludes this part with a picture of the British academics and their current political and structural postures on teaching.

Part Six comprises two chapters. The first, by Robert Menges, recapitulates the traditional approaches to "faculty development," particularly with respect to teaching motivation, and then reconceptualizes the topic in the light of the preceding chapters. The final chapter attempts to capture the highlights of the book, relying in part on the insights of the previous chapters and in part on some different perspectives that emerge from their juxtaposition and integration.

No one book alone can include all of the approaches to understanding the complexity of human behavior, even in a limited domain of work. This book is no exception. Indeed, for a variety of reasons (including space limitations), some critical areas have admittedly been neglected. There are, nevertheless, at least three merits to bringing together at least some of the broad and varied modes of understanding faculty motivation to teach included in this volume. One is that the book offers an overview of the richness and variety of outlooks that should be useful to would-be change agents. A second is that the subject matter is intrinsically interesting to consider. The third is that the array of new conceptualizations become "data" for further scholarship, making possible a more integrated explanation of the phenomena. It is hoped that readers will find all three of value.

References

Bess, J. L. (1977). The motivation to teach. *Journal of Higher Education, 48,* 243–258.
Bess, J. L. (1980). The profession: Critical themes for development. In J. L. Bess (Ed.), *Academic work: Doing it well/doing it better* (pp. 4–10), Proceedings of a conference at Teachers College, Columbia University, April 14–15, 1978 (ERIC Document, ED180 289).
Bess, J. L. (1982). *University organization: A matrix analysis of the academic professions.* New York: Human Sciences Press.
Bess, J. L. (1992). Collegiality: Toward a clarification of meaning and function. In J. C. Smart (Ed.), *Higher education: Handbook of theory and research* (Vol. 8, pp. 1–36). New York: Agathon Press.
Boyer, E. L. (1989). Foreword to Carnegie Foundation for the Advancement of Teaching, *The condition of the professoriate: Attitudes and trends, 1989.* Princeton: Carnegie Foundation for the Advancement of Teaching.
Boyer, E. L. (1990). *Scholarship reconsidered: Priorities of the professoriate.* Princeton: Carnegie Foundation for the Advancement of Teaching.
Kanfer, R. (1990). Motivation theory and industrial and organizational psychology. In M. E. Dunnette & L. M. Hough (Eds.), *Handbook of industrial and organizational psychology* (2d ed., Vol. 1, pp. 75–170). Palo Alto, CA: Consulting Psychologists Press.
Katzell, R. A., & Thompson, D. E. (1990a). An integrative model of work attitudes, motivation, and performance. *Human Performance, 3*(2), 63–85.
Katzell, R. A., & Thompson, D. E. (1990b). Work motivation, theory and practice. *American Psychologist, 45*(2), 144–153.
von Bertalanffy, L. (1950). The theory of open systems in physics and biology. *Science, 111,* 23–29.

I

Approaches to
Studying the
Motivation to Teach

1 The Meaning of Human Motivation

CHARLES J. WALKER AND
CYNTHIA SYMONS

Dr. Ralph Connors and Dr. Carol Raynor have been colleagues for eleven years. They have adjoining offices in the modern science center of Eastern State University. Both teach introductory physics to undergraduates. They have much in common, but they are entirely different teachers. Among the undergraduates, Dr. Connors is known as "Dr. Snores." As he lectures, Ralph has the curious habit of looking down at his weathered boots while constantly counting and recounting his pocket change. Occasionally his right hand emerges from the side of the podium to add emphasis to what is being said or to flip pages. But only his hand is animated. His speech is soft and slow. There is little life in what he says or in the way he says it. All the fraternities have copies of his notes, copies of copies that date from 1984. But he is popular with them because "Snores only gives two multiple-guess tests, and if you've got his notes, you can skate his class."

Dr. Raynor has a different reputation on campus. Students call her Dr. Rap because in the spring of 1990 she invited to class a local group to rap about Ohm's law. Midway through their performance she suddenly turned off the lights and told her two hundred students to join in: "The louder you sing, the brighter the lights will become." Sing they did, much louder than she ever expected. The lights swiftly rose to glaring intensity and then flickered and began to fail. After their applause she said, "Now let's talk about the role that resistance can play when circuits get overloaded."

Carol no longer needs the rap group; it has become a tradition for students to rap on their own on the day that Ohm's law is scheduled. She constantly works on her teaching. She enjoys physics and shares her enthusiasm with students. When asked by a campus reporter about the best class she ever taught, she replied "Teaching is a work in progress; I've been pleased with some of my classes, but I have yet to teach my best class."

Although it may be obvious that Carol has more motivation to teach than Ralph, the reason is not as evident. Human motivation is complex. When we attempt to explain why one teacher is more motivated than another, we must consider all the internal and external variables that affect behavior and use the most veridical theories to account for the differences. We must try to answer what is perhaps the oldest question in human history, Why do people do what they do?

What Is Motivation?

Until recently the concept of motivation was considered obsolete by most research psychologists. Courses on it were dropped, and the American Psychological Association considered replacing it as a search term in the Psychological Abstracts. As a concept, it had too much meaning and therefore was not very useful. To some extent, the present text has inherited this problem. However, several new theories have been published which provide better definitions of human motivation. These new theories constrain the meaning of human motivation and provide surer footing for those who want to do research on it or design interventions to enhance it.

Drawing on these new theories, in this chapter we define motivation as "the conditions and processes that activate, direct, and sustain behavior." However, before turning to current views of human motivation, we would like to review some classic ideas on motivation.

Old Answers to an Old Question

Teaching was an honored profession among the ancient Greeks. Philosophers such as Thrasymachus and Socrates gave vivid accounts of teachers and the reactions of students to them. How would Thrasymachus and Socrates react to the teaching of Dr. Connors and Dr. Raynor? Thrasymachus believed that human beings are motivated only by self-interest. To guard against the inherently hedonistic tendencies of people, he felt that rules and guidelines had to be established and enforced to protect society. Thrasymachus would probably conclude that Ralph was taking advantage of a laissez-faire culture of teaching. In this same culture, Carol was motivated by self-interest too; he might guess that she taught the way she did because she needed the adoration of students.

In contrast, Socrates believed that people are motivated to do what is right. Although he conceded that people may not know what is right, once they do know what is right, even against their own self-interest, they will do the right thing. Socrates would probably say that Ralph had poor mentors and never acquired standards for excellent teaching whereas Carol was privileged to be schooled by great teachers. To make Ralph more motivated, Socrates would suggest simply exposing him to inspiring teachers and declaring exactly what the standards of good teaching are. While Thrasymachus would agree that standards must be declared, he would say it is naive to rely on Ralph's presumed tendency to do something right for its own sake; in addition, he would penalize bad teaching and reward good teaching.

The views of Thrasymachus and Socrates on human motivation are quite modern; in particular, their ideas underpin current theories that focus on external or internal causes of behavior. In the present text, Parts Three, Four, and Five emphasize external influences on behavior, whereas Part Two and some chapters in Part Four (e.g., assimilated organizational culture) emphasize internal influences on behavior. Several chapters integrate these views—in particular, the chapters on intrinsic motivation, goal setting, self-determination, and flow theory. In turn, we now introduce these modern theories of human motivation.

External Influences on Human Motivation

Learning and Reward Systems

Through the writings of Thomas Hobbes, the ideas of Thrasymachus have made their way into modern learning theory. A fundamental assumption of the theories of Pavlov and Skinner is that the external environment controls behavior. Motivation is an unnecessary concept. According to this view, Ralph and Carol merely express different behaviors in the classroom; internal states such as their motivations and emotions are irrelevant. Both are attempting to obtain reinforcement and avoid punishment. Ralph stares at his boots because he is escaping and avoiding the bored looks of his students. Carol involves students because she has been rewarded for doing this in the past. Students control her too. Carol would appear to lack motivation with a class that did not respond to her. Conversely, Ralph might appear to have a great deal of motivation with students to whom he had not acquired a conditioned fear response; for example, he might display more enthusiasm around friendly graduate students. According to the theory of Pavlov, Ralph's fear of students in his large classes could be reduced by counterconditioning, or according to the theory of Skinner, he could be trained to reinforce students in his large classes when they express friendly nonverbal behaviors like those of his graduate students. Either method would make Ralph *look* more motivated.

Through a similar management of the environment, reward systems influence behavior. Like behavior modification, reward systems assume that extrinsic rewards exert more influence on behavior than intrinsic rewards. In individual-centered cultures, merit pay systems and bonus systems have been shown to increase productivity and decrease costs (Lawler, 1981). On the surface it would appear that merit pay systems would be useful in higher education. However, defining good teaching performance, measuring it, and then gaining consensus to implement a reward system to reinforce it is a difficult endeavor (Schuster & Zingheim, 1992). For example, Ralph might teach better if his pay was contingent on the amount of learning of his students. But Ralph could be handicapped because Carol attracts more capable students. Moreover, among the many influences on student learning, it may be impossible to isolate and measure the singular effect of Ralph's teaching on his students. In addition, the culture of the host institution can play a critical role. If Ralph and Carol taught at a teaching-intensive community college, the assessment of teaching would probably gain immediate acceptance, and over time it would continually be revised and improved. However, Ralph and Carol teach at a comprehensive university with an unclear mission. Eastern State University is an organization in which it is difficult to forge agreement about what good teaching is and quite impossible to gain consensus on what the rewards for good teaching should be or who should receive these scarce rewards. Ralph and Carol may display differences in their motivation to teach because they have adapted differently, but equally well, to a dysfunctional organization.

Job Design

Theories of job design also assume that the environment highly influences human motivation—that is, it is the work, not the worker, which affects persistence and performance. Although theories of job enrichment and job enlargement may point out job characteristics that make some work more motivating than other work (Campion & McClelland, 1993), the theory of job design by Hackman and Oldham (1980) does this and prescribes what can be done to improve work. These theorists propose that work will be more motivating when it is meaningful, allows autonomy, and provides feedback. According to their theory, work is most meaningful when it requires a multiplicity of skills, is a whole unit rather than an unintelligible part, and is clearly important to others. Work supports autonomy when the worker is given control of what, how, and when the work is done. Finally, the work itself is a source of motivation when the worker has knowledge of results. Like goal-setting theory and flow theory, job design theory recommends that workers receive immediate, unambiguous feedback on their performance (Griffin & McMahan, in press).

College teaching, at first glance, may appear to be well-designed work: It is meaningful and autonomous, and feedback is readily available. However, as practiced by some instructors, college teaching can be dreary work. While some forms of teaching can be inspiring for the instructor as well as the student, this is not likely to be so with the most common form of college teaching, the traditional lecture. The traditional lecture requires few skills; it is segmental and inconsequential. It bridles autonomy because of the imperative to cover certain content; that is, curricula, syllabi, and texts are often predetermined. Autonomy is further abridged by the architecture and size of most lecture halls. Finally, because the lecture emphasizes covering content, not teaching it, performance feedback is mostly internal and cognitive, not external and social. Put simply, if we assume that lecturing is the predominant work of college instructors, as practiced, the work of most college instructors is poorly designed and unstimulating.

Ralph Connors may be merely a victim of the traditional lecture. Perhaps our assumptions about the quality of work life of college teachers need to be reexamined. We assume that college teaching is good work and that those who do it poorly, therefore, are bad workers. In fact, their bad performance may reflect more about the need to change the work than the worker. Carol may be more motivated because she has redesigned her work. She does not give traditional lectures. Without collegial or institutional support she has improved her work on two of the three dimensions of job design: (1) She has made her work more meaningful, and (2) she has opened up channels of communication for feedback. Although she has acquired more autonomy than Ralph, she may still not have all the autonomy she needs; for example, she may prefer to teach twenty students in a seminar room rather than two hundred in an impersonal lecture hall.

Job design theory is useful and provocative in the way it explains the motivation of instructors like Ralph and Carol, but it does not give an account of how they set and manage the goals of their work. Goal-setting theory, which we turn to next, does this.

Goal Setting

According to Locke and Latham (1990), human motivation is enhanced when people have challenging goals. Their goals should be specific enough to be operational, and they may be set by themselves or assigned by legitimate authorities. Regardless if goals are set or assigned, persistence and high achievement are only seen when people pursue difficult goals and receive feedback on goal performance. Difficult goals alone or feedback alone is not associated with highly motivated performance.

Locke and Latham (1990) have found that for people to achieve high levels of performance, optimal internal and external conditions have to be present. Their theory suggests that workers must be competent and possess high self-efficacy, and to help workers maintain high performance, they recommend that administrators reward successful performance and do it in a manner that is fair and equitable. Like expectancy theory, this theory suggests that both extrinsic rewards *and* intrinsic rewards are needed to sustain the motivation of college instructors.

These theorists predict that instructors will be most persistent when they have clear, feasible goals to achieve. No goals, vague goals, easy goals, impossible goals, or too many goals will not inspire high performance according to the theory. But wise goal setting alone will not necessarily improve performance or increase the motivation of an instructor. Frequent performance feedback is also needed to obtain good results. Neither end-of-the-semester evaluations nor mid-semester evaluations should be sufficient. The theory predicts that the highest performance and most motivation will be seen with goal achievement feedback that is specific, unambiguous, and *continuous*.

From the perspective of goal-setting theory, Ralph and Carol are vastly different instructors. Ralph appears to have few work-relevant goals; for example, his goals do not obviously include student learning. The feedback he does receive appears only to serve the function of reinforcing his preconceptions of himself and his students, not assessing goal achievement. In contrast, Carol does have goals. Most important, her goals concern student learning. The way she teaches is calculated to produce specific effects on students, and because she demands participation from her students, she not only keeps them active, but she gets immediate feedback from them. Both she and her students know when they have achieved their goals. From the standpoint of goal-setting theory, the way Carol teaches is both challenging and inspirational.

Thus far we have described and discussed theories that explain human motivation by accounting for conditions in the environment of a person. We now turn to theories that explain motivation by appealing to cognitive structures and processes within individuals.

Internal Influences on Human Motivation

Expectancy Theory

Later revisions to behavioristic theories considered the role of internal motivating factors on behavior. Although social learning theory (Bandura, 1982) does not appeal to motivational constructs to explain behavior, its development led many theorists to begin to explore the internal influences that motivate and maintain behavior. One motivational theory that emerged out of industrial-organizational psychology was expectancy theory (Vroom, 1964).

Supporters of expectancy theory (Lawler, 1981; Mitchell, 1982) propose that the motivation to engage in a particular activity is dependent on the outcome of a "motivational calculus" we compute before behaving. First, we assess the probability of success if we perform a certain behavior; this is termed *effort-to-performance expectancy*. Even if our effort-to-performance expectancy is high, we may still choose not to emit the behavior. According to expectancy theory, whether or not we actually choose to act is dependent on our *performance-to-outcome expectancy*, that is, our expected probability that a skilled performance will obtain certain outcomes. Outcomes may be positive or negative. Moreover, outcomes can be intrinsic (e.g., they make us feel good or enhance self-esteem) or extrinsic (e.g., money). Lawler also distinguishes between first- and second-level outcomes. First-level outcomes are those that have (or can have) inherent value for motivating behavior. For example, for a particular person, money may have value in and of itself as an indicator of the person's value in the organization, a value that may go far beyond its buying power. When money is valued because it is necessary for buying desired possessions, it has *instrumentality*. The first-level outcome (money) has instrumentality for achieving second-level outcomes that the person desires.

An assessment of an individual's motivation is arrived at by multiplying the effort-to-performance probability by the product(s) of the performance-to-outcome probability and their respective valences. Note, then, that if the effort-to-performance expectancy is zero ("I do not expect to succeed at this behavior, even if I try"), motivation will be very low. In turn, if either performance-to-outcome expectancies are zero ("Even if I am successful, there is no reason to perform this behavior; there is nothing in it for me") or the valences are negative, motivation will be low.

Expectancy theory has been used to predict several important indicators of work behavior, including satisfaction, performance, and effort. In the cases of Carol and Ralph, we can see how expectancy theory can be applied to predict their levels of motivation to teach. Consider Carol and her use of the "rap technique" in her class. She probably has a high effort-to-performance expectancy: She expects to be successful in the performance of her teaching activities, as she has been in the past. Moreover, we can consider at least one potential outcome that probably enters into her decision to try new teaching techniques. Specifically, she received a very positive response to the rap technique. That response constitutes a positive extrinsic outcome gained as a consequence of engaging in the behavior. Other outcomes to be considered are, for example, the feeling of competency she experiences (an intrinsic outcome) and the higher probability of subsequent promotion because of good teaching evaluations (an extrinsic outcome). Because of her motivational "calculations," Carol is likely to have high motivation to teach and to improve her teaching.

Ralph's motivation, on the other hand, seems to be lower, on the basis of everyday observation. According to expectancy theory, this may be due to a number of possibilities. Ralph may have low effort-to-performance expectancies (he doesn't expect to succeed if he tries), a combination of low performance-to-outcome expectancies and outcome valences (i.e., he doesn't expect any notable outcomes for trying, and the outcomes are not rewarding to him), or both. For example, Ralph's effort-to-performance expectancy may be low because past experience has taught him that trying new teaching techniques doesn't seem to work. In this case, his motivation to try again should be low. It is possible that his effort-to-performance expectancy is high; however, note that (a) high expectations of success do not mean that he will be successful, and (b) it would be possible to have high effort-to-performance expectancies because he is oblivious to (or ignores) the effect he has on his students—that is, he may have the delusion that he is someone who is very successful when he tries. If Ralph expects to be successful when he puts out effort but his motivation to try new techniques is still low, it may be the case, according to expectancy theory, that his low motivation is caused by a low expectation of attractive outcomes (performance-to-outcome expectancy and outcome valence). For example, perhaps Ralph believes that even if he would be successful at trying new teaching strategies, the outcomes that he will receive are not sufficient to warrant putting forth a great deal of effort. Perhaps his pay is too low, or perhaps he has learned that even good teaching evaluations don't help to ensure promotion or other second-level outcomes.

An analysis using expectancy theory offers some possible solutions for low motivation, assuming we can identify the point in the motivational configuration where expectancies are low. If effort-to-performance expectancies are low, we might offer workshops to improve teaching ability and give teachers a safe environment in which to practice their new skills and experience success. If performance-to-outcome expectancies are low, we could attempt to increase the positive outcomes available for performing the behavior or increase the instrumentality of the first-level outcomes for obtaining second-level outcomes (e.g., rewarding good teaching performance with pay incentives and promise of promotion or public acknowledgment).

Self-efficacy Theory

Expectancy theory focuses on the internal calculations that we undertake to assess whether increased effort is worth it, taking both intrinsic and extrinsic outcomes into account. Self-efficacy theory (Bandura, 1982) also takes our outcomes into account but focuses more heavily on the internal, intrinsic rewards that accumulate when we are successful. Self-efficacy can be defined as a feeling of competence and effectiveness. It is a sense of mastery over the environment.

Bandura has observed self-efficacy in numerous people who have overcome phobias. Their self-efficacy is evident in their willingness to explore new areas. Recent research in the area of self-efficacy has focused on the importance of personal control. People who are high in self-efficacy exhibit a greater sense of personal control over the environment. Unlike learned helplessness, in which one might fail to respond because one has learned that no matter what response is attempted, it will be ineffective, the person with high self-efficacy will attempt to exert control in situations in which it is lost (cf. Fiske & Taylor, 1991).

Bandura (1982) also discusses certain expectations that can influence attempts to perform some behavior, called self-efficacy beliefs. Self-efficacy beliefs are control-related beliefs concerning one's ability to perform instrumental behavior specific to particular situations. People with strong self-efficacy beliefs view themselves as able to perform a task in an efficacious manner. The result is persistence and a high level of effort to complete the task. Research has shown that attempts to try new things, put forth effort on a task, or try to reach certain goals are directly related to self-efficacy beliefs in particular situations. In our example, Carol seems to have a strong sense of self-efficacy. Her sense of effectiveness in the classroom situation seems to give her freedom to continue to explore new techniques and to work on her teaching. We would expect that, were she to have a bad teaching experience, her first reaction would be to attempt to exert personal control by reevaluating the situation and perhaps trying a new strategy or involving her students in the process of problem solving. Her sense of self-efficacy would lead her to continue to explore new avenues to improve her teaching.

Although we could not say with certainty that Ralph is low in self-efficacy, it is clear that he is exhibiting some patterns consistent with learned helplessness or low self-efficacy because he does nothing to improve his classroom techniques in what must surely be an aversive situation. If anything, his demeanor seems to indicate withdrawal and apathy, and it is clear that he communicates these emotions to his students.

One commonality that we see when comparing self-efficacy theory and expectancy is the importance of successful experiences in teaching. Both theories predict that some history of success (at some level) is necessary to maintain high levels of motivation to improve one's teaching skills. Expectancy theory suggests that low expectancies of success will result in low motivation before one has ever engaged in the behavior. Self-efficacy theorists, on the other hand, say that without successful experiences, a sense of mastery and personal control will not emerge. Taken together, these theories make a compelling case for training instructors early in their careers; in contrast with current practice, these theories would propose a form of training which built on success rather than risk failure during such a critical period in professional development.

Integrations of Internal and External Influences

Some theories blur the line between internal and external sources of human motivation. For example, the theory of goal setting looks at internal conditions such as the competence of the performer and external conditions such as the clarity of feedback. Likewise, job design theory assumes that properly designed jobs will stimulate effort only when the performer is skilled and possesses growth needs. The explanatory power of some theories clearly depends on both internal and external accounts of human motivation. Optimal experience theory, self-determination theory, and recently published theories on social motivation are even more difficult to classify. By merging internal and external perspectives, these theories give us a third distinctive account of human motivation.

Optimal Experience Theory

According to optimal experience theory (Csikszentmihalyi, 1990; Csikszentmihalyi & Csikszentmihalyi, 1988), a kind of euphoria is experienced by performers when the challenges they face are gracefully dispatched by their competence (i.e., they have had a *flow experience*). Like goal-setting theory, optimal experience theory predicts that the greatest improvements in intrinsic motivation will occur when there is harmony between the competencies of an individual and the challenges of his or her task environment. The theory predicts that performers will experience anxiety when challenges outreach skills and boredom when performers are overqualified for their tasks. When this theory is applied to college teaching, it recommends eliminating challenges that are beyond competencies of instructors, or helping them improve their competencies, or a combination of these two (Froh, Menges, & Walker, 1993). If these actions are taken, Csikszentmihalyi predicts that instructors will find teaching to be more intrinsically rewarding because they will be more likely to have *flow* experiences while they teach.

Unlike Carol Raynor, Ralph Connors probably does not have flow experiences while he teaches; he probably feels apathy and boredom. Ralph may be having these unpleasant experiences because he is too knowledgeable to teach an introductory course to sophomores. According to Csikszentmihalyi, Ralph could improve the quality of his experiences by teaching a course that is more challenging, for example, an honors course in theoretical physics. This suggestion assumes that the referent point (i.e., a performance criterion) for Ralph's flow experience is the correct articulation of complex ideas. However, if the referent point is effective communication (i.e., student learning), then the teaching of introductory physics still holds the promise of enhancing Ralph's motivation. If student learning matters to Ralph and if he discovers that he lacks critical pedagogical skills, suddenly introductory physics will become more challenging for him. In fact, at first it may overwhelm him with anxiety and may make him very receptive to improvements in his teaching skills. This shift in his perspective, when accompanied by increases in relevant skills, according to optimal experience theory, should give Ralph a kind of "born again" experience in college teaching.

Self-determination Theory

According to Csikszentmihalyi, Ralph cannot be forced to change his perspective or required to increase his teaching skills. Flow experiences cannot be caused by external agents; they happen only when a person has a hyper–sense of control. The idea that autonomy and self-control are necessary conditions for heightened human motivation is the core of self-determination theory.

Deci and Ryan (1985, 1991) propose that human beings have three fundamental needs: a need for competence, a need for relatedness, and a need for self-determination (i.e., autonomy). According to Deci and Ryan, self-determination is felt when a person has a sense of choice in the initiation and regulation of his or her actions. These investigators have found that for most people, self-determination is important; however, for people who must do creative, complex work, like that of college teachers, it is essential. When such work is externally controlled, not only is the motivation of workers deflated and their performance impaired, but they also develop feelings of distrust and alienation. In contrast, when self-determination is supported, workers perform more creatively, are more trusting, and report higher levels of job satisfaction.

Theoretically, self-determination is supported by environments that provide choice and informative feedback. To create such environments, Deci and Ryan suggest that supervisors must respect the autonomy of subordinates, give them noncontrolling positive feedback, and acknowledge their perspective. Indeed, when this has been done in educational settings, the self-esteem and intrinsic motivation of students have been enhanced (Ryan & Grolnick, 1986). What has been shown to be effective with students may be equally effective with teachers.

From the standpoint of self-determination theory, Ralph is probably not as motivated as Carol simply because he does not want to teach introductory physics to undergraduates. His motivation will increase, according to theory, when he is given the freedom to pick the courses he teaches and the students he teaches. Moreover, if he is given feedback on his teaching, it should be informative and positive, not evaluative and implicitly controlling. When these things are done, Ralph should begin to take a greater interest in his students than in his weathered boots.

Whereas theories such as self-determination theory, self-efficacy theory, and optimal experience theory emphasize the individual and can only secondarily consider the social context of teaching, recent theories of social motivation describe how and why the motivation of individuals changes when they must perform in different social contexts. These theories allow us to acknowledge the most conspicuous feature of college teaching: It is done in the midst of others. Although no chapter covers these theories, we believe they complement and enlarge the other views of human motivation presented in this text. We turn to these theories next.

Social Motivation Theories

Much of the professional life of college teachers is spent performing in front of students. In the career of a typical college instructor, an uncountable number of lectures are delivered, numerous discussions are led, and many tutorials are conducted. At times, even colleagues serve as an audience when the scholastic work of a college teacher is presented. Although there are moments when college teachers work alone, most often the work of college teachers is done in the presence of others. Like entertainers, college teachers must perform frequently in front of or among others. This fact must be considered when we attempt to explain and predict the motivation of instructors in higher education.

For example, Leary and Kowalski (1990) would predict that among college teachers, the avoidance of and escape from social anxiety is a strong source of motivation. This would be particularly so for those college teachers who define themselves in terms of the reactions of others (Brickler & Greenwald, 1986). Anxiety should be felt by these instructors when they believe the favorable impression they would like to make on students is not possible—for example, when they must lecture on a topic they know to be boring, or when they believe they do not possess the scholastic background to prepare and deliver certain lectures or the pedagogical skills to manage spontaneous student reactions to some lectures. Separately, or in combination, these things may conspire to undermine the attempts of college instructors to present themselves as good, rational, and competent people.

According to Leary and Atherton (1986), when people believe they can not make a favorable impression on an audience, social anxiety is felt. On the other hand, when people are confident in their ability to make the right impression but see their audience as unappreciative, anger will be felt. Researchers have found that in response to prolonged anxiety, cognitive deconstruction occurs, that is, the performer withdraws into the self and becomes closed-minded and preoccupied with senseless details (Baumeister, 1990). In response to anger, a confident performer preserves his or her self-esteem by rejecting or derogating the audience. For college teachers, these theories predict that over their professional lives, they will be inclined to fear students early in their careers and despise them later in their careers. Students will be feared by new instructors because new instructors lack confidence in their ability to teach; however, with time and practice, soon they will master their disciplines and eventually discover that some students do not respect their expertise or, for other reasons, are not ready for their level of teaching.

From the standpoint of social motivation theories, Carol and Ralph have quite different motives for teaching. Whereas for Carol social anxiety was a reason to perfect her teaching early in her career, for Ralph it was a reason to retreat into a private world. Ralph apparently learned to escape social anxiety through cognitive deconstruction. When Ralph was younger, getting in front of two hundred students was highly anxiety provoking; however, now it may not seem so because of his maladaptive habit of counting change and staring at his boots.

Although these social motivation theories may have implications for older instructors like Ralph, they have definite implications for new instructors. Like some of the other theories we have discussed, such as expectancy theory and self-efficacy theory, they strongly support the value of pedagogical training early in the career of an instructor. Nonetheless, for more experienced instructors, they also propose some interesting possibilities. For example, these theories support the idea of giving highly competent faculty the opportunity to teach only advanced students. For some exceptional faculty, advanced students may be limited to colleagues and peers. When this is not possible, it is consistent with social motivation theories that these instructors be trained to accelerate their students' learning through preclass assignments such as critical thinking tasks or self-guided exercises. Doing this should improve the preparation of less advanced students and thus make them more receptive for learning and a more appreciative audience. An instructor like Ralph might try doing something like this, not because it is good practice, which it is, but because it has the potential of revitalizing his teaching.

Summary and Conclusion

Although we have described and discussed a sample of theories under the headings of internal and external influences on motivation, we would like to conclude by drawing attention to the themes that are common to both of these perspectives. As noted in a previous review of the literature (Walker & Quinn, 1996), when the leading theories on human motivation are viewed as a whole, five themes emerge: Human motivation is at its highest when people (1) are competent, (2) have sufficient autonomy, (3) set worthwhile goals, (4) get feedback, and (5) are affirmed by others. These ideas are not independent; they are interdependent like spokes on a wheel. They are the minimum elements of a self-renewing motivational system.

Many of the theories we have discussed include most of these ideas, but no theory includes and integrates all of them. Yet, especially when we consider the complexity of college teaching, it seems evident that all these elements are needed to support high levels of performance. And the complexity of college teaching is only part of the challenge for theories of motivation: The career of an average college professor frequently extends more than thirty years, and, increasingly, the entirety of it is spent in the same institution (Blackburn, Lawrence, Bieber, & Trautvetter, 1991). The fact that many colleges and universities are currently undergoing tremendous social change adds still another dimension of challenge for psychologically based theories of motivation. Because of the nature of their work, where they do it, how long they do it, and for whom they do it, understanding and supporting the motivation of college teachers is a formidable task. The authors of the coming chapters attempt to cast this task in new light and reveal intriguing, unique ways to accomplish it.

References

Bandura, A. (1982). Self-efficacy mechanisms in human agency. *American Psychologist, 37,* 122–147.

Baumeister, R. E. (1990). Anxiety and deconstruction: On escaping the self. In J. M. Olson & M. P. Zanna (Eds.), *Self-inference process: The Ontario symposium* (Vol. 6, pp. 5–38). Hillsdale, NJ: Erlbaum.

Blackburn, R. T., Lawrence, J. H., Bieber, J. P., & Trautvetter, L. (1991). Faculty at work: Focus on teaching. *Research in Higher Education, 32,* 363–382.

Brickler, S. J., & Greenwald, A. G. (1986). Motivational facets of the self. In R. M. Sorentino & E. T. Higgins (Eds.), *Handbook of motivation and cognition* (pp. 145–164). New York: Guilford.

Campion, M. A., & McClelland, C. L. (1993). Follow-up and extension of the interdisciplinary benefits of enlarged jobs. *Journal of Applied Psychology, 78,* 339–351.

Csikszentmihalyi, M. (1990). *Flow: The psychology of optimal experiences.* New York: Harper & Row.

Csikszentmihalyi, M., & Csikszentmihalyi, I. (1988). *Optimal experience: Psychological studies of flow in consciousness.* Cambridge: Cambridge University Press.

Deci, E. L., & Ryan, R. M. (1985). *Intrinsic motivation and self-determination in human behavior.* New York: Plenum Press.

Deci, E. L., & Ryan, R. M. (1991). A motivational approach to self: Integration in personality. In R. Dienstbier (Ed.), *Nebraska symposium on motivation* (Vol. 38). Lincoln: University of Nebraska Press.

Fiske, S. T., & Taylor, S. E. (1991). *Social cognition* (2d ed.). New York: McGraw-Hill.

Froh, R. C., Menges, R. J., & Walker, C. J. (1993). Revitalizing faculty work through intrinsic rewards. In R. Diamond (Ed.), *New directions in higher education* (Vol. 81, pp. 87–95). San Francisco: Jossey-Bass.

Griffin, R. W., & McMahan, G. C. (in press). Motivation through job design. In J. Greenberg (Ed.), *Organizational behavior: The state of the science*. Hillsdale, NJ: Erlbaum.

Hackman, J. R., & Oldham, G. R. (1980). *Work redesign*. Reading, MA: Addison-Wesley.

Lawler, E. E. (1981). *Pay and organization development*. Reading, MA: Addison-Wesley.

Leary, M. R., & Atherton, S. C. (1986). Self-efficacy, social anxiety, and inhibition in social encounters. *Journal of Social and Clinical Psychology, 4,* 256–267.

Leary, M. R., & Kowalski, R. M. (1990). Impression management: A literature review and two-component model. *Psychological Bulletin, 107,* 34–47.

Locke, E. A., & Latham, G. P. (1990). *A theory of goal setting and task performance.* Englewood Cliffs, NJ: Prentice-Hall.

Mitchell, T. R. (1982). Expectancy-value models in organizational psychology. In N. T. Feather (Ed.), *Expectations and actions: Expectancy-value models in psychology* (pp. 293–312). Hillsdale, NJ: Erlbaum.

Ryan, R. M., & Grolnick, W. S. (1986). Origins and pawns in the classroom: Self-report and projective assessments of individual differences in children's perceptions. *Journal of Personality and Social Psychology, 50,* 550–558.

Schuster, J. R., & Zingheim, P. K. (1992). *The new pay: Linking employee and organizational performance.* New York: Lexington Books.

Vroom, V. H. (1964). *Work and motivation.* New York: Wiley.

Walker, C. J., & Quinn, J. W. (1996). Fostering instructional vitality and motivation. In R. Menges & M. Weimer (Eds.), *Teaching on solid ground: Using scholarship to improve practice* (pp. 315–336). San Francisco: Jossey-Bass.

2 Wanting to Be a Good Teacher: What Have We Learned to Date?

WILBERT J. MCKEACHIE

When people in the same situation with similar backgrounds differ in behavior, it is natural for us to attribute the differences to motivation. Compare the following two senior faculty members.

Henry is sixty-three. As a graduate student and as a faculty member he was very effective as both a teacher and a researcher until his late forties. He completed an extensive major study when he was in his early forties—a study that now provides the dominant conceptual base for a major area of his field. This was followed by some related studies and a five-year term as department head. Since then he has taught adequately, but his courses are in areas that are not of great intrinsic interest to most students in his discipline. He is currently doing no research. He enjoys tennis, friends, and entertaining with his wife and has a good sense of humor.

Joe, seventy-one, is also energetic. Hired primarily for teaching, he has continued to do research and publish, but in recent years most of these activities have been joint efforts with colleagues and graduate students. He too served as department Chair. Although officially retired, he is still teaching and doing research with enjoyment and satisfaction. He enjoys sports, music, and travel.

The author has benefited from comments by Diane Cordova, Martie Maehr, and Paul Pintrich.

How Can We Account for Differences in Faculty Motivation?

As we consider Henry and Joe, we note that they were both highly motivated as graduate students and assistant professors; both were working hard, beginning to achieve national reputations. Both were active in faculty athletics and had high energy levels. Up to about age fifty both received a good deal of recognition, although Henry reports that real recognition of his achievement came later—"twenty years too late," he says. At the time he published his major study, the field he worked in was not a hot area, and his contribution was probably not appreciated as much then as it has been in recent years.

One account of differences in faculty motivation is a developmental one (e.g., see Baldwin & Blackburn, 1981). Approached from a developmental point of view, the problem of faculty motivation can be understood in terms of the differing needs and situational pressures experienced by faculty at different career stages. Thus Henry's loss of motivation with aging might be at a normal decline. Although there have been some studies showing a decline in scholarly productivity in later life, Blackburn concluded his review of the research (1982) with the statement that "the existence of career phases in motivation to teach cannot be supported by the existing evidence," and he begins his chapter in this volume by stating that "little demonstrable evidence exists to support predictable phases for academics."

Thus we need to look at more general motivational principles to account for the differences between Henry and Joe. In this chapter, I introduce some theoretical concepts that I believe are helpful in understanding faculty motivation. Then I look at some of the motivational characteristics of faculty members—both those that are common human motives and those in which faculty members differ from individuals in other occupations. I then touch briefly on some of the contextual variables that influence faculty motivation at different points in faculty careers, and I conclude with a few thoughts about the future.

Motivation Theory

I approach motivational problems primarily from the perspective of cognitive expectancy-value theory (McKeachie, 1961). Basically, this theory says that one's motivation for a particular behavior or set of behaviors is a function of the expected value of a goal or incentive to be obtained by successful implementation of the behaviors and the expectancy (expected probability) that the behaviors will achieve the expected value or satisfaction.

When I use the terms *goal, reward, satisfaction,* or *motive,* I am referring to the *value* term of the equation. In any situation there are many potential goals as well as potential costs or negative consequences.

When I use the terms *expectancy, perceived probability,* or *self-efficacy,* I am referring to the *expectancy* term. The expectancy term covers two kinds of expectancies—the expectancy that successful behavior will lead to the goal, and the expectancy or perceived probability that one can do the required behavior successfully.

When I talk about the amount of effort, or persistence, or choice of one activity versus another in a particular situation, I am referring to *motivation*—the other side of the equation. Note that I use *motive* to refer to a latent characteristic of an individual and *motivation* to refer to the activated motive in a particular situation.

The product of the value and expectancy for one set of behaviors is compared with that of other sets of behaviors leading to this and other values. Thus, one could explain Henry's reduced motivation as resulting from three possible changes: (1) The perceived value of research and teaching has decreased; (2) the expectancy of success in research and teaching has decreased; that is, he has lower self-efficacy (Bandura, 1986); or (3) other goals have become stronger, and their values now dominate the choice of behaviors.

Henry's loss of motivation for academic life can well be a product of all three of these variables. Note that one critical feature is his perception that recognition came late and that his work is still not adequately appreciated by his own department.

Extrinsic versus Intrinsic Satisfactions

We can also gain some additional understanding by considering a distinction between two kinds of values—extrinsic and intrinsic (Deci & Ryan, 1985). *Extrinsic* values are those rewards that come after successful completion of an activity. Probably the most common extrinsic reward is money; for students it may be grades; for faculty members it might be a salary raise or promotion to a higher rank. *Intrinsic* satisfactions, on the other hand, inhere in the activity itself. Thus delight in satisfying curiosity, the satisfaction in doing a good job, of meeting one's own standards of achievement, the pleasure from participating in a stimulating discussion— these are intrinsic satisfactions. To the degree that they, and other intrinsic satisfactions, are inherent in college teaching, teaching will be fun. But they too can be lost if the teaching situation is one that diminishes the chances to receive such satisfactions.

The first thought of those attempting to motivate someone to behave in a desired direction is to promise rewards or threaten punishment. And rewards and punishments can control behavior to some extent. But the long-term results may not be those desired. When people perceive rewards or punishments as attempts to induce a particular behavior, the behavior begins to lose its former intrinsic satisfaction. On the other hand, if a reward is seen as appreciation for work the individual has done, motivation is maintained or enhanced (see Chap. 4 in this volume).

Returning to the cases of Henry and Joe, both Henry and Joe enjoyed recognition, but Joe feels that he no longer needs it. In one joint publication with graduate students and other faculty members, he suggested that they list the authors in the order in which they needed recognition, with his name last and a job-seeking doctoral candidate first. This does not mean that he does not enjoy recognition. He glows when he receives a note of appreciation or some indication that his work has had an impact. But for him this is frosting on the cake. Most of his satisfactions are intrinsic—preparing for class, teaching, talking about research with his students and colleagues, supervising graduate and undergraduate research, trying to figure out why his research results came out as they did.

Note that Henry is not unmotivated—he's just more motivated for tennis than for teaching. Faculty motivation for teaching is part of a larger complex including many other motives competing for time and energy. It is affected by satisfactions and problems in the rest of life. For example, Henry was divorced about age fifty and remarried a few years later. Could this have affected Henry's career satisfactions? Or is it simply that after achieving the major goal of his research other work seemed trivial? There are certainly many examples of individuals who achieved such great success at an early age that they felt unable to do anything later that might detract from their reputation.

Unhappiness at home may tie up cognitive and emotional resources that are needed for successful academic functioning. On the other hand, when home life is unpleasant, some professors may spend more time with students or in other academic activities. In any case, family and personal relationships are important for most faculty members and have an impact upon motivation for teaching (Braskamp, Fowler, & Ory, 1982).

The cases of Henry and Joe illustrate some of the puzzles motivation theory tries to explain. Clearly individuals differ in motivation, and the motivation of an individual may change over time. This chapter examines both individual differences and changes in motivation for teaching in terms of values (rewards or satisfactions) derived from teaching and the expectations that effort devoted to teaching will result in those rewards. The rewards may be extrinsic, such as a high salary, promotion, an award, prestige, or recognition, or they may be intrinsic, such as the satisfaction of gaining new insights while preparing a lecture or satisfaction in seeing students' progress.

Using these concepts, I propose to review some of the research relevant to the following questions:

1. What are the satisfactions (values) faculty members report as being important?
2. How do faculty members' motives differ from those of individuals in other occupations?
3. What motives are particularly salient for faculty members at different career stages?

What College Teachers Value

We know a good deal about why people choose to become academicians, what they find satisfying, and how they differ from people in other jobs. Data on faculty motivation go back to studies by Jack Gustad (1960) and by Ruth Eckert and John Stecklein (1961), who studied all faculty members in the state of Minnesota. Later studies by Blackburn (1982), Clark and Corcoran (1985), and Blackburn and Lawrence (1995) added to our understanding. The Carnegie Foundation for the Advancement of Teaching 1969 and 1989 National Surveys of Faculty supported many of the insights gained from the earlier studies, as well as revealing changes occurring as the economic and social situation changed. Sampling unsuccessful and successful faculty members, Bowen and Schuster (1986) uncovered some of the sources of dissatisfaction in academic life. Finkelstein (1984) has summarized a number of these studies. Perhaps most revealing are the studies by Caplan, Cobb, French, Harrison, and Pinneau (1980) comparing the motives and satisfactions of academics with those of individuals in other occupations.

Although these studies occurred in different decades and with different samples, there are a number of characteristics of faculty motivation for teaching which seem quite robust even though there are some differences in the relative levels of different values contributing to faculty satisfaction.

First of all, most faculty members are quite satisfied with their occupation, and the percentage that are dissatisfied is small compared with that in most other occupations. Even though their study occurred during a period of retrenchment (1985), Eble and McKeachie (1985) found that 90 percent of the faculty in their sample were satisfied, a finding similar to that obtained by Gustad (1960) a quarter of a century earlier and by Armour, Fuhrmann, and Wergin in 1990. Both Eble and McKeachie (1985) and Simpson (1992) found women to have higher levels of satisfaction than men, even though extrinsic rewards, such as rank and salary, were often not as great for women. On the other hand, Gmelch (1993) reported that married women professors experience more stress than men or unmarried women. These results are not necessarily in contradiction. One can still experience a great deal of satisfaction in teaching but feel stress because of competing life demands. Overall, Gmelch reports that data from the National Institute for Occupational Health and Safety rank college professor as the least stressful occupation of those requiring higher education.

What are the sources of satisfaction? The array of these studies extending over several decades and with differing samples reveals a good deal of commonality in the motives that characterize academicians. Faculty members report that they are motivated by and find satisfaction in the following:

- open-ended problem solving;
- being helpful (listed in Simpson's study [1992] as a factor in choice of career along with a desire to do research and teach);
- a sense of making a difference, for example, seeing students develop;
- interaction with students;
- the sense of being appreciated by department Chair, colleagues, students, and family;
- a sense of competence—increasing skill, knowledge;
- opportunities to use skills and knowledge;
- opportunities for learning;
- autonomy-independence (self-determination; see Chap. 4 in this volume).

Most of these are common motives for many human beings in our culture, and faculty members differ from one another in the strength of each of these motives. Moreover, even though Blackburn found no general relationship of motivation to career stages, individual faculty members may change in the relative strengths of one or more or all of these motives at different times or in different circumstances during their lives. In addition, faculty members in universities may, in general, differ from those in liberal arts colleges. Maehr and Braskamp (1986) found that college professors more often emphasized concern for others as a guiding value (see also Braskamp & Ory, 1994).

Note that most of these motives are intrinsic—they are part of the job, not dependent upon rewards and punishments extrinsic to the job. What is the role of extrinsic rewards, such as money? Faculty members are less motivated for money than are members of other professions (Matthews & Weaver, 1989). Vocational choice studies suggest that young people strongly motivated for money are not likely to choose college teaching as a career. Nonetheless, among faculty members money is a more important concern for assistant professors and those with lower pay (a not-surprising finding).

Generally we take satisfactions for granted unless they are missing; for example, we don't appreciate oxygen unless we have asthma. Moreover, we judge our deprivation not simply in absolute but also in relative terms. Money is very important if salary levels are low compared with those at other comparable institutions. In a study of University of Oregon faculty members, Kerlin and Dunlap (1993) found that money was a primary concern. (At that time Oregon ranked 111th out of 121 research universities in faculty salaries.)

Cook, Kinnetz, and Owens-Misner (1990) found that faculty members felt that their colleges rewarded scholarly activity more than teaching, but the faculty members rated teaching as more rewarding to them personally than scholarly work. Nonetheless, the system of evaluating faculty for merit pay and promotion has a major motivational impact upon faculty's preferred allocation of time. In his study of Stanford faculty, Dornbusch (1979) found that faculty members perceived research as the predominant factor determining university rewards, and this perception was related to their desire to reduce time spent teaching and increase time for research. More than half of the respondents wanted to have more emphasis placed on teaching in the evaluation criteria. (And this was at Stanford, a major research university!) Diamond and Adam's volume (1993) describes efforts to move reward systems in the direction of greater emphasis on teaching, and recent volumes by Centra (1993) and Braskamp and Ory (1994) describe methods of evaluation which should both provide better evidence and contribute to faculty development.

Although a sense that teaching is unrecognized, unappreciated, and not rewarded is likely to have a corrosive effect upon the motivation of the good teacher, a heavy emphasis upon financial incentives may not be the best way to improve teaching. Good teachers need to feel that they are being treated fairly, but they are not likely to teach better in order to receive an award for teaching. Quite probably investment in improving the

158,274

LIBRARY
College of St. Francis
JOLIET, ILLINOIS

conditions that enhance intrinsic rewards will be a better investment, although awards as a *symbol* of an institution's values may be of value (McKeachie, 1979; Kohn, 1993).

The evaluation system also comes into play in affecting one's self-efficacy as a teacher, that is, one's *expectancy* that one can obtain satisfaction by teaching. One of the unfortunate features of providing norms for student ratings of teaching is that if one provides percentiles or quartiles or in some way compares the individual's mean rating with that of other faculty members, approximately half of the faculty find that they are below average, even though most of their students rate them as very good or excellent.

Goal theory (Maehr & Pintrich, 1991; Urdan & Maehr, 1995) deals with the way that different goals may become salient in a situation; for example, does the person focus on doing the task well or on competing with others? Goal theory suggests that a focus on one's ability relative to that of others is likely to be damaging to long-term achievement. Although finding that one is below average may, in some cases, motivate increased effort, for many faculty members being "below average" is discouraging and results in less enthusiasm for teaching. Moreover, if the ratings are public, or are perceived as being known by one's colleagues, one's relationships with others may also be threatened. Faculty members may handle a below-average rating by defining themselves as "researchers" for whom teaching is only of secondary importance.

Do Faculty Members Differ in Motivation from Individuals in Other Fields?

We have seen that motivation for a given individual may differ from time to time and that faculty members differ in motivation. Nonetheless, are there some ways in which faculty members as a group differ in motivation from other occupational groups? The answer is yes.

In the Institute of Social Research studies comparing faculty members with individuals employed in twenty-three other occupations (half blue collar), a number of interesting findings indicate the relatively high morale of faculty members (French, Caplan, Harrison, & Pinneau, 1976; Caplan, Cobb, French, Harrison, & Pinneau, 1980). For example, college teachers were the second-highest occupation in intrinsic interest in work, as indicated by hours worked. Only physicians worked longer hours (52–56 hours for professors vs. 58 hours a week for physicians). Physicians felt an overload of about three hours; faculty members reported an overload of

1.5 hours a week—about the same perceived overload as workers in oc-cupations working 40 hours a week. However, Eble and McKeachie (1985) found that "too much to do" was the biggest concern of about two-thirds of their respondents—mostly in the lower academic ranks. And Boice's studies of new faculty members (1992) document the great stress experi-enced in not having enough time to meet all of the perceived demands of the job.

One of the strengths of the Institute of Social Research studies is that the interviewees were asked not only what they preferred but also how well their jobs provided the kind of stimulation or opportunities relevant to that preference, so that the reports of satisfaction are directly tied to self-perceptions and perceptions of the context of the work situation. "Per-son-environment fit" theory suggests that satisfaction and productivity are not dependent simply upon the strength of motivation but rather upon the degree to which one's motives fit with the capacity of the situation to use and satisfy those motives. Thus the Caplan, Cobb, French, Harrison, and Pinneau studies not only describe faculty motives compared with those of people in other occupations; they also describe how well the academic sit-uation provides a fitting situation for satisfying these motives.

Faculty members report that they are motivated by, and find satisfaction in, *open-ended problem solving*. They are high in *need for achievement* (Fink-elstein, 1984). They like *complexity* and report a higher level of job com-plexity than those in other occupations, except for administrators and physicians. Similarly, faculty members like to feel that their *abilities are uti-lized*, and they report high utilization. White, Spencer, and Peterson (1993) report that faculty members' perception of *challenge* is related to in-stitutions' resources for faculty and instructional development. (Note that the balance between skills and challenges is one of the factors contributing to Csikszentmihalyi's "flow"; see Chap. 5 in this volume.)

Professors have a sense of *responsibility* for other persons and feel there is a good fit between their motive and their job. They like to feel that they can *participate in decisions* that affect them and feel that they do participate (more than those in other occupations). Professors also feel that *support from peers and from family and friends* is important and generally report that they feel such support. Professors and physicians report the least boredom and most satisfaction with their jobs, and professors report the fewest ill-nesses of the occupations studied—probably a good indication of relative freedom from stress.

Person-environment fit theory suggests that satisfaction, stress, and ef-fectiveness depend upon the fit of the person's abilities, personality, and motives with the demands of the environment and the opportunities the environment affords. This theory has been used productively for half a century and is particularly relevant to our discussion in this chapter. We have already seen that in general, the academic environment provides a good fit for typical college teachers. But it is well to remember that our general picture of faculty members would be misleading if one forgot the enormous variability found in the college teaching ranks. Fortunately there are also a great variety of situations as well. A faculty member who fits well in one college or department might well be ill fitted for another. Moreover, situations change and individuals change, so that a college environment that provides optimal stimulation and satisfaction for a faculty member at one time may not be optimal later.

In general, studies of faculty motivation suggest that when faculty members report satisfactions, they emphasize intrinsic motives; when they report dissatisfactions, they mention extrinsic factors such as money, administrative policies, and working conditions. Because many of the intrinsic factors are relatively stable despite changes in budgets or administration, those who are intrinsically motivated are, perhaps, more likely to have lasting satisfaction from teaching.

How Do Motives Differ at Different Stages of Faculty Careers?

As Blackburn points out (Chap. 16 in this volume), events, rather than life stages, are likely to account for changes in motivation over a faculty member's career. Certainly chance plays a large role. Nonetheless, examination of the contextual and motivational factors likely to be influential at different stages of an academic career may help us better understand motivation for teaching.

Choice of College Teaching

To the best of my knowledge there are no longitudinal studies that have traced academic careers from the initial choice to retirement, but we do have some data from retrospective accounts. Clark (1987) interviewed 170 faculty members in diverse institutions and found diverse reasons for choosing the academic life. For example, one science professor became intrigued with dinosaurs at an early age and continued to be fascinated with science on through college and graduate school into an academic career. Clark found that many science teachers followed similar pathways, some having diverted from premedicine or other curricula during undergraduate days and others attracted earlier. But like many college teachers in other disciplines, they were attracted by intrinsic interest in the field of study and research, not by the prospect of teaching.

Clark contrasts the scientists with professors of English, who reported moving from subject to subject in college, sometimes spent time in other occupations, such as secondary school teaching, and in general entered full-time academic careers later. Many of those in the humanities and social sciences were first attracted to college teaching in their undergraduate years, and those in the humanities are most likely to report that they were attracted to academia by a desire to teach (Sorcinelli, 1988; Armour, Fuhrmann, & Wergin, 1990).

Simpson (1992) found that women, more than men, were likely to cite "desire to write" and "influence of a faculty member." Men were more likely to cite "attraction of the academic life style."

Beardslee and O'Dowd (1962) reported that undergraduate students' perceptions of college professors' lives were generally very positive. College professors were seen to have great intellectual competence as well as sensitivity to aesthetic experience. Professors were perceived to be unselfish individualists with colorful, interesting lives (albeit coupled with rashness and emotional difficulty) (see also O'Dowd & Beardslee, 1961).

For many faculty members, however, the first attraction to college teaching came as a result of experience as a teaching assistant. Although for many this brings satisfactions, a sizeable number complain of poor training and supervision (Diamond & Gray, 1987). Thus, for them, the expectancy of success may be low.

The Nontenured Years

The first extensive study of new faculty members was carried out by Dee Fink (1984) in the late 1970s; the most recent are those carried out by Bob Boice (1992) and Deborah Olsen (1993). These studies found that teaching dominated the time and energy of the new faculty members. Despite their knowledge that promotion to a tenured position would depend upon research, the new teachers devoted great amounts of time to preparation of classes and other aspects of teaching. This suggests to me that most of us are motivated by a desire to do a good job, particularly in a public setting. At the very least, we don't want to appear incompetent. It also indicates that new faculty members have an expectancy that increased time spent on preparation will lead to success or at least avoid failure.

Although new faculty members expected to spend about half of their time on teaching and half on scholarly writing, they spent much more time on teaching. During each of the first four semesters they expected to be able to achieve a better balance by the following semester—an expectation that was never realized. Sorcinelli's study (1988) of second-year teachers produced similar results. Mager and Myers (1983) reported that increased time for research and writing is possible only by increasing the workweek to more than seventy hours.

Both Fink and Boice reported that new teachers feel that there is no time for innovation or risk taking; rather, they teach cautiously and defensively, attempting to avoid public embarrassment and criticism. In this situation there is a danger that students will be perceived as adversaries—consuming time that is needed for research and writing. Nonetheless, teaching successes were the most frequently cited source of satisfaction and self-esteem, and despite the stress of lack of time, the majority reported satisfaction with their positions. (It may be worth noting that feeling time pressure is not limited to the first years of teaching. Using data from three national surveys, Elaine El-Khawas [1991] reported that more than 70 percent of faculty members over fifty years of age reported stress from time pressures.)

These first experiences in teaching are likely to have significant impact upon academic careers. For those who find satisfaction in teaching, approaching the classroom with joyful expectancy is likely to elicit positive responses from students and lead to continuing interest in teaching and development as a teacher. For those whose first experiences are unpleasant, the anticipation of negative student responses may lead to avoidance of interaction with students and to a retreat to lecturing with as little attention as possible to cues of student inattention or confusion.

As compared with tenured faculty members, new faculty members show (quite realistically) greater concern about extrinsics (promotion and salary). There is also a greater sense of competition—more anxiety—not unexpected in today's academic job market.

In an institution in which only a small proportion of assistant professors are promoted to tenure, the climate of interpersonal support is almost inevitably corroded. Loss of valued friends is almost always painful, even more so if one has been involved in the decision to tell that friend to leave. Senior faculty members may, therefore, be reluctant to establish warm personal ties with younger colleagues who may, after a few years, be denied tenure and released. As a result, even those who achieve tenure may find the tenuring process unpleasant and embittering. Boice (1992, p. 231) quotes one young faculty member's reaction: "I will never, ever, forget this [tenuring process]. I'm left feeling that they didn't really want me, that they begrudged me the tenure and promotion."

An additional complication for the cohort of younger and middle-aged faculty members is the problem of finding fulfilling positions for both members of a dual-career family. In the post–World War II period there was actually a decline in the proportion of female faculty members as compared with the 1920s; it was expected that women would be primarily devoted to homemaking, and if they had doctorates, their academic careers were likely to be part-time, nontenured, and if married to an academic, they followed their husbands to the college or university best suited to his motivations. Today the situation is much different.

> A promising young assistant professor was recruited to a major research university from a smaller institution in another state where her spouse had a tenure-track teaching position at a nearby college. The university acknowledged her spouse's situation and provided reassurances of eventual employment, but there was no guarantee of employment before the wife had to accept the position.
>
> With good intentions all around, the wife accepted, as it was clear advancement for her. While her spouse was on leave from his college for one year, some avenues were explored for him, but nothing developed in his field. The wife at that point could not return to her previous position, for it had been filled. (Rathbun, 1993)

Dilemmas such as this couple face must inevitably affect motivation and satisfactions in their academic careers. Institutions are, in many cases, trying to adapt to this and other changes in the lives of academicians, but in times of tight budgets, flexibility is often curtailed, and the intrinsic satisfactions of teaching may be overwhelmed by external stresses.

Midcareer

The posttenure years are typically ones in which faculty members settle into their careers. Tenure is intended to confer the sort of security which will free up one to be creative—able to take risks in exploring new research areas and new methods of teaching. Obviously this is not always the case.

Although we do not have the extensive research on the middle years which is reported in Boice's book about new faculty members, there is evidence that many faculty members do settle into their roles in teaching and research in ways that are both satisfying and productive. Pelz and Andrews (1966) report that research contributions peak for researchers in their late thirties and early forties, drop in the late forties, and peak again in the late fifties (see also Chap. 16 in this volume). In general, university scientists showed higher intrinsic motivation for research and less decline in motivation with age than scientists in government or industry.

However, extrinsic pressures may still weigh heavily. In recent years, as research funding has become more difficult, many faculty members report feelings of stress from administrative pressures to obtain outside funding. This is particularly troubling when viewed in the context of Pelz and Andrews' finding that the decline in research productivity in later life found in both university and nonuniversity settings was much less for those scientists with strong intrinsic motivation for research.

We do not have comparable data about motivation for teaching. One might hypothesize that extrinsic pressures for research funding would lead faculty members to turn to teaching for more satisfaction, but it seems likely that stress in one area of academic life (research) may have detrimental effects on other areas, rather than resulting in increased motivation and satisfaction from teaching.

Nonetheless, motivation for teaching probably remains high. In the national surveys carried out by the Carnegie Foundation, 56 percent of the faculty members under forty years of age report being more interested in teaching than research while 74 percent of those over forty prefer teaching (Boyer, 1990, table A-26).

Most studies suggest that extrinsics tend to be less important, and intrinsic satisfactions more important, for older as compared with younger faculty members. This fits with anecdotal and other data, but it is possible that there are substantial differences between cohorts entering academic life at different times.

In many institutions faculty members experience changing demands. They were hired for one role—teaching—and now find that their college or university is putting more emphasis on research. Although intrinsic satisfactions may still sustain teaching, motivation may be corroded by a lowered expectancy of support and respect from younger faculty members and administrators.

It may well be that with the current increased emphasis upon undergraduate teaching, the converse will also be true—those who have made their career in research and graduate teaching will now experience unwelcome stress when they are expected to be competent undergraduate teachers. Similarly, many faculty who entered academic life expecting to teach eighteen- to twenty-two-year-old predominantly American-born white students are now coping with diversity and wondering, "Do I have the skills needed?"

What about Older Faculty?

The concerns above may be accentuated for older faculty members. Some report anxiety about keeping up with their field. Others report difficulties in their relations with students—a sense of not being in touch with the students' culture. As faculty members approach retirement age, they wonder, "Is it worth investing effort in developing new skills, new courses? Do younger colleagues feel that I contribute?"

The end of mandatory retirement may make investment in new skills and competencies more appealing to older faculty members, since there is increased expectancy that these skills can be used in satisfying ways. Yet older faculty members must consider whether the support of peers, which has been so important to their satisfaction, will still be as strong when they continue to occupy a position and draw a salary that might be used to recruit fresh new faculty members.

The intrinsic rewards of interactions with students may still be very satisfying; yet it may be more difficult to communicate effectively with students as one becomes less a part of the common culture of youth. Expectancy of satisfying results may be threatened.

Faculty members' motivation for teaching may also be affected by their own perceptions of the aging process. Many view intellectual and biological changes in aging as greater and more threatening than is justified by the research evidence. Although there is some inevitable decline, the amount of decline depends a great deal upon the individual's activities. To the degree that one remains intellectually active, verbal intelligence declines relatively slowly, so that faculty members actually decline less than most other people. An assumption that one is no longer capable of creative, innovative ideas for teaching and research after age sixty-five, seventy, or seventy-five produces lower expectations and ends in the very results that have been assumed.

Despite these problems the well-being of faculty members in retirement tends to be high. About 90 percent of faculty members continue doing some teaching or research after formal retirement and report continued satisfaction (Finkelstein, 1984).

I have stressed the fact of individual differences in introducing this chapter. Here I should point out that individual differences tend to increase with age, so that the variability among older faculty is even greater than that among young faculty members.

What of the Future?

What will be the impact of current trends—more centralization of decision making, heavier teaching loads, larger classes, increased emphasis upon evaluation and assessment, the loss of the sense of being valued by society (for example, attacks by the former secretary of education and other political figures)? Each of these has an impact upon intrinsic satisfactions of college teaching.

Greater centralization of decision making in state agencies and in the administrative structures of colleges and universities and increased emphasis upon evaluation and assessment are likely to have a negative effect upon faculty members' feeling of autonomy, responsibility, and opportunity for creativity and innovation. Heavier student loads and larger classes reduce opportunities for satisfying interactions with students. Thus enthusiasm, innovativeness, and flexibility may be reduced.

Nonetheless, I believe that college teachers will continue to find college teaching one of the most satisfying of occupations, for there are also positive features in the present academic trends. One of these is the increased emphasis both in public discussions and in academia on the value of excellent undergraduate teaching. More and more institutions are providing training in teaching for doctoral students; more and more institutions are providing skilled consultants for faculty development as teachers. As faculty members perceive the fascinating complexity of the college classroom and of course planning—as they gain additional skills for coping with the dynamics of teaching—they gain a new vision of themselves as experts in teaching and learning. This enhanced vision of a possible self will in itself provide strong motivation for teaching (Markus & Nurius, 1986). Some of the intrinsic values of teaching may be diminished by budget-cutting axes, but there will always be opportunities for creativity, for satisfying interpersonal relations, and for intellectual stimulation.

References

Armour, R. A., Fuhrmann, B. S., & Wergin, J. F. (1990). Senior faculty career attitudes: Implications for faculty development. In L. Hilsen (Ed.), *To improve the academy: Resources for student, faculty, and institutional development* (Vol. 10, pp. 217–230). Stillwater, OK: New Forums Press.

Baldwin, R. G., & Blackburn, R. T. (1981). The academic career as a developmental process: Implications for higher education. *Journal of Higher Education, 52*(6), 598–614.

Bandura, A. (1986). *Social foundations of thought and action.* Englewood Cliffs, NJ: Prentice-Hall.

Beardslee, D. C., & O'Dowd, D. D. (1962). Students and the occupational world. In N. Sanford (Ed.), *The American College.* New York: Wiley.

Blackburn, R. T. (1982). Career phases and their influence on faculty motivation. In J. L. Bess (Ed.), *Motivating faculty to teach effectively.* San Francisco: Jossey-Bass.

Blackburn, R. T., & Lawrence, J. H. (1995). *Faculty at work: Motivation, expectation, satisfaction.* Baltimore: Johns Hopkins University Press.

Boice, R. (1991). New faculty as teachers. *Journal of Higher Education, 62*(2), 150–173.

Boice, R. (1992). *The new faculty member.* San Francisco: Jossey-Bass.

Bowen, H. R., & Schuster, J. H. (1986). *American professors: A national resource imperiled.* New York: Oxford University Press.

Boyer, E. L. (1990). *Scholarship reconsidered: Priorities of the professoriate.* Princeton: Carnegie Foundation for the Advancement of Teaching.

Braskamp, L. A., Fowler, D. L., & Ory, J. C. (1982). Faculty development and achievement: A faculty's view. Paper presented at the annual meeting of the American Educational Research Association, New York.

Braskamp, L. A., & Ory, J. C. (1994). *Assessing faculty work.* San Francisco: Jossey-Bass.

Caplan, R. D., Cobb, S., French, J. R. P., Jr., Harrison, R. V., & Pinneau, S. R., Jr. (1980). *Job demands and worker health.* Ann Arbor: Institute of Social Research, University of Michigan.

Carnegie Foundation for the Advancement of Teaching. (1989). *The condition of the professoriate: Attitudes and trends, 1989.* Princeton: Carnegie Foundation for the Advancement of Teaching.

Centra, J. A. (1993). *Reflective faculty evaluation: Enhancing teaching and determining faculty effectiveness.* San Francisco: Jossey-Bass.

Clark, B. R. (1987). *The Academic life: Small worlds, different worlds.* Princeton: Carnegie Foundation for the Advancement of Teaching.

Clark, S. M., & Corcoran, M. (1985). Individual and organizational contributions to faculty vitality: An institutional case study. In S. M. Clark & D. R. Lewis (Eds.), *Faculty vitality and institutional productivity: Critical perspectives for higher education* (pp. 112–138). New York: Teachers College Press.

Cook, E. P., Kinnetz, P., & Owens-Misner, N. (1990). Faculty perceptions of job rewards and instructional development activities. *Innovative Higher Education, 14*(2), 123–130.

Deci, E. L., & Ryan, R. M. (1985). *Intrinsic motivation and self-determination in human behavior.* New York: Plenum Press.

Diamond, R. M., & Adam, B. E. (Eds.). (1993). *Recognizing faculty work: Reward systems for the year 2000.* New Directions in Higher Education. No. 81. San Francisco: Jossey-Bass.

Diamond, R. M., & Gray, P. J. (1987). *National study of teaching assistants.* Syracuse: Syracuse University, Center for Instructional Development.

Dornbusch, S. M. (1979). Perspectives from sociology: Organizational evaluation of faculty performances. In D. R. Lewis & W. E. Becker, Jr. (Eds.), *Academic rewards in higher education* (pp. 41–60). Cambridge, MA: Ballinger.

Eble, K. E., & McKeachie, W. J. (1985). *Improving undergraduate education through faculty development.* San Francisco: Jossey-Bass.

Eckert, R. E., & Stecklein, J. E. (1961). *Job motivations and satisfactions of college teachers: A study of faculty members in Minnesota colleges.* Washington, DC: U.S. Government Printing Office.

Eckert, R. E., & Williams, H. Y. (1972). *College faculty view themselves and their jobs.* Minneapolis: College of Education, University of Minnesota.

El-Khawas, E. (1991). *Senior faculty in academe: Active, committed to the teaching role.* ACE Research Briefs. Washington, DC: American Council on Education.

Fink, L. D. (1984). *The first year of college teaching.* New Directions for Teaching and Learning. No. 17. San Francisco: Jossey-Bass.

Finkelstein, M. J. (1984). *The American academic profession: A synthesis of social inquiry since World War II.* Columbus: Ohio State University Press.

French, J. R. P., Jr., Caplan, R. D., Harrison, R. V., & Pinneau, S. F., Jr. (1976). Job demands and worker health: A symposium. Paper presented at the 84th annual convention of the American Psychological Association, Washington, DC.

Gmelch, W. H. (1993). Coping with faculty stress. Newbury Park, CA: Sage.

Gustad, J. W. (1960). The career decisions of college teachers. Washington, DC: U.S. Department of Health, Education, and Welfare.

Kerlin, S. P., & Dunlap, D. M. (1993). For richer, for poorer: Faculty morale in periods of austerity and retrenchment. Journal of Higher Education, 64(3), 348–377.

Kohn, A. (1993). Why incentive plans cannot work. Harvard Business Review, September–October, 1–7.

Maehr, M. L., & Braskamp, L. A. (1986). The motivation factor: A theory of personal investment. Lexington, MA: D. C. Heath.

Maehr, M. L., & Pintrich, P. (1991). Advances in motivation (Vol. 7). Greenwich, CT: JAI Press.

Mager, G. M., & Myers, B. (1983). Developing a career in the academy: New professors in education (Tech. Rep. 143). Washington, DC: Society of Professors of Education.

Markus, H., & Nurius, P. (1986). Possible selves. American Psychologist, 41, 954–969.

Matthews, M. D., & Weaver, C. N. (1989). What college professors want from a job. Psychological Reports, 65, 792–794.

McKeachie, W. J. (1961). Motivation, teaching methods, and college learning. In M. R. Jones (Ed.), Nebraska symposium on motivation (Vol. 9, pp. 111–142). Lincoln: University of Nebraska Press.

McKeachie, W. J. (1979). Perspectives from psychology: Financial incentives are ineffective for faculty. In D. R. Lewis & W. E. Becker, Jr. (Eds.), Academic rewards in higher education (pp. 5–20). Cambridge, MA: Ballinger.

O'Dowd, D. D., & Beardslee, D. C. (1961). The image of a college professor. AAUP Bulletin, 47(3), 216–221.

Olsen, D. (1992). Interviews with exiting faculty: Why do they leave? In D. H. Wulff & J. D. Nyquist (Eds.), To improve the academy (Vol. 11, pp. 35–47). Stillwater, OK: New Forums Press.

Olsen, D. (1993). Work satisfaction and stress in the first and third year of academic appointment. Journal of Higher Education, 64(4), 453–471.

Pelz, D. C., & Andrews, F. M. (1966). Scientists in organizations: Productive climates for research and development. New York: Wiley. Also see revised edition (1976). Ann Arbor: Institute for Social Research, University of Michigan.

Rathbun, J. (1993). Dual career couples: Decisions and dilemmas. University Record, 49(5), 4. University of Michigan.

Simpson, E. L. (1992). Gender differences in faculty perceptions of factors that enhance and inhibit academic career growth. In D. H. Wulff & J. D. Nyquist (Eds.), To improve the academy (Vol. 16). Stillwater, OK: New Forums Press.

Sorcinelli, M. D. (1988). Satisfactions and concerns of new university teachers. In J. G. Kurfiss (Ed.), To improve the academy (Vol. 7, pp. 121–133). Stillwater, OK: New Forums Press.

Urdan, T. C., & Maehr, M. L. (1995). Beyond a two-goal theory of motivation and achievement: A case for social goals. Review of Educational Research, 65, 213–243.

White, T. H., Spencer, M. G., & Peterson, M. W. (1993). Institutional climate and the quality of the academic workplace. Review of Higher Education, 17(1), 69–93.

3 Beyond Male Theory: A Feminist Perspective on Teaching Motivation

JUDITH S. GLAZER

It was not until the 1970s that women's voices were heard in motivational psychology, and then only tangentially. Even today, more than two decades later, mainstream psychologists and organizational theorists continue to use concepts rooted in androcentric values and to disregard evidence that universities, for example, are gendered organizations (Acker, 1990; Calas & Smircich, 1992; Hearn & Parkin, 1983). Theories of intrinsic and extrinsic motivation are derived largely from male-designed and -administered studies that treat gender as a variable, if at all (Stewart & Chester, 1982).[1] Even guides to effective teaching offer only a gender-neutral approach in their analyses of motivation, focusing on interaction with students, enthusiasm for and knowledge of the subject, and socialization to the job (see, e.g., Dill & Assoc., 1990; Eble, 1988; McKeachie, 1986).

As a consequence, motivation theory offers only a partial view of human behavior. Its underlying assumption is that internal and external influences affect human behavior and attitudes and that, through modifying one or more elements, individual motivation can be enhanced. The elements most frequently mentioned are performance and learning goals, feedback and rewards, personal and professional autonomy, and self-efficacy. There are a number of motivational theories in the management literature, which Barry Staw (1984) subdivides into "three theoretical camps": *reinforcement theories* concerned with behavior modification, demonstrating the power of extrinsic rewards in changing behavior; *need theories,* which argue that knowledge of the need state of any individual is essential to behavioral prediction; and, largely allied with need theorists, *expectancy theories,* which claim that individuals seek to maximize valued outcomes through their capacity to achieve high performance, the probability of success, and the institutional reward system (p. 64). Although Staw is aware that reinforcement and need theories have been attacked on both methodological and theoretical grounds, he notes that need theory, in particular, continues to play a strong indirect role in several models of organizational behavior (p. 65). There is also a growing recognition among organizational theorists that motivational behavior is enhanced through a combination of intrinsic factors (ability, competence, self-efficacy) and the expectation of valued outcomes or rewards (Lawler, 1977).

Models of Teaching Motivation

Explanatory models of teaching motivation utilize concepts derived from need, expectancy, and reinforcement theories. Process-product, or teaching-effectiveness, research has developed within the tradition of applied behaviorist psychology, and, according to Ross, Cornett, and Mc-Cutcheon, it "represents the mainstream of research on teaching since 1965" (1992, p. 4). The main purpose of process-product research has been to examine the relationship between "what teachers do in the classroom (the processes of teaching) and what happens to their students (the products of learning)," controlling for such context variables as gender, subject matter, and ability levels and leading to the development and promotion of effective practices to improve instruction (p. 5). This approach is closely allied with reinforcement theory in its emphasis on the importance of external influences for teaching performance. In this construct, the individual is motivated, not through interactions, self-understanding, or cognitive development, but by adhering to externally imposed goals, standards, and measures of teaching effectiveness and the expectations of rewards for positive performance. Women (and men) who adopt a more critical approach to "effective teaching" question the underlying assumptions of the process-product model, with its emphasis on the use of such pedagogical techniques as critical thinking, mastery learning, and assertive discipline in producing anticipated measurable and observable responses. This interpretive approach replaces "nomothetic, decontextualized, universal" theorizing with an "understanding [of] teaching and curriculum making as universes of activity influenced by personal experiences and interactions among individuals and contexts" (p. 17).

Humanistic models of teaching motivation assume that "particularistic and universal needs . . . adhere in all faculty" and that strong motivation and commitment to the teaching role are derived from a recognition that the teaching enterprise can be a continuing source of profound satisfaction (Bess, 1977, p. 245). Recent models that combine elements from need and expectancy-values theories attempt to reconceptualize the traditional reward system by assigning greater value to the outcomes of classroom teaching despite both anecdotal and statistical evidence that, in higher education, prestige, status, and remunerative rewards accrue more readily for scholarly productivity than for pedagogical excellence (Fairweather, 1993; Glazer, 1993).

In assuming a gender-neutral stance, each of these theories of teaching motivation overlooks almost entirely the differential treatment accorded to women faculty, the contexts in which they work, and the multiple influences on their professional and personal lives. Gender issues are largely ignored in research conducted almost exclusively by men who affirm a masculine ideal as the universal norm through which male/female motivation is measured and compared. There is a general failure to acknowledge the views of feminist faculty who adhere to dissimilar values and beliefs and whose expectations are thwarted by unresponsive systems. Their positions, which have evolved within changing social, political, and economic contexts during the past thirty years, convey different convictions and result from different experiences than those of their male colleagues, with the result that "malestream" motivation theory provides only a partial vision of human behavior.[2]

In her comparative analysis of feminism, postmodernism, and psychoanalysis, Jane Flax (1990) suggests that women need to articulate and reflect on their social worlds, particularly existing power/knowledge relationships, and to formulate ways in which these worlds can be transformed. In this context, I propose to undertake a feminist critique of mainstream motivation theory as a socially constructed metaphor for power/ knowledge relationships within organizations and then to consider the role of feminist pedagogy in redefining teaching motivation to reflect more accurately the intellectual and social worlds of women faculty. From the multiplicity of motivation theories, I limit my analysis to a discussion of need and expectancy-value theories that have been applied and tested in feminist psychological research and that have emerged from the twin traditions of developmental psychology (Maslow, 1954) and social psychology (McClelland, 1984b; McClelland, Atkinson, Clark, & Lowell, 1953).

Hierarchies of Need: The Maslow Tradition

The Maslow tradition presupposes that "human needs arrange themselves in hierarchies of prepotency [and that] the appearance of one need
usually rests on the prior satisfaction of another, more prepotent need [as]
man is a perpetually wanting animal" (1943, p. 374). In this model of
human development, which was organized in opposition to behaviorist
psychology, social relationships and self-esteem are merely the third and
fourth stages in a hierarchy of prepotent or higher needs leading to a fifth
stage of self-actualization. In the 1960s and 1970s, organizational theorists
adopted and modified Maslow's theoretical construct, while retaining the
dualisms that separate dominant/subordinate needs into satisfiers (intrinsic motivators) and dissatisfiers (extrinsic hygienes) (Herzberg, Mausner,
& Snyderman, 1959) or into higher order/lower order, primary/secondary
needs (Alderfer, 1972) or, in the case of expectancy theorists, into quality-
of-life/organizational effectiveness needs (Lawler, 1977).

Herzberg's motivation-hygiene theory uses two sets of factors to explain
the relationship between an individual and his or her work: intrinsic *motivators,* which he views as the main determinants of job satisfaction, for example, recognition, achievement, responsibility, and personal growth, and
extrinsic *hygienes,* which he characterizes as sources of dissatisfaction derived from organizational policies, working conditions, and reward systems. As Hackman points out in his essay on work redesign, neither
Herzberg's motivation-hygiene model nor his own job characteristics
model, which is concerned with matching the characteristics of jobs to the
abilities and needs of jobholders (person-environment fit), addresses
"managerial, social, technical, or situational moderators of how people
react to their work" (Hackman, 1977, p. 111).

For Alderfer, existence-relatedness-and-growth (ERG) theory "is derived from an open-systems view of man," consisting of a three-stage hierarchy of basic needs in which existence and relatedness are viewed as
lower-order needs and growth is perceived as a higher-order need to be
achieved through individual differentiation-integration (1972, pp. 11–13).
Although he acknowledges the persistence of male/female, dominant/sub-
ordinate hierarchies within work organizations, he subscribes to the view
that women's acquiescence to male superiority in intergroup relations may
be evidence of female acceptance of the status quo within work organizations (1977, p. 273). Lawler's reward system also consists of a two-stage hierarchy: at one level are individual quality-of-work-life issues related to
equity and the satisfaction of basic security needs, and at a higher level are

organizational effectiveness concerns related to individual performance, reward distribution patterns, and organizational membership (1977, p. 172). Implicit in Lawler's model of an equitable reward system is the assumption that good performance leads to desirable rewards.

In the humanistic tradition, the underlying assumptions for persistent differences in male and female motivation are not addressed, and women's motivational behavior is frequently portrayed as deficient, aberrant, and problematic (Crawford & Marecek, 1989). Recent scholarship on the psychology of women, however, has begun to generate feminist frameworks through which to rethink the questions that are asked, the methodologies that are used, and the concepts that are identified as correlates of human behavior (Bohan, 1992; Unger & Crawford, 1992). The use of gender as an analytic category rather than an abstract variable is fundamental in comprehending as well as changing organizational structures and processes that thwart women's motivation, for, as Joan Acker (1990) argues, "the deeply embedded gendering of both organizational processes and theory" provides the "subtext for arrangements of domination, subordination, and control."

Betty Friedan drew on Maslow for her pathfinding study of the disparity between the reality of women's lives and the biological and cultural stereotypes that thwart their ability to move from domesticity to professionalism (1963).[3] She was not alone in shaping her arguments along traditional theoretical lines, thinking that women's lives could be reinterpreted through the use of existing ideologies. As Flax (1990) aptly remarks, "By conceptualizing woman as the problem, we repeat rather than deconstruct or analyze the social relations that construct or represent us as a problem in the first place" (p. 138).

Maslow's influence on Friedan is an excellent example of this contradiction. Although he believed that women's fulfillment was achieved through the domestic sphere and through "strong men defined culturally in terms of power, status, wealth, rank, athletic prowess rather than through self-fulfillment" (1979, p. 1139), Friedan argued that a greater emphasis on women's equality, rights, and human potential in the public (societal) sphere would eradicate such cultural stereotypes. She contended that sexual emancipation and self-realization came from meaningful work, that "the same range of potential ability exists for women as for men, [who] can only find their identity in work that uses their full capacities," without which they commit "a kind of suicide" (p. 293). Recognizing the differential treatment accorded women faculty in the 1960s, Friedan exhorted universities to desist from treating unmarried women scholars "as lepers" and to recruit married women scholars as "role models who have combined marriage and motherhood with the life of the mind" (p. 321).

It is not surprising, in retrospect, that Friedan embraced Maslow's need theory. As Jean Grimshaw points out in a critique of Maslow, his ideal society, Eupsychia, was ruled by "an elite of self-actualizers" (1986, p. 151), based on "notions of hierarchy, superiority, inferiority, dominance, and submission" (p. 153). Even though his theory of self was clearly antiegalitarian, elitist, and hierarchical, it appealed to Friedan and to other followers of the human potential movement by virtue of its "vigorous image of self-assertion, self-affirmation, and independence" (Grimshaw, 1986, p. 153).

By 1970, the slow progress of the women's movement and women's inability to make significant gains as faculty or administrators in higher education motivated feminists to reject Friedan's liberal feminist vision and to advocate a radically different agenda. Espousing the belief that masculinity and femininity are essentially conflictual, they ambitiously sought to transcend the artificiality of disciplinary boundaries and, as part of the feminist agenda, to transform the university system. This agenda was reaffirmed in an ethnographic study of women faculty in academe as recently as 1988 when Aisenberg and Harrington called for the adoption of

> countervalues [that] add up to a countersystem of social order, one that opposes excessive hierarchy and exclusivity in the holding of authority, one that incorporates diversity, spreads authority through processes of cooperation, resists centrality both in the holding of political and intellectual authority and in the defining of truth and value, and protects individuality through the legitimizing of a personal component in professional life, a personal component to a professional voice. (p. 137)

Achievement and Power: The McClelland Tradition

Another strand of motivational research which is less concerned with humanistic hypotheses than with those incentives that act as motivational determinants of human behavior is exemplified by the many studies conducted over a period of three decades by David McClelland and his colleagues.[4] He and his followers have developed a vast body of research, using the Thematic Apperception Test (TAT) to measure three motives: achievement, affiliation, and power (McClelland, 1984b; McClelland, Atkinson, Clark, & Lowell, 1953). In concentrating his attention on recording the thoughts and actions of male subjects, McClelland has formulated a "balanced motivational profile" of the successful man with moderately high power, affiliation, and achievement motivation scores. This has led to a four-stage theory of power motivation and levels of maturity, embodying three motivational determinants of male leadership behavior: a strong concern for influence (high power motivation), a lesser concern for being liked (low affiliation motivation), and strong self-control (high activity inhibition) (1975, p. 277).

Although McClelland acknowledges that psychologists have tended to regard male behavior as the norm and female as deviant, he perpetuates gender stereotypes in the imagery he uses, the interpretations he gives to his data, and the conclusions he draws (1975, 1984a). Comparing sex differences in power motivation, he finds evidence of traditional male and female roles, and his essay "Power and the Feminine Role" stresses the importance of biological and social determinants of women's motivational behavior, suggesting that women make better teachers and office workers because they are more contextual than analytic, have a more complex interdependent relationship to the world than men, and are more interested in people than things (1975, p. 86).

In an early feminist critique of McClelland's work, Matina Horner maintained that women's achievement is more concerned with social acceptability, whereas men's is more closely tied to the life cycle (1972). In their 1953 study of the achievement motive in male undergraduates, McClelland and his colleagues had identified two subtypes of a more general motive which they referred to as "fear of failure" and "hope of success." Horner noted a third subtype in her research on female undergraduates which she called "the motive to avoid success" (p. 158). She argued that "femininity and competitive achievement in American society [continued] to be viewed as two desirable but mutually exclusive ends" and that, as a result, many achievement-oriented women, "when faced with the conflict between their feminine image and developing their abilities and interests, disguise[d] their ability and abdicate[d] from competition in the outside world" (1972, p. 181). In effect, this was the flip side of the feminine mystique coin; women were now gaining access to professional careers in male-dominated fields, but when confronted with major career decisions, they were reverting to internalized values and beliefs about appropriate female roles (p. 183). In a later study of the impact of liberal arts education on men and women, McClelland mused that college attendance "*may* hurt women by 'maintaining' their fear of success, but more research [was] needed to be sure" (1984a, p. 282). What became known in popular parlance as "the Cinderella complex" provided a plausible explanation for a phenomenon in which "women's shortcomings [were] seen as arising from gender-related motives, fears, or self-concepts that [caused them] to act against [their] own best interests" (Crawford & Marecek, 1989, p. 152).

More than two hundred subsequent studies of the fear-of-success construct attempting to replicate Horner's findings brought mixed results, leading Rhoda Unger and Mary Crawford (1992, p. 471) to conclude that the achievement motive cannot be understood without considering gender socialization in both women and men. A further critical appraisal by Michelle Paludi of the validity and reliability of sixty-four of these studies also determined that fear of success, ability in women, sex-role orientation, and other behavioral measures appear to be unrelated. She suggests that fear of success is a methodological rather than a societal issue and recommends that this label be abandoned, "since its continued use serves only to reinforce the popular and widespread, but scientifically unfounded, idea that sex differences in occupational or academic participation are attributable to an intrapsychic difference between men and women, an approach that blames the victim" (1987, p. 200).

Abigail Stewart and Nia Chester (1982) had already undertaken a comprehensive review of studies of gender differences in achievement, affiliation, and power motives in the McClelland tradition, leading them to conclude that (1) most research on women's motivation takes findings with male subjects as the norm and then compares them with findings from research on female subjects; (2) the evidence that all three motives can be similarly aroused and measured in men and women is ignored or misinterpreted; and (3) minor variations are more attributable to social norms and expectations than to differences in gender (p. 174). Stewart and Chester portray members of the research community as blinded by their belief that "the need for achievement could be aroused in women only under special conditions, even as they developed evidence that this was not true," and note that only research designed to produce more directly comparable data can finally settle the question (p. 189).

Cultural Feminism and Teaching Motivation

Self-in-Relation Theory

Recent feminist conceptualizations of human motivation link achievement, affiliation, and power as mutually reinforcing motives. This approach contradicts need theorists in the Maslow tradition who view affiliation and achievement needs as midway points in a hierarchy of lower- and higher-order needs and who emphasize the importance of individuation-differentiation as evidence of self-actualization and personal growth. It also rejects empirical research in the McClelland tradition which isolates motivational determinants of behavior from other aspects of human thought and actions—for example, values, beliefs, attitudes, and skills. Cultural or self-in-relation feminists assert that "women are repositories of qualities of affiliativeness, relatedness, empathy, and nurturance, [qualities that] are devalued and distorted in male-dominant culture and by men" (Chodorow, 1993, p. 120).

The cultural feminist position is persuasively argued by Jean Baker Miller and her colleagues at the Stone Center for Developmental Studies at Wellesley College (Braude, 1988; Jordan, Kaplan, Miller, Stiver, & Surrey, 1991). Miller speculates that women may be strongly motivated to take a "different, critical, and creative stance" to power and to seek new ways of negotiating power with others in their personal and professional lives (Miller, 1988, p. 8). She supports an alternative vision in which women's self-development is "organized around being able to make and then to maintain affiliation and relationships" (Miller, 1991, p. 83).

Studies undertaken by two of Miller's colleagues, Janet Surrey and Judith Jordan, attempt to move beyond the dualisms of person/society, dependence/independence, and separation/individuation to a model based on relationship-differentiation, defined as "a dynamic process that encompasses increasing levels of complexity, structure, and articulation within the context of human bonds and attachments" (Surrey, 1991, p. 36). In this paradigm, women's self-development does not occur through a hierarchical sequence of defined separations implicit in androcentric models but through relationships and relational competencies that facilitate and create "new growth-enhancing structures for women" (p. 43). Motivation and empowerment are achieved through "mutual intersubjectivity," interpreted as "an interest in, attunement to, and responsiveness to the subjective, inner experience of the other at both a cognitive and affective level" (Jordan, 1991, p. 165). Jordan acknowledges the difficulties of motivating group interdependence in contemporary work settings that adhere to hierarchical power/knowledge relationships as incentives to individual achievement (p. 94). The position taken by Miller, Jordan, and Surrey is supported by the work of Carol Gilligan (1977), who has written extensively on women's different voices and the importance of relationships throughout women's lives, and by the research of Mary Belenky and her colleagues (1986), who find that women's personal growth and intellectual development move them toward connected learning, mutual empathy, and self-understanding (Surrey, 1991, p. 171).

In writing on the "state of the art" in American feminist psychology, Martha Mednick (1991) distinguishes between this work, which she characterizes as "essentialist," and that of the social constructionists. Essentialist theories locate gender within the individual "in terms of fundamental attributes that are conceived as internal, persistent, and generally separate from the ongoing experience of interaction with the daily sociopolitical contexts of one's life," whereas social constructionist theories regard gender as those "interactions that are socially constructed or gendered" (p. 616). Social constructionists challenge the essentialist view, asserting that feminist research should be grounded in the social/situational constraints that women encounter rather than culturally determined or innate qualities that differentiate them from males (Mednick, 1991, p. 617). Their position equates motivational determinants of behavior with the constructed and frequently fragmented realities of women's lives rather than with sex/gender variables. When applied to education, these two views are not mutually exclusive, and a cultural feminist perspective combining elements of essentialism and social constructionism provides a useful conceptualization through which to reframe motivation as a gendered theory.

Feminist Pedagogical Theory and Practice

What are the pedagogical principles that motivate feminist faculty? In teaching the sociology of women's education at the University of Waikato in New Zealand, Sue Middleton finds that "feminist pedagogy requires us as teachers to make visible to and explore with our students the aspects of our own life histories that impact on our teaching. We must analyze relationships between our individual biographies, historical events, and the broader power relations that have shaped and constrained our possibilities and perspectives as educators" (1993, p. 17).

The rationale for feminist pedagogy is closely allied with Paolo Freire's theory of critical or liberatory pedagogy, which asserts that teaching and learning should be "participatory, experiential, and non-hierarchical" based on such concepts as empowerment, student voice, dialogue, and critical thinking (Finke, 1993). However, as Kathleen Weiler (1992) observes in her introduction to a series of essays on the practice of critical pedagogy in schools, critical or Freirian pedagogy has tended to exclude gender or race from consideration, being concerned mainly with class reproduction and resistance in schools. She challenges her white male colleagues who teach in research universities to "address the implications of their own positions of privilege in gender, race, and class terms and to consider ways in which they also implicitly made priveleged and universal claims" in their critical theorizing (p. 4).

For two decades, feminist pedagogy has flourished largely in women's studies programs, focusing on classroom practices, curriculum choices, and evaluative strategies that emphasize empowerment and relationality among a community of women learners (Shrewsbury, 1987, p. 6). This process, in which "feminism and pedagogy converge at the point of inter-section between personal experience and commitment to transformative politics" (Lewis, 1993), has fostered the growth of interdepartmental net-works, sounding boards for feminist theorizing about subject matter con-tent, scholarly research, and classroom teaching. In subjecting disciplinary knowledge to feminist analysis, the dynamics and content of classroom discourse have become more collaborative, leading to what Belenky, Clinchy, Goldberger, and Tarule (1986) refer to as "connected teaching," in which women students are encouraged to articulate and expand their tacit knowledge, to integrate it with their personal experiences, and to develop their own authentic voices.

More recently, however, influenced by postmodern theory, feminist fac-ulty now take a more active political stance, broadening the dialogue to question the viability of pedagogical theory within institutional contexts based on traditional power/knowledge relationships and to subject texts and theories embedded in them to closer critical scrutiny in terms of gen-der, race, ethnicity, sexual orientation, and class (Weedon, 1987). They argue from a constructionist perspective that "gender is not a trait of indi-viduals at all, but simply a construct that identifies particular transactions that are understood to be appropriate to one sex" (Bohan, 1993, p. 7). No longer willing to be relegated to extradepartmental courses based on femi-nist concepts, they employ more active intervention strategies to extend pedagogical knowledge in their disciplines. Teaching motivation becomes a matter of confronting the power/knowledge polarities, recognizing that women "need not take established meanings, values and power relations for granted" and that in the context of gender relations, traditional theories are relative, shifting, and often contradictory (Weedon, p. 174).

The orchestration of class, race, and gender-related experiences in the feminist classroom provides a direct challenge to the notion of knowledge as received wisdom and the teacher as dispenser of knowledge (Lewis, 1990; Weiler, 1991). Those "pedagogical moments [that] arise in specific contexts" are described by Magda Lewis as "the social location of the teacher and students; the geographic and historic location of the institution in which they come together; the political climate in which they work; the personalities and personal profiles of the individuals in the classroom; the readings selected for the course; and the academic background of the students" (1990, p. 487). Lewis defines feminist pedagogy as "those teaching practices aimed at creating the conditions for understanding the possibilities for and restrictions on women's autonomy and self-determination" (1993, p. 52). In viewing the feminist classroom as the site of "political struggle over meaning," she recognizes the risks inherent in challenging assumptions of male privilege and in overcoming institutional and student resistance to feminist perspectives (p. 153).

To some extent, this conflictual attitude arises from the difficulties that Lewis, Middleton, and other feminists encounter in implementing their pedagogies. As Laurie Finke observes in her essay on the relationship between feminism, voice, and the pedagogical unconscious, when feminist pedagogues ask students to discover their own voices, in reality they seek a "particular voice that corresponds to [their] own desires as teachers, desires which have been authorized by the discursive practices of [their] disciplines and fields: English, anthropology, history, and more specifically, feminism" (1993, p. 17). The question becomes whether empowerment can be actualized within existing institutions based on traditional teacher/student, power/knowledge relationships. Finke describes the acquisition of knowledge, revealed in students' diaries for a term project on feminist theorizing, as filled with "conflict and struggle, continually being renewed, recreated, and rethought in light of specific classroom practices" (p. 26).

During the past three years, a female colleague and I have been teaching a course in contemporary educational issues on different suburban campuses of our university. Like Finke, we have also experimented with the use of journal writing by cohorts of women teachers. Our goal has been to encourage students to develop greater reflexivity about their teaching and to understand how social problems and policy making affect their professional lives. By encouraging a climate of feminist inquiry, we consciously seek to re-create our role as "teacher trainers," challenging students to develop their critical voices, to engage more directly with course topics, to integrate professional experience and academic knowledge. In addition to providing us with more spontaneous avenues for two-way communication, journal writing expands opportunities for self-expression, self-understanding, and self-renewal of adults for whom student-teacher relationships are frequently construed in self-other rather than collegial terms. On occasion, journal comments disclose a disjuncture between their diverse academic backgrounds, their daily work lives, and the theoretical stance of their course work. Journal entries also reveal attitudes of powerlessness, anger, ambivalence, and confusion about the overwhelming social problems and remote policy decisions that filter into their personal and professional lives and which have an indirect impact on their work. By inviting students who are also teachers into an ongoing dialogue throughout the semester, we consciously seek to move beyond mainstream theories that have little relevance to their lives and to utilize feminist pedagogies as a platform for constructing more interactive, collaborative models.

Conclusions

Women approach teaching from different perspectives than their male colleagues, but they are not a monolithic group. Their motivation to teach, their socialization to the profession, the dual reward systems that sustain them, and their interactions with students derive from their gendered experiences. At one end of the spectrum may be the non-tenure-track instructor with a fifteen-credit workload, little job security, and large classes of underprepared and undermotivated students. At the other extreme may be the tenured research professor whose laboratory is supported by federal grants, whose teaching load may be limited to one course during the academic year, and whose satisfaction is derived from scholarly pursuits and national recognition. Somewhere in between are the vast majority of faculty who must balance the contradictory responsibilities of teaching, research, and service in their professional careers.

In subjecting representative motivation theories from developmental and social psychology to feminist critique and in reviewing the research of feminist psychologists who have analyzed and applied these theories, I have sought evidence of their validity and meaning for women faculty. It is my view that the use of male-derived motivation theories as explanatory frameworks is unpersuasive, particularly if not only gender but also race/ethnicity, social class, sexual orientation, and age are excluded from the investigation. When applied to college and university teaching, mainstream psychology and organizational behavior ignore the institutionalized discrimination and asymmetric roles of women faculty, the frequently contradictory impact of gender relations, and the differential reward systems that permeate gendered organizations.

There is ample documentation that dual reward systems continue to discriminate against women faculty who lag behind men on *all* measures that can be termed intrinsic motivators—salary, tenure, academic rank, interpersonal relationships with male colleagues and supervisors, working conditions—with the result that job satisfaction is seriously compromised (Tack and Pattitu, 1993). Such inequities sustain male power relationships and raise questions about the validity of traditional rationales for engaging women with high achievement and power motives in gender-neutral faculty development programs. Current data on faculty salaries indicate, for example, that despite an increase of 6 percent in the number of women faculty in the past decade, the disparity between women's and men's salaries remains unchanged (AAUP, 1993b, p. 12). These data also show that "part-time faculty are disproportionately female" and that the disparity is even greater, "fully two to one," for women in non-tenure-track positions (AAUP, 1993a, p. 42). Their cumulative impact is to call into question the liberal feminist perspective that equalizing opportunity through changes in laws and customs sufficiently motivates academic institutions to remove barriers to women's advancement.

The relative lack of progress being made by women faculty is in dramatic contrast to the shift occurring in male-female student enrollment ratios. National enrollment data for fall 1992 indicate that women are now 55.7 percent of all undergraduates and 56.4 percent of all graduate students (Snyder & Hoffman, 1994, p. 208). This shift in the ratio of female to male students and the lagging progress of women in the professoriate emphasize the urgency for reassessing institutional as well as pedagogical practices. It also provides further evidence that women's so-called fear of failure is a culturally constructed myth unsupported by the data on women's growing participation in graduate and professional schools. Underlying the need for reassessment is the recognition that academic institutions are gendered organizations, that gendered subtexts are embedded in academic departments and disciplines, that the epistemological development of students is not a gender-neutral process, and that, as Stewart and Chester (1982) observe, variations in gender motivation are due less to gender differences than to disparate social norms and expectations.

Cultural or self-in-relation feminists link achievement, affiliation, and power as mutually reinforcing motives rather than as lower-order/higher-order stages in women's development. Their research demonstrates that relationality, empathy, and personal growth are not intermediate stages leading to separation-individuation and that their centrality in women's lives should be considered in devising more responsive models of teaching and learning. Constructionist feminists challenge the foundational claims of cultural feminism, asserting that motivational determinants of behavior are socially constructed rather than culturally determined qualities derived from sex/gender variables. I have concluded that, when applied to education, a cultural feminist perspective combining elements of both essentialism and social constructionism can provide the basis for reframing motivation as a gendered theory. In this construct, feminist pedagogies can serve as mediating frameworks to replace traditional notions of teaching motivation with more innovative and collaborative approaches.

Men can begin to adopt elements of these pedagogies, applying multifocal perspectives in listening to women's voices, reflecting on pedagogical practice, subjecting texts and theories to critical scrutiny, and starting a dialogue with their colleagues in women's studies programs. For example, feminists reject transmission-of-knowledge approaches and positivistic methodologies as antithetical to collaborative discourse. Therefore, the material that is taught and the methodology that is used are apt to reflect an interest in elevating women's critical voice, nurturing their potential as autonomous learners, and fostering their personal growth. Whereas the cultural feminist position affirms the importance of women's self-development in relational contexts, the constructionist view asserts that pedagogical practice is grounded in experience rather than being culturally determined. A feminist perspective on teaching motivation opens the door to many possibilities for change in colleges and universities. The gendering of pedagogical theory and practice, building on the knowledge gained through two decades of feminist pedagogy, provides an important mechanism for initiating that process.

Notes

1. For example, in a comprehensive study of fifty motivational theories of personality, learning, and cognition constructed between 1930 and 1971, none of the numerous explanatory concepts and hypotheses that are used "to describe, explain, and predict" purposive or goal-directed behavior measure male/female differences in their research. See K. B. Madsen, *Modern theories of motivation: A comparative metascientific study* (New York: Wiley, 1976).

2. See Shulamit Reinharz, *Feminist methods in social research* (New York: Oxford University Press, 1992), for a discussion of "malestream" research methods.

3. Friedan drew on two of Maslow's studies in framing her argument: A. Maslow, "Dominance, personality, and social behavior in women," *Journal of Social Psychology, 10* (1939), 3–39; and A. Maslow, "Self-esteem (dominance-feeling) and sexuality in women," *Journal of Social Psychology, 16* (1942), 259–294.

4. A useful bibliography of McClelland's work can be found in A. J. Stewart (Ed.), "Chronological bibliography of David C. McClelland," in *Motivation and society* (San Francisco: Jossey-Bass, 1982), pp. 344–359.

References

Acker, J. J. (1990). Hierarchies, jobs, and bodies. *Gender and Society, 4,* 139–158.

Aisenberg, N., & Harrington, M. (1988). *Women in academe.* Amherst: University of Massachusetts Press.

Alderfer, C. P. (1972). *Existence, relatedness, and growth: Human needs in organizational settings.* New York: Free Press.

Alderfer, C. P. (1977). Group and intergroup relations. In J. R. Hackman & J. L. Suttle (Eds.), *Improving life at work: Behavioral science approaches to organizational change* (pp. 227–296). Santa Monica, CA: Goodyear Publishing.

American Association of University Professors [AAUP]. (1993a). The status of non-tenure-track faculty. *Academe, 79,* 39–51.

American Association of University Professors [AAUP]. (1993b). Treading water: The annual report on the economic status of the profession, 1992–1993. *Academe, 79,* 8–14.

Belenky, M. F., Clinchy, B. M., Goldberger, N. R., & Tarule, J. M. (1986). *Women's ways of knowing: The development of self, voice, and mind.* New York: Basic Books.

Bess, J. L. (1977). The motivation to teach. *Journal of Higher Education, 48,* 243–258.

Bohan, J. S. (Ed.). (1992). *Seldom heard, rarely seen: Women's place in psychology.* Boulder, CO: Westview Press.

Bohan, J. S. (1993). Regarding gender: Essentialism, constructionism, and feminist psychology. *Psychology of Women Quarterly, 17,* 5–21.

Braude, M. (Ed.). (1988). *Women, power, and therapy: Issues for women.* New York: Haworth Press.

Calas, M. B., & Smirich, L. (1992). Re-writing gender into organizational theorizing: Directions from feminist perspectives. In M. Reed & M. Hughes (Eds.), *Rethinking organizations: New directions in organizational theory and analysis* (pp. 227–253). Newbury Park, CA: Sage.

Chodorow, N. J. (1993). What is the relation between psychoanalytic feminism and the psychoanalytic psychology of women? In D. Rhode (Ed.), *Theoretical perspectives on sexual difference* (pp. 114–130). New Haven: Yale University Press.

Crawford, M., & Marecek, J. (1989). Psychology reconstructs the female, 1968–1988. *Psychology of Women Quarterly, 13,* 147–165.

Dill, D. D., and Associates. (1990). *What teachers need to know: The knowledge, skills, and values essential to good teaching.* San Francisco: Jossey-Bass.

Eble, K. (1988). *The craft of teaching.* San Francisco: Jossey-Bass.

Fairweather, J. (1993). Academic values and faculty rewards. *Review of Higher Education, 17,* 43–68.

Finke, L. (1993). Knowledge as bait: Feminism, voice, and the pedagogical unconscious. *College English, 55,* 7–27.

Flax, J. (1990). *Thinking fragments: Psychoanalysis, feminism, and postmodernism in the contemporary West.* Berkeley: University of California Press.

Friedan, B. (1963). *The feminine mystique.* London: Penguin Books.

Gilligan, C. (1977). In a different voice: Women's conceptions of self and morality. *Harvard Educational Review, 47,* 481–517.

Glazer, J. S. (1993). *A teaching doctorate? The doctor of arts, then and now.* Washington, DC: American Association for Higher Education.

Grimshaw, J. (1986). *Feminist philosophers: Women's perspectives on philosophical traditions.* London: Harvester Wheatsheaf.

Hackman, J. R. (1977). Work design. In J. R. Hackman & J. L. Suttle (Eds.), *Improving life at work: Behavioral science approaches to organizational change* (pp. 96–162). Santa Monica, CA: Goodyear Publishing.

Hearn, J., & Parkin, P. W. (1983). Gender and organizations: A selective review and a critique of a neglected area. *Organizational Studies, 4,* 219–242.

Herzberg, F., Mausner, B., & Snyderman, B. (1959). *The motivation to work* (2d ed.). New York: Wiley.

Horner, M. (1972). Toward an understanding of achievement-related conflicts in women. *Journal of Social Issues, 28,* 157–175.

Jordan, J. V. (1991). The meaning of mutuality. In J. V. Jordan, A. G. Kaplan, J. B. Miller, I. P. Stiver, & J. L. Surrey (Eds.), *Women's growth in connection: Writings from the Stone Center* (pp. 81–96). New York: Guilford Press.

Jordan, J. V., Kaplan, A. G., Miller, J. B., Stiver, I. P., & Surrey, J. L. (Eds.). (1991). *Women's growth in connection: Writings from the Stone Center.* New York: Guilford Press.

Lawler, E. E., III. (1977). Reward systems. In J. R. Hackman & J. L. Suttle (Eds.), *Improving life at work: Behavioral science approaches to organizational change* (pp. 163–226). Santa Monica, CA: Goodyear Publishing.

Lewis, M. G. (1990). Interrupting patriarchy: Politics, resistance, and transformation in the feminist classroom. *Harvard Educational Review, 60,* 467–487.

Lewis, M. G. (1993). *Without a word: Teaching beyond women's silence.* New York: Routledge.

Maslow, A. H. (1943). A theory of human motivation. *Psychological Review, 50,* 370–396.

Maslow, A. H. (1954). *Motivation and personality.* New York: Harper.

Maslow, A. H. (1979). *The journals of A. H. Maslow* (Vol. 2). Edited by R. J. Lowry. Monterey, CA: Brooks/Cole.

McClelland, D. C. (1975). *Power: The inner experience.* New York: Irvington.

McClelland, D. C. (1984a). The Harlequin complex. In D. C. McClelland (Ed.), *Motives, personality, and society: Selected papers* (pp. 119–146). New York: Praeger.

McClelland, D. C. (1984b). How motives, skills, and values determine what people do. In D. C. McClelland (Ed.), *Motives, personality, and society: Selected papers* (pp. 213–236). New York: Praeger.

McClelland, D. C., Atkinson, J. W., Clark, R. A., & Lowell, E. L. (1953). *The achievement motive.* New York: Appleton-Century-Crofts.

McKeachie, W. (1986). *Teaching tips: A guidebook for teachers* (8th ed.). Lexington, MA: D. C. Heath.

Mednick, M. T. (1991). Currents and futures in American feminist psychology: State of the art revisited. *Psychology of Women Quarterly, 15,* 611–621.

Middleton, S. (1993). *Educating feminists: Life histories and pedagogy.* New York: Teachers College Press.

Miller, J. B. (1988). Women and power. In M. Braude (Ed.), *Women, power, and therapy: Issues for women* (pp. 1–10). New York: Haworth Press.

Miller, J. B. (1991). The development of women's sense of self. In J. V. Jordan, A. G. Kaplan, J. B. Miller, I. P. Stiver, & J. L. Surrey (Eds.), *Women's growth in connection: Writings from the Stone Center* (pp. 11–26). New York: Guilford Press.

Paludi, M. (1987). Psychometric properties and underlying assumptions of four objective measures of fear of success. In M. R. Walsh (Ed.), *The psychology of women: Ongoing debates* (pp. 185–203). New Haven: Yale University Press.

Ross, E. W., Cornett, J. W., & McCutcheon, G. (1992). Teacher personal theorizing and research on curriculum and teaching. In E. W. Ross, J. W. Cornett, & G. McCutcheon (Eds.), *Teacher personal theorizing: Connecting curriculum practice, theory, and research* (pp. 3–18). Albany: State University of New York Press.

Shrewsbury, C. M. (1987). What is feminist pedagogy? *Women's Studies Quarterly, 15,* 6–13.

Snyder, T., & Hoffman, C. (1994). *Digest of educational statistics.* Washington, DC: U.S. Government Printing Office.

Staw, B. (1984). Motivation research versus the art of faculty management. In J. L. Bess (Ed.), *College and university organizations: Insights from the behavioral sciences* (pp. 63–83). New York: New York University Press.

Stewart, A. J., & Chester, N. L. (1982). Sex differences in human social motives: Achievement, affiliation, power. In A. J. Stewart (Ed.), *Motivation and society: A volume in honor of David McClelland* (pp. 172–218). San Francisco: Jossey-Bass.

Surrey, J. L. (1991). The 'self-in-relation': A theory of women's development. In J. V. Jordan, A. G. Kaplan, J. B. Miller, I. P. Stiver, & J. L. Surrey (Eds.), *Women's growth in connection: Writings from the Stone Center* (pp. 51–66). New York: Guilford Press.

Tack, M. W., & Pattitu, C. L. (1993). *Faculty job satisfaction: Women and minorities in peril.* ASHE-ERIC Education Report No. 4. Washington, DC: Association for the Study of Higher Education.

Unger, R., & Crawford, M. (1992). *Women and gender: A feminist psychology.* New York: McGraw-Hill.

Weedon, C. (1987). *Feminist practice and poststructuralist theory.* Oxford: Basil Blackwell.

Weiler, K. (1991). Freire and a feminist pedagogy of difference. *Harvard Educational Review, 61,* 449–474.

Weiler, K. (1992). Introduction. In K. Weiler & C. Mitchell (Eds.), *What schools can do: Critical pedagogy and practice* (pp. 3–10). Albany: State University of New York Press.

II Theories of Internal Motivation to Teach

4

Self-Determined Teaching:
Opportunities and Obstacles

EDWARD L. DECI, TIM KASSER, AND RICHARD M. RYAN

Guiding the intellectual and emotional development of students, whether in nursery school or graduate school, can be profoundly gratifying for teachers, satisfying their psychological needs and contributing to their growth as individuals. Yet all too often, at each level of education, one finds teachers who are frustrated, disaffected, or just plain bored. Public school teachers, for example, can often be heard complaining about students, parents, or the educational system; and the scenario of a professor lecturing from aged, yellowing notes may, at least metaphorically, be more real than apocryphal. In this chapter we consider both the motivating opportunities provided by teaching at the college or university level, and the obstacles to that motivation (i.e., the factors responsible for the frustration and disinterest).

Although there are noteworthy similarities in the opportunities and obstacles faced by faculty members at all educational levels, the motivational dynamics of college or university professors are in some ways more complex than those of other teachers, because the nature of the tasks performed by many professors is more varied. Whereas the job of a nursery, elementary, or secondary school teacher is to teach—that is, to nurture the

Preparation of this chapter was supported in part by grants from the National Institute of Mental Health (MH 18922) and the National Institute of Child Health and Human Development (HD 19914) to the Human Motivation Program in the Department of Psychology at the University of Rochester.

cognitive and personal development of students—it is less clear just how salient the activity of teaching is in a professor's job description and self-concept. To be sure, teaching is the primary task of faculty members at some colleges and universities, but at others, particularly the major research universities, the job of a faculty member comprises research, writing, fund-raising, administration, professional service—and, oh yes, teaching. Of course, individual professors vary in terms of how central teaching is to their view of the job, but the unwritten, though nonetheless pervasive, value structure in the research university culture seems to place teaching fairly low in the importance hierarchy, and in the respect afforded its exemplary practitioners.

For some professors the motivation to teach was the primary reason for entering the profession; they were intrinsically motivated. Therefore, the critical question for them is: What factors in the college or university setting will support versus undermine their intrinsic motivation to teach? For other professors, however, the desire to teach had relatively little to do with their career choice. Hence, the relevant motivational question for them is: What factors could facilitate their developing a value for and commitment to teaching once they have arrived at their first jobs?

We address both questions from the perspective of self-determination theory (Deci & Ryan, 1985b, 1991). We thus begin with a brief overview of the theory and then use it to explore professors' motivational dynamics within the college or university setting.

Self-Determination Theory

Self-determination theory posits that the nature of human beings is to grow and develop through the operation of what is called the organismic integration process (Ryan, 1993). By striving to master one's environment, by internalizing experiences, values, and attitudes, and by integrating all this material with intrinsic aspects of oneself, a person develops a progressively more elaborated, refined, and adaptive sense of self. Operating in concert with the three innate psychological needs for competence, autonomy, and relatedness (Deci & Ryan, 1991), the organismic integration process is the means through which one's motivated behavior can become increasingly self-determined—that is, increasingly choiceful and expressive of oneself.

Self-determination theory has been concerned with differentiating various types of motivation to allow a refined analysis of the factors that facilitate versus diminish the quality of motivated behavior. The most important distinction is whether a motivated behavior is autonomous (i.e., self-determined) or controlled. *Autonomous,* or self-determined, actions are freely chosen and experienced as emanating from oneself. In the words of deCharms (1968), they have an internal perceived locus of causality. *Controlled* actions, in contrast, are coerced or seduced by some force external to one's integrated sense of self. Such actions are accompanied by the experience of pressure or tension and have an external perceived locus of causality.

The concept of self-determination is of particular importance for understanding effective teaching at the postsecondary level because a great deal of research across many different types of activities has shown convincingly that self-determined behavior involves higher-quality functioning than controlled behavior. With subjects ranging in age from children to the elderly, in laboratory and field settings, in cultures ranging from America to Japan, and in domains such as education, sports, work, and religion, studies have indicated that, when self-determined, people perform better on complex tasks (McGraw, 1978), process information more flexibly (Grolnick & Ryan, 1987), are more satisfied at work (Deci, Connell, & Ryan, 1989), learn better (Benware & Deci, 1984), are more creative (Amabile, 1983), persist more (Deci, 1971), and achieve better (Grolnick, Ryan, & Deci, 1991). In addition, self-determination has been linked to better adjustment and psychological health (Deci, Schwartz, Sheinman, & Ryan, 1981; Kasser & Ryan, 1993; Ryan, Rigby, & King, 1993).

These results have emerged from work with general personality constructs (Deci & Ryan, 1985a), domain-specific individual differences (Ryan & Connell, 1989), and environmental influences (Deci & Ryan, 1987), and in each case advantages of being self-determined have been clear. Because many of the identified consequences of being self-determined (e.g., enhanced creativity, conceptual understanding, cognitive flexibility, enthusiasm, and persistence) are important attributes for being a college or university teacher, an understanding of how to promote self-determined teaching is of considerable importance.

To explicate the autonomy-versus-control distinction, we begin by differentiating intrinsic and extrinsic motivation. Intrinsically motivated behaviors, which represent the prototype of self-determination, are performed for the spontaneous experience that accompanies them (i.e., the reward is inherent in the doing of the activity itself), whereas extrinsically motivated behaviors are performed for some contingent outcome, whether that be interpersonally or intrapsychically administered.

Intrinsic Motivation

Intrinsic motivation is based in the inherent proactivity of the human organism. By nature people are active agents, operating on the environment to satisfy their needs and working to integrate and assimilate their experience. When intrinsically motivated, people engage in activities out of interest and enjoyment, out of the satisfactions that accrue spontaneously as they involve themselves in the activities. For example, people may climb mountains or solve crossword puzzles because they find the activities themselves rewarding—that is, because the rewards for the activities are the spontaneous feelings of engagement, excitement, accomplishment, or awe which accompany them. Intrinsically motivated behaviors represent the clearest instance of engaging in an activity with a true sense of freedom and choice.

Considerable research and theorizing have indicated that tasks themselves influence whether people are intrinsically motivated (Deci, 1975). Activities that are optimally challenging and responsive to one's initiations and provide meaningful feedback and allow freedom for self-expression are likely to be intrinsically motivating (Csikszentmihalyi, 1975; Danner & Lonky, 1981; Deci, 1975). Of course, people differ in terms of what they find optimally challenging and which activities they find interesting, but when a person finds an activity intrinsically interesting, it will almost surely contain these elements.

Teaching at the college or university level involves many features that can make it intrinsically rewarding. The task of fostering the development of conceptual understanding, aesthetic appreciation, and personal growth in students is certainly challenging, and seeing students respond with enthusiasm and excitement about new ideas can be a source of great satisfaction, for it indicates that one has had a meaningful impact. Professors are typically allowed substantial freedom to innovate and teach in their own way, and there is less surveillance and overt evaluation by supervisors than in most jobs. Furthermore, college or university settings offer considerable opportunities for professors to relate to colleagues and students as they engage in interesting activities and discuss interesting ideas.

It seems clear that teaching at a college or university offers professors the types of challenge which can stimulate intrinsic motivation, and it can provide them opportunities to satisfy their fundamental psychological needs—for competence, autonomy, and relatedness. It is also the case that many people generally think of college or university teaching as intrinsically rewarding. For example, a study by Benware and Deci (1984) showed that when subjects were offered the opportunity to teach college students, they reported a high level of interest and enthusiasm, suggesting that they had the expectation that teaching is intrinsically interesting.

Although postsecondary teaching does offer many potentially motivating features, some people simply do not find the activity interesting, and some do not have the skills necessary for doing it well. For them, the task may be overly challenging and thus not intrinsically motivating. Such people were, no doubt, attracted to the profession by other aspects of the job, aspects such as research or writing. For these people, teaching would be an extrinsically motivated aspect of their job.

Extrinsic Motivation

Extrinsic motivation refers to any instance in which the reasons for one's actions are some separable consequences, whether they be interpersonally administered (e.g., praise, monetary payments, or the opportunity to do other, more interesting tasks) or self-administered (e.g., praising self-statements or presents to oneself). Extrinsic rewards are frequently used and widely advocated as a means of motivating individuals—for example, as a way of motivating professors to teach.

Our primary aim in researching extrinsic motivation has been to understand its relation to self-determination (i.e., to autonomy versus control) and to the qualities of functioning associated with it. Many early studies explored the effects of extrinsic rewards and prompts on intrinsic motivation as a way of beginning to assess the relation of extrinsic motivation to self-determination. These studies uniformly indicated that extrinsic inducements or constraints tended to impair the experience of autonomy and undermine intrinsic motivation (e.g., Deci, 1971; Lepper, Greene, & Nisbett, 1973), thus implying that extrinsically motivated behavior is not self-determined.

Subsequent research has indicated, however, that although extrinsic rewards do often undermine intrinsic motivation, they sometimes enhance or leave it unchanged. These findings suggest that extrinsically motivated behavior can be self-determined (e.g., Ryan, Mims, & Koestner, 1983), so we have differentiated the concept of extrinsic motivation to take account of this. Behaviors that are extrinsically motivated can become autonomous through the developmental processes of internalization and integration (Schafer, 1968). A regulatory process that is initially external, one that takes the form of an offer, a prod, or a threat, for example, can be taken in, so the person begins to value the activity and self-initiate the behavior without the external prompt. In time, the regulation may be wholly integrated with other aspects of the person's self and thus become the basis for truly autonomous extrinsic motivation.

According to the theory, there are two important types of internalized extrinsic regulation which differ in the degree to which the internalization and integration processes have progressed and thus the degree to which the regulation is autonomous versus controlled. *Introjected* regulation involves behaving because one feels one "should," because there is an internalized pressure to behave a certain way in order to bolster one's self-esteem or avoid guilt. *Integrated* regulation, in contrast, involves having accepted the value or personal importance of a behavior and integrated it with other aspects of oneself. This allows the person to engage in the behaviors in an unconflicted, nonpressured, and truly choiceful way. To be integrated with respect to an extrinsic motive is to be autonomous, and integrated regulation and intrinsic motivation represent the most autonomous forms of regulation. External regulation and introjected regulation represent the more controlled forms of motivation.

Those who do not find teaching intrinsically motivating perform the relevant behaviors for extrinsic reasons. The critical question for them, therefore, is how can their extrinsic motivation become integrated rather than remaining external or being merely introjected? Stated differently, the key question is, What factors in the social context of the college or university will facilitate professors' integrating the value of teaching and becoming autonomous in doing it? Again, we emphasize that the importance of this issue derives from the fact that the more autonomous forms of extrinsic motivation—like intrinsic motivation, which is by nature autonomous —have been found to be positively associated with high-quality functioning.

Human Needs and Social Contexts

The self-determination analysis of the influence of contextual events, social climates, and job design on autonomous functioning is done in terms of the relation of those elements to the three fundamental psychological needs. We have hypothesized and consistently found that people will be more self-determined in performing a particular behavior to the extent they have the opportunity to experience autonomy, competence, and relatedness with respect to it (Deci & Ryan, 1985b; Ilardi, Leone, Kasser, & Ryan, 1993). More specifically, maintaining intrinsic motivation tends to be facilitated primarily by feeling competent and autonomous, and integration tends to be promoted by feeling satisfaction of all three needs.

The need for *autonomy* involves experiencing oneself as the origin of one's behavior, rather than feeling like a pawn coerced by circumstances (deCharms, 1968). That is, one is autonomous when the "perceived locus of causality" for one's actions is in factors within oneself (e.g., interest in or valuing of a behavior) rather than from reasons based in pressures, compulsions, or rebellion (Ryan & Connell, 1989). When people feel autonomous, their behavior is choiceful and congruent with their organismic self (Ryan, 1993). *Competence* involves feeling efficacious (White, 1960), feeling a sense of accomplishment. An expression of humans' need for competence is that they often engage in behaviors to meet optimal challenges, even in the absence of prods, prompts, or pressures. People want to expand their capacities and feel effective, and they engage in a wide range of activities toward that end. *Relatedness* involves feeling close to and connected with other individuals (Ryan, 1993). When operating with regard to specific individuals, this need leads to developing intimate relationships, and when operating with respect to groups, it leads to joining formal and informal organizations and to feeling a sense of belonging to their community, work group, or culture.

In considering teaching at the college or university level, then, we would look to whether the interpersonal context and job design afford opportunities to experience autonomy, competence, and relatedness, although our research has focused more on autonomy and its support than on the other two needs. We now consider research relevant to this issue with respect to both intrinsic motivation and the internalization of extrinsic motivation.

The Job and Context of Teaching

A substantial amount of research has explored the effects of social contextual factors on autonomy, suggesting that policies of the institution and relationships between professors and their administrators and colleagues can either bolster their excitement and creativity or turn those qualities into frustration and cynicism.

Studies have shown that for a job to be intrinsically motivating it must be optimally challenging for the individual (e.g., Danner & Lonky, 1981); in other words, there must be a good match between the professor and the teaching demands. Then, even with a good match, there are numerous other factors that can affect intrinsic motivation.

Several studies have shown, for example, that making extrinsic rewards salient as a means of motivating people to do some activity undermines their intrinsic motivation for the task (Deci, 1971). Threats of punishment, the imposition of deadlines, competition, and evaluations when made salient to motivate people have also been found to have the same deleterious effects (Amabile, DeJong, & Lepper, 1976; Deci, Betley, Kahle, Abrams, & Porac, 1981; Deci & Cascio, 1972; Smith, 1974). Of course, professors must be paid and evaluated, and they deal with deadlines regularly, but the point is that the more salient these factors are made and the more they are used in an attempt to motivate or control, the more likely their consequences will be negative. Indeed, studies have shown that when rewards are used as a means of conveying positive feedback or appreciation, rather than as a control strategy, their effects may be positive (Ryan, Mims, & Koestner, 1983). The problem is that rewards and other such motivators are all too often used in an attempt to control—or at least people experience them that way, which leads to the same negative effects.

Additional studies have shown that the style and locution of a person's communications can affect the intrinsic motivation of others (Ryan, 1982; Ryan, Mims, & Koestner, 1983). The more the communication emphasizes controls—through the use of direct commands or words like "should"—the more likely it is to have an adverse effect. Similarly, the general climate or ambience of a setting, such as an academic department or college, can affect the experience of autonomy and thus intrinsic motivation (Deci, Schwartz, Sheinman, & Ryan, 1981; Ryan & Grolnick, 1986). Interpersonal contexts that feel controlling rather than autonomy-supportive have been found to have negative consequences for motivation and well-being (Deci, Connell, & Ryan, 1989).

As a complement to these results, other studies have shown that intrinsic motivation can be enhanced by the provision of choice, the minimization of controlling language and style, and the acknowledgment or reflection of people's feelings and perspectives (Koestner, Ryan, Bernieri, & Holt, 1984; Zuckerman, Porac, Lathin, Smith, & Deci, 1978). When administrators provide more choice with respect to teaching, when they provide a general climate of autonomy support, when they acknowledge faculty members' perspectives, and when they provide meaningful rationales for requests, it is likely that the intrinsically motivated teachers will maintain their enthusiasm and commitment to teaching. To some extent, of course, this will need to be done in an individualized way. New faculty members will typically need greater support than more seasoned ones. They may need a kind of mentor to turn to with problems, perhaps even to help them in planning courses. And even people with the same years of experience will differ in their teaching strengths, so it is useful to take these into account in the match of professors with teaching assignments if intrinsic motivation is to be maintained.

Studies of internalization and integration have found results that parallel those for intrinsic motivation. For example, Grolnick and Ryan (1987), in a study of parents and their elementary-school-aged children, found that parents who were more autonomy-supportive with respect to nonintrinsically motivating activities such as doing homework and chores around the house had children who demonstrated more internalization of the regulation for these activities and who were more autonomous in performing them than the children of controlling parents.

A study by Deci, Eghrari, Patrick, and Leone (1994) also showed that being autonomy-supportive by providing choice, minimizing pressures, presenting a meaningful rationale, and reflecting individuals' feelings led to greater internalization than being controlling. Further, this study showed that people do sometimes internalize regulations presented in a controlling manner, but when they do, they merely introject them, whereas when people internalize regulations in autonomy-supportive contexts, they are more likely to integrate them. Introjected regulations are accompanied by pressure, tension, and the experience of not liking the activity, whereas integrated regulations are accompanied by the experience of greater freedom and enjoyment. Integration of extrinsic motivation is the means by which one can be autonomous when extrinsically motivated, and, as the Deci, Eghrari, Patrick, and Leone and other studies have shown, being autonomous has important positive consequences.

Taken together, the various studies indicate that the same type of factors which support intrinsic motivation also facilitate the integration of values and regulations. There is, however, one particularly important point with respect to internalization and integration—namely, that they involve taking in and making one's own the values that are extant in one's social milieu. Insofar as institutions or administrators wish to promote the value of teaching, they must make this value salient so that faculty members who were not initially interested in teaching will internalize and integrate the value and become more autonomous in carrying out their teaching responsibilities.

One might wonder just how pervasive the value of good teaching is in institutions of higher learning, particularly the research universities. Do administrators and colleagues really value good teaching? Disconcertingly, the answer is probably, "Not particularly." It is not at all clear that one's teaching skills are given much weight in hiring decisions, promotion decisions, or salary decisions. And to the extent that they are not, the message is clear—teaching is not valued. In making this point, we are not suggesting that departments and colleges should become more controlling about teaching; on the contrary, we are advocating their being autonomy-supportive. But the autonomy support must be accompanied by a valuing of teaching, with those values being consistent and clear and being considered in important personnel decisions.

There are a variety of other studies that help to clarify factors in the social context which support one's being autonomous. For example, an experiment by Deci, Spiegel, Ryan, Koestner, and Kauffman (1982) indicated that the more strongly administrators emphasize performance standards, the less autonomous teachers feel and the more controlling they become with their students. In that experiment, half the teachers were told that it was their responsibility to make sure their students performed up to high standards in solving problems; the other teachers were told that their job was to help their students learn to solve problems. Independent judges listened to tapes of the sessions and rated the teachers' styles. Those teachers who were told to make sure their students performed up to standards talked more, gave more directives, used more "should"-type statements, asked more controlling questions, and let their students self-initiate less than did teachers who were not pressured about standards. The former teachers were also rated as more controlling and demanding and less effective than the latter teachers. Furthermore, the students whose teachers had not been pressured actually evidenced more independent problem solving than the students whose teachers had been reminded of performance standards.

Professors need administrators and colleagues who respond to and support their autonomy, creativity, and self-initiation with respect to teaching if they are to be autonomous in that activity and to experience the interest and spontaneity that are necessary to sustain excellent teaching.

Because of what seemed to be very clear advantages to autonomy support, Deci, Connell, and Ryan (1989) studied whether it is possible to teach managers to be more autonomy-supportive of their subordinates and, if so, whether their changed management styles would have positive effects on these workers. The researchers trained supervisors in a large corporation to provide their employees with more choices and more inputs to decision making, to better acknowledge their subordinates' feelings and perspectives, and to give them more informational competence-relevant feedback. Deci, Connell, and Ryan found that the trained supervisors became more autonomy-supportive and their workers reported increased satisfaction with their jobs and more trust in the organization. One presumes that similar benefits would result if administrators and colleagues at a university were to provide more support for professors' psychological needs rather than attempt to control the professors' behavior.

Unfortunately, it may be the case that the conditions supportive of professors' autonomy are slowly eroding. Revenue from both federal sources and tuition is dwindling, which puts greater pressure than ever on professors to produce. People completing their doctoral degrees need several publications to be considered for university faculty positions, and promotions require not only a very strong publication record but also evidence of obtaining extramural funding. In the face of these pressures—and in some cases with increased teaching loads—teaching is likely to be given even less weight in promotion decisions and is likely to be given less attention by faculty members. In other words, professors may be less likely to use teaching as a realm in which to direct their mastery attempts, and, if that is so, they will be less likely to teach well and to feel competent as teachers.

As Mann and others (1970) have pointed out, the teaching culture has an important impact on professors. The ambience created by a group of colleagues affects each member, and as university resources shrink, colleagues tend to become more competitive, which can decrease the experience of autonomy (Deci, Betley, Kahle, Abrams, & Porac, 1981). With this egocentrism, colleagues are less concerned about one another and more concerned about their own fate.

The challenge facing administrators is thus a large one indeed, for they are vulnerable to the same pressures as everyone else. To resist being more controlling in response to these pressures, to be able to encourage mutual support rather than competition and strain among colleagues during difficult times, is asking quite a bit of administrators. But it is a request that must be made, for it is critical if we are to promote more effective teaching.

Of course, a professor's administrators and colleagues are not wholly responsible for his or her effectiveness as a teacher. Substantial research indicates that professors with a more autonomous personality orientation (Deci & Ryan, 1985a; Koestner, Bernieri, & Zuckerman, 1992) are more self-initiating, energetic, and creative, suggesting that they would be more effective teachers. However, because the theme of this book is *promoting* effectiveness, we focus our attention on social-contextual facilitators of effective teaching rather than on personality determinants.

A final set of contextual influences that have a substantial impact on the motivation and experience of professors and thus deserve mention are the behaviors of the students professors encounter. Students, like professors, bring their own personalities, projections, and motivational orientations into the classrooms, and these influence their behavior and the subsequent course of teaching and learning.

In one study conducted by Jelsma (1982), experimental accomplices who posed as learners were taught to solve anagrams by adult subjects who served as teachers. Learners were trained to be interested and cooperative with some teachers and to be less interested and slightly unruly with others. Jelsma found that subjects who taught the restless students became more controlling and enjoyed the experience less than those who taught the more cooperative students. It seems that when students evidence lack of interest, faculty members experience that as pressure and respond by being controlling. That, of course, as the research has consistently shown, will in turn have a negative effect on the learning of the students.

Other research has shown that students' expectations about professors (based on the kinds of things they hear in the student union, perhaps) affect those students' behaviors. For example, Wild, Enzle, and Hawkins (1992) conducted a study in which some subjects were led to believe that their teacher had been paid (and thus was extrinsically motivated) while others were led to believe that their teacher had volunteered (and thus was intrinsically motivated). Even though all subjects received the same lesson, subjects who thought the teacher was intrinsically motivated reported enjoying the lesson more, said they would like to learn more, and explored their new skills more. They also thought the teacher exhibited greater enjoyment, enthusiasm, and innovation. These findings indicate that the students' beliefs about their professors will affect their perceptions and behaviors and, as the Jelsma study showed, the students' behavior will in turn affect the professors' motivation.

These studies suggest that the relationship between students and faculty is an interactive one that can be either positively or negatively synergistic. Students affect the faculty's motivation and behavior just as faculty affect the students'. But it is important to keep in mind that part of the task of teaching is to engender in students the enthusiasm that facilitates a positive rather than negative cycle. For teachers to recognize that students' lack of enthusiasm affects them negatively can be important and useful information for their own self-regulation, but it does not absolve them of responsibility for not devoting themselves to teaching.

Self-Determined Teaching: A Summary

Self-determined education involves having proactivity at the heart of the endeavor (e.g., Rogers, 1969). It means having professors encourage and support students' intrinsic motivation to create, explore, learn, and experiment. It means having professors be an inspiration and a resource—a guide for students' active and self-initiated learning—so that active minds will have the opportunity to meet together in an arena of interesting ideas which can change each participant's way of seeing the world. Such a learning climate for students requires professors to be enthused and involved in the teaching process and in the material they are teaching. This, we suggest, results from the professors' being self-determined in their teaching.

The motivational bases for professors' feeling autonomous and committed in their teaching are intrinsic motivation and integrated extrinsic motivation. Being intrinsically motivated to teach means being interested in teaching and finding it spontaneously satisfying; being autonomously extrinsically motivated means involving oneself fully in the activity because of having internalized and integrated the importance of the activity.

Substantial research now indicates that when professors have the opportunity to feel autonomous, competent, and related, they will be able to assimilate their experiences and express them in stimulating ways. When administrators and colleagues value and support teaching, professors are more likely to maintain whatever intrinsic motivation they have and to integrate extrinsic motivation. Valuing and supporting teaching means giving it importance in decision making and being consistent and honest about its importance. It also means encouraging faculty to be self-initiating, to experiment and try new approaches; it means freeing them from pressures to comply or to focus on imposed standards. Supporting self-determined teaching entails matching a person's skills with the demands of the job and then both placing the locus for decision making about teaching with the teachers themselves and providing informative structures that acknowledge competence and facilitate improvement.

The aim of administrators and others who wish to facilitate effective teaching would usefully be to instill and support a self-responsibility in which professors would be effective because of their own desires to be competent and autonomous in their teaching, to be related to those around them, and to feel that through effective teaching they could grow as both professors and individuals in the environment of the college or university.

References

Amabile, T. M. (1983). *The social psychology of creativity.* New York: Springer-Verlag.

Amabile, T. M., DeJong, W., & Lepper, M. R. (1976). Effects of externally imposed deadlines on subsequent intrinsic motivation. *Journal of Personality and Social Psychology, 34,* 92–98.

Benware, C., & Deci, E. L. (1984). Quality of learning with an active versus passive motivational set. *American Educational Research Journal, 21,* 755–765.

Csikszentmihalyi, M. (1975). *Beyond boredom and anxiety.* San Francisco: Jossey-Bass.

Danner, F. W., & Lonky, E. (1981). A cognitive-developmental approach to the effects of rewards on intrinsic motivation. *Child Development, 52,* 1043–1052.

deCharms, R. (1968). *Personal causation: The internal affective determinants of behavior.* New York: Academic Press.

Deci, E. L. (1971). Effects of externally mediated rewards on intrinsic motivation. *Journal of Personality and Social Psychology, 18,* 105–115.

Deci, E. L. (1975). *Intrinsic motivation.* New York: Plenum Press.

Deci, E. L., Betley, G., Kahle, J., Abrams, L., & Porac, J. (1981). When trying to win: Competition and intrinsic motivation. *Personality and Social Psychology Bulletin, 7,* 79–83.

Deci, E. L., & Cascio, W. F. (1972, April). Changes in intrinsic motivation as a function of negative feedback and threats. Paper presented at the meeting of the Eastern Psychological Association, Boston.

Deci, E. L., Connell, J. P., & Ryan, R. M. (1989). Self-determination in a work organization. *Journal of Applied Psychology, 74,* 580–590.

Deci, E. L., Eghrari, H., Patrick, B. C., & Leone, D. R. (1994). Facilitating internalization: The self-determination theory perspective. *Journal of Personality, 62,* 119–142.

Deci, E. L., & Ryan, R. M. (1985a). The general causality orientations scale: Self-determination in personality. *Journal of Research in Personality, 19,* 109–134.

Deci, E. L., & Ryan, R. M. (1985b). *Intrinsic motivation and self-determination in human behavior.* New York: Plenum Press.

Deci, E. L., & Ryan, R. M. (1987). The support of autonomy and the control of behavior. *Journal of Personality and Social Psychology, 53,* 1024–1037.

Deci, E. L., & Ryan, R. M. (1991). A motivational approach to self: Integration in personality. In R. Dienstbier (Ed.), *Nebraska symposium on motivation: Vol. 38. Perspectives on motivation* (pp. 237–288). Lincoln: University of Nebraska Press.

Deci, E. L., Schwartz, A. J., Sheinman, L., & Ryan, R. M. (1981). An instrument to assess adults' orientations toward control versus autonomy with children: Reflections on intrinsic motivation and perceived competence. *Journal of Educational Psychology, 73,* 642–650.

Deci, E. L., Spiegel, N. H., Ryan, R. M., Koestner, R., & Kauffman, M. (1982). The effects of performance standards on teaching styles: The behavior of controlling teachers. *Journal of Educational Psychology, 74,* 852–859.

Grolnick, W. S., & Ryan, R. M. (1987). Autonomy in children's learning: An experimental and individual difference investigation. *Journal of Personality and Social Psychology, 52,* 890–898.

Grolnick, W. S., Ryan, R. M., & Deci, E. L. (1991). The inner resources for school achievement: Motivational mediators of children's perceptions of their parents. *Journal of Educational Psychology, 83,* 508–517.

Ilardi, B. C., Leone, D., Kasser, T., & Ryan, R. M. (1993). Employee and supervisor ratings of motivation: Main effects and discrepancies associated with job satisfaction and adjustment in a factory setting. *Journal of Applied Social Psychology, 23,* 1789–1805.

Jelsma, B. M. (1982). Adult control behaviors: The interaction between orientation toward control in women and activity level of children. Unpublished doctoral dissertation, University of Rochester.

Kasser, T., & Ryan, R. M. (1993). A dark side of the American dream: Correlates of financial success as a central life aspiration. *Journal of Personality and Social Psychology, 65,* 410–422.

Koestner, R., Bernieri, F., & Zuckerman, M. (1992). Self-determination and consistency between attitudes, traits, and behaviors. *Personality and Social Psychology Bulletin, 18,* 52–59.

Koestner, R., Ryan, R. M., Bernieri, F., & Holt, K. (1984). Setting limits on children's behavior: The differential effects of controlling versus informational styles on intrinsic motivation and creativity. *Journal of Personality, 52,* 233–248.

Lepper, M. R., Greene, D., & Nisbett, R. E. (1973). Undermining children's intrinsic interest with extrinsic rewards: A test of the "overjustification" hypothesis. *Journal of Personality and Social Psychology, 28,* 129–137.

Mann, R. D., Arnold, S. M., Binder, J. L., Cytrynbaum, S., Newman, B. M., Ringwald, B. E., & Rosenwein, R. (1970). *The college classroom.* New York: Wiley.

McGraw, K. O. (1978). The detrimental effects of reward on performance: A literature review and a prediction model. In M. R. Lepper & D. Greene (Eds.), *The hidden costs of reward* (pp. 33–60). Hillsdale, NJ: Erlbaum.

Rogers, C. (1969). *Freedom to learn.* Columbus, OH: Merrill.

Ryan, R. M. (1982). Control and information in the intrapersonal sphere: An extension of cognitive evaluation theory. *Journal of Personality and Social Psychology, 43,* 450–461.

Ryan, R. M. (1993). Agency and organization: Intrinsic motivation, autonomy, and the self in psychological development. In J. Jacobs (Ed.), *Nebraska symposium on motivation: Developmental perspectives on motivation* (Vol. 40, pp. 1–56). Lincoln: University of Nebraska Press.

Ryan, R. M., & Connell, J. P. (1989). Perceived locus of causality and internalization: Examining reasons for acting in two domains. *Journal of Personality and Social Psychology, 57,* 749–761.

Ryan, R. M., & Grolnick, W. S. (1986). Origins and pawns in the classroom: Self-report and projective assessments of individual differences in children's perceptions. *Journal of Personality and Social Psychology, 50,* 550–558.

Ryan, R. M., Mims, V., & Koestner, R. (1983). Relation of reward contingency and interpersonal context to intrinsic motivation: A review and test using cognitive evaluation theory. *Journal of Personality and Social Psychology, 45,* 736–750.

Ryan, R. M., Rigby, S., & King, K. (1993). Two types of religious internalization and their relations to religious orientations and mental health. *Journal of Personality and Social Psychology, 65,* 586–596.

Schafer, R. (1968). *Aspects of internalization.* New York: International Universities Press.

Smith, W. E. (1974). The effects of social and monetary rewards on intrinsic motivation. Unpublished doctoral dissertation, Cornell University.

White, R. W. (1960). Competence and the psychosexual stages of development. In M. R. Jones (Ed.), *Nebraska symposium on motivation* (Vol. 8, pp. 97–141). Lincoln: University of Nebraska Press.

Wild, T. C., Enzle, M. E., & Hawkins, W. L. (1992). Effects of perceived extrinsic versus intrinsic teacher motivation on student reactions to skill acquisition. *Personality and Social Psychology Bulletin, 18*(2), 245–251.

Zuckerman, M., Porac, J., Lathin, D., Smith, R., & Deci, E. L. (1978). On the importance of self-determination for intrinsically motivated behavior. *Personality and Social Psychology Bulletin, 4,* 443–446.

5   Intrinsic Motivation and Effective Teaching: A Flow Analysis

MIHALY CSIKSZENTMIHALYI

There is a great deal of confusion concerning teaching at the university level. Labeling it "teaching" and those who do it "teachers" is part of the problem. To teach implies a transfer of information, and that is not the main purpose of higher education. In fact, those who teach in universities are called "professors," because their primary function is to profess an intellectual discipline. The most relevant meaning of the act of professing is the Middle English connotation of being bound by a vow or the even older Latin one that refers to one's faith in, or expressing allegiance to, some idea of goal.

Thus, at least originally and ideally, an effective university teacher is one who believes in what he or she does to the point of identifying with it. This view does not simply reflect a quaint historical or etymological curiosity. It continues to represent the most important contribution that teachers at a university can make to the education of their students. Higher education succeeds or fails in terms of motivation, not cognitive transfer of information. It succeeds if it instills in students a willingness to pursue knowledge for its own sake; it fails if students learn simply in order to get a degree. The best way to get students to believe that it makes sense to pursue knowledge is to believe in it oneself. Thus, an effective professor is one who is intrinsically motivated to learn, because it is he or she who will have the best chance to educate others.

When we try to improve the organizational design of schools by changing reward contingencies and feedback systems (see Chaps. 6 and 10 in this volume), we are essentially trying to bring the behavior of teachers in line with some a priori criterion of effectiveness. These attempts are useful for improving the teaching component of a professor's job, but they tend to leave the more essential professing component unaffected. In fact, such attempts might make an allegiance to knowledge for its own sake more unlikely. It may be difficult for an intelligent human being to identify with an institution run by administrators whose main question is: "How can environmental conditions be developed so as to increase the frequency and intensity of 'good' teaching?" (as Nord suggests in Chap. 6 of this volume that they should be). Contemporary research suggests that external control and manipulation of this sort may destroy intrinsic motivation (see Chaps. 2 and 4 in this volume). Thus, we might safely conclude that efforts to improve teaching which result in a professor's attributing to an outside agency control over his or her actions will lead to the exact opposite outcome from the one intended (that is, to inefficient education owing to a loss of a professor's intrinsic motivation).

The Loss of Intrinsic Motivation

Before developing this argument further, it might be worthwhile to clarify a few points concerning intrinsic motivation. The importance of this concept is not so much that motivation is an efficient means toward some outside goal—such as becoming a good teacher, learning all there is to learn about a certain subject, or making a great deal of money—but that such motivation reflects an experience that is an end in itself, a dynamic psychological state that is valued for its immediate rewarding qualities.

The intrinsic reward from learning is the enjoyment one gets here and now, from the act of learning itself, and not from what follows later from having acquired the knowledge. Of course, it is possible to derive both intrinsic and extrinsic rewards from the same learning process. For instance, one might enjoy the fascination of learning how the anatomy of the human body works and at the same time enjoy the rewards of good grades that will eventually lead to a medical degree. Yet it seems that if the extrinsic outcome is emphasized at the expense of enjoying the experience as it occurs, the effectiveness of learning is greatly diminished.

In most cultures, and especially in Western cultures since the Industrial Revolution, it has been taken for granted that productive work must be a burden, to be put up with whether one likes it or not. School learning, like work, is expected to be a generally negative experience for both students and teachers. Compulsory education (as if education could ever be compulsory) is generally seen as a painful necessity for all concerned. When workers report their experiences at work, and students at school, it is clear that the motivations that keep them at their task are rarely intrinsic (Csikszentmihalyi, Larson, & Prescott, 1977; Csikszentmihalyi & Graef, 1980; Csikszentmihalyi & Larson, 1984). Even students who are highly talented in science or mathematics would prefer to do almost anything else rather than pursue those subjects in school (Csikszentmihalyi, Rathunde, & Whalen, 1993). Most people believe that studying and working are naturally unpleasant activities to be avoided if at all possible.

In the nineteenth century, when factory operatives worked fourteen and more hours a day, six days a week, with a forty-five-minute break for dinner (Thompson, 1963; Wallace, 1978), few people asked what enjoyment the workers were getting out of their jobs. The goal of workers was to serve the needs of production. Productivity justified their existence and assured their eternal salvation. How workers felt while accomplishing this was entirely irrelevant.

By now most people accept as common sense that work has to be boring or exhausting. It is seen as a means of obtaining financial rewards that then can be used, in the worker's free time, to achieve the real goals that justify existence. Intrinsic rewards are not expected from work itself. This view has almost achieved the status of an inevitable law of nature. By sixth grade, our children have learned to distinguish reliably between activities that they consider to be work (studying, straightening out their room, taking out the garbage) and those they consider to be play (watching television, hanging out with friends, shooting baskets). When they do something like "work," they report very negative moods and low self-esteem; when engaged in "play," they claim to be happy and high on self-esteem (Csikszentmihalyi & Whalen, 1993). Yet there is evidence to suggest that making a living need not conflict with a person's well-being.

A few surviving societies based on hunting and gathering give us a glimpse of productive systems that do not require adults to spend their lives doing things they would rather not be doing. As Sahlins (1972), Turnbull (1962), and others have shown, work in preagrarian cultures was not only much less demanding than it later became—on the order of three to five hours a day—but it was also considerably more free, challenging, and enjoyable. Work was not distinguished from the rest of life, an undesirable means to a desirable end, but integrated in such a way that one could not tell work from socializing, performance, worship, or simply having fun. In a few contemporary traditional cultures, this happy synergy between playful work and serious play still survives (Delle Fave & Massimini, 1988).

At present, our relationship to work in the United States is strangely paradoxical. Most adults report being more satisfied, strong, creative, and generally in a better mood when they work than when they have free time. Despite this fact, they declare a preference for less work and more free time (Csikszentmihalyi & LeFevre, 1989; Csikszentmihalyi, 1990). Apparently, when it comes to evaluating work, cultural prejudices take precedence over actual experience. At the same time, the work environment could be vastly improved upon if we understood better the necessity for work to produce optimal experiences.

One reason for the negative attitudes toward work, including schoolwork, is that the rationalization of productive techniques in industrial societies has isolated work from most other meaningful experiences. The typical assembly-line or clerical worker operates in a restricted environment; attention must be concentrated on a strictly limited stimulus field, one that allows only the most routine forms of human experience to occur. The same pattern of operating efficiency has spread to other jobs, whether educational, bureaucratic, or technical. With the advent of operant system designs, this pattern threatens to shackle even the liberal profession of university teaching. We have grown accustomed to thinking that work is something to be tolerated in order to achieve future goals and leisure, even though in itself work may be a fundamentally alienating experience. Industrial psychologists have given their blessing to this state of affairs, advising, as it were, workers to resign themselves to their meaningless jobs for the sake of the paycheck at the end of the week. By and large, this is also the attitude taken by most unions.

Like the king's invisible clothes, the irrationality of this view is rarely questioned. What is the purpose of producing more, of saving, of accumulating material resources, if one's productive activity is, from the worker's point of view, wasted? If work is not enjoyable, if it does not allow a sense of growth and freedom, what makes one suppose that the rest of life will be enjoyable, free, and growth producing? Not only does the job take up a substantial amount of time and energy (and become, therefore, quantitatively a large part of one's life); it is also a qualitatively unique aspect of life. As Marx argued in his early manuscripts (Tucker, 1978), and as many social scientists have recognized ever since, productive work provides essential feedback to the human self which cannot be obtained from any other source. Acquiescing to the alienation of work means giving up the possibility of developing an integrated self.

Intrinsic Motivation and the Process of Higher Education

In human terms, any act that is not intrinsically rewarding is wasteful. An activity is intrinsically rewarding when the actor experiences it as worth doing for itself, not just as a means to future, external goals (Csikszentmihalyi, 1975; Csikszentmihalyi & Rathunde, 1993). Life is wasted to the extent that it is spent doing things that one does not wish to do. These considerations, which apply to work in general, are particularly relevant to higher education. The point is that for a professor, intrinsic motivation is both the product of the activity and the means by which the product is realized.

Basically teaching involves changing the learners' cognitive structures, and, more important, changing their goal structures. The product of teaching is a socialized individual, a young person who shares the goals valued in a given society. At the university level, this socialization includes a set of intellectual goals. To accomplish this end, according to the operant model on which teaching machines are based, the teacher is supposed to transmit information and award rewards and punishments (or positive and negative feedback) contingent on the learner's progress.

But this is a very impoverished view of what teaching is about, because transmission of information is of marginal importance to the primary goals of teaching. In this respect, Carl Rogers was right when he said: "It seems to me that anything that can be taught to another is relatively inconsequential and has little or no significant influence on behavior. . . . I have come to feel that the only learning which significantly influences behavior is self-discovered, self-appropriated learning. In such self-discovered learning, truth has been personally appropriated and assimilated in experience, and cannot be directly communicated to another" (quoted in Marty, 1979, pp. 196–197).

Although it is true that information is transmitted in lectures and seminars, the real task of a professor is to enable the learner to enjoy learning. Education works when the student becomes intrinsically motivated to acquire the information or the goals to be transmitted; at that point, the major part of the teacher's task is accomplished. Learning motivated by extrinsic rewards is costly to maintain and easy to extinguish in the absence of reward contingencies. Recent experimental evidence suggests that, contrary to behaviorist assumptions, extrinsic rewards might in some circumstances inhibit rather than promote learning (Lepper & Greene, 1978; see also Chaps. 2, 4, and 10 in this volume).

The product of teaching, then, is an intrinsically motivated learner. A teacher has done his or her job when the students enjoy learning and look upon the activity of learning as an end in itself, rather than as a means to an external goal—a grade, a diploma, or a job. Admittedly, it is difficult to measure teaching effectiveness by this criterion. It is easier to measure it by the amount of information transmitted to the student, but such a criterion is not terribly useful unless one knows whether the student wants to retain, use, and increase the information learned. Knowledge that is not intrinsically motivated is not much good to anybody.

Intrinsic Motivation and Students

If the product of teaching is a student who enjoys learning, what are the means by which a teacher can accomplish this purpose? How does one get students to enjoy learning? Here, again, the answer is in principle very simple: by enjoying learning. A teacher who is intrinsically motivated to learn has a good chance to get students to seek the intrinsic rewards of learning.

Young people are more intelligent than adults generally give them credit for. They can usually discern, for instance, whether an adult they know likes or dislikes what he or she is doing. If a teacher does not believe in his job, does not enjoy the learning he is trying to transmit, the student will sense this and derive the entirely rational conclusion that the particular subject matter is not worth mastering for its own sake. If all the teachers they are exposed to are extrinsically motivated, students might well conclude that learning in general is worthless in and of itself.

Such a reaction on the part of young people is eminently adaptive. Why should they want to spend their lives being bored? Why should they emulate a model who is already alienated from his or her life activity? The young are in general less resigned than adults to the prospect of a meaningless life. They look around them for adults who seem to enjoy their jobs, who believe in what they are doing, and take them as models. Of course, young people can also be fooled, like everyone else. They get fooled by people whose job it is to pretend to enjoy what they are doing even when they do not—that is, professional athletes and entertainers who try to convince the uncommitted youth that it is worth growing up because adult life can be enjoyable (Csikszentmihalyi, 1981).

At close quarters, it is more difficult to dupe a young person into believing that something matters when it does not. Professors who are cynical about their jobs, who do not enjoy what they are doing, do not help the transmission of knowledge; they only spread cynicism down another generation. At the same time, a teacher who loves the subject and enjoys the process of thinking is the most convincing argument for the usefulness of knowledge. This does not mean, of course, that if Ms. X enjoys mathematics, all of her students will adopt her for a model and become intrinsically motivated to pursue mathematics. Too many other variables help to determine the process: the students' talents, competing interests, the degree to which they are already convinced that math is boring or meaningless. But even those students who will never be turned on to math will know that it is indeed possible to love it, because Ms. X bore witness to that unlikely possibility. And that knowledge might in the long run be more useful than facility in calculus.

When students are asked about teachers who were influential in their lives, and the reasons for such influence, their answers do not fit into the theories that social scientists have developed to account for the effectiveness of role modeling. According to the classical theories, a young person wants to imitate an adult who has status and power, someone who has control over desired resources, who can reward and punish (Bandura & Walters, 1963; Bronfenbrenner, 1973). Socialization is supposed to be based primarily on fear, envy, and greed. Somehow this neat explanation manages to ignore the rather obvious fact that young people will imitate adults who find life worth living—even in the absence of status, power, and control over resources.

The most influential teachers—those who are remembered, who made a difference in the way we see ourselves and the world, who stirred us in new directions, and who revealed unexpected strengths in us or made us aware of our limitations—are not necessarily the ones who had more status, power, or control. They might or might not have been exceptionally intelligent or knowledgeable, but they were usually the ones who loved what they were doing, who showed by their dedication and their passion that there was nothing else on earth they would rather be doing (Csikszentmihalyi & McCormack, 1986).

Students we studied often described their most influential teacher with some variation of: "Oh, he was such a nut!" This is not, as it turns out, because the teacher was funny or entertaining but simply because his or her involvement in the subject matter seemed, by normal standards, to be excessive—in fact, almost crazy. Yet it is such holy fools who keep the fabric of knowledge from unraveling between one generation and the next. If it weren't for them, who would believe that knowledge really mattered?

It is the teacher who cares about his or her craft who makes students want to care for others. As I first drafted these pages, one of the teachers I had had in college died. At his funeral, I was trying to figure out how he had managed to make such a difference in my life and in the lives of several other former students who had come to mourn his passing. Robert Nickle, who taught design at the University of Illinois for several decades, was a terrible teacher. He could not explain what he wanted from us, nor did he try to; he did not demonstrate how to do things; his feedback to students was erratic and arbitrary. We were in a constant state of uncertainty and confusion in his classes. He violated all the rules of rational transmission of information; he was the exact antithesis of a well-designed teaching machine. Yet what a great professor he was! His concern for good design, for the integrity of vision and execution, was clear to everybody; it was etched in the lines of pain on his face when confronted with a facile drawing, or in the look of exultation that—alas, much more rarely—passed over his features when someone broke away from a conventional cliché. It was clear that he enjoyed every minute of his work, even though most of it was painful. He could not fake enthusiasm, conviction, or belief either for our sake or for his own, but this very submission to the rules of art generated enthusiasm, conviction, and belief on our parts.

If I think back on the other teachers since college who have had similar effects on me—and how few they were—the same characteristics emerge. Whether the subject matter was philosophy, or statistics, or psychology, it is not the knowledge or prestige of teachers that I remember, or the correctness of their methods. It is, rather, the conviction they conveyed that what they were doing was worth doing, that it was intrinsically valuable. This is the means by which the goal of education can be achieved, and it is not something teaching machines or audiovisual aids can be built to simulate. It is not the transmission of information but the transmission of meaning which is involved (Nehari & Bender, 1978). Information can be conveyed in many ways, such as through books, instruments, machines, and so forth. Meaning, which refers to information that is integrated in terms of a person's life goals, cannot be taught; it can only be demonstrated in one's own actions. This is essentially the kind of learning Carl Rogers, in the quote above, has called "self-discovered." A person who professes a set of meanings has a chance to stimulate such discovery, or the meaningful integration of information, in others.

On the most general level, education refers to the process by which youths agree to become adults. It is not just a question of behaving like adults but of liking to be adults. That this process is not an automatic one is shown by the 300 percent increase in adolescent suicides over the past thirty years (Social Indicators, 1981; Wynne, 1978; Csikszentmihalyi,

1990) and by the similar increases in drug addiction, delinquency, and other forms of deviance. These trends indicate that young persons in our society are refusing, in increasing numbers, to grow up into adulthood. Education fails when becoming an adult is no longer a desirable option.

From this point of view, the main function of the teacher is not to teach science, math, or literature; it is to make being an adult seem like a worthwhile option. Of course, this modeling responsibility is not peculiar to teachers alone, but rests upon every adult member of our society. The task specific to teachers is to demonstrate, by their own example, that being an educated adult is a goal worth striving for.

It is possible that the survival of a culture over time depends on whether the older generations are able to convince the younger ones that growing up makes sense. To be convinced, a youth has to feel that being an adult can be meaningful. This in turn requires exposure to persons who derive intrinsic rewards from adult roles. Similarly, young people will not want to become philosophers or scientists if their teachers do not enjoy philosophy or science. Even within a given field, the development of subfields seems to be a function of differential intrinsic rewards. As Kuhn (1970) suggests, young scholars will move to research areas that promise to be exciting and enjoyable and will abandon those that seem boring. Thus, intrinsic motivation is a crucial link in the transmission of cultural forms across time.

Enjoyment in the History of Pedagogy

It would be easy enough to dismiss this emphasis on intrinsic rewards in learning as a modern conceit. Yet few strands of thought in the history of education have a longer pedigree. When Plato wrote about the conditions necessary for learning in the Symposium and Phaedrus, the major part of his argument revolved around the importance for young people to enjoy what they were being taught.

Closer to our time, John Dewey formulated most clearly the pedagogical function of enjoyment. He saw that to be effective, teaching had to achieve two complementary results: It had to produce an experience of pleasure at the moment, and it had to convey knowledge that made future growth possible. For instance:

> Everything depends upon the quality of experience which is had. The quality of an experience has two aspects. There is an immediate aspect of agreeableness or disagreeableness, and there is its influence upon later experience. . . . Hence, the

central problem of an education based upon experience is to select the kind of present experiences that live fruitfully and creatively in subsequent experience. (Dewey, 1938, p. 27)

True education, according to Dewey, is a spiral and dialectical process. The task of the teacher consists in stimulating students' enjoyable experiences in a learning context, so that they would want to repeat such experiences on their own.

> It is part of the educator's responsibility to see equally two things. First, that the problem grows out of the conditions of the experience being had in the present, and that it is within the capacity of students; and, secondly, that it is such that it arouses in the learner an active quest for information and for production of new ideas. The new facts and new ideas thus obtained become the ground for new experiences in which new problems are presented. The process is a continued spiral. (Dewey, 1938, p. 79)

Similarly William James, the great early American psychologist, understood that without enjoyment there could not be genuine learning. "For to miss the joy is to miss all," he writes, quoting Robert Louis Stevenson. "In the joy of the actors lies the sense of any action" (James, 1917, p. 7). This insight, too, has a long history, going back to Aristotle and to medieval Western philosophy (Csikszentmihalyi, 1993). For instance, more than six hundred years ago the poet Dante wrote that "in every action . . . the main intention of the agent is to express his own image; thus it is that every agent, whenever he acts, enjoys the action. Because everything that exists desires to be, and by acting the agent unfolds his being, action is naturally enjoyable" (Alighieri, 1317, I, 13).

Of course, joyful learning occurs only if students in schools are allowed to act, thereby "unfolding their being." Unfortunately, however, all they are allowed to do is re-act. As is generally the case with complex insights, the ideas of Plato, Aristotle, Dewey, and James were often trivialized in their application to educational practice. Instead of trying to combine enjoyable experience with hard work, teachers took the easier route of substituting the former for the latter. Yet Dewey had been very clear that neither of these approaches was effective in isolation from the other. Mere playfulness without concentrated work is just as inimical to learning as drudgery. "To be playful and serious at the same time . . . defines the ideal mental condition" (Dewey, 1933, p. 286). How to integrate these two quite different aspects in the same experience is the main challenge that educators face.

A Model of Intrinsically Rewarding Learning

The argument thus far has striven to establish that lack of enjoyment in teaching deprives the activity of its main value for both the teacher and the student. Teachers who do not find their subject matter worthwhile in and of itself but teach it only for extrinsic reasons—pay or prestige—waste their own time and convey the message to students that learning lacks intrinsic value and is only a means to other ends.

The question then becomes, What makes teaching enjoyable? Is it possible to learn to enjoy teaching? While one can certainly learn to enjoy teaching, I have argued that learning cannot be taught. The intrinsic rewards and the meaning of the activity must be discovered on one's own. It is possible, however, to reflect on those aspects of teaching which have the greatest potential for providing intrinsic rewards and to experiment with them until a personally meaningful combination of rewards is discovered. To facilitate this task, we shall review a general model of enjoyment which has been found useful in a variety of contexts and then apply it to the activity of teaching.

Research with intrinsically motivated individuals suggests that whenever a person has fun, whether it is dancing or playing chess, climbing a mountain, or studying in a classroom, a similar set of inner experiences and environmental conditions is present (Csikszentmihalyi, 1975, 1978a, 1978b, 1979, 1990, 1993; Csikszentmihalyi & Larson, 1978; Csikszentmihalyi & Csikszentmihalyi, 1988; Csikszentmihalyi & Rathunde, 1993). The experience of enjoyment, or flow, as we came to call it, is characterized above all by a deep, spontaneous involvement with the task at hand. In flow, one is so carried away by what one is doing and feels so immersed in the activity that the distinction between "I" and "it" becomes irrelevant. Attention is focused on whatever needs to be done, and there is not enough left to worry or to get bored and distracted. In a state of flow, a person knows what needs to be done moment by moment and knows precisely how well he or she is doing. In flow, a person usually does not worry about the consequences of his or her performance. The sense of time becomes distorted; hours seem to pass by in minutes, but afterward one might feel that an eternity has elapsed. The ego that surveys and evaluates our actions disappears in the flow of experience. One is freed of the confines of the social self and may feel an exhilarating sense of transcendence, of belonging to a larger whole.

These qualities describe how people feel when they enjoy what they are doing. Surgeons in the operating room or laborers on the assembly line use the same words to describe their work when it is enjoyable and rewarding. What we know about flow is that its presence depends a great deal on two conditions: how the activity is structured objectively, and how the person perceives the structure of the activity. For instance, every game is structured so as to make the focusing of attention on the play activity easy, and it provides clear goals, rules, and feedback. These structural features engage the player's attention, producing a flow experience. However, a person might restructure stimuli in his or her consciousness so as to produce flow without assistance from prestructured patterns in the environment and thus experience flow outside ready-made cultural play forms. This is what children, yogis, mathematicians, artists, and countless unsung average people can do at times.

A decisive structural factor for enjoyment is the balance of challenges and skills. At any given moment, we process in consciousness two crucial pieces of information: "What can be done here?" and "What am I capable of?" The first question deals with the opportunities for action in the environment, or challenges. The second concerns one's own capacity to act, or skills. When challenges overwhelm skills, we feel anxious; when skills outweigh challenges, we feel bored. Flow occurs when we come close to matching the two. Here, again, we meet the external and internal dialectic of flow: Challenges and skills are partly objective features of the situation; partly they are the results of one's subjective attitude. The two are related, and both are important in producing the experience.

An essential feature of this structure of challenges and skills is that the balance is not static. If the complexity of challenges one faces does not increase with time, flow gives way to boredom. As we practice an activity, our skills in it increase until they outweigh the challenges. Hence, to maintain flow, provisions must be made to find new things to engage our attention and skill, lest what used to be fun drift into tedium.

In summary, learning, like any activity, can become rewarding if it meets the following conditions:

1. *There must be clear goals.* The person should know what is to be done at every moment and why. In a classroom situation, it is not enough for students to have only a general idea of the purpose of the lecture or the assignment. In order to enjoy learning, they should have a continuous sense of what is going on, just as a person playing basketball or a surgeon performing an operation knows at every instant what needs to be done. Similarly, teachers will enjoy teaching if they always know what they are doing and why.

2. *There must be immediate feedback.* In order to enjoy learning, students

should receive information as quickly and frequently as possible about how well they are doing. At first, feedback has to come from the outside—from the teacher or some other external source—but eventually students will learn to administer feedback to themselves. Learning is completed when a person knows whether he or she is right or wrong without external help, and at that point feedback will be continuous and therefore learning enjoyable. (The teachers' feedback is the students' learning: the look of comprehension on their faces, the questions they ask, the answers they give. Without a constant stream of feedback from students to teachers, the job of teaching becomes dry and mechanical.)

3. *Challenges and skills must be in balance.* Students should have the option of increasing or decreasing the difficulty of the task so they can match as well as possible their abilities with the requirements for action. The teacher's task is to help provide new challenges when old ones are mastered and to model new skills if the challenges become overwhelming. Preferably a broad range and variety of challenges should be presented, so that students with different abilities can become involved. For instance, it makes sense to test knowledge in a course by a variety of different tests and assignments, some measuring memory, others rational abilities, empirical relations, and emphatic understanding. If the teacher does not increase his or her challenges continuously, by trying new methods and integrating new material, the job soon becomes boring.

4. *Concentration is essential.* In classrooms, students pay attention to what teachers say or do only a fraction of the time. Yet without focusing attention no learning can occur. At first, the teacher may have to attract attention by connecting with students' already existing interests and motivation. It is essential, however, to know how to transfer attention from these to the subject matter fairly soon. When the previously described conditions are present and the student begins to concentrate, the flow experience usually follows, and learning becomes intrinsically rewarding.

5. *Distractions must be avoided.* Irrelevant stimuli—a lecturer's mannerisms or self-indulgent stories, emphasis on meaningless details or bureaucratic procedures—destroy the concentration that makes involvement in the learning process enjoyable. A common source of distraction is an unnecessary threat to the students' ego, such as emphasizing grades or ridiculing performance. Creating self-consciousness is a sure way to distract the learner. Whatever the teachers can do to cut out distractions from their main task will increase the enjoyment of teaching.

6. *Control must be made possible.* All too often, teachers satisfy their own need for power and self-esteem by depriving students of any control over

the learning process. Yet without a sense of choice, it is impossible for students to act in the Aristotelian sense of expressing their being. And without the possibility of control, it is very difficult to enjoy what one is doing. Obviously one cannot give complete freedom of choice to students in a classroom. But whatever a teacher can do to transfer the responsibility for the learning process to students ought to bring great dividends in intrinsic motivation. Similarly, teachers may need to get involved in bringing about structural changes in their schools to achieve greater control in their own jobs.

7. *Growth and self-transcendence must be enhanced.* Although a person usually forgets him- or herself in flow, afterward one feels that as a result of the experience one has achieved a higher level of skills, an expanded sense of self. It is important for teachers to make students aware that learning is a matter not just of absorbing information but of becoming part of a community of learners. The original meaning of education in Latin was to "lead out," in other words, constantly to expand the limits of the self. Excessive mystification of the learning process is not a good idea, but a certain amount of ritual and symbolism is appropriate and can lead to an easier focusing of attention. After all, we have all sorts of rituals before football and basketball games, which help the audience's involvement with the action to follow, whereas classroom activities often lack clear demarcation from the attentional structures of everyday life.

8. *The autotelic nature of true learning must be highlighted.* It is important for teachers and parents not to emphasize too much the instrumental aspects of education. The more learning is talked about as simply a ticket to a well-paying job, the less easy it will be for students to realize its intrinsic rewards. The most effective message is one that is embodied in the adults' living example. A parent or teacher who reads complex books for enjoyment, who listens to stimulating music in free time, who gets involved in ideas and in challenging conversations, is a concrete proof that learning can be rewarding in and of itself.

Establishing Flow in Teaching

In teaching, two main action systems provide intrinsic rewards. One is the educational process itself (i.e., the changes in the student's performance attributable to the teacher's actions). The challenges here are to attract and maintain the students' attention and to motivate them to pursue goals valued by the teacher. The second set of intrinsic rewards is provided by the subject matter. The challenges here refer to the continuing integration of new information on the teacher's part. In other words, it is the teacher's own learning that is enjoyable. Although these two aspects are independent of each other—one can enjoy teaching without learning much that is new about the subject matter and vice versa—they are not mutually exclusive. In fact, teaching is probably most effective when the teacher enjoys both processes at the same time.

Subject Matter

Presumably there are subject matter differences in the ease of establishing flow in a classroom. Science and math, for instance, have the initial disadvantage of presenting too many challenges to students, who start out being anxious and often remain in that state without ever enjoying the learning process. But once skills are matched to challenges, it is probably easier to sustain the flow experience in science and math than in humanities or social sciences because the goals, the rules, and the feedback are much less ambiguous in the former. Certain subjects, such as art, music, or drama, have the advantage of clearly demarcating the field from everyday life and therefore admitting greater concentration with fewer distractions. Our studies have shown that students find intrinsic rewards much more easily in art and music than in math and science. But it is very difficult to develop high levels of proficiency even in math and science if one does not enjoy the subject (Csikszentmihalyi, Rathunde, & Whalen, 1993). Presumably, any subject can be taught enjoyably if the teacher understands the principles of flow.

Classroom Structure

Structural aspects of the classroom situation will also have an effect on how much enjoyment teaching can bring. For instance, lecturing to a large class makes it almost impossible for the teacher to monitor individual changes in students. Similarly, if students are seen for only a semester or a year, the teacher will have little opportunity to get feedback about how they have changed. Without such feedback, there is little enjoyment to be derived at the educational level. A class that consists of students with widely different levels of preparation also detracts from the enjoyment of teaching because the challenges facing the teacher are incongruent with each other. A structurally adversary relationship between teacher and students, as in required courses, also has the same result. If for these or other reasons teaching cannot be turned into a flow activity, the effectiveness of the class will be reduced for both teacher and students because the experience will cease to be intrinsically rewarding.

Under conditions that make teaching unrewarding, the professor may change the rules and shift into a performing mode. As a performer, he or she need not be concerned with specific changes in individual students; the feedback that counts is the audience's spellbound attention. Charismatic teachers—those who have the skills to project emotions and meanings—might enjoy classroom conditions that would make others bored or anxious. Such teaching is effective insofar as it communicates to the students that the teacher values knowledge for its own sake and therefore enjoys the symbolic manipulation of knowledge. Of course, other things might be communicated as well, messages that conflict with the educational goal, for instance, that the teacher enjoys being the center of attention, that his rewards derive from being powerful or entertaining.

It is outside the scope of this chapter to detail techniques that might turn teaching into a flow activity. Research could help identify and describe such techniques, but at this point there are virtually no studies of intrinsic motivation in teaching. The chapters in this volume, particularly Chapters 2, 4, and 7, suggest techniques that are congruent with the flow model by demonstrating either how distractions can be eliminated or how conditions for involvement with challenges can be enhanced. General studies of teachers, such as the ones by Lortie (1975), Dubin and Champoux (1977), and Miskel, de Frain, and Wilcox (1980), have started to explore the motivational structure of educators, but their perspective is still too broad to provide the kind of detail needed to know how teaching is to be turned into an enjoyable experience. Apparently there is no study relating a teacher's motivation to the effectiveness of his or her teaching—in other words, to the students' motivation. One pilot study by Plihal (1981) shows that grade school students pay more attention in the classes of teachers who rate enjoyment as the highest reward of teaching. Obviously, we need more studies of this type at higher levels of education.

In fact, a great many questions arise if one accepts as testable the propositions advanced here. To accept them, one must modify current assumptions about the effectiveness of teaching. Instead of emphasizing transmission of information as the criterion of good teaching, the importance of intrinsic motivation, both as a means and as a goal of education, should be recognized.

References

Alighieri, D. (1317). De monarchia. [Translation by the author from the Latin text].

Bandura, A., & Walters, R. H. (1963). *Social learning and personality development*. New York: Holt, Rinehart, & Winston.

Bronfenbrenner, U. (1973), *Two worlds of childhood*. New York: Pocket Books.

Csikszentmihalyi, M. (1975). *Beyond boredom and anxiety*. San Francisco: Jossey-Bass.

Csikszentmihalyi, M. (1978a). Attention and the holistic approach to behavior. In K. S. Pope & J. L. Singer (Eds.), *The stream of consciousness* (pp. 335–358). New York: Plenum Press.

Csikszentmihalyi, M. (1978b). Intrinsic rewards and emergent motivation. In M. R. Lepper & D. Greene (Eds.), *The hidden costs of reward* (pp. 205–218). New York: Erlbaum.

Csikszentmihalyi, M. (1979). The concept of flow. In B. Sutton-Smith (Ed.), *Play and learning* (pp. 257–294). New York: Gardner.

Csikszentmihalyi, M. (1981). Leisure and socialization. *Social Forces, 60*(2), 332–340.

Csikszentmihalyi, M. (1990). *Flow: The psychology of optimal experience*. New York: Harper/Collins.

Csikszentmihalyi, M. (1993). *The evolving self: A psychology for the third millenium*. New York: Harper/Collins.

Csikszentmihalyi, M., & Csikszentmihalyi, I. (Eds.). (1988). *Optimal experience: Psychological studies of flow in consciousness*. New York: Cambridge University Press.

Csikszentmihalyi, M., & Graef, R. (1980). The experience of freedom in daily life. *American Journal of Community Psychology, 8*(4), 401–414.

Csikszentmihalyi, M., & Larson, R. (1978). Intrinsic rewards in school crime. *Crime and Delinquency, 24*(3), 322–335.

Csikszentmihalyi, M., & Larson, R. (1984). *Being adolescent*. New York: Basic Books.

Csikszentmihalyi, M., Larson, R., & Prescott, S. (1977). The ecology of adolescent activity and experience. *Journal of Youth and Adolescence, 6*(3), 281–294.

Csikszentmihalyi, M., & LeFevre, J. (1989). Optimal experience in work and leisure. *Journal of Personality and Social Psychology, 56*(5), 815–822.

Csikszentmihalyi, M., & McCormack, J. (1986). The influence of teachers, *Phi Delta Kappan*, February, 415–419.

Csikszentmihalyi, M., & Rathunde, K. (1993). The measurement of flow in everyday life: Toward a theory of emergent motivation. In J. E. Jacobs (Ed.), *Nebraska symposium on motivation* (Vol. 40, pp. 57–97). Lincoln: University of Nebraska Press.

Csikszentmihalyi, M., Rathunde, K., & Whalen, S. (1993). *Talented teenagers: The roots of success and failure*. New York: Cambridge University Press.

Csikszentmihalyi, M., & Whalen, S. (1993). Flow and the development of a work ethic during adolescence. Chicago: Annual Meeting of the Midwestern Psychological Association.

Delle Fave, A., & Massimini, F. (1988). Modernization and the changing contexts of flow in work and leisure. In M. Csikszentmihalyi & I. Selega Csikszentmihalyi (Eds.), *Optimal experience: Psychological studies of flow in consciousness* (pp. 193–213). New York: Cambridge University Press.

Dewey, J. (1933). *How we think*. Lexington, MA: D. C. Heath.

Dewey, J. (1938). *Experience and education*. New York: Macmillan.

Dubin, R., & Champoux, J. (1977). Central life interests and job satisfaction. *Organizational Behavior and Human Performance, 18*, 366–377.

James, W. (1917). *Selected papers on philosophy*. London: Dent.

Kuhn, T. S. (1970). *The structure of scientific revolution*. Chicago: University of Chicago Press.

Lepper, M. R., & Greene, D. (Eds.). (1978). *The hidden costs of reward*. New York: Erlbaum.

Lortie, D. C. (1975). *Schoolteacher.* Chicago: University of Chicago Press.

Marty, M. A. (1979). Teaching history today. *Theology Today, 36*(2), 195–199.

Mayers, P. L., Csikszentmihalyi, M., & Larson, R. (1978). The daily experience of high school students. Presented at the American Educational Research Association annual meeting, Toronto.

Miskel, C., de Frain, J. A., & Wilcox, K. (1980). A test of expectancy work motivation theory in educational organizations. *Educational Administration Quarterly, 16*(1), 70–92.

Nehari, M., & Bender, H. (1978). Meaningfulness of a learning experience: A measure for outcomes in higher education. *Higher Education, 7,* 1–11.

Plihal, J. F. (1981). Intrinsic rewards of teaching. Paper presented at the American Educational Research Association meeting, Los Angeles.

Sahlins, M. (1972). *Stone age economics.* Chicago: Aldine.

Social Indicators, III. (1981). Washington, DC: Department of Commerce.

Thompson, E. P. (1963). *The making of the English working class.* New York: Vintage.

Tucker, R. C. (1978). *The Marx-Engels reader.* New York: Norton.

Turnbull, C. M. (1962). *The forest people.* New York: Simon & Schuster.

Wallace, A. F. C. (1978). *Rockdale.* New York: Knopf.

Wynne, E. A. (1978). Behind the discipline problem: Youth suicide as a measure of alienation. *Phi Delta Kappan, 59*(5), 397–415.

III Theories of External Motivation to Teach

6

Behavior Modification in a Loosely Coupled System of Higher Education

WALTER R. NORD

The general task of administration is the translation of policy and organizational objectives into procedures and operational goals that direct the efforts of others toward the successful achievement of these objectives. In varying degrees all administrators face uncertainty about whether the particular outcomes that they intend will result from their actions. The degree of this uncertainty is a function of many things that affect the tightness of coupling among components of an organization. Generally speaking, the degree of uncertainty university administrators face is often quite high because the tightness of coupling is often low. In fact, Weick's (1976, 1979) term *loosely coupled* describes important parts of systems such as universities well. The purpose of this chapter is to suggest how adoption of an orientation derived from behavior modification (B-mod) might be useful to university administrators in promoting effective teaching in such loosely coupled systems.

In this chapter, *loose coupling* is used in what Orton and Weick (1990) called the "voice of topology." Loose coupling refers to the connection (albeit a loose one) between parts of an organization, such as between hierarchical levels or among subunits, for example, administration (including deans or academic vice president and so on) and the professional core. In

The author gratefully acknowledges the helpful comments of Ann F. Connell on earlier versions of this chapter.

loosely coupled systems, changes along any one dimension or changes within one subsystem are expected to have fewer or less intense ramifications upon other dimensions and subsystems than comparable changes in more tightly coupled systems would have.

At a practical level this difference means that typically university administrators are apt to experience greater uncertainty in comparison with managers of most business and governmental units in their attempts to influence the behavior of individuals and units elsewhere in the system. In addition, at least at present, in many respects the task of teaching is less routine and less measurable than many tasks in other organizations. Normally, this state of affairs would be expected to reduce the utility of B-mod, since it is often assumed that to employ behavior modification successfully, both easily measurable performance criteria and tight control over the conditions surrounding the individuals whose behavior we might be seeking to modify are required. Therefore, at first glance, B-mod may not appear to be a viable approach for motivating teaching performance. This is a very reasonable expectation; however, things are not that simple. Although the use of B-mod is aided by control over a situation, I argue that the approach has a number of potential benefits for administrators of loosely coupled systems as well (even those engaged in nonroutine tasks, such as teaching). These advantages accrue from three factors.

First, in loosely coupled systems, the total amount of control available to administrators is apt to be small; therefore, the incremental utility of even a modest amount of control is apt to be larger than in more tightly coupled systems where administrators have many levers available to use in directing the actions of subordinates. In more tightly coupled organizations that do routine tasks, sources of control are apt to be embedded in technology, rules, and procedures, input and output controls, and so forth. Although even there unanticipated consequences are frequent, administrators of such systems can have more confidence than their counterparts in less tightly coupled systems that, once their wishes are appropriately communicated, their subordinates will be constrained to act on them. Consequently, the marginal value to them of any incremental control that a B-mod or some other approach might yield is often small in a tightly coupled system. In contrast, administrators of loosely coupled systems (especially those in which nonroutine tasks are performed) cannot expect high levels of certainty and do not have many institutionalized sources of control. Thus, the marginal value to them of any given source of influence is apt to be large.

A second source of advantage of the B-mod orientation for administrators of the particular class of loosely coupled systems in which colleges and universities are located is similar to the first. In addition to being loosely coupled, these systems are often characterized by a rather extreme form of decentralized power which permits members of the "operating core" (Mintzberg, 1979)—the faculty, in the case of universities—to exercise substantial influence over many aspects of both their own work and the organization as a whole. (In other, more centralized or bureaucratic organizations, these aspects would be controlled more unilaterally by managers, administrators, or what Mintzberg termed the "technostructure.") Obviously, university administrators are not powerless; as Mintzberg observed, they often exercise considerable power; however, they use it informally, subtly, and indirectly by influencing one individual or group who may exercise influence on some third party. In addition, they often move incrementally.

Seen this way, administration is a process of designing systems and introducing stimuli that change the probabilities of certain behaviors that are themselves goals or that increase the chances that certain, more remote actions will occur. Several key questions that the B-mod perspective encourages the educational administrator to ask are: How can environmental conditions be developed which will increase the frequency and intensity of "good" teaching? What behaviors make for good teaching? Furthermore, faculty members exercise considerable control over the day-to-day operations and what behaviors colleagues are rewarded for. Because faculty members are apt to have substantial impact on one's motivation to teach, the administrator must ask: How can faculty members serve to stimulate their colleagues in ways to support better teaching?

A third advantage from a B-mod orientation is the congruence between the way of thinking it stimulates and the nature of the administration of loosely coupled systems. Administrators in these systems are well advised to think probabilistically; their success depends on introducing stimuli and processes that produce only moderate changes in the probabilities of behaviors. Accordingly, often they should think in terms of sequential probabilities, encouraging behaviors that, although removed from the desired goals in themselves, are necessary before other ultimate behaviors or outcomes are possible. For example, the development of a "professional" climate (i.e., a setting in which the actions one views as being professional are modeled and responded to positively) is not an end in itself but a means to stimulating participants in the system to behave as "professionals." This sequential perspective overlaps with the view fostered by the concepts of shaping and response hierarchies which are central in the B-mod view.

Behavior Modification and Motivation

The focus of B-mod is on changing the probabilities of the behaviors of focal individuals. Users of this approach usually adopt an external perspective, centering their attention on manipulating elements (stimuli and the relation of stimulations) in the environment to produce and sustain desired behavior. They generally avoid making inferences about what inner psychological processes might account for the behavior. Consequently, they typically eschew the term *motivation,* as used in psychology and everyday language. Instead, they prefer to refer to the frequency or intensity (or both) of the occurrence of particular behaviors. In order to be consistent with the B-mod terminology, although I personally believe the focus on behavior is productive, I do not share the inhibition about assuming the importance of internal events. However, I limit my use of the term *motivation,* and when I do use it, I enclose it in quotation marks to call attention to this inconsistency with the strict B-mod position. Therefore, when the term *motivation* is used, the reader should understand by the quotation marks that the external focus of B-mod is being emphasized.

The external focus with its emphasis on behavior has a major advantage for administrators; it encourages them to specify what particular actions they want and to examine what happens when a person acts in this way. Even if no other changes are introduced into the system, the focus on behavioral specificity can have important consequences both in clarifying the administrator's own thoughts and in operationalizing the desired behavior in concrete terms. For example, telling teachers that they are encouraged "to experiment with and evaluate, according to a specified procedure, the success of techniques A, B, and C" gives much clearer information than do general phrases such as "being innovative" or "be motivated to try new things." This is not to say that "good teaching" can be made into a programmable task. It is only to say that it is both possible and useful to make many aspects of teaching (or steps leading to better performance) much more concrete than abstract labels of "good," "dedicated," or "motivated" teachers have led us to do.

In addressing the question of how teaching behavior can be modified by an administrator, I consider four general approaches from the B-mod literature: respondent conditioning, ecological design, modeling, and operant conditioning. These are well-established techniques, and detailed treatments of them can be found throughout the B-mod literature (see Nord & Peter, 1980, for a more detailed treatment of these specific four).

Respondent Conditioning

Pavlov's famous classical conditioning experiments with dogs provide the basic paradigm for understanding the process of respondent conditioning. Respondents are a class of behaviors that are controlled by stimuli that precede them. These behaviors include reflexes, glandular responses, and the responses normally called emotions. Usually these behaviors are thought to be governed by the autonomic nervous system and therefore not under a person's conscious control. For present purposes, the class of respondent behaviors normally called emotions are of most interest.

Although it is possible to conceive of an administrator arranging pairs of stimuli to condition certain feelings or emotions, such an application is unlikely to be feasible very often. However, what administrators can do is try to design climates that are relatively rich in stimuli that are apt (via prior conditioning) to elicit certain desired feelings and, conversely, create climates that are relatively free of stimuli that are apt to elicit undesired emotions. In this respect, B-mod would direct effort to the same type of symbolic and ritualistic stimuli which are highlighted by students of organization culture. Three possible sets of applications are treated here: the development of climates generally, communication processes, and symbolism and ritual.

Climates

Organizational climates have a powerful influence on people's feelings. For example, the allocations of resources to create classroom and other facilities that connote a professional, academic, or some other specific type of atmosphere may deserve far more conscious priority than they often receive. Although this approach might at first consider the physical aspects of classroom design, it is apt to spread more widely to such things as eliminating activities (certain committee assignments, administrative routine, and so on) which are in conflict with experiencing oneself as a professional.

Communication Processes

The respondent view also might serve to center attention on aspects of communication which influence the development of an organization climate or culture. All modes of communication—written, meetings with large groups, and one-on-one sessions—entail many stimuli that elicit emotions. In each mode, administrators who have clear images of the climates they wish to create may benefit by viewing communication not only as a way to accomplish a short-run goal of information transmission but also as an opportunity to present stimuli that evoke the feelings they wish to develop. For example, use of words such as *colleagues* and *excellence* is apt to evoke quite different feelings than terms such as *teachers* and *acceptable performance*. Not only will different feelings be evoked from receivers, but using the different terms is quite likely to influence the feelings of the speaker as well. Of course, words are only examples to illustrate the general notion of how stimuli may be used to create climates by the feelings they elicit.

All aspects of interaction, including nonverbal communication and the processes employed to disseminate information to obtain feedback, can be influential. In this respect, the value of the respondent view is not that it contributes anything substantively new but that it directs attention to the possibility of influencing climates (quite inexpensively) via everyday behavior—by both the deliberate and repetitious presentation of certain stimuli and the consistent avoidance of others. As with other applications of B-mod, a major advantage of the approach is that it drives the administrator to examine the current state of the system in concrete terms and to specify the behavior he or she wishes to stimulate.

Rituals and Ceremonies

The respondent perspective can center attention on a third set of topics—the use of ceremonies, rituals, and symbols. Pfeffer (1981) has summarized how a variety of these mechanisms operate in organizations. Sayles (1979) described a related set of activities in a leadership context. For example, Sayles noted how "leaders generally 'work up' the group to prepare them to be responsive" (p. 34). Both Pfeffer and Sayles observed how leaders enhance their influence by appealing to past successes and shared values.

Clearly, colleges and universities have numerous ceremonies and rituals that elicit strong feelings. Unfortunately, many of them contribute little of direct relevance to the stimulation of teaching excellence. Many of the ceremonies seem to be directed mainly at external audiences and not at the creation of a climate for teaming. Other rituals, such as graduation and convocation, employ more traditional academic trappings that may elicit feelings related to teaching performance, but unfortunately, many of them (not convocations, of course) occur at the end of the academic year, and their potential effects dissipate over the summer.

Finally, many of the settings (e.g., orientation programs) which might be opportunities to present relevant symbols are directed at quite specific ends of their own, causing administrators often to fail to take advantage of them as opportunities to elicit emotions that would energize teaching excellence by the faculty and a demand for teaching excellence by the students. For academic administrators concerned with improving teaching performance, searching for ways to schedule and utilize ritualistic activities and ceremonies as opportunities to arouse the faculty emotionally and keeping the faculty audience in mind seem extremely worthwhile.

Ecological Design

Ecological design refers to the deliberate structuring of environments to modify behavior. Clearly, some of the ideas suggested in the discussion of respondent conditioning fit this definition. However, ecological design also includes such things as the arrangement of spatial, physical, and temporal relationships and even location of personnel to facilitate some behaviors and constrain others.

To illustrate the thought processes stimulated by an ecological view, consider the goal of increasing the "motivation" to be innovative and imaginative in one's teaching. The probability of a teacher attempting to employ a new technology is constrained by ecological factors (for example, a classroom in which all the chairs are bolted to the floor in long rows facing a lectern makes using small-group discussions very difficult). The arrangement of schedules and personnel can similarly affect the likelihood that use of new techniques will be attempted. Clearly, variations in the "motivation" to use new teaching technologies can be influenced by modification of features of the system's physical, spatial, and temporal arrangements—in short, by ecological design.

Modeling

Modeling (or vicarious learning) refers to a process that is designed to alter behavior by having an observer watch the actions of another person (a model) (Bandura, 1969). Modeling can be particularly useful for increasing the frequency and effectiveness of new behaviors and in decreasing the frequency of undesired behaviors.

The potential value of modeling for changing teaching behavior is considerable. Teachers often may not try a particular approach because they cannot visualize how it looks or do not have a ready repertoire of backup responses in case an initial effort goes awry. In such situations, one picture is probably worth much more than the proverbial one thousand words. For example, role-playing the use of a particular learning technique or demonstrating it on videotape can provide someone wanting to use the technique with a gestalt of the approach as well as examples of on-line adjustments to unanticipated situations, which can contribute to the readiness of a learner to try the technique and also increase the chances that he or she will use the technique competently and hence successfully and therefore be likely to repeat it. Similarly, the opportunity to observe ineffective behavior can help the learner to realize how some of his or her actions may lead to dysfunctional consequences.

There are a number of modeling methods that can increase the frequency of effective teaching behavior. Obvious examples include films and role-playing. Opportunities to observe other teachers who are particularly skilled in some special method or style are useful in themselves and serve as stimuli that contribute to the creation of a professional atmosphere and demonstrate a concern with teaching excellence. They can also serve as stimuli to encourage teachers to discuss methodology and learn from one another. Modeling that has already been proven to be an effective means for modifying behavior in industry (Goldstein & Sorcher, 1974; Hamner & Hamner, 1976) would seem to be a productive means to help people enhance their teaching performance. Academic administrators who realize the potential of modeling can do two quite specific things to improve teaching. First, they can find ways to help faculty members observe people who are behaving in desired ways. Second, they can call positive attention to those individuals who are in the system and are doing the desired things.

Operant Conditioning

Operant conditioning is the best-known component of the B-mod approach. I have deliberately left it for last in the hope of emphasizing the potential value of the other components.

The operant approach is concerned with responses that are normally considered to be under the conscious control of the individual. The most important feature of these responses is that the probability of repeating them in the future is a function of stimuli or consequences that have followed the response in the past. For present purposes, an exposition of the details of operant conditioning will be omitted (see Skinner, 1953, and Reese, 1966, for this information). Its central principle is that the arrangement of consequences following behavior influences the probabilities of the specific behavior being repeated. Application of this principle requires, among other things, inquiry into and specification of the particular behaviors that are desired and those that are not desired. As previously mentioned, this process itself can make important contributions to improving performance. In addition, attention must be given to what consequences (positive, negative, and neutral) are available and how they can be made contingent upon the behaviors in question.

Hamner and Hamner (1976) provided a useful summary of how to develop an operant program. First it is necessary to define performance in behavioral terms (that is, what specific actions constitute "good" and "bad" performance). Once performance has been defined behaviorally, then a "performance audit" can be conducted to determine current levels of performance. This audit often makes people aware that they are not performing nearly as well as they expected and makes them more responsive to a program for improvement. Stages two to four include setting specific goals for each individual, encouraging each person to keep a record of his or her own performance, and positively reinforcing desired performance.

Implementing the program requires that one know what consequences will act as positive reinforcers. (I deal only with positive reinforcement in this chapter. For a discussion of the use of punishment, see Skinner, 1953; Solomon, 1964; and Church, 1963.) Positive reinforcers can be administered either internally, such as when a person feels he or she has performed well, or externally in the form of material or social rewards given by some other person, such as a supervisor or through some organizational routine. Of course, different things act as positive reinforcers for different people; consequently, what will work for each individual and when it will work need to be discovered. Some advocates of B-mod (especially the so-called radical behaviorists) have argued that the *only* valid way to determine what is a positive reinforcer is empirically—that is, if a consequence increases the frequency of a behavior that it follows, the consequence is a positive reinforcer. Practically, when one is dealing with people, this can entail an unnecessarily cumbersome procedure. This extreme position is a correlate of the heavy use of lower-level animals as subjects and skepticism about the explanatory value of internal causes of behavior. This latter concern is a carryover of the efforts of Skinner, as Bandura (1986) put it, "to avoid spurious inner causes" (p. 12). These efforts lead to the appearance of rejecting internal causes of behavior. However, even many radical behaviorists may not hold this extreme a position. Rather, as Bandura (1986) observed: "Radical behaviorists do not deny that inner events are linked to behavior, but they express little interest in them because they are assumed to be caused by external stimuli. Through the presumption that inner events transmit but cannot create influences, internal determinants get dubbed as a redundant link in the causal chain. Behavior thus becomes fully explainable by relating external stimuli to actions without regard to the intervening inner link" (p. 12).

In my view, this lack of interest often unfortunately leads to a rejection of verbal reports as having any utility. Although I believe there may be good reason to be cautious in accepting the validity of verbal reports, that does not mean they cannot be used to practical advantage. Thus, in my view, it is useful to ask individuals what outcomes they desire. This acceptance of the value of internal data does not mean that the consequences of behavior are unimportant. Rather, it suggests a convenient and inexpensive way to learn what consequences are likely to have the desired effects on behavior. If this is known, one thing that can be done is to place people and help people place themselves into situations in which these outcomes are likely. Practically speaking, one can get cues as to what might serve as positive reinforcers by asking people what they would like and using intuitive judgments and past experiences. Once these are known, "all" that needs to be done is to make them contingent upon the desired behaviors.

Unfortunately, making external rewards contingent on effective teaching is not easy. Mintzberg (1979) noted that although in theory competent performance of professionals in professional bureaucracies is ensured by fellow professionals, in practice such control is not always exercised. Universities are no exception; in many of them there are strong norms against colleagues or administrators observing a professor's teaching performance especially in order to evaluate it. Interestingly, such norms contrast sharply with the behavior of most faculty members with respect to their research work, where most are eager to have as many colleagues as will take the time to read it critique their research work. I point to this inconsistency not because the situations are identical but because the analogy to research may be useful in thinking about ways to improve teaching performance by indicating that, at least under certain conditions, professors seek criticism. In what ways could such behavior be enhanced with respect to teaching? Perhaps the analogy itself can provide a useful point of departure to stimulate faculties to explore these differences and examine their own behaviors. The analogy may be useful in another way. Clearly, one can choose people whom one respects to provide preliminary critiques of one's research. Perhaps if this volunteerism in selection were incorporated into the design of peer reviews of teaching, they would be more readily accepted.

In any case, research on leadership, conducted using the behavior modification perspective, has indicated the important positive effects that frequent monitoring of performance can have, even in the absence of direct manipulation of performance consequences. In reviewing this research, Komaki (1986) wrote: "Effective managers were not found to provide more performance consequences than marginally effective managers, but they did monitor performance more often. Furthermore, the effective managers were found to monitor performance by directly sampling performance" (p. 313). Of course, this conclusion leaves open the possible reasons for the effectiveness of more frequent work sampling. One may speculate, however, that such monitoring, if nothing else, provides an occasion for discussing performance. Such discussions of teaching in a loosely coupled system such as a university might have quite favorable effects and would certainly be consistent with common professional norms.

Further, such discussions might serve as opportunities for administrators to work with faculty members to help identify the type of outcomes which each desires from teaching. These might include exploring new areas and helping students develop specific skills. Teaching assignments could then be designed to increase the likelihood that the desired rewards would be attainable. In a way this is an extension of ecological design, but it focuses on facilitating the placement of individuals in contexts based on the relationship between the outcomes they desire and those apt to occur in a particular setting rather than designing the setting per se.

Of course, implementing such placements will have costs. One way to proceed might be to allocate a certain pool of money to each individual faculty member to be used for this end. Individual faculty members could spend the money to purchase equipment or training activities that would seem likely to help them teach so as to gain the rewards from teaching they desired. (Some colleges already do something similar with respect to supporting faculty research.) Since decisions about how to spend money that is allocated to people often cause them to think seriously about how to spend it, if nothing else, systems of the type suggested would stimulate faculty to think through what they need to do to make their teaching more effective and rewarding. Stimulating this type of thinking about teaching might be a substantial accomplishment in itself and also a first step toward other things such as discussions with colleagues about teaching. Such discussions might help overcome the reluctance noted earlier of colleagues to draw on one another to help improve their teaching.

In many colleges and universities such discussions might serve as early steps in the desired direction. Of course, the desirability of such actions is not peculiar to a B-mod approach. However, the rationale for them and the process I have described for generating them are consistent with the basic B-mod premises that the frequency and intensity of behavior directed to improving teaching performance are functions of its consequences and that the lack of contingent consequences is apt to be associated with the absence of the desired behavior. From the administrator's perspective, introducing such contingencies is a sequential task that might well begin with efforts to educate the faculty on the importance of contingencies rather than proposing any particular system or even proposing any system at all.

Of course, finding ways to make consequences contingent upon performance is only one of many problems in "motivating" professionals. Some evidence suggests that many extrinsic rewards such as money might actually reduce performance of intrinsically rewarding tasks (see Chap. 4 in this volume), although the results of research on this matter are by no means clear-cut (Staw, 1976; Guzzo, 1979). Even if extrinsic rewards often do undermine intrinsic motivation, that would not be adequate justification to ignore the role of extrinsic rewards in university teaching. For one thing, many aspects of teaching may not be intrinsically rewarding for some teachers. Furthermore, many teachers may not be able to perform well enough to receive the intrinsic rewards that are dependent on competent teaching performance; to the degree this is true, the intrinsic consequences these instructors receive from teaching are aversive. Consequently, a sequential strategy that employs extrinsic rewards to reinforce behaviors that enable good performance (and hence the receipt of intrinsic rewards) may be useful. In this regard, however, please note that the B-mod approach I have presented above encourages administrators to consider all sources of rewards, including outcomes that are intrinsically rewarding to specific people. This approach could easily lead to designing systems rich in intrinsic rewards. However, it is still possible that the process this entails might still be one that Deci and Ryan (1985) and their followers would suggest undermines intrinsic motivation.

Even if that is so, it seems reasonable to assume that if appropriately designed and framed, attempts to link extrinsic rewards to teaching performance and the development of behaviors contributing to such performance can yield some important benefits. However, successful implementation will depend upon the ability and willingness of administrators to find ways to have performance measured and to make rewards contingent upon performance or steps that are apt to lead to desired behavior. Often the unwillingness of administrators to make these discriminations seems to be responsible for their failure to develop and employ performance measures.

Thus, it becomes important to consider the reinforcement contingencies of administrators—that is, how administrators are administered. Among other things, administrators should be encouraged (i.e., positively reinforced) to develop and use relevant performance measures. (Obviously, a precondition for such measures is specification of the desired behaviors and outcomes. Such specification by itself might have a considerable impact.) Unfortunately, administrators are often rewarded on the basis of an efficiency measure (such as student credit hours) which constrains administrators through compensation systems that leave little or no discretion for discriminating among teachers on the basis of performance. Clearly, blanket salary increases for faculty reward tenure in the system rather than performance.

From the operant perspective, such systems result in an inefficient use of the resources used to "motivate" people. Teaching performance can be improved by making rewards contingent upon desired behavior. Obviously, reviews of and feedback about performance by administrators can provide opportunities to give such rewards. In addition, it needs to be recognized that some of the most direct feedback faculty get about their teaching in many of today's universities is from evaluations made by students. One problem with student evaluations is that they are often a peripheral activity "squeezed in" in one of the last class meetings of a course and are often designed to permit rapid completion. Detailed feedback about specific things an instructor has done during the course is unlikely to result from this process. Therefore, it may behoove administrators to support redesign of the evaluation process to increase the chances of such feedback occurring on an appropriate schedule. This might be done by hiring a sample of students and training them to provide the type of feedback desired at a time when it would be most meaningful to the instructor. This step would be highly consistent with the known benefits of frequent performance monitoring described earlier.

A second general matter raised by the B-mod approach takes the issue of misuse even further. Often our systems not only fail to reward people for desired behavior; they actually reward people for undesired behavior or for behavior in conflict with the desired behavior. Kerr's (1975) famous paper "On the Folly of Rewarding A, While Hoping for B" makes this point well, by showing how throughout our society we reward behavior we do not desire. To take but one of numerous examples, he argued that in universities we want people to work hard at teaching. However, the significant rewards (salary, tenure, promotion) are primarily contingent upon research. As another example, to the degree that reinforcement contingencies induce teachers to spend their time on routine administrative or monitoring tasks, they are "motivating" teachers to spend their time and energies in ways that are inconsistent with performance in the classroom. In short, we often reward teachers for A while hoping they will do B. It comes as no surprise to a student of B-mod that often they do so little B.

I would like to emphasize two other concepts from B-mod which, I believe, have particular relevance to administration in loosely coupled systems. The first is the concept of shaping. In simple terms, shaping involves positively reinforcing approximations of or approaches to desired behavior. For example, consider a teacher who has fallen well behind recent developments in disciplines related to his or her field. Dealing with such a problem often requires a number of steps (e.g., summer study, attending seminars, taking formal coursework, and so on). This teacher needs to be rewarded for taking these intermediate steps. If the administrator waits for the problem to be completely solved before giving rewards, the opportunity to give the rewards may seldom occur. What needs to be done is to determine a sequence of steps that appear likely to lead to improved performance and to positively reinforce successful completion of these even though they may be early on the path to the ultimately desired behavior. It might be a mistake to rely only on the typical salary administration process to deliver rewards. In fact, the delivery of the rewards itself could be used as a climate-setting event. In delivering rewards for excellent teaching, administrators could orchestrate events so as to signal special messages about what is valued in the system. Specifically they might create ceremonies in which students honor faculty and faculty honor one another for their teaching effectiveness, in a manner done by at least one university that has an elaborate ceremony annually to honor master teachers.

Another concept from the operant tradition which might be useful is the notion of a response repertoire, which calls attention to the fact that, at any given time, individuals have a finite set of behaviors that they are capable of emitting. Many people may simply not have the behaviors that they need to have in their response repertoires. Consequently it is necessary to help them broaden their response set in order to help them improve their teaching. In such cases, something like training in improvisational theater might be helpful. Of course, the suggestion for such training is not unique to the B-mod perspective, but it is the focus on behavior which this perspective encourages which might increase the likelihood of such a creative action.

Conclusion

In this chapter I have argued that four components of the B-mod approach can be surprisingly useful in organizations such as educational systems, even though they are both loosely coupled and engaged in nonroutine tasks. It is important to realize that this argument can be made at two different but at least partially overlapping levels. At one level the approach offers a technology; at another level it offers an orientation.

At the level of technology the approach suggests some rather clear-cut actions that can be taken. For example, one could attempt to specify desired behavior and to set up a system to reward it directly by making extrinsic rewards contingent on desired behavior. Similarly, one could establish a program to use models to develop particular skills. These activities are all possible with current knowledge and have demonstrated utility. This is not to say the applications would be free of problems; it is only to say that they are feasible.

As an orientation, B-mod encourages the administrator to focus on the relationship between external factors and behavior. I suggest that the orientation itself is fruitful because it guides one to specific actions that work. Few of these are unique to B-mod. Most of them are similar to elements derived from other perspectives. For example, the program outlined by Hamner and Hamner (1976) is only partially based on B-mod principles as they are usually conceived. In particular, the use of goals is something that does not fall conveniently into traditional B-mod perspectives. Yet students of goal setting Erez (1977) and Wood and Locke (1990) stress the importance of feedback. In fact, one could argue that the success of programs in companies such as Emery Air Freight (see Dowling, 1973), which students of B-mod like to cite as evidence for the utility of their approach, was due to the cognitive processes emphasized by students of goal setting.

The actual reasons why B-mod works are of both theoretical and practical importance. However, application need not await such knowledge; one can benefit greatly from the orientation. The approach used at Emery was derived from an external orientation that sought to modify behavior by altering stimuli in the environment. The approach led people to specify what behaviors were desired and what stimuli were available for use and to monitor the consequences of arranging these stimuli systematically with respect to the behavior. The orientation led people to administrative actions that were clearly productive. However, although the external orientation is useful, as I implied in my brief comments concerning radical behaviorism, too doctrinaire commitments to it can be dysfunctional.

Despite this potential problem, B-mod, both as a technology and as an orientation, has demonstrated its value for the management of organizations. The notion that the B-mod approach may be particularly valuable in loosely coupled, nonroutine organizations is speculative but consistent with organization theory, such as Child's (1972) argument that there are a variety of ways to exercise control in an organization. He suggested that where tasks can be formalized, control can be decentralized; where tasks cannot be formalized, control is often centralized. My argument is based on the assumption that in educational systems teaching performance cannot be formalized or controlled via centralization. Consequently, an alternative perspective for control, which centers on influencing the probabilities of behavior by the somewhat incremental rearrangements of stimuli, may be especially useful.

Finally, we should note that recent trends in the application of behavior modification to organizations seem to be moving us away from one of the most serious problems of the approach—the manipulation of directly acting contingencies by allowing a greater role for verbal communication of contingencies. Scott and Podsakoff (1985) implied that an important role for an effective leader may be to describe the contingencies that are operative in their organization. More recently Malott (1992) introduced the idea of "rule," which he defined as a verbal description of a behavioral contingency to describe a key role of leaders of cultures. These developments are especially interesting for revealing how the advantages of the behavioral perspective can be sustained in complex organizations by abandoning the constraints imposed by radical behaviorism which stem from its historical roots in the study of animals that appear to not use language as humans do.

References

Bandura, A. (1969). *Principles of behavior modification.* New York: Holt, Rinehart, & Winston.

Bandura, A. (1986). *Social foundations of thought and action: A social cognitive theory.* Englewood Cliffs, NJ: Prentice-Hall.

Child, J. (1972). Organization structure and strategies of control: A replication of the Aston study. *Administrative Science Quarterly, 17,* 163–177.

Church, R. M. (1963). The varied effects of punishment on behavior. *Psychological Review, 70,* 369–402.

Deci, E. L., & Ryan, R. M. (1985). *Intrinsic motivation and self-determination in human behavior.* New York: Plenum Press.

Dowling, W. F., Jr. (1973). At Emery Air Freight: Positive reinforcement boosts performance. *Organizational Dynamics, 1,* 41–50.

Erez, M. (1977). Feedback: A necessary condition for the goal setting performance relationship. *Journal of Applied Psychology, 62(5),* 624–627.

Goldstein, A. P., & Sorcher, M. (1974). *Changing supervising behavior.* New York: Pergamon Press.

Guzzo, R. A. (1979). Types of rewards, cognitions, and work motivation. *Academy of Management Review, 4,* 75–86.

Hamner, W. C., & Hamner, E. P. (1976). Behavior modification and the bottom line. *Organizational Dynamics, 4,* 3–21.

Kerr, S. (1975). On the folly of rewarding A, while hoping for B. *Academy of Management Journal, 18,* 769–783.

Komacki, J. L. (1986). Applied behavior analysis and organizational behavior: Reciprocal influence on the two fields. *Organizational Behavior, 8,* 297–334.

Locke, E. A., & Bryan, J. F. (1969). Knowledge of score and goal level as determinants of work rate. *Journal of Applied Psychology, 53,* 59–65.

Malott, R. W. (1992). Two theories of rule-governed behavior: A theory of rule-governed behavior and organizational behavior management. *Journal of Organizational Behavior Management, 12,* 45–65.

Mintzberg, H. (1979). *The structuring of organizations.* New York: Prentice-Hall.

Nord, W. R., & Peter, J. P. (1980). A behavior modification perspective on marketing. *Journal of Marketing, 44,* 36–47.

Orton, J. D., & Weick, K. E. (1990). Loosely coupled systems: A reconceptualization. *Academy of Management Review, 15,* 203–223.

Pfeffer, J. (1981). *Power in organizations.* Marshfield, MA: Pitman.

Reese, E. P. (1966). *The analysis of human operant behavior.* Dubuque, IA: William C. Brown.

Sayles, L. R. (1979). *What effective teachers really do . . . and how they do it.* New York: McGraw-Hill.

Scott, W. E., Jr., & Podsakoff, P. M. (1985). *Behavioral principles in the practice of management.* New York: Wiley.

Skinner, B. F. (1953). *Science and human behavior.* New York: Macmillan.

Solomon, R. L. (1964). Punishment. *American Psychologist, 19,* 239–253.

Staw, B. M. (1976). *Intrinsic and extrinsic motivation.* Morristown, NJ: General Learning Press.

Weick, K. E. (1976). Educational organizations as loosely coupled systems. *Administrative Science Quarterly, 21,* 1–19.

Weick, K. E. (1979). *The social psychology of organizing* (2d ed.). Reading, MA: Addison-Wesley.

Wood, R. A., & Locke, E. A. (1990). Goal setting and strategy effects on complex tasks. In M. Staw & L. L. Cummings (Eds.), *Research in organizational behavior, 12,* 73–109.

7

Expectancy Theory Approaches to Faculty Motivation

RICHARD T. MOWDAY AND
SANG H. NAM

Announcements of corporate restructuring have become commonplace in the business press. Some of the largest and most visible corporations in America have announced massive layoffs in an effort to survive in an increasingly competitive global business environment. The goal is to achieve far greater productivity with fewer employees, a strategy made possible by changing technology and fundamentally different approaches to organization design and management.

Although restructuring in the corporate context is more visible in the press, major organizational changes are also evident in government and educational organizations. Higher education, long immune from radical organizational change, has not been spared from financial and competitive pressures. The 1980s and 1990s, in particular, have been a period of increasing financial pressure for most universities in North America (Levin, 1991; Small, 1994). Shortfalls in state tax revenues, eroding local support, and cutbacks in federal programs have all contributed to mounting financial pressures on higher education (St. John, 1991). As a result, higher education faces the challenge of restructuring its activities to become more productive and cost efficient (Levin, 1991).

Higher education, at least historically, is labor intensive, which constrains its ability to reduce labor costs (Levin, 1991). At the margin, many schools have increased the size of their part-time or adjunct instructional staff. The need to maintain a core of faculty members, especially in graduate programs, limits the extent to which this strategy can be implemented on a widespread basis, however. Thus, the strategy for increasing productivity shifts to the revenue side of the equation. As this chapter was being written, for example, the president of the University of Oregon held a press conference to announce his intention of meeting increasing budget pressures by increasing tuition and admitting twelve hundred additional students to the university without increasing the size of the faculty or the instructional staff. The University of Oregon, like most business corporations, is seeking to attain far greater productivity, albeit by a somewhat different method.

The implications of this strategy for the faculty are dramatic. Not only will the faculty be asked to accommodate more students in their classes, but a better job must be done teaching classes. With rising tuition (Small, 1994) and the increasing importance of tuition as a source of revenue (Hauptman & Hartle, 1987), high-quality instruction becomes critical in attracting and retaining students. Sacken (1990) also noted that, given recent interest in assessing quality and effectiveness of teaching within higher education, particularly among legislators, teaching effectiveness has become an issue of increasing importance for most universities.

If recent events at the University of Oregon are indicative of broader trends in higher education, the teaching role of faculty will take on increased importance in coming years. Universities have been criticized for neglecting their teaching mission relative to research and scholarship (Anderson, 1992). For instance, former U.S. secretary of education William Bennett argued that higher education is characterized by gross inefficiencies owing to "absurdly low teaching responsibility of faculty" (quoted by Levin, 1991). In the face of increasing financial and competitive pressures, neglecting teaching responsibilities or offering students less than high-quality instruction will be a luxury that universities can ill afford.

An important challenge facing university administrators is how faculty members can be motivated to increase the time and attention they devote to teaching and to students. Encouraging faculty members to take teaching seriously in higher education, however, will be a difficult task (Sacken, 1990). A former president of the American Association for Higher Education, for instance, noted that those attempting to improve teaching effectiveness were "swimming against the tide" (Heller, 1988). In a culture that has long held research and publication in higher esteem than classroom instruction, how can the faculty be motivated to become more effective teachers?

How one approaches this challenge depends a great deal on one's perspective on motivation. Different theories of motivation can lead to quite different administrative actions. The theory of motivation discussed in this chapter, expectancy theory, is a cognitive choice theory that focuses attention on how people make decisions about where to allocate their effort. It is perhaps the most influential theory of motivation in organizational behavior, because of both its intuitive conceptual appeal and its clear implications for management practice. One goal of this chapter is to highlight the major theoretical propositions of expectancy theory, and to discuss some of its implications for motivating faculty to become more effective teachers. We also explore how important changes taking place in universities relating to teaching may make it more difficult to motivate faculty using expectancy theory.

Expectancy Theory

The most influential statement of expectancy theory in work settings was offered by Vroom (1964). Since his pioneering effort, there have been a number refinements and extensions of his basic model (Graen, 1969; Lawler, 1973; Porter & Lawler, 1968). In more recent years, research on expectancy theory has focused less on substantive revisions to the basic theory and more on methodological efforts to improve the precision of its predictions of behavior (cf. Kanfer, 1990). Because we are less interested in methodogical fine points relative to the general implications of the theory for improving teaching effectiveness, we only touch briefly on some of the current research issues.

Moreover, the goal here is not to present Vroom's theory and later refinements in specific detail. Rather, the intention is to provide a general understanding of expectancy theory which can be applied to teaching in universities. Readers interested in a more in-depth treatment of expectancy theory and the research evidence supporting it are referred to Kanfer (1990) and Pinder (1984).

All of the different approaches to expectancy theory make similar assumptions about people and share key theoretical variables in common. Three assumptions are commonly made. First, people have expectations or beliefs about the outcomes of their behavior. For example, if one sets out to teach a class to graduate students, she or he has a high (or low) expectation of performing well. Second, individuals have preferences among the different outcomes of their behavior. In other words, some outcomes will be preferred to others. Third, people behave hedonistically when choosing among different tasks or levels of effort to exert in performing a task. For instance, if the probability of receiving a pay raise is the same whether high

Fig. 7.1   Nadler and Lawler's (1977) Expectancy Theory Model of Behavior

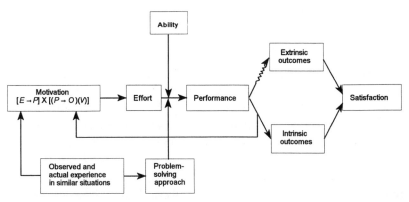

Source: Reprinted from Nadler and Lawler (1977) with permission.

or low levels of effort are exerted in accomplishing a task, most people are likely to exert low levels of effort.

Figure 1 presents the basic motivation-behavior sequence identified by Nadler and Lawler (1977). It is useful in understanding the basic components of expectancy theory and their linkages.

Effort-to-Performance Expectancies

Expectancies are beliefs or subjective probabilities that certain outcomes are likely to follow from behavior. The most basic outcome in expectancy theory is the level of performance or task accomplishment (Lawler, 1973). Following an example presented earlier, individuals have beliefs about the likelihood that effort invested in teaching a class will lead to successful task accomplishment. If the class has been taught successfully many times before, this expectancy will be rather high. If the class is a new preparation or covers unfamiliar material, the expectancy of task accomplishment may be lower.

An important characteristic of expectancies is that they are subjective probabilities or individual beliefs, not objective likelihoods. Two faculty members facing exactly the same teaching task may have quite different expectancies depending upon a host of factors, including individual differences (e.g., self-esteem) and contextual influences (e.g., role clarity). From a motivational perspective, the critical issue is not whether expectancies are realistic. Whether effort will be directed toward a teaching task depends on the faculty member's beliefs that good teaching can be accomplished, not on what others think. It stands to reason that faculty are unlikely to put forth effort beyond the minimum level on assigned teaching tasks that they view as impossible to perform well.

Performance-to-Outcome Expectancies

A second set of expectancies or beliefs link performance with other outcomes. A given level of teaching performance is positively valent if faculty believe that it will lead to other outcomes such as rewards. In other words, if a faculty member believes that good teaching performance is instrumental for the acquisition of attractive rewards (e.g., pay raise), or for avoiding punishment (e.g., increased teaching loads), she will be motivated to improve her teaching performance (Pinder, 1984). Thus, if a faculty member receives one of the highest student teaching evaluations in the department, for instance, he may expect to be rewarded with a merit pay increase. Alternatively, an individual who receives unsatisfactory student teaching evaluations may expect to receive no merit pay increase. As with effort-to-performance expectancies, performance-to-outcome beliefs are subjective. To motivate behavior, they need not be realistic or even objectively likely.

Outcomes can be of different types. One distinction that is commonly drawn is between extrinsic and intrinsic outcomes. Extrinsic outcomes are controlled by people or forces external to the individual. They include such things as pay raises, awards, letters of commendation, promotions, and so forth. In contrast, intrinsic rewards are controlled by the individual. Self-esteem, personal growth, and feelings of accomplishment for a job well done are examples of intrinsic rewards that individuals control.

A second distinction is sometimes drawn between first- and second-level outcomes. A reward such as a pay raise would be viewed as a first-level outcome for performance that is valued because it is instrumental for achieving second-level outcomes. Pay raises may be valued because they allow us to take a vacation we have promised to our family or allow us to move to a house in a neighborhood with better schools for our children. The perceived likelihood that a first-level outcome leads to a second-level outcome is called instrumentality in some variations of expectancy theory (cf. Nadler & Lawler, 1977).

Valence of Outcomes

The final major component of expectancy theory is the valence of outcomes. Valence represents the value or anticipated satisfaction that comes from different outcomes of our behavior. Common rewards such as pay raises are positively valent for most people. In contrast, being assigned a less desirable class to teach or a heavier teaching load would be viewed as negatively valent.

Because individuals differ widely in their needs and values, the valence component of expectancy theory is one major way in which individual differences can influence the motivation process. Some individuals may value extrinsic rewards such as pay and promotions, for instance. For other individuals, a high value is placed on intrinsic rewards such as the feeling of accomplishment which comes from helping a struggling student master a difficult concept.

The valence of outcomes can also be influenced by the organizational culture of the university where a faculty member works. For instance, private liberal arts campuses that depend on attracting students who pay a large tuition generally have a culture on campus which values classroom instruction. This is necessary to attract and retain students, as well as to convince students they are receiving value for their tuition dollar. In contrast, large public universities that have funded research as a major part of their mission may place less emphasis on teaching than on scholarship and obtaining grants. Although the valence component of expectancy theory reminds us that individual differences in valued outcomes are important, we should also recall that what individuals value can be powerfully shaped by environmental forces.

Motivational Force

The three components of expectancy theory come together to determine motivational force. From the previous discussion, it should be clear that the highest levels of motivation are associated with high effort-performance expectancies, high performance-outcome expectancies, and highly valent outcomes. In other words, high motivation results when individuals believe that effort will lead to successful task accomplishment and that successful task accomplishment will lead to outcomes with positive valence. In early formulations of the theory, motivational force was viewed as the multiplicative outcome of the major components of the theory. More recent research by Harrell and Stahl (1986) found that individuals often combined expectancy and valence information additively instead of multiplicatively. The combinatorial strategy used appears to differ both across and within individuals.

As a cognitive choice theory, expectancy theory applies to situations in which individuals choose among alternative activities in which to engage and among different levels of effort to invest in a particular activity. For instance, a faculty member might choose between spending time on preparing a lecture or working on the draft of a research paper. Alternatively, a faculty member may decide how much effort to invest in, for instance, preparing a lecture. If low to moderate levels of effort lead to outcomes similar to those resulting from high effort, the theory predicts that lower levels of effort will be invested.

Because expectancy theory focuses on individual choice, research on the theory using between-subjects designs has been criticized as less appropriate than within-subject designs (Mitchell, 1982). In addition, the theory has been viewed as focusing only on expectancies and valences for specific behaviors in specific situations (cf. Kanfer, 1990). In this regard, the theory may be less relevant in understanding behavior that occurs in response to ongoing events or to changes in behavior which occur in the absence of changes in expectancies or valences (cf. Kuhl & Atkinson, 1984). For this reason, Kanfer (1990) classified Vroom's version of expectancy theory as a "cognitive-episodic" theory of motivation. The extent to which this feature of the theory limits its applicability to understanding faculty motivation to teach may not be great, however. The nature of the teaching role in universities may be viewed less as a continuing process and more as a discrete series of episodes (i.e., classes) that confront faculty members as terms change.

Encouraging More Effective Teaching

Encouraging more effective teaching in university settings is a difficult process owing to the number and complexity of factors influencing faculty judgments on where to invest their time and energy. One value of a theory such as expectancy theory is that it focuses our thinking by highlighting key components of the motivation process. Expectancy theory suggests that faculty motivation for effective teaching would be primarily determined by two factors: positive effort-performance expectancies and offering attractive rewards for good teaching performance. Both factors are required to encourage faculty to improve their teaching effectiveness.

Managing Performance Expectancies

One of the more intractable problems in applying expectancy theory to motivating faculty teaching performance is the difficulty associated with specifying and measuring performance itself. Teaching in higher education is an inherently ambiguous technology because outcomes are often complex, multifaceted and nonspecified and may take years to become apparent (Halpern, 1987).

There are some generally accepted characteristics of "good" teaching: enthusiasm, knowledge of the subject area, stimulation of interest in the subject matter, organization, communication clarity, concern for students, use of higher cognitive levels for discussions, encouragement of active learning and student participation, and provision of constructive feedback (Goodwin & Stevens, 1993). It is also generally agreed, however, that it is difficult to measure teaching effectiveness, and this is still a major concern that is unresolved today (Goodwin & Stevens, 1993; McKeachie, 1963).

Student evaluations of teaching effectiveness are probably the most thoroughly studied of all forms of teaching evaluation and one of the best in terms of being supported by empirical research (Marsh & Bailey, 1993). Although student evaluations are undoubtedly a legitimate source of information, many faculty members remain skeptical about the validity of this method. Boice (1991) found that faculty members often blame invalid rating systems for teaching failures as indicated by student ratings (for a discussion of the role of causal attributions in the motivation process, see Weiner, 1986). Many campuses are experimenting with multiple methods of evaluating teaching, including peer observations. Even less is known about the validity of alternative evaluations methods, however. Moreover, methods such as peer observation have often been used to provide developmental feedback to faculty members. Using this same information for evaluation purposes may limit its utility as a developmental tool.

Even in the face of problems associated with specifying what constitutes good teaching performance, university administrators can still play an important role in influencing effort-performance expectancies. First, faculty members have to be assigned to classes that they believe they are capable of teaching. The question of whether faculty members are capable of being more effective teachers if so motivated has not received the attention it perhaps deserves. Expectancy theory suggests that people are more likely to engage in behaviors when they see a high probability that effort will lead to high performance. Faculty members who are assigned to unfamiliar courses or to teaching situations that do not match their skills are less likely to have a high effort-to-performance expectancy. They will teach courses because the system demands it, but they may not teach with much enthusiasm or invest the energy required to become better teachers.

Second, university administrators can manage situational factors to create a favorable teaching environment conducive to the faculty's success as instructors. Success experiences are an important determinant of positive expectancies (Pinder, 1984). The teaching environment in higher education, however, is often characterized by many situational constraints that interfere with faculty members' teaching performance (Mathieu, Tannen-baum, & Salas, 1992). Examples are lack of materials and supplies, con-flicting obligations, insufficient time allowed to complete tasks, techno-logical problems, and lack of information (Peters, O'Connor, & Eulberg, 1985). Faculty members confronted with such situational constraints be-come frustrated because they believe their effort will not be translated into good teaching performance. Frustration produced by situational con-straints would reduce faculty members' motivation by reducing their ex-pectancy perceptions. According to one survey, faculty felt that better physical resources and more support staff would contribute to their class-room performance (Olsen, 1993). It was also found that work motivation was negatively affected when individuals perceived that many situational constraints prevented good performance (Phillips & Freedman, 1984).

The effect of reducing situational constraints is perhaps most important for new faculty members. The faculty development literature suggests that junior faculty members often suffer from substantial role anxiety, high stress, and low satisfaction during the first three years of their appointment (Olsen, 1993). Their teaching pattern is cautious and defensive to avoid public failures at teaching. They are also surprisingly slow in establishing comfort, student acceptance, moving beyond defensive teaching strategies, and looking for support in improving teaching (Boice, 1991). Thus, it is critical to provide new faculty with social, intellectual, and physical sup-port to facilitate successful teaching experiences. Although such a recom-mendation seems commonplace, heavy first-year teaching loads, lack of re-sponse to requests for equipment or personnel, and the interpersonal indifference of senior faculty members were all frequently cited phenom-ena by junior faculty members (Olsen, 1993).

More and more campuses have centers for effective instruction which can work with faculty members to improve their teaching skills. In addi-tion, seminars are held to acquaint faculty members with effective teaching methods. Participation in these activities is most often voluntary, however. It is possible that faculty members who would benefit the most from such seminars are least likely to see the need, in part because they can easily ra-tionalize their poor teaching performance. It is all too easy, for instance, for instructors to blame students for the problems that occur in a specific class. In addition, instructors can and often do retreat behind institution-ally sanctioned norms (e.g., high standards for student performance) which can mask problems in classroom instruction. With increasing inter-est in faculty mentoring programs (Olsen, 1993), personal guidance can be provided to faculty through consultation with the Chair or senior faculty in helping them participate in useful seminars. Such efforts will be most helpful if they happen early in a faculty member's career.

Managing Rewards

Expectancy theory highlights the importance of the reward system in motivating more effective teaching. If rewards do not follow for high levels of teaching performance or if the rewards that follow are not valued, it is unrealistic to expect that most faculty members will invest time in the classroom. The most obvious rewards are extrinsic outcomes such as pay increases and promotions. The value of pay raises, in particular, appears to have become increasingly important as academic incomes have failed to keep pace with increases in the cost of living and levels of compensation in other professional domains (Bok, 1993; U.S. Department of Education, 1990). Alternative rewards would be other types of faculty benefits such as money placed in an individual faculty account that could fund travel, research, and other amenities for the faculty member (Olsen, 1993).

Many faculty members believe that good teaching is not rewarded on most campuses, at least not relative to other aspects of their performance (cf. Kerr, 1975). The evidence on the relationship between teaching performance and monetary outcomes, while limited, suggests that this belief may be correct. In a study of management professors at a variety of higher education institutions, Gomez-Mejia and Balkin (1992) found no relationship between teaching evaluations and either nine-month salary or average annual raises over a three-year period. Interestingly, the only significant relationship found between teaching evaluations and pay was among individuals who had above-average records of publishing in the top-tier journals. In other words, good teaching "counts" if you are a prolific researcher but not if you are a less productive scholar.

Although developing a strong linkage between teaching performance and extrinsic rewards like pay is a clear implication of the theory, some have argued that such efforts are likely to be futile. For example, Bok (1993) claims that devising financial incentives to reward good student ratings or for teaching overload classes is likely to "result only in large outlays of money in exchange for small changes in behavior" (p. 166). Bok argues that most faculty members are already conscientious teachers, a contention with which not everyone might agree. For those faculty members who neglect their teaching in favor of outside activities such as consulting and research, institutions may not be able to offer a sufficient level of rewards to change behavior.

Expectancy theory makes clear that intrinsic rewards also play an important role in motivating behavior. The intrinsic rewards of an academic career have traditionally been viewed as central to faculty satisfaction (Olsen, 1993). Given that extrinsic rewards have been seen as sources of dissatisfaction in higher education (Bess, 1981; Carnegie Foundation for the Advancement of Teaching, 1989), the role of intrinsic rewards could be particularly salient for faculty. Examples of intrinsic rewards include feelings of accomplishment and the satisfaction that comes from opportunities to contribute to student growth and development. The extent to which faculty members value teaching and derive intrinsic satisfaction from effective performance can have a critical impact on their behavior.

Institutional norms and the culture of universities can have an important influence on the intrinsic satisfaction associated with good teaching. Faculty members are often socialized to believe that research and scholarship are the most critical components of their professorial role. If they work on campuses that reinforce this view, faculty members are less likely to place emphasis on teaching or to find performance in the classroom rewarding. If the culture on campus supports the importance of good classroom instruction and rewards teaching performance, faculty members are more likely to place a higher value on teaching and derive intrinsic satisfaction from effective classroom performance. Developing a campus culture that supports teaching begins with a strong statement of values. It is not enough to simply say that teaching is important, however. In addition, the value of teaching must be continually reinforced in tangible and visible ways. For instance, pay raises, teaching awards, and informal expressions of appreciation, such as a congratulatory note from the president or lunch with the department Chair to celebrate teaching excellence, communicate a teaching-oriented culture to faculty (Baldwin, 1990). Bardwick (1986) suggested that the "specific form of recognition is much less important than the reward of being singled out." Many different symbols of merit can help foster a teaching-oriented culture by recognizing and reinforcing good teaching performance by faculty (Baldwin, 1990) .

Achieving the appropriate balance between extrinsic and intrinsic rewards to motivate teaching presents even experienced educators with something of a dilemma. It was already noted that the former president of Harvard, Derek Bok, felt that financial incentives for good teaching are unlikely to produce changes in faculty behavior sufficient to justify the expenditures involved. At the same time, Bok (1993) clearly argues that institutions would be unwise to act as if financial incentives are unimportant. He feels that university professors are among the least accountable professions in America and that every effort must be made to keep faculty committed to serving their institutions and satisfying the needs of their students. If universities are to achieve their goals of motivating more effective faculty teaching, attention must be given to both extrinsic and intrinsic rewards.

Conclusion

Expectancy theory makes clear that any efforts to encourage more effective teaching must address both motivation and teaching skills. In this chapter, we suggested various ways of both increasing faculty members' efforts toward effective teaching and helping them improve their teaching skills. Programs that address either one of these to the exclusion of the other are probably doomed to failure.

In addition, more attention needs to be given to teaching as a process that ranges from identifying topics to cover in a course to effective delivery of information in a classroom setting. The teaching function is complex and calls upon a variety of skills. The person who is entertaining in front of a group may not necessarily be good at organizing material in a logical manner that students can comprehend. We tend to focus on what the instructor does in the actual classroom. However, hours of work are normally required to prepare for the time spent in the classroom. Effective teaching depends on the ability both to prepare good classes and to deliver a learning experience for students.

Finally, we emphasized the importance of being sensitive to how changes on campus and in the environment influence faculty motivation. Traditionally, higher education in North America has maintained organizational cultures that encourage their administrators to take a sink or swim approach to faculty teaching. Expectancy theory suggests that such an approach would be ineffective in promoting teaching effectiveness. One of the primary responsibilities of policy makers in higher education is to create a supportive organizational culture and environment for faculty development. Most important, the policy makers have to perceive support of faculty as an investment in the success of a faculty career as teachers and ultimately of an institution that is truly committed to high-quality teaching (Olsen, 1993).

Institutions must also be sensitive to how other changes in the environment impact the teaching roles of faculty. The traditional model of instruction in most universities has been defined by one faculty member in front of one class. However, rapidly changing technology now makes it possible for a single faculty member to offer instruction in widely dispersed classroom settings. There will be strong pressures on institutions to employ such technology, since it increases the productivity of individual faculty members. For faculty members to be effective in the new instructional settings made possible by technology, however, may require an institutional investment in training to use the new technology. The faculty member comfortable in leading a small-group discussion may find her or his skills less effective in more technologically sophisticated settings (e.g., distance learning). Moreover, as expectancy theory reminds us, faculty members unfamiliar with the new technology may be less motivated to master it unless they believe their efforts will lead to effective performance.

It is important to recognize that the challenge facing higher education administrators may extend beyond motivating individual faculty members to be more effective teachers in their own classes. Bok (1993) argued that "the most important question facing American universities today is whether to transform themselves from institutions in which individual professors teach classes into communities joined in a common effort to find better ways to help students learn" (p. 175). This is a daunting challenge in the best of times but may be particularly difficult if public support for higher education, both monetary and other kinds, continues to erode. Faculty members are used to a great deal of autonomy in teaching. Motivating them to become actively involved in the creation of the learning communities envisioned by Bok may be the greatest challenge of all.

References

Anderson, M. (1992). *Imposters in the temple.* New York: Simon & Schuster.

Baldwin, R. G. (1990). Faculty vitality beyond the research university: Extending a contextual concept. *Journal of Higher Education, 61,* 160–180.

Bardwick, J. M. (1986). *The plateauing trap.* New York: American Management Association.

Bess, J. L. (1981, March). Intrinsic satisfaction from academic versus other professional work: A comparative analysis. Paper presented at the meeting of the Association for the Study of Higher Education, Washington, DC.

Boice, R. (1991). New faculty as teachers. *Journal of Higher Education, 62,* 150–173.

Bok, D. (1993). *The cost of talent.* New York: Free Press.

Brinko, K. T. (1990). Instructional consultation with feedback in higher education. *Journal of Higher Education, 61,* 65–83.

Carnegie Foundation for the Advancement of Teaching. (1989). *The condition of the professoriate: Attitudes and trends, 1989.* Princeton: Carnegie Foundation for the Advancement of Teaching.

Gomez-Mejia, L. R., & Balkin, D. B. (1992). Determinants of faculty pay: An agency theory perspective. *Academy of Management Journal, 35,* 921–955.

Goodwin, L. D., & Stevens, E. A. (1993). The influence of gender on university faculty members' perceptions of good teaching. *Journal of Higher Education, 64,* 166–185.

Graen, G. (1969). Instrumentality theory of work motivation: Some experimental results and suggested modifications. *Journal of Applied Psychology* Monograph, 53 (2, Pt. 2).

Hackman, J. R., & Oldham, G. R. (1980). *Work redesign.* Reading, MA: Addison-Wesley.

Halpern, D. F. (Ed.). (1987). *New directions for higher education: Student outcomes assessment: What institutions stand to gain* (No. 59). San Francisco: Jossey-Bass.

Harrell, A., & Stahl, M. (1986). Additive information processing and the relationship between expectancy of success and motivational force. *Academy of Management Journal, 29,* 424–433.

Hauptman, A. W., & Hartle, T. (1987). Tuition increases since 1970: A perspective. *Higher Education and National Affairs,* Newsletter of the American Council on Education, February 23.

Heller, S. (1988, April 16). Higher-education reformers take up challenge to give teaching—and teachers—more clout. *Chronicle of Higher Education,* A1, A14, A15.

Kanfer, R. (1990). Motivation theory and industrial and organizational psychology. In M. E. Dunnette & L. M. Hough (Eds.), *Handbook of industrial and organizational psychology* (2d ed., Vol. 1, 75–170). Palo Alto, CA: Consulting Psychologists Press.

Kerr, S. (1975). On the folly of rewarding A, while hoping for B. *Academy of Management Journal, 18,* 769–783.

Kuhl, J., & Atkinson, J. W. (1984). Perspectives in human motivational psychology: A new experimental paradigm. In V. Sarris & A. Parducci (Eds.), *Perspectives in psychological experimentation: Toward the year 2000* (pp. 235–252). Hillsdale, NJ: Erlbaum.

Lawler, E. E. (1973). *Motivation in work organizations.* Monterey, CA: Brooks/Cole.

Levin, H. M. (1991). Raising productivity in higher education. *Journal of Higher Education, 62,* 241–262.

Marsh, H. W., & Bailey, M. (1993). Multidimensional students' evaluations of teaching effectiveness: A profile analysis. *Journal of Higher Education, 64,* 1–18.

Mathieu, J. E., Tannenbaum, S. I., & Salas, E. (1992). Influences of individual and situational characteristics on measures of training effectiveness. *Academy of Management Journal, 35,* 828–847.

McKeachie, W. J. (1963). Research on teaching at the college and university level. In N. L. Gage (Ed.), *Handbook of research on teaching* (pp. 1118–1172). Chicago: Rand McNally.

Mitchell, T. R. (1982). Expectancy-value models in organizational psychology. In N. Feather (Ed.), *Expectations and actions: Expectancy-value models in psychology* (pp. 293–312). Hillsdale, NJ: Erlbaum.

Nadler, D. A., & Lawler, E. E. (1977). Motivating individuals in organizational settings. In J. R. Hackman, E. E. Lawler, & L. W. Porter (Eds.), *Perspectives on behavior in organizations.* New York: McGraw-Hill.

Olsen, D. (1993). Work satisfaction and stress in the first and third year of academic appointment. *Journal of Higher Education, 64,* 453–471.

Peters, L. H., O'Connor, E. J., & Eulberg, J. R. (1985). Situational constraints: Sources, consequences, and future considerations. In G. Ferris & K. O. Rowland (Eds.), *Research in personnel and human resources management* (Vol. 3, 79–114). Greenwich, CT: JAI Press.

Phillips, J. S., & Freedman, S. M. (1984). Situational performance constraints and task characteristics: Their relationship to motivation and satisfaction. *Journal of Management, 10,* 321–331.

Pinder, C. C. (1984). *Work motivation: Theory, issues, and applications.* Glenview, IL: Scott, Foresman.

Porter, L. W., & Lawler, E. E. (1968). *Managerial attitudes and performance.* Homewood, IL: Dorsey Press.

Sacken, D. M. (1990). Taking teaching seriously: Institutional and individual dilemmas. *Journal of Higher Education, 61,* 548–564.

Small, J. M. (1994). Reform in Canadian universities. *Canadian Journal of Higher Education, 24*(2), 1–15.

St. John, E. P. (1991). A framework for reexamining state resource-management strategies in higher education. *Journal of Higher Education, 62,* 263–287.

U.S. Department of Education. (1990). *Digest of education statistics.* National Center for Educational Statistics. Washington, DC: U.S. Department of Education.

Vroom, V. H. (1964). *Work and motivation.* New York: Wiley.

Weiner, B. (1986). *An attributional theory of achievement motivation and emotion.* New York: Springer-Verlag.

8 Implications of Goal-Setting Theory for Faculty Motivation

GARY P. LATHAM,
SOOSAN DAGHIGHI, AND
EDWIN A. LOCKE

How many faculty members come to a classroom with the enthusiastic belief that they will impart knowledge and wisdom that will enhance the mind and spirit of those with whom they will come in contact? How can faculty members be motivated, energized, and inspired to want to impart their knowledge and release their creativity? A theory that can assist us in responding effectively to these questions is goal setting (Locke & Latham, 1990). This theory provides a means of instilling a sense of challenge in and recognition from performing tasks that are frequently perceived by the performer as having little value to anyone.

The importance of people taking personal interest in what they do is illustrated dramatically by an event described by Frank (1983) which occurred in 1944 when Allied aircraft began bold air strikes into Germany. After a German factory was hit by bombs, the Germans ordered prisoners to one end of the building remains, commanding them to shovel the debris into carts and drag it to the other end of the compound. The next day the prisoners were ordered to move the high pile of debris back to the other end of the compound. Day after day the prisoners hauled the same mountain of rubble back and forth from one end of the camp to the other. After several weeks of this drudgery, one man began sobbing uncontrollably and

Preparation of this chapter was supported in part by a grant from the Social Science and Humanities Research Council of Canada to the first author.

was led away by the guards. Another screamed until his captors beat him into silence. Then another man, who had survived three years of prison, darted away from the group and threw himself on an electrified fence. This activity continued until dozens of prisoners went mad and ran from their work only to be shot by the guards or electrified by the fence.

Why did the Germans require this activity? The commandant of the camp later explained that this was an experiment to see what would happen when people were given a task again and again which was not valued by them.

What are the implications of this finding for understanding why faculty eventually lose interest in teaching students? In a university setting, many of us teach the same undergraduate subject matter year after year. Unlike in the graduate student seminars that we teach, the undergraduate students who take our courses are often nameless and faceless to us. This is especially true in large survey courses. At best, if we do know the students, it is only for one quarter or one semester before they disappear from us. Through casual conversation we often learn that the majority of students have little or no interest in the subject matter that we are teaching them. They are taking the course only to satisfy a requirement for receiving their degree. Unlike our research, there appears to be little opportunity from teaching for us as faculty to discover or acquire new knowledge, skills, or abilities. Thus for many faculty, teaching undergraduate students is devalued. How then can faculty be motivated to teach effectively? In responding to this question, we discuss the theory of goal setting and its effect on performance success and self-satisfaction. We examine who should set the goals and the type of goals which should be set. We then look at ways of gaining faculty commitment to teaching goals. Finally, we examine how goal-setting theory was applied effectively to management education. Management development education is focused upon because it is an area in which many deans find it difficult to generate faculty involvement.

Goal-Setting Theory

Motivation is concerned with factors that affect the direction, arousal, and duration of action. Goals affect all three elements of action (Locke & Latham, 1990). Goals have two attributes: content and intensity. Goal content refers to what is being sought; goals may differ in terms of difficulty and clarity or specificity. Goal intensity is reflected mainly in commitment to the goal.

There is a linear relationship between degree of goal difficulty and performance until faculty reach the limits of their ability. The explanation for this linear effect is that given that goals are accepted, hard goals lead to greater effort and persistence than do easy goals. Moreover, hard goals (e.g., get more students to take one's elective course; receive 4.0 or higher on a 5-point scale on student ratings of teaching effectiveness in a required course) make self-satisfaction contingent on a higher level of performance than do easy goals.

A second finding of the theory is that specific, difficult goals (e.g., help *x* percent of culturally disadvantaged students get on the dean's list) lead to a higher level of performance than vague, nonquantifiable goals such as "do your best" or no specific goals. Since the goal to do one's best is in itself a hard goal, it is interesting that it does not translate into as high a level of motivation as do specific hard goals. This is because a vague goal allows people to give themselves the benefit of the doubt in evaluating their own performance (Kernan & Lord, 1989). In the case of a specific hard goal, only attaining a specific, high score (e.g., getting 90% of the students in a fourth-year honors class accepted by a graduate school) is compatible with labeling one's performance a success.

Finally, goals are most effective when there is feedback showing progress in relation to the goal and when there is commitment to the goals. Commitment is especially important when the goals are difficult. High commitment is most likely to be present when people believe that the goals are important and when they believe that they can make substantial progress toward attaining them.

The generality of these conclusions is impressive. Goal-setting experiments have been conducted with at least eighty-eight different tasks including air traffic control, bargaining, engine overhaul, faculty research, logging, maintenance and technical work, management training, engineering and R&D work, and United Fund campaigns. The subjects used in goal-setting studies range from students to factory workers, to managers, to college professors. The studies have been conducted in North America, Australia, Germany, the Caribbean, Israel, England, and Japan. Criteria used to date include grades, costs, performance quantity and quality, time spent on a task, performance appraisal results, faculty teaching and research, and learning. The time spans of these studies range from 1 minute to thirty-six months. In short, the evidence is overwhelming in both laboratory and field experiments that goal-setting effects generalize over a wide range of tasks, settings, subjects, countries, criteria, and time spans (Latham & Lee, 1986; Locke & Latham, 1990). Few theories in organizational psychology or human resource management can claim such consistent and wide-ranging support.

In a review of thirty-two theories in organizational science, Miner (1984) showed that goal-setting theory was one of only four theories that are "high" on validity and usefulness in application. In another assessment, Pinder (1984) concluded that "goal setting theory has demonstrated more scientific validity to date than any other theory or approach to work motivation" (p. 169). Finally, Lee and Earley (1988) asked 127 scholars in the fields of organizational behavior and industrial-organizational psychology to rate fifteen motivation theories on the criteria of scientific validity and practical usefulness. Goal-setting theory was rated first in validity and a close second in practical usefulness among the full sample of raters. Among the scholars who were high in research productivity, it ranked first on the combined criteria.

Goal Mechanisms

To understand and explain the effect of goals on action, it is necessary to understand the mechanisms by which goals produce their results. As noted above, the three most direct goal mechanisms are primarily motivational; the fourth is cognitive. Goals affect arousal by regulating the intensity of effort a faculty member expends on a task, and they affect its duration by leading faculty to persist in their actions (e.g., finding a job for a newly minted doctoral student) until the goal is attained. Goals affect choice by leading faculty to direct their attention to and take action with respect to goal-relevant activities while ignoring those that are non–goal relevant (e.g., interacting with colleagues in the faculty lounge).

The course syllabus, for example, is a specific goal self-set by a professor and assigned to the students. It tells both the professor and the students what to study and when to study it. The syllabus directs the actions of both parties toward course-relevant activities.

Goals define for the faculty member what constitutes an acceptable level of performance. Actions that fall short of desired ends (e.g., receiving teacher ratings below 3.5 on a 5-point scale) are appraised by them as nonsatisfactory and lead to negative self-evaluations (Bandura, 1986). Such negative evaluations can stimulate actions aimed at eliminating the source of the dissatisfaction by improving subsequent performance (e.g., getting teacher ratings from students which range from 3.5 to 5.0). Actions that attain or exceed desired ends lead to positive self-appraisals. If a positive self-appraisal results in the anticipation that attaining the same performance level again will lead to a neutral or negative appraisal, a person will set a higher goal for the future (Bandura & Cervone, 1986). Thus, once a college professor has a goal (e.g., receive a teaching award), and once he or she commits to act on it, the three direct mechanisms, effort, choice, and persistence, are brought into play more or less automatically. People learn from an early age that to achieve a goal, they must exert effort, persist over time, and pay attention to what they are doing and what they want to achieve (Duda, 1986).

When these mechanisms are insufficient for goal attainment, an individual must also engage in a process of problem solving in order to discover how the goal can be attained. This process involves discovering suitable task strategies. For example, an assistant professor who receives low teacher ratings will usually try to discover the reasons for them and then search for improved teaching techniques. Task strategies are conscious or deliberate action plans motivated by goals. Numerous studies have shown that when given a goal, individuals develop task strategies on their own to achieve it (e.g., Latham & Baldes, 1975; Latham & Saari, 1982; Latham, Winters, & Locke, 1994). Thus there are cognitive as well as motivational benefits of setting a goal.

It might be argued that goal progress for teaching activities is exceedingly difficult to measure. Student ratings of teaching skill are one measure that is useful, especially concerning such issues as preparation of the lecture, organization of the material, clarity of instruction, taking an interest in students, and showing enthusiasm for the subject matter. Student ratings are less meaningful for determining whether the teacher was teaching the right facts or theories correctly; the latter can be measured by a visit to the classroom by one's colleagues. Teachers, of course, also set their own goals for what they want the students to learn. Success here can be measured by how well the students answer examination questions or complete the course syllabus.

Performance Success and Satisfaction

A goal is at the same time a target to aim for and, as noted above, a standard by which to evaluate the adequacy of one's performance. Thus goals specify the conditional requirements for positive self-evaluation. By making self-satisfaction conditional on matching one's goals, faculty give direction to their actions and create self-incentives to persist in their efforts until their performance matches their goal (Bandura, 1988). Thus faculty with hard goals have to perform at higher levels to be satisfied than do their colleagues with easy goals. Having high goals means not being satisfied with less than high performance.

The greater the success experienced in attaining the goal, the greater the degree of satisfaction experienced. Similarly, dissatisfaction is experienced when there is goal blockage (Locke, 1976). This is because goals are used as value standards for appraising one's performance. If a faculty member chronically believes that the goal is unattainable, the result can be depression. The same holds true for students.

Kanfer and Zeiss (1983) found that depressed students had goals for home, social, and work activities similar to those of nondepressed students but felt much less capable of attaining those standards. Depressed students may set unrealistically high goals for themselves and thus doom themselves to disappointment (Bandura, 1986, 1988). Often these goals are adopted uncritically from peers without considering the student's personal context and abilities. When the arbitrary goals are not met, the student may engage in self-belittlement. This may in turn be followed by setting even higher and more unrealistic goals leading to further disappointment, or to apathy leading to no action and therefore no sense of achievement. A solution is for faculty to assign proximal in addition to distal goals and to sequence the tasks so as to increase the probability that the proximal goals will be attained, not only for their students, but for themselves.

The relation of success to satisfaction is also affected by the significance or importance of success to the person. If faculty tie their self-concept to task performance (e.g., ability to generate student interest and proficiency in the subject matter), success on the task will be much more important to them than it is to those who do not consider performance to be self-relevant. Phillips and Freedman (1988) gave one group of students goals with no explanation or rationale, whereas others were told that their performance in relation to goals would indicate how well they were performing in relation to other students. Those who were given this information felt more task and goal satisfaction from working at this task than did those who were not given this information. The wider principle here is that a person's reactions to specific situations are colored by basic assumptions about or regarding that person's own self. Faculty who believe subconsciously that they are fundamentally incompetent will tend to view success as less significant and failure as more significant than those who have high self-efficacy, namely, the conviction "yes I can" (Korman, 1976). This is because we often respond more to feedback that agrees with our self-concept, whether it is positive or negative, than we do to feedback that is inconsistent with our self-concept.

Who Should Set the Goal?

Deci and Ryan (1985) argued that intrinsic motivation is based on a need for self-determination (choice) and competence. It is allegedly aroused by freedom from external constraints, the faculty member feeling a strong locus of causality, undertaking challenging tasks, and receiving positive noncontrolling feedback regarding performance. Intrinsic motivation is usually measured by allowing a person a free choice of activities and observing how much time the individual chooses to spend on them. However, this is an inadequate measure of intrinsic interest or motivation because time can be spent on an activity for many reasons other than interest (Bandura, 1986).

A critical problem with this theory is that it seems incongruous that the need for self-determination and competence is said to lie at the core of all human motivation and at the same time is said to be so fragile that its effects can be negated by such common everyday exigencies as pressure, anxiety, conflict, feelings of obligation to others, surveillance, and performance appraisals. Thus it is not surprising that the extant research shows that little can be concluded about the effect of different methods of setting goals on intrinsic motivation. One might assume that participation in goal setting would lead to higher intrinsic motivation than assigned goals, but the results are not consistent. For example, Chang and Lorenzi (1983) found that both participatively set and assigned goals enhance intrinsic motivation on an interesting relative to a boring task. But on the boring task, assigned goals led to greater intrinsic motivation than participatively set goals. Mossholder (1980) found that assigned goals reduced intrinsic motivation on an interesting task as compared with no goals but increased it on a boring one. Shalley, Oldham, and Porac (1987) found that assigned goals led to greater intrinsic motivation than participatively set goals on a task described as "moderately interesting." To this date, research on Deci and Ryan's theory has yet to measure the mediating variables that are said to be responsible for its effect on performance.

Extensive research conducted in both field and laboratory settings shows that when goal difficulty is held constant, the motivational effects, as defined by effort, choice, and persistence of assigned versus participative versus self-set goals, are the same (Locke & Latham, 1990). However, participatively set goals sometimes lead to the setting of more difficult goals than is the case when a department chairperson sets them unilaterally (Latham, Mitchell, & Dossett, 1978). From a motivational aspect, high goals lead to higher performance than easy goals.

From a cognitive standpoint, task strategy and self-efficacy have been found to be the mediators of participation in decision making (pdm) and performance (Latham, Winters, & Locke, 1994). That is, pdm is effective only if it leads to the discovery of strategies that lead to goal attainment. This in turn increases one's self-efficacy. Conversely, to the extent that pdm increases self-efficacy, a faculty member is apt to persist in the search for effective task strategies that will lead to goal attainment.

In summary, from a motivation standpoint, if assigned goals from a dean or department chairperson are given in a supportive manner, if they are given with a rationale, and if the goals fall within the perceived legitimacy of the authority figure's role, they can be as effective in energizing the performance of a faculty member as are goals that are set participatively (Latham, Erez, & Locke, 1988).

Process versus Outcome Goals

Who sets the goal is not as important as the type of goal which is set. Earley, Lee, and Lituchy (1989) found in three separate studies that untrained subjects performed better with do-your-best rather than specific hard goals. The subjects with specific hard goals thoughtlessly switched strategies. Similarly, Kanfer and Ackerman (1989) found that air force students who had yet to master a complex learning task performed poorly when they were assigned specific hard goals. Winters and Latham (in press) discovered that the fault was not in the setting of specific hard goals but rather in the nature of the goals themselves. Specifically they found that when people have the requisite knowledge and skill to perform a task, performance outcome goals (e.g., getting teacher ratings of 4.0 or higher) should be set. When a person has yet to acquire the knowledge or skill, learning goals should be set (e.g., discover x strategies for improving your teaching ratings). This is because people lack prior experience or training; thus they have no proven strategies or problem-solving processes to draw upon. The motivational mechanisms of effort, persistence, and choice are not sufficient to bring about high performance. Therefore faculty members must learn the best strategy to use. If before this is done they are given specific hard outcome goals, they may develop tunnel vision and try too hard to get immediate results when instead they should be learning the optimum way of performing the task.

A department chairperson who assigns an outcome goal to an assistant professor who has minimal teaching experience in terms of a teacher rating from students (e.g., 4.0 or higher) may inadvertently hurt that faculty member's performance. Instead, the chairperson might assign a process or behavioral goal to the faculty member to discover x behaviors within the first year to increase the student's appreciation for and mastery of the subject matter. This is because a process goal shifts the focus from a specific quantity or quality of something to be achieved to task processes in terms of strategy development. It cues the faculty member to direct attention to the formulation and use of strategies to perform the tasks. Thus, rather than inform a faculty member that she should strive for at least a 3.5 rating on a 5-point scale from her students, a department chairperson should suggest that the faculty member identify five specific strategies that she can use to improve her teacher ratings.

Locke (1975) found that in course work, students often have to learn how to study before they can successfully earn high course grades. In addition, they often have to learn course-specific and teacher-specific strategies. Thus a professor, whose goal it is for students to master the course material, must help them set process goals regarding the discovery of specific strategies that will facilitate learning. It can be as frustrating for the teacher as it is for the student to see that knowledge has not been gained, that skills have not been attained.

In summary, specific, challenging outcome goals

1. direct attention and action;
2. stimulate task persistence;
3. motivate effort expenditure;
4. require high performance in order to ensure self-satisfaction;
5. reduce ambiguity about what constitutes high or good performance; and
6. promote the search for suitable task strategies.

When the requisite ability is lacking, faculty should set process goals for themselves and their students.

Gaining Goal Commitment

A primary way of gaining goal commitment is to build or enhance a person's self-efficacy. Self-efficacy is defined as "one's judgment of how well one can execute courses of action required to deal with prospective situations" (Bandura, 1982, p. 122). Self-efficacy is significantly and positively related to future performance. This has been demonstrated in three studies of student grade performance (Wood & Locke, 1987).

Assigned goals not only affect one's personal goals, but they also can affect self-efficacy even before any performance has taken place. This is because the assigned goal conveys normative information to us by suggesting the level of performance we can expect to attain (Meyer & Gellatly, 1988). In short, assigned goals affect self-efficacy and one's personal goals, while self-efficacy affects personal goals and performance. The joint effect of self-efficacy and goals on performance shows that performance is affected not only by what one is trying to do but by how confident one is of being able to do it.

The most direct way of increasing self-efficacy is through enactive mastery, in which task sequencing ensures that people will experience early successes. Bandura and Schunk (1981) found that proximal goal setting showed a greater positive effect on school children's self-efficacy, persistence, and performance on arithmetic problems than did distal goal setting or no goals.

Enactive mastery is experienced when goals are attained. Mossholder (1980) found that those who succeeded in attaining a specific, hard goal viewed themselves as more competent at the task than did those who failed to reach it. This does not imply that people with low goals will have higher self-efficacy than those with high goals. The reverse is true; people with low goals will succeed more, but they will feel less able to attain higher levels of performance than will those with challenging goals. Thus low standards provide a fool's paradise, namely, self-satisfaction with incompetence. This may explain why many American and Canadian public schools graduate a large number of students who are not able to function in a high-technology world.

A second way of increasing self-efficacy is through persuasion from a significant other. A goal assigned from a significant other such as the dean can be a signal that the faculty member is capable of reaching it. In this way the assigned goal can increase a faculty member's self-efficacy or confidence in teaching students. Significant others include people whose authority to assign the goal is viewed by the faculty as legitimate, who foster a sense of achievement, and who are viewed by the faculty as supportive and trustworthy. Lyman Porter, the former dean at the University of California, Irvine, tells the story of how he became an organizational psychologist. He arrived at Berkeley as a newly minted Ph.D. in experimental psychology. The department chairperson, Edwin Ghiselli, gave him the teaching assignment of an introductory organizational psychology course. He then convinced Porter of how easy it would be to master the subject matter so that Porter could teach the course well if he simply read the lecture notes of a previous undergraduate student and drew upon his own knowledge of experimental psychology.

Observing a model is also an effective method of increasing one's self-efficacy (Bandura, 1988). Thus faculty can improve their teaching skills by observing colleagues who are effective in the classroom and by combing their colleagues' syllabi for ideas.

As noted earlier, it is the content or type of goal which is set which affects self-efficacy. When ability is not an issue, setting a specific challenging outcome goal can increase a faculty member's self-efficacy because it triggers the use of strategies that have proven to be task effective for that person. However, if ability is an issue, the very same goal (teach a course outside one's level of expertise) can have a deleterious effect on one's confidence and performance. Hence a process or learning goal should be set. Elliot and Dweck (1988) assigned either learning or outcome goals on a concept formation problem to fifth-grade students. Children with high self-efficacy performed equally well with either type of goal. But children with low self-efficacy demonstrated less persistence and lower performance when given outcome rather than learning goals.

Applying Goal-Setting Principles to Management Development

Organizations are increasingly turning to the university, especially its schools of business, engineering, and education, to form partnerships for the purpose of providing their workforce with continuing education. Progressive organizations are approaching education from a strategic perspective, with the goals of their educational programs related directly to their strategic goals. In this way the process of education becomes a primary means to attaining the organization's vision. The challenge for faculty members is to motivate the participants, most of whom are experienced and educated individuals with management responsibilities, to commit to the superordinate goal of their organization, namely, its vision. Conceptualizing and setting in motion such educational programs can lead to positive changes in the behavior of educators through the application of goal-setting principles.

An underlying assumption that often results in the failure of management development programs is the false premise by a dean that faculty members are sufficiently motivated to participate in and learn about the client organization, that they share common goals with the client, and that there is consensus among them as to the desired outcome. The motivation to participate in management development programs is often lacking among faculty who

1. have research or other priorities that relate directly and positively to their performance evaluation;

2. prefer to operate within the university primarily as an individual rather than as a member of a team;
3. have developed specific teaching methodologies and are unwilling to (or perceive themselves as incapable of) change;
4. perceive a lack of reward for teaching in the university's management development programs; or
5. perceive a lack of peer recognition for teaching management development courses.

The challenge for a dean is how to motivate faculty to participate in such partnerships in a manner that achieves an integrated program approach and one that leads to the attainment of both the school's and the client's goals as well as the faculty member's objectives. Through the application of goal-setting theory to the development process of partnership education programs, the satisfactory delivery of such programs can lead to feelings of accomplishment and recognition among faculty.

A case in point is the Stentor organization, an alliance of the ten telephone companies across Canada, which launched a partnership program with the University of Toronto for its managers. A superordinate goal that effectively motivates people conveys to them that what they are doing contributes not only to the betterment of their organization but to the betterment of society. Together with business school faculty, the following superordinate goal was articulated by Stentor, namely, to create "a national organization providing seamless service with a local touch." This superordinate goal appealed to the faculty's national pride. Implicit in this goal is to compete effectively with the American telephone companies who have entered the Canadian marketplace.

Once this superordinate goal had been set, process goals were established as to specific strategies for attaining it. These broad goals were set jointly by Stentor and the faculty, namely, to increase each participant's leadership ability, business acumen, and team-playing skills. Each faculty member then set specific process goals with regard to this subject matter. The faculty who participated in the Stentor program were given the opportunity to work directly with Stentor senior management as well as potential participants in the program as to their perceived program needs. The faculty then articulated their individual teaching objectives, which, integrated into a program concept, were in alignment with Stentor's three objectives and the overall superordinate goal.

Expert teaching to a group of managers with immense organizational knowledge and experience can be a challenge to those faculty who have become accustomed to teaching relatively subservient students with little "real-world" experience. An educator's ability to impart and exchange knowledge in ways that will bring about a commitment to a client's superordinate goal was especially challenging for junior faculty.

To increase their self-efficacy through "persuasion," the client's senior executives reviewed and endorsed the course learning objectives, and through their own active participation throughout the program, they enhanced the self-confidence of the junior faculty. The presence of a "model" can bring about a dramatic increase in the self-efficacy of inexperienced faculty to teach in such programs. This can be done by having a senior faculty member co-teach the course. Specifically, the senior member can introduce the subject matter and provide support for difficult questions from the participants. But the course is taught primarily by a junior faculty member who initially doubted his or her ability to do so.

The appropriate "incentives for goal commitment" are a critical factor for motivating faculty to teach in management development programs. Therefore, rewards for teaching in these programs must be clearly defined and articulated. A primary reason why faculty motivation to teach decreases over the years is the belief that no one is learning or using what is being taught. In short, what is being taught is "going in one ear and out the other." Thus, once involved in such programs, sustaining a high level of faculty commitment becomes the next step in ensuring ongoing attainment of program goals. This may be accomplished by showing that the superordinate goal is being attained.

In the Stentor situation, the level of enthusiasm for teaching increased during the program as the faculty saw that the individual participants' and Stentor program goals were being attained. Short-term measurement of goal attainment was embedded in the design of the Stentor curriculum. This was done through the use of simulation exercises that assessed participant learning at the end of the program. Long-term measurement of success was the extent to which participants were able to apply their learning to the attainment of specific goals that each person set on the last day of the program. Stentor's success as an organization is shared regularly with the faculty. The faculty can see that what they are doing is "making a difference." The goals that were set are being attained.

Other incentives that have enhanced goal commitment to the school's management development programs include the following. First, faculty who are asked to participate in these programs are viewed as the outstanding teachers in the business school by colleagues. The dean himself teaches in the program. Second, the faculty not only receive monetary incentives for participating in the programs but, third, they are recognized explicitly by the dean as contributing to the school's reputation in the community. Fourth, the faculty have found that this is an excellent forum for gaining converts to their theories. Fifth, in many instances participant interest has led to research sites for faculty to conduct research. In this way, Kurt Lewin's dictum—"no research without action; no action without research"—is realized. The mediating variable in this dictum is teaching managers who apply the ideas of faculty and then ask for additional knowledge that in turn leads to additional research.

Observe that this approach to management education contains the key elements of goal-setting theory. The faculty goals were both challenging and specific. Feedback was provided to them. This plus suitable incentives and rewards ensured commitment to the goals. The self-efficacy of junior faculty was raised through persuasion and modeling. Only the most able faculty were used: standards were high but achievable. As a result both the faculty and the "students" gained useful and relevant knowledge.

Conclusion

Goals provide people with a sense of purpose. Goal attainment provides a means for people to receive recognition and derive a sense of pride in and competency from what they accomplish. To return to our concentration camp example, even moving dirt from one location to another can be perceived as worthwhile if there is a valued goal at the end. Suppose, for example, that the German prisoners used the moving of dirt as an opportunity to hide new dirt from an escape tunnel they were building. Would the prisoners go mad performing the task under these circumstances, or would they experience excitement and hope? The answer is obvious.

Goals exist in a hierarchy. Attaining one goal usually facilitates the attainment of the next one in the hierarchy. For the German prisoners, the hierarchical chain of goals in the above example might have been as follows: move dirt → disguise escape tunnel → escape → freedom. In teaching students, there is the confluence of two sets of goals. For a teacher, the goal chain might be: learn and organize material → communicate effectively → help students attain their learning goals → achieve pride from helping students master the material → reward. For the students, the goal chain might be: learn course material → achieve pride from gaining knowledge → earn degree → job and career benefits.

For a faculty member, goal attainment in terms of inculcating knowledge or skills effectively in students can be measured by seeing how the students perform on examinations and in terms of student ratings of the teacher's effectiveness. Teacher goals for student ratings affect the actual ratings teachers obtain (Locke, Smith, Erez, Chah, & Schaffer, 1994). Concomitantly, a faculty member may urge students to set a specific, challenging goal for the grades to be earned in the course. The goals students set affect the grades that they receive (Locke & Bryan, 1968).

A key aspect for effective teaching is to address the question of why the curriculum exists, what its goals are, and what void would exist for the faculty member and the student if the goal is not attained. In answering these questions, teachers and students can create a shared vision or superordinate goal regarding mastery of knowledge and skill regarding a given subject matter. Once educators and students commit to a goal, they usually ask: "How do I achieve it?" "How can I get it?" And they start planning a strategy to attain the goal.

Once the goal is set, there is a sense of purpose in communicating information (inside and outside the classroom) and searching for the methods (e.g., videos, lectures, cases, workshops, simulation exercises) and the resources (e.g., visiting speakers, computing networks, networking) to attain it. It is from goals that a person derives a sense of accomplishment. In the absence of goals, people do not know whether they have performed well. Worse, there is a tendency to give oneself the benefit of the doubt by assuming that performance is better than it is in fact (Kernan & Lord, 1989).

It is crucial that we as faculty have goals in order for us to change and grow. Goals provide targets for us to aim toward, to look forward to the future. Equally important, goals give feedback significance. Once we commit to a goal, we become alert to where we are in relation to it. Thus feedback, whether from students, colleagues, department chairpersons, or deans, allows faculty to make adjustments so that they can grow and develop in ways to attain the goals, which in turn gives them the confidence to set even higher goals. When feedback, however, is given in the absence of goals, it has no effect on behavior (Latham, Mitchell, & Dossett, 1978). Feedback or knowledge of results only affects behavior to the extent that it leads to the setting of and commitment to specific challenging goals (Locke & Latham, 1990).

How can a department chairperson or dean motivate professors to commit to setting and attaining teaching goals? We professors traditionally have high autonomy, have multiple demands on our time, and may even prefer conducting research to teaching students. Goal theory argues that people will commit to goals when they believe that they are important and when they believe that they can attain them (Locke & Latham, 1990). Chairs and deans can help make teaching important to us by emphasizing its importance at faculty meetings, recognizing outstanding teaching by means of awards, and rewarding it with pay raises. Ultimately, teaching effectiveness also should be linked directly to promotion and tenure decisions if it is to be taken seriously by faculty.

Some faculty members view their role as a professor as being one of having equal power with chairpersons and deans—a position that might lead them to question the power of such administrators to motivate teaching effectiveness. This view, we believe, underestimates the role of goal setting to leadership (Locke & Associates, 1991). Setting a superordinate goal or vision can inspire faculty to take teaching seriously, especially if it is rewarded, as noted previously, and if the resources are provided by administrators to help professors improve their teaching and self-development.

References

Bandura, A. (1982). Self-efficacy mechanism in human agency. *American Psychologist, 37*, 122–147.

Bandura, A. (1986). *Social foundations of thought and action: A social-cognitive view.* Englewood Cliffs, NJ: Prentice-Hall.

Bandura, A. (1988). Self-regulation of motivation and action through goal systems. In V. Hamilton, G. Bower, & N. Frijda (Eds.), *Cognitive perspectives on emotion and motivation* (pp. 37–61). Dordrecht: Kluwer Academic Publishers.

Bandura, A., & Cervone, D. (1986). Differential engagement of self-reactive influences in cognitive motivation. *Organizational Behavior and Human Decision Processes, 38*, 92–113.

Bandura, A., & Schunk, D. H. (1981). Cultivating competence, self-efficacy, and intrinsic interest through proximal self-motivation. *Journal of Personality and Social Psychology, 41*, 586–598.

Chang, G. S., & Lorenzi, P. (1983). The effects of participative versus assigned goal setting on intrinsic motivation. *Journal of Management, 9*, 55–64.

Deci, E. L., & Ryan, R. M. (1985). *Intrinsic motivation and self-determination in human behavior.* New York: Plenum Press.

Duda, J. L. (1986). Toward a developmental theory of children's motivation in sport: The consideration of variations in goals. Paper presented at North American Society for the Psychology of Sport and Physical Activity, Scottsdale, AZ.

Earley, P. C., Lee, C., & Lituchy, T. R. (1989). Task strategies and judgements in goal setting: The effects of a learning emphasis and training sequence on performance. Unpublished manuscript, Management and Policy, University of Arizona.

Elliot, E. S., & Dweck, C. S. (1988). Goals: An approach to motivation and achievement. *Journal of Personality and Social Psychology, 54*, 5–12.

Frank, J. (1983). *Dostoevsky: Years of ordeal.* Princeton: Princeton University Press.

Kanfer, R., & Ackerman, P. L. (1989). Motivation and cognitive abilities: An integrative/aptitude-treatment interaction approach to skill acquisition. *Journal of Applied Psychology, 74,* 657–690.

Kanfer, R., & Zeiss, A. M. (1983). Depression, interpersonal standard setting, and judgments of self-efficacy. *Journal of Abnormal Psychology, 92,* 319–329.

Kernan, M. G., & Lord, R. G. (1989). The effects of explicit goals and specific feedback on escalation processes. *Journal of Applied Social Psychology, 19,* 1125–1143.

Korman, A. K. (1976). Hypothesis of work behavior revisited and an extension. *Academy of Management Review, 1,* 50–63.

Latham, G. P., & Baldes, J. J. (1975). The "practical significance" of Locke's theory of goal-setting. *Journal of Applied Psychology, 60,* 122–124.

Latham, G. P., Erez, M., & Locke, E. A. (1988). Resolving scientific disputes by the joint design of crucial experiments by the antagonists: Application to the Erez-Latham dispute regarding participation in goal setting [Monograph]. *Journal of Applied Psychology, 73,* 753–772.

Latham, G. P., & Lee, T. W. (1986). Goal setting. In E. A. Locke (Ed.), *Generalizing from laboratory to field settings* (pp. 101–117). Lexington, MA: Lexington Books.

Latham, G. P., Mitchell, T. R., & Dossett, D. L. (1978). Importance of participative goal setting and anticipated rewards on goal difficulty and job performance. *Journal of Applied Psychology, 63,* 163–171.

Latham, G. P., & Saari, L. (1982). The importance of union acceptance for productivity improvement through goal setting. *Personnel Psychology, 35,* 781–787.

Latham, G. P., Winters, D. W., & Locke, E. A. (1994). Cognitive and motivational effects of participation: A mediator study. *Journal of Organization Behavior, 15,* 49–63.

Lee, C., & Earley, P. C. (1988). Comparative peer evaluations of organizational behavior theories. Unpublished manuscript, College of Business Administration, Northern University.

Locke, E. A. (1975). *A guide to effective study.* New York: Springer.

Locke, E. A. (1976). The nature and causes of job satisfaction. In M. E. Dunnette (Ed.), *Handbook of industrial and organizational psychology* (pp. 1297–1349). Chicago: Rand McNally.

Locke, E. A., & Associates. (1991). *The essence of leadership.* New York: Lexington Books.

Locke, E. A., & Bryan, J. (1968). Grade goals as determinants of academic achievement. *Journal of General Psychology, 79,* 217–228.

Locke, E. A., & Latham, G. P. (1990). *A theory of goal setting and task performance.* Englewood Cliffs, NJ: Prentice-Hall.

Locke, E. A., Smith, K., Erez, M., Chah, D., & Schaffer, A. (1994). The effects of intra-individual goal conflict on performance. *Journal of Management, 20,* 67–91.

Meyer, J. P., & Gellatly, I. R. (1988). Perceived performance norm as a mediator in the effect of assigned goal on personal goal and task performance. *Journal of Applied Psychology, 73,* 410–420.

Miner, J. B. (1984). The validity and usefulness of theories in an emerging organizational science. *Academy of Management Review, 9,* 296–306.

Mossholder, R. W. (1980). Effects of externally mediated goal setting on intrinsic motivation: A laboratory experiment. *Journal of Applied Psychology, 65,* 202–210.

Phillips, J. S., & Freedman, S. M. (1988). The task-related competency and compliance aspects of goal setting: A clarification. *Organizational Behavior and Human Decision Processes, 41,* 34–49.

Pinder, C. C. (1984). *Work motivation*. Glenview, IL: Scott, Foresman.

Shalley, C. E., Oldham, G. R., & Porac, J. F. (1987). Effects of goal difficulty, goal-setting method, and expected external evaluation on intrinsic motivation. *Academy of Management Journal, 30,* 553–563.

Tice, L. E. (1989). *A better world a better YOU*. Englewood Cliffs, NJ: Prentice-Hall.

Winters, D. W., & Latham, G. P. (in press). The effect of learning versus outcome goals on a simple versus a complex task. *Group and Organization Management.*

Wood, R. E., & Locke, E. A. (1987). The relation of self-efficacy and grade goals to academic performance. *Educational and Psychological Measurement, 47,* 1013–1024.

IV Organizational Conditions as Motivators

9 Organizational Cultures and Faculty Motivation

JANICE M. BEYER

Cultural processes underlie much of what happens in modern organizations. Culture filters the ways in which people see and understand their worlds. Culture prescribes some behaviors and forbids others. Culture colors the emotional responses that people have to events. Given the central role of culture in channeling human behavior, its relative neglect in the study of organizations is unfortunate. (Trice & Beyer, 1993, p. xiii)

The dearth of research noted by Trice and Beyer holds for universities and colleges. Relatively few empirical studies have specifically focused on their cultures and fewer still on the cultural aspects of teaching. Nevertheless, there is considerable research on organizational cultures and on higher education in general which is relevant to understanding how university and college cultures are likely to affect teaching. The goal of this chapter is to begin to integrate both sets of research in a way that will throw fresh light on how the cultures of higher education affect the motivations of faculty. It does not, however, attempt a comprehensive analysis or summary of either literature but rather focuses on what I believe to be the most distinctive and important aspects of cultures in colleges and universities and how these are likely to affect faculty motivation.

One of the benefits of taking a cultural perspective on higher education is that it highlights the importance of collective, shared understandings, identities, and activities. Individual faculty members derive much of the meaning and motivation for their efforts from collective sense making that goes on in the cultures to which they belong. As members, they in turn contribute to collective sense making and motivation through a variety of social processes in which they engage. Shared experiences (Berger & Luckmann, 1967), socialization (Beyer & Lutze, 1992), communication (Putnam & Pacanowsky, 1983), and leadership (Trice & Beyer, 1991) are some of the most obvious of these interactive sense-making processes.[1]

People who live in modern complex societies belong to multiple cultures. Faculty in higher education are not only members of their national cultures; they also belong to various subcultures based in many other social distinctions and groupings. Especially relevant for an analysis of faculty motivation are the subcultures and organization-wide cultures that arise within colleges and universities. Before discussing their likely effects, I provide the definitions and conceptions of culture and motivation which informed my analysis.

Definition and Concepts

Culture and Motivation

Theories of motivation deal with two different aspects of the motivational process: the preferred end states toward which people strive, and the means by which they strive for those ends. Texts in organizational behavior typically refer to these two types of theories as content and process theories, respectively. Content theories, like Maslow's hierarchy of needs or McClelland's acquired needs theory (Schermerhorn, Hunt, & Osborn, 1994), presume that people's needs activate them toward behaviors intended to satisfy those needs. Process theories seek to explain why people engage in some behaviors and not others in trying to satisfy their needs. Applying these two types of motivation theories to higher education focuses attention on (1) determining the personal needs that faculty attempt to satisfy by the efforts they expend in their educational activities, and (2) the cognitive, social, and behavioral processes that encourage, sustain, or discourage them in those efforts.

The cultures in higher education influence both motivational content and processes. The needs specified in various theories of motivation vary in their susceptibility to cultural influence. To illustrate, the so-called basic needs in Maslow's theory—those whose minimal satisfaction is necessary for survival—undoubtedly exist in all cultures. Although their existence may transcend cultural influence, their satisfaction is channeled by cultural prescriptions. Cannibal societies permitted the eating of human flesh; some cultures forbid the eating of animal flesh altogether; most cultures prescribe which animals are considered acceptable food. As we move up the Maslow hierarchy of needs to security, social belonging, self-esteem, and self-actualization,[2] culture is likely to play an increasingly important role in not only how people satisfy their needs but also how they conceive of those needs. Being socialized into a culture means learning to see and experience some needs as more important than others. Cross-cultural research on Maslow's hierarchy of needs has revealed substantial differences in the relative ordering of needs in different cultures (Adler, 1991). Being socialized into a particular social role, like gender, may also engender different sets or ordering of needs (see Chap. 3 in this volume). As McClelland (1961, 1971) argues about the needs for achievement, affiliation, and power, people probably acquire some of their needs over time as a result of their life experiences. The long debates over the presence and grouping of needs suggest that needs are not uniform across individuals. One reason is that what people experience and learn as active members of their cultures helps to determine which needs they will develop and therefore the ends they are motivated to seek.

The connection between process theories of motivation and culture is more obvious because process theories contain many elements that are culturally defined or influenced. Equity theory, for example, rests on evaluations of equity and inequity, the values assigned to various rewards, and the values assigned to various inputs. Expectancy theory involves beliefs about outcomes and the ways to achieve them, and the values assigned to various work-related outcomes. Attributional theory focuses on people's beliefs about causes and effects. All of these elements—evaluations, values, and beliefs—are rooted in culture. To illustrate, a recent analysis of equity theory concluded that all of the components of the equity theory model are likely to be affected by societal-level cultures. Members of cultures with values favoring uncertainty avoidance (Hofstede, 1993), for example, tend to distort their perceptions of inputs and outcomes rather than respond by changing behavior (Kilbourne & O'Leary-Kelly, 1994). Similar reanalyses of expectancy and attributional theories would come to similar conclusions. By what they favor and identify as possible and desirable, cultural beliefs and values shape all of the elements included in our theories of motivation. By what they ignore or hold in disfavor, cultural values and beliefs inhibit motivation in other directions (Ortner, 1984).

General Features of Organizational Cultures

Although scholars disagree somewhat on their relative importance, organizational cultures have two major elements—substance and forms.

Clifford Geertz pointed out that people are "meaning-seeking animals" (1973, p. 140); they strive to understand their worlds and their place in them. The *substance* of cultures consists of those meanings or sets of ideas which people come to share and pass on from one generation to the next. Because these ideas are arrived at, with difficulty, as people face the uncertainties of life, they tend to invest them with strong emotions. Members of universities and colleges are no exception. The substance of their organizational cultures includes emotionally charged ideologies, values, and norms. Ideologies are shared belief systems that bind people together and explain their worlds to them in terms of causes and effects (Beyer, 1981). Founding ideologies at two "plate-glass" English universities endowed particular modes of teaching—tutorials and small seminars—with superior learning outcomes (Lodahl & Mitchell, 1980). Values are preferred means or ends (Beyer, 1981). In higher education, values express preferences for learning outcomes—a well-rounded informed citizen or a technically proficient engineer, for example. Values can also express preferences for means of educating; examples are a general education curriculum or interdisciplinary courses. Norms express what other members of the culture expect—participative class activities, extensive writing assignments, or predetermined grading distributions.

Nowhere is the persuasiveness and strength of cultural substance in higher education better illustrated than in Clark's well-known study of the sagas of three distinctive colleges. As he describes it,

> Ideology is carried in a generalized memory culture expressed in dozens of ways in everyday life. The legend initiated at Antioch in the twenties is found in the sixties in the beliefs expressed in catalogues and at commencements, in the repetitious cry of students and faculty that the college is not living up to what it has always stood for, in the sustained meaning given to certain buildings and patches of sidewalk, in the interpretation assigned to the faces and figures of retired deans who still stroll the grounds. (1992, p. 254)

The second element of cultures, *cultural forms*, is the vehicle through which people express, affirm, and celebrate their cultural ideologies, values, and norms. All those entities that Clark mentions as expressing the ideologies of Antioch—catalogues, commencements, repeated cries of students and faculty, buildings and sidewalks, and even the faces and figures of retired deans—functioned as cultural forms.

A recent analysis broke cultural forms into four major categories, given in table 9.1. All of these cultural forms have flourished in universities and

Table 9.1   Categories and Examples of
Cultural Forms

Category	Examples
Symbols	Objects, natural and manufactured
	Settings
	Performers, functionaries
Language	Jargon, slang
	Gestures, signals, signs
	Songs
	Humor, jokes, gossip, rumors
	Metaphors
	Proverbs, slogans
Narratives	Stories, legends
	Sagas
	Myths
Practices	Rituals, taboos
	Rites, ceremonials

Source: Trice & Beyer (1993), p. 78.

colleges over the centuries, and most have important consequences for their cultures. *Symbols* are the most general and pervasive of cultural forms. Most organizations use many kinds of symbols to convey all sorts of abstract ideas. The cap and gown, doctoral hood, plaques on the wall, classroom settings, and even the overhead projector carry cultural messages about higher education. *Language* is a system of categories and rules through which people both communicate and structure their perceptions and understandings. Every college and university has its own slang, humor, slogans, and songs which, when heard, revive shared meanings among its alumni. *Narratives* give accounts of events and experiences that help people to make sense of their situations and to express their feelings and beliefs. Whether true or invented, the myths, stories, and legends about former deans and professors tell new students what kinds of ordeals to expect before they graduate. *Cultural practices* usually involve specific sets of behaviors performed in relatively standardized or traditional ways; they can express cultural meanings because human behaviors have an inherent duality of both doing and saying things (Leach, 1968). The rituals of hiring new faculty and granting tenure have not only the manifest practical consequences of selecting the worthy but also the latent consequences of affirming the importance of professors, their value to society, and their commitment to high standards.

In applying the cultural perspective to higher education, I focus on the expressive side of organizational life—the shared meanings that reside in cultural substance and cultural forms. There are many other perspectives and approaches that focus on the practical and technical sides of organizations. Other chapters in this volume represent some of those approaches.

Table 9.2 presents six characteristics of cultures which apply to organizational as well as other cultures. Cultures originate from people interacting together and coming to share certain ways of seeing their worlds and acting within them. In particular, cultures result from the ways that people learn to manage their anxieties and mask the fundamental insecurities of life. Ideas and practices so developed are bound to be infused with emotion. People often cling to their cultural ideas and practices long after they have outlived their usefulness (Ferguson, 1936, p. 29). Because these ideas and practices will reflect the circumstances from which they sprang, cultures contain residues of the unique history of a particular group of people or a particular organization (Clark, 1992). Thus cultures create continuity and tend to persist over time. As Cameron and Ettington (1988, p. 362) pointed out, "a majority of these definitions [of culture] focus on attributes of culture that are enduring. . . . These attributes distinguish the concept of culture from the concept of climate, which . . . centers on individual attitudes and perceptions . . . [that] change much more quickly than organizational cultures."

It is, however, a mistake to see cultures as static. Various internal processes ensure that cultures are dynamic. Cultures cannot exactly reproduce themselves over time because of such factors as the inevitable slippage and inaccuracies in socialization, the unavoidable discretion of individuals, and the importing of new individuals and ideas from a changing environment. Moreover, the very fact that much cultural communication is symbolic makes it imprecise. In addition, because cultures develop over time in response to changing circumstances, they tend to incorporate so many different sets of ideas that they become rather fuzzy and full of confusion and contradictions. The colleges and universities of today bear some resemblance to those of earlier times, but they clearly have changed in many important ways.

All of these general characteristics of cultures are evident in colleges and universities. However, because of their unique missions and history,

Table 9.2   Some Characteristics of Culture

Collective	Inherently symbolic
Emotionally charged	Dynamic
Historically based	Inherently fuzzy

Source: Trice & Beyer (1993), p. 5.

organizational cultures in higher education are bound to have somewhat different properties than those of corporations or governments. Two characteristics stand out as especially important in motivating faculty: (1) the many strong subcultures in colleges and universities; and (2) the wide variance in the strength of their organizational-level cultures.

Multiple Subcultures

Certain social conditions tend to give rise to subcultures. These include differential levels of interaction between people, shared experiences, similar personal characteristics, and social cohesion. Various groups of participants in higher educational organizations experience these social conditions and thus usually form subcultures consisting of "distinctive clusters of ideologies, cultural forms, and other practices" (Trice & Beyer, 1993, p. 174). Subcultures are important not only because they constitute a social reality that shapes, guides, and to some extent dictates behavior but because they can disable their members from seeing alternative social realities (S. Ortner, 1984, p. 152). The many subcultures in higher education create many boundaries and require many boundary crossings by its members (Becher, 1989). I discuss below three sets of boundaries: those that arise between roles and statuses, between disciplines, and between demographic groupings.

Faculty, Students, and Administrators

Members of all of these groups meet the conditions listed above. Persons in each group tend to interact more with one another than with members of other groups; have similar experiences as they carry out their assigned tasks; more often resemble one another in age and education (and often in gender or social class, as well) than members of other groups; and, for all of these reasons, tend to be attracted to one another and form friendships within groups rather than between them.

In addition, the very fact that participants in higher education are frequently referred to by these categories signals that institutionalized expectations vary for these groups (Scott, 1987). In cultural terms, the categories applied to them mean that these groups differ in accepted and expected ways. Faculty members are experts who have acquired specialized knowledge that presumably qualifies them to perform certain professional activities including teaching. College and university students are persons who have completed other levels of education and presumably qualify in terms of ability and motivation to continue their education. Administrators are persons who, by virtue of experience or special training, are expected to have specialized knowledge that qualifies them to manage the structures of higher education.

One way to look at the differences between these groups is to realize that they are engaged in different occupations. Sociologists who study occupations recognize that their members frequently form occupational subcultures (Trice, 1993). Most occupational subcultures transcend the boundaries of specific organizations, although such subcultures are usually evident within organizations, as well. They are certainly evident in higher education, where faculty, administrators, and students hold and celebrate quite diverse values. For example, although precise data are lacking, faculty may value scholarship, administrators may value accountability and efficiency, and students may value personal development.

Table 9.3 lists six characteristics of especially strong occupational subcultures that have been called occupational communities (Van Maanen & Barley, 1984). All of these apply to faculty, administrator, and student subcultures in higher education. Students exhibit their consciousness of kind when they flock to Florida or Texas beaches during spring break or when they form study and social groups that practice various distinctive rituals and exchange stories and myths about how to succeed in their specific academic programs. Faculty and administrators celebrate their subcultures when they attend meetings of their professional associations or the organizational subunits to which each belongs.

Because they have different belief and value systems, students, faculty, and administrators often come into cultural conflict. I discuss two possible sets of conflicts in this chapter, between faculty and administrators and between students and faculty. I address the cultural conflict that arises between the relatively permanent organizational subcultures of faculty and administrators first because I believe it is especially potent in shaping the cultures of most institutions of higher education. That between students and faculty is addressed in the final section on implications.

Table 9.3 Characteristics of Occupational Subcultures

Consciousness of kind	Favorable self-image and social identity
Reference groups	Extension into nonwork life
Unusual emotional demands	Ethnocentrism

Source: Adapted from Trice & Beyer (1993), pp. 181–185.

Faculty-Administrator Conflict

The primary arena for cultural conflict between faculty and administrators is the control of task performance. Like members of other occupations, especially the professions, faculty feel they alone have sufficient knowledge about their tasks to know how they should be performed. Administrators in higher education, on the other hand, feel they also have special knowledge—especially about how to achieve efficiency, predictability, and order and how to meet the demands of legislatures, donors, parents, and regulatory agencies. Each group thus seeks to control in different ways how the university or college operates (Rhoades & Slaughter, 1991). At issue is the balance of control between administrative and occupational principles (Trice, 1993)—between such administrative devices as rules and regulations, hierarchies of authority, and standardization, and the professional controls associated with training, extensive socialization, professional associations, and codes of ethics.

Teaching seems to become more readily an arena for faculty-administrator conflict than does research. Among the reasons for this difference is that administrators cannot possibly know the technical details needed to do more than try to channel the general directions that research takes. In addition, in research-oriented universities, faculty gain some independence from administrative control over their research by bringing in grant money and enhancing the prestige of the institution with their publications. In their study of universities, Lodahl and Gordon (1973a) found that only faculty in physics departments with relatively low prestige—and fewer publications and research grants (Lodahl & Gordon, 1973b)—reported that their administrators tried to influence the areas in which they did research. Administrators are no wiser about how to teach than their faculty, but the faculty has no expert power in the teaching domain. In the presence of equal ignorance, legitimate power wins out. College and university administrators everywhere have developed ways to try to control teaching activities and performance. Three pervasive ways are teaching evaluations, the promotion process, and curriculum reform. To the degree that administrators, including deans, influence these processes, they are exerting administrative control over teaching.

Teaching Evaluations

The evaluation of teaching by student surveys is an especially interesting example of administrative control because these surveys have all the trappings of rationality—the underlying value for the administrative principle. Although scientific-sounding terms such as *statistical norms, reliability,* and *validity* are frequently used to legitimate survey-type teaching evaluations, it is unclear exactly what such evaluations measure and clear that they do not adequately measure many aspects of teaching. Yet they are widely used. Why? The manifest reasons are (1) to allow students (the clients) to express their satisfaction with the services received, and (2) to give feedback to professors, ostensibly to improve their teaching. A latent reason is that they function as bureaucratic administrative controls over the teaching process. Administrators can use the numbers generated by such surveys to document ostensibly good or poor performance, to reward or punish groups or individuals, and above all, to signal to themselves and others that they are exerting some rational control over the teaching process.[3] A second latent reason is that carrying out these evaluations signals to parents, donors, and legislators that attention is being paid to students' interests.

From a cultural perspective, all three—teaching evaluations, promotion processes, and curriculum reforms—function as rites of renewal (Trice & Beyer, 1984); they refurbish and strengthen existing structures and systems of authority rather than change them. This does not mean, however, that they do not have powerful effects on individual faculty motivation. Student evaluations of teaching, to the degree they are rewarded with outcomes faculty desire, can motivate faculty to manipulate the ratings by behaviors not likely to improve educational outcomes. Just a few I have heard about include giving easy grades on quizzes or midterm examinations, excusing or postponing assignments due just before the evaluation, testing on only predesignated portions of assigned materials, and giving students time off for several class periods before the evaluation. Whether or not these practices actually occur, the stories about them are cultural forms that express the anxieties and temptations faculty experience about student evaluations, and their existence highlights how strong a motivational factor these evaluations and the ways they are used can become.

Promotions

Promotion processes, which usually include consideration of teaching evaluations, are probably the most powerful motivational levers in academia. The outcomes of promotion processes send powerful signals to faculty of what is valued by an academic culture. In particular, the criteria that faculty perceive as being used to judge candidates are likely to motivate them to pursue certain ends more than others. Junior faculty who perceive that research productivity is more important than teaching evaluations will bend most of their efforts toward research if they wish to achieve tenure. They are likely to do the reverse if teaching evaluations seem to be weighted more heavily than research in determining who gets tenure. When junior faculty perceive the relative weighting of these "traditional" criteria to be unpredictable or arbitrary across individual cases, they are likely to become disillusioned, feel threatened, and be motivated to resolve their uncertainty in some way. One possibility is to try to form strong political alliances with one or more senior faculty; another is to just leave. Only when teaching performance has clear and consistent effects on promotion decisions are desires for promotion likely to have positive effects on junior faculty's motivation to teach.

Curriculum Reforms

Periodic attempts at curriculum reform influence faculty motivation by the educational goals and means they emphasize, the rewards they offer, and the level of participation individual faculty have in making decisions involved in the reforms. Faculty are likely to be more highly motivated to pursue new educational goals or means that they can believe in than those they have doubts about. Because curriculum reform involves change, it usually involves discrediting past practices to some degree (Biggart, 1977). Cultural leadership that advances appealing visions of the new educational goals and means is probably required to persuade faculty of the value of the new approaches. Since change always involves extra effort, reforms that reward faculty for their participation and efforts will help to avoid feelings of inequity. Rewards might involve summer salary to develop new courses, temporarily lighter teaching loads, or extra teaching assistance. Participation in decisions gives faculty increased "ownership" of the decisions reached and thus increases their motivation to implement the spirit and substance of the reforms in their own educational activities.[4]

Disciplines and Subdisciplines

The second potent set of subcultures in colleges and universities develops from the cognitive and social structures of academic disciplines. Theories and methodologies of fields of knowledge become paradigms that structure the way their members see the world (Kuhn, 1970). Such paradigms act as subcultures that channel behavior by suggesting which problems are worth studying, which methods are appropriate for studying different problems, and which criteria to use in weighing the worth of theories and answers (Trice & Beyer, 1993). The central ideas and theories of a paradigm are its cultural substance; the methods, procedures, artifacts, and language used in its teaching and research constitute its cultural forms.

Paradigms and Education

Although the possibility has not been specifically investigated, it seems highly likely that the paradigms of fields of knowledge incorporate ideas and values about appropriate methods and goals for teaching that knowledge. Most of these are taken for granted and do not ordinarily get noticed. When the British "plate-glass" universities were founded in the 1960s, however, specific teaching methods were encouraged at each institution. The University of Sussex, for example, initially adopted an ideology that favored teaching by tutorials. Later, the physical scientists, mathematicians, and others in fields with developed paradigms pressed for and got lecture halls built. Because of the amount of agreed-upon, cumulative knowledge in these fields it is not surprising that faculty members in the physical sciences would favor knowledge acquisition in lectures and labs. Given the controversy and lack of agreement endemic in their disciplines, it is equally understandable that faculty in the humanities would favor critical thinking and discussion in small seminars or tutorials. Educational reforms that ignore such disciplinary differences and the value systems that accompany them risk damaging the motivation of some groups of faculty by prescribing teaching methods seen as unfitting or impractical by their members.

The structure of knowledge affects educational processes in various other ways. The initial research on paradigm development in university departments (Lodahl & Gordon, 1972) found that faculty in fields with relatively developed paradigms (physics and chemistry) found it easier to agree within their departments on course content and degree requirements than faculty in fields with less developed paradigms (sociology and political science). In addition, as Salancik, Staw, and Pondy (1980) argued, the chains of prerequisites are longer in the more paradigmatically developed fields. The basic courses in these fields tend to cover knowledge that is relatively well established, and therefore those who teach them can spend years polishing the best ways to present their material without having to worry about changing it very much to keep up with the latest research developments. Members of fields with less developed paradigms must expend some of their educational efforts on updating their materials, reviewing new texts, and developing new lectures or other methods of presenting the material. Thus, to achieve comparable educational outcomes may demand more effort and higher motivation to teach well in fields with less developed paradigms than in fields with more developed paradigms.

Disciplinary Boundaries

In U.S. higher education, the cultural boundaries of most disciplines are expressed and reinforced by the structural boundaries of departments and colleges. These boundaries are further heightened by the reward systems of science and academia, in which both external and internal rewards typically go to those faculty who are productive in terms of currently held standards set by dominant paradigms. Most scholars and scientists value the esteem of other members of their fields of study above all other rewards (Hagstrom, 1965).

Being oriented toward earning their colleagues' esteem undoubtedly leads many academics to exert more effort in their research and scholarship than in their teaching. This desire for peer approval may also lead some academics, especially nontenured faculty, to be extremely conventional in their approach to teaching. For example, they may tend to pattern the style and content of their teaching after that of the senior faculty in their field. Such tendencies are likely to discourage teaching innovations and experimentation by the junior faculty and smother any impulses they may have to look outside their field for course content or teaching methods.

There are other effects of the subcultural boundaries that grow up around knowledge paradigms. The cultural differences between disciplines make interdisciplinary efforts in either teaching or research notoriously difficult, as Lodahl and Mitchell (1980) showed in their study of two English universities that aspired to interdisciplinary programs of study. As control over socialization of new faculty passed from founders to subunits of colleagues, the initial ideals of these universities weakened (pp. 194–195). Taking a cultural perspective shows that members of different paradigm groups literally speak different languages and see different things when they look at the same phenomena. Working with a member of another paradigm group is like working with a person from another national or ethnic culture. It takes strong and consistent motivation on both sides to overcome such cultural barriers. When most rewards reside primarily in the paradigm group, faculty must be either intrinsically motivated to do interdisciplinary work or else receive new types of extrinsic rewards specifically given to reinforce such efforts. One result is that genuinely interdisciplinary courses are rare and usually depend heavily on the efforts of specific faculty members.

Conflicts

Cultural barriers are not confined to differences between disciplines but occur within them as well. When members of a discipline disagree over what are for them significant values, beliefs, and symbols, cultural division arises and conflict ensues (Kempner, 1991). In disciplines with low consensus, in particular, members are likely to break into conflicting factions who disagree over the important problems, methods, and criteria for scholarship. These factions, in turn, often become subdisciplines or schools of thought. Needless to say, members of these different groups do not agree very well on what to teach or how to teach it. They usually coexist by practicing avoidance, discretion, overlooking (Meyer & Rowan, 1977), and loose coupling of their activities (Weick, 1976) when possible. But hiring, tenure decisions, and especially curriculum reform tighten the coupling and thus can easily become occasions for bitter contests in which each subdiscipline seeks to gain or protect power and resources. With such stakes, any improvement in teaching may be a by-product of these periodic rituals. As mentioned earlier, curriculum reforms usually end up as rites of renewal because those groups with the most power and resources manage to maintain them. Only if administrators intervene strongly or other stakeholders make extremely strong demands is much real change likely to ensue. Since hiring and tenure decisions also tend to rely on the criteria professed by those with the most power, they are also unlikely to produce drastic change. As Kanter (1977) observed about top management, senior faculty in a position to influence hiring decisions often prefer candidates similar to themselves.

An unfortunate likely by-product of the conflict between and within disciplinary subcultures is that members of in-groups who are in power often apply sanctions of various kinds to out-groups. These maneuvers cannot be hidden from students, especially graduate students, and provide very poor examples to them regarding the value of openness to new ideas in their own learning. If these conflicts and any associated sanctions serve to muffle some sets of ideas or devalue them among groups of students, they impoverish the diversity of intellectual and value frameworks that are available to them for their learning. It goes without saying that members of out-groups will have great difficulty maintaining their motivation for expressing their ideas through either teaching or research if they are punished for doing so. Unless tolerance for diversity is encouraged and intolerance sanctioned within the larger culture—whether departmental, collegewide, or universitywide—subcultural conflicts concerning the substance and methods of disciplines can have withering consequences on the motivation and efforts of individual faculty.

Another interesting instance of faculty disciplinary conflict arises around the issue of teaching undergraduate students to write well. The determination of faculty to control their own teaching becomes especially strong when members of other disciplines develop expectations about how or what they should teach. Nowhere is this difficulty more evident than in the counterpressures that English departments have applied when complaints were heard from faculty in other departments that undergraduate students were not learning how to write.[5] Although virtually all undergraduate students are required to take freshman English, and although many universities list this as a writing course, English faculty become indignant that they should be held responsible for teaching students to write; they insist it is not their job but the job of all faculty. The ideology apparently underlying their arguments says that students cannot learn to write in just one year-long course; it takes their whole undergraduate career. A strong, but not publicly advertised, motivating factor for all sides of this issue is that grading writing assignments thoroughly is very time-consuming and in no way contributes to faculty scholarship and publishing.

Demographic Differences

Although probably less potent than disciplines or subdisciplines, demographic differences provide possible bases for the formation of academic subcultures, especially within departments. Gender, ethnicity, age, type of degree, and status could all provide the basis for social attractions that lead to the formation of subcultures.

One extremely common basis for subculture formation in departments that hire non-tenure-track faculty is the rather large gap between them and the tenure-track faculty. Similar distinctions occur between "regular" faculty and those who work for extension divisions, laboratories, or other units affiliated with the college or university but do not teach in the degree-granting programs. The latter type of faculty, no matter what degrees they have earned, are typically not accorded the status given to the teaching faculty by either the administration or members of the teaching faculty. As Martin recently pointed out, "There is nothing the matter with difference; the problem is that one of the two categories in each dichotomy is devalued. Thus, the issue is neither similarity nor difference, but power" (Martin, 1994, p. 406). Where such dichotomies arise, power differences that affect motivation in many different ways follow. Those in the powerful group usually manage to acquire more of whatever resources are available to assist them than those with less power. Those with less power soon realize that they cannot succeed with fewer resources by criteria that disadvantage them. In expectancy theory terms, they develop low expectations of their effort leading either to successful performance (as judged by the powerful) or to conventionally valued outcomes (which the dominant group will capture in disproportionate amounts). In equity theory terms, the less powerful will feel underrewarded if they believe they are exerting the same efforts as are those in the dominant group but realizing lower levels of benefits.

In order to remain positively motivated, these theories suggest, the less powerful may have to define successful performance differently than members of the dominant group, learn to value different outcomes, and choose referent others who are equally powerless. Some of this may benefit educational programs—for example, by channeling the efforts of part-time faculty solely into teaching. But this is a far from assured outcome. The less powerful part-timers may simply withdraw some of their effort if they feel underrewarded and seek satisfactions of their needs in other social roles. Or they may band together and develop countercultures to resist the domination of the full-timers. The least likely alternative is that they will accept the dominant group's criteria as legitimate and fair and struggle against the odds to meet them. Overall, then, what seems especially important for teaching outcomes in situations in which status differences split faculty into groups is whether the powerful group of faculty uses criteria and procedures that reward teaching performance in ways that are equitable to all groups.

Unfortunately, other subcultural issues further complicate the issue of equitable rewards for teaching. Prominent among these is how gender affects teaching evaluations. A substantial body of research, reviewed by Lott (1985), has documented that both male and female students evaluate male instructors more favorably than female instructors in terms of intelligence, skills in motivating them, power, and effectiveness. Although research has detected differences between male and female students in the degree of bias they exhibit against women, the pattern of results strongly suggests a general bias against women within the student subculture.[6] Similar biases may exist against members of other groups for which there are strong cultural stereotypes, particularly when belonging to the stereotyping category is evident, as it is for many of the disabled and for members of certain ethnic groups. Until rewards for teaching take these culturally derived biases in student ratings into account, programs that rely heavily on them in rewarding faculty are creating substantial disincentives for women and others subject to such biases to continue to remain highly motivated in their teaching.

Another possibility, especially in some large departments or schools, is that subcultures may form around cohorts of faculty who are hired at about the same time (McCain, O'Reilly, & Pfeffer, 1983). Those who arrive on a campus at the same time will experience the same anxieties and threats at about the same time, will frequently be similar in terms of age and experience, and thus may find one another's company congenial and reassuring. Over time, with repeated contact and greater familiarity, small subcultures may develop from those cohorts to provide mutual support and facilitate sense making (Pfeffer, 1985). Such cohort subcultures could have positive effects on the motivation and performance of their members by speeding their learning of and adjustment to their new role. New faculty lacking a cohort group may feel adrift and lack socializing agents. At the same time, however, tight cohort subcultures can have deleterious effects on the motivation of those faculty who are excluded from them if cohorts become ethnocentric and begin to believe in and assert their superiority. Through extensive in-group interaction, they can develop values different from those of other faculty and use their collective influence solely to advance those values and thus their own interests. Whether these values center on teaching, research, or governance issues, the motivation of faculty who feel left out and ignored is likely to be reduced. Academic departments with dominant cohorts and large gaps between cohorts have higher rates of voluntary retirement, resignations, and expired appointments (McCain, O'Reilly, & Pfeffer, 1983).

Organization-Wide Cultures

Martin (1992) argues that organization-wide cultures can be viewed from three perspectives: integration, differentiation, and fragmentation. The integration perspective focuses on organization-wide consensus, the differentiation perspective on subculture consensus, and the fragmentation view on multiple views with little or no consensus. Although colleges and universities could presumably be analyzed using any of these perspectives, the integration perspective seems more appropriate for colleges than for universities. The differentiation perspective, on the other hand, seems to fit either universities or colleges. A fragmentation perspective on either is also possible, as exemplified by Cohen, March, and Olsen's (1972; Cohen and March, 1976) analyses of decision making and ambiguity in higher education.

Prevalency

Clark's (1992), Chaffee and Tierney's (1988), and Tierney's (1991a) observations of colleges' sagas and identities seem to indicate that organization-wide cultures exist in some but not all colleges. They describe colleges whose members agree not only on their central mission but also on whole sets of beliefs about the educational process and affirm those beliefs through distinctive curricula, teaching practices, and other cultural forms. Such organizations fit Martin's integration perspective. Tierney also observed several colleges and one state university that lacked clear identities and consensus over their mission. Such organizations, if viewed from an integration perspective, lack organization-wide cultures. If the other two perspectives are used, these organizations could be viewed as having differentiated or fragmented cultures. The culture is differentiated if many different subcultures are formed around a single basis of differentiation—for example, different disciplines. If one subculture becomes clearly dominant—for example, the physical science disciplines—the organization-wide culture is no longer differentiated but rather integrated around and shaped by that single family of disciplines (Becher, 1987b). This could be the situation at technical universities such as Rice, Carnegie, or MIT. If several crosscutting subcultures are present and none is dominant, the organization-wide culture is fragmented.

Martin argues that alternating between these perspectives can provide beneficial insights providing each is kept separate enough to preserve "its conceptual and political integrity" (Martin, 1992, p. 187). In effect, she seems to be arguing that all organizations can be characterized as having at least one of these types of organization-wide cultures. As already explained, the perspective on culture taken in this chapter allows for the presence of ambiguity, conflict, and contradictions within cultures but also insists on some shared core of cultural substance and forms as a defining characteristic of culture. From this perspective, all organizations do *not* have organization-wide cultures.

One reason is that organizational cultures do not form in all social circumstances. Their emergence requires frequent interactions among members, some consensus over cultural meanings, and the development of cultural forms. These social processes require at least two structural conditions: the ability of potential members to communicate, and some reasonable duration in their interaction with one another over time (Richardson, 1971). Large size, newness, and member turnover greatly lessen those conditions. Communication becomes less dense as the number of members increases; consensus takes time to achieve. Large universities are therefore less likely to have recognizable organization-wide cultures than are small colleges; large colleges are also probably less likely to have organization-wide cultures than are small ones; and colleges or universities that are very new or have large numbers of temporary faculty will have difficulty forming or maintaining genuine organization-wide cultures.[7] In the absence of organization-wide cultures, faculty will depend on their subcultures to give meaning to their teaching efforts.

There are always exceptions, of course. One is the University of Chicago during Hutchins' presidency. The second is Texas A&M University, which has maintained a distinctive and pervasive culture since its founding. It is interesting to note that the distinctive cultures of these universities are or were centered in the ideologies and cultural forms embodied in their undergraduate students and programs, but it also seems reasonable to argue that the strength of these cultures is or was such that they affected everyone in the university to some degree. As Shils (1975) pointed out, cultures have centers and peripheries; all members of a culture are not equally committed to its tenets or involved in its practices. Faculty motivation connected with educational activities endorsed at the center of a culture is likely to be weaker at the peripheries. Thus, motivation of faculty who teach only graduate students at these schools may be less influenced by the organization-wide culture than is the motivation of those who teach mostly undergraduates.

Given the cultural and structural boundaries around departments, distinctive academic subcultures can emerge within departments at a single university, but such subcultures will be shaped in various ways by the larger institutions of which they were a part. Van Maanen's (1984) accounts of business school cultures at MIT and Harvard provide good illustrations of such subcultures and also reveal how powerfully the student subculture can affect educational outcomes. Such accounts also remind us that faculty subcultures exist in constant interaction with student subcultures, which are thus likely to affect faculty teaching motivation at least indirectly. For example, student denigration may damage faculty self-esteem, or it may lead faculty to develop negative feelings about students (see Chap. 1 in this volume).

Cultural Leadership

Although it is theoretically possible that organizational cultures could emerge spontaneously from the interactions of members of organizations (Trice & Beyer, 1993, p. 414), such births have not been recorded in the literature. Rather, the literature documents the crucial role of early leaders, usually the founders, in creating distinctive organization-wide cultures (Kimberly, 1980; Sonnenfeld, 1988; Schein, 1985; Clark, 1992; Lodahl & Mitchell, 1980; Chaffee & Tierney, 1988). In an article reporting research on the founding of two of the English "plate-glass" universities, Lodahl and Mitchell conclude that "founders have only a short time in which to place their unique stamp on the way things are done—shorter, perhaps, than anyone might have imagined. Here, in what was perhaps the most favorable environment for innovation in the long history of university foundations, we see organizational drift setting in clearly by the fourth year. Shaping new behaviors in academia is clearly no easy task" (1980, p. 197). This account and these conclusions contrast sharply with what Clark (1992) saw in the founding and subsequent history of three distinctive U.S. colleges. He reports that not only were distinctive cultures created by the founders or a founding group but these cultures were maintained over time. As he comments, "The question of how distinctiveness is achieved must at least be broken into the two parts of how it was initiated and how it is sustained" (p. 256). He goes on to suggest that a founder or small founding group may initiate a distinctive culture, but it is the tenured faculty who are committed to its distinctive features who maintain it.

In a similar vein, Trice and Beyer (1991, 1993) identified two basic types of cultural leadership: that which produces cultural innovation and that which produces cultural maintenance (table 9.4). Cultural leaders, often charismatics, innovate when they create or change cultures; other cultural leaders maintain existing cultures when they personally embody their cultures' ideas and values or when they integrate existing subcultures. By addressing the issue of the maintenance, as well as the creation, of cultures, both sets of scholars call our attention to the fact that the presence of organization-wide cultures depends on the active leadership efforts of multiple leaders besides the founder.

While creating and changing cultures seem to require strong cultural leaders at the top, these leaders achieve their impacts on the organizational

Table 9.4   Types of Cultural Leadership

	Core Problem
Innovation	
To create a culture	To attract followers and unite them
To change a culture	To weaken and replace elements of the old culture
Maintenance	
To embody a culture	To keep an existing culture vital
To integrate subcultures	To reconcile diverse values and interests

Source: Adapted from Trice & Beyer (1993), p. 264.

culture by communicating their visions broadly and motivating "their middle managers to play a similar kind of leadership role for their own divisions, departments, and groups" (Kotter & Heskett, 1992, p. 146). Eventually, in successful cultural leadership, cultural ideologies and values that were articulated by top leaders are internalized throughout the organization (Roueche, Baker, & Rose, 1989; Clark, 1990). Such ideologies and values can motivate faculty toward effective teaching by channeling their efforts and providing goals that pull them in directions consistent with the culture.

All leadership is a social process and not the property of certain persons. As a social process, cultural leadership involves (1) a leader with certain personal qualities (2) and visions of what is possible and desirable (3) acting in particular ways (4) in a particular social situation (5) so as to attract and influence a set of followers who come to believe in the leaders' vision (Trice & Beyer, 1993).

Given the difficulties of creating and maintaining organization-wide cultures, it is not surprising that they are relatively rare in universities and not common in small colleges. Trice and Beyer (1993) remind us that charisma must be routinized to have more than transitory effects; many factors in modern organizations interfere with routinization, including the pressures on top executives to get involved in the mundane details of administration, which tarnishes their charisma by diluting their aura of exceptionalness (p. 293). Higher education of today—perhaps because of its pervasive fragmentation and the multiple, often contradictory, societal pressures it faces—seems to lack leaders who have the exceptional qualities needed to attract and unite faculties and students around new shared visions. The current crises in funding, enrollments, and general societal support for higher education have not sparked drastic changes in the educational missions of most universities and colleges. Some community colleges may be the exception (Clark, 1990).

Without exceptional leaders, it is hard to see how new organization-wide cultures can be created. It may be more realistic to look for cultural leadership that maintains existing cultures and keeps them vital through expressive activities. University and college presidents who model behaviors consistent with some traditional cultural values and not others can thereby refocus and revitalize a culture and promote its continuity. In particular, it matters what they say and do about teaching. In large universities, however, because of their sheer size and fragmentation, such behaviors are not always visible to all the faculty. As a practical matter, therefore, most academic institutions must look more to their deans and department chairpersons for cultural leadership that will motivate faculty. Sadly, it is often lacking there as well, as academic leaders at all levels get pulled toward the research imperative (Gumport, 1991) and into the demanding orbit of attending to their outside constituencies.[8] Without consistent messages from leaders at all levels that teaching matters and is vital to an institution's mission, faculty will attend to the cultural voices emanating from their subcultures, with uncertain consequence for their motivation to teach.

Implications

The cultural perspective taken in this chapter shows why most universities and colleges have differentiated cultures. Indeed, so many forms of cultural differentiation are present, and some of them, most notably disciplinary differences, are so strong, that it is unusual to find distinctive organization-wide cultures in higher education. Cultural influences on faculty motivation to teach therefore come from many different sources. Only if the ideologies and values promulgated by the subcultures in higher education communicate that educational outcomes are important professional goals and that such goals are achievable and rewarded are individual faculty members likely to be highly motivated to teach well.

It seems clear, however, that many academic subcultures carry ideologies and values that tend to decrease faculty motivation to teach in various ways. The very mechanisms designed to establish some administrative controls over teaching—teaching evaluations, promotions, and curriculum reform—often become rites of renewal which serve the interests of the powerful more than they serve to improve education. Moreover, faculty identify with disciplinary subcultures that value and reward research over teaching (Nisbet, 1971), prefer different modes of teaching, bifurcate areas of study, and often generate destructive conflicts among faculty. In addition, demographic differences along gender, cohort, and other lines hold the potential for creating other damaging subcultural conflicts.

Given these circumstances, it is not enough to exhort university and college presidents to become cultural leaders of the educational process—although that is no doubt desirable. Other levels of cultural leadership are needed to advance and sustain ideologies and values that make faculty want and like to teach well. Deans and department chairpersons must also be sensitive to their role as symbolic, cultural leaders—especially to the messages they send by their actions and decisions about teaching. In large and differentiated university cultures, consistent cultural leadership at all levels is probably needed to achieve and sustain high teaching motivation. Achieving cultures that support teaching efforts does not necessarily require cultural change, however. Cultural leadership can also be directed toward maintaining cultures. Revitalizing and strengthening traditional educational values already present in the history of an institution may often be a better alternative. As Lockwood (1987) pointed out, these traditional values have stood the test of time and have been adapted to varying demands in the past. Higher education also needs cultural leaders who can reconcile differences between the many competing cultures within academia and thus help faculty arrive at and work toward common educational goals.

Unfortunately, the internal cultural differentiation described in the chapter is only part of the cultural confusion and contradictions affecting higher education. External constituencies are making powerful demands on colleges and universities to serve varied interests. Many parents and students want training and high grades (Reibstein, with King, Rosenberg, and Biddle, 1994; "Making the Grades," 1994) that will lead surely to jobs (Tierney, 1991a). Employers want vocationally relevant education as well as strong basic skills. There are relatively fewer constituents crying for a liberal education or for education for good citizenry. These external forces seem to be pulling university and college administrators toward ever more instrumental views of education (Slaughter, 1991). When such views conflict with those of faculty, they can undermine faculty motivation to teach. Universities and colleges therefore need strong integrative cultural leadership that can reconcile these pressures with traditional faculty values.

Conclusions

There are many cultural influences both within and outside academic organizations which draw faculty members away from concern for their teaching and toward other pursuits. Even those pressures specifically intended to make faculty take more notice of their teaching are ineffective and often damaging to faculty motivation in the complex structure of power and subcultures that exist in modern higher education.

One remedy for conflicting demands is to accommodate them by further differentiating a system (Clark, 1983). As Lockwood (1987) argues, leaders in higher education must find ways to resist pressures toward uniformity and create greater acceptance of the idea that diversity within the system is a strength. To manage this diversity requires cultural leadership that can (1) integrate the diverse concerns of members of the academic community and the general society around superordinate educational goals, and (2) develop or revitalize ideologies and practices that make teaching an exciting and rewarding enterprise for faculty at all levels of academic organizations.

Notes

1. See Trice and Beyer (1993, pp. 83–85) for information about other collective sense-making processes.

2. The Maslow hierarchy of needs is being used here in an illustrative sense only; I am aware of the many criticisms and augmentations it has received.

3. Some institutions, of course, provide assistance to faculty whose student evaluations are disappointing or considered unsatisfactory. One of the first was the University of Texas, whose Center for Teaching Effectiveness is more than twenty years old ("CTE Is 20!," 1993).

4. There has been considerable controversy over whether and how strongly participation affects subsequent motivation. Recent research (Latham, Winters, & Locke, 1994) shows that the effects of participation on motivation are indirect, being mediated by self-efficacy and task strategies.

5. Of course, potential employees and parents share these concerns as well. Pressures from these stakeholders are discussed in a later part of this chapter.

6. One explanation of this bias against women instructors is that they do not fit the cultural stereotype for femininity—in particular, that they be warm and nurturing. Men instructors are not expected to be responsive and friendly, and when they are, they are considered "really good guys" (Bridges & Hartman, 1975, p. 77).

7. The current trends to hire more part-time faculty, especially in community colleges, clearly operate to discourage genuine organization-wide cultures.

8. See chapters in Tierney (1991b) for a critical perspective on many of the issues created by these pressures. See Cousins (1994) for one faculty member's account of how the pressures for research from accrediting agencies and subsequent changes in the reward system damaged the teaching motivation of faculty at what had been a teaching-oriented university.

References

Adler, N. J. (1991). *International dimensions of organizational behavior* (2d ed.). Boston: PWS-Kent.

Becher, T. (1984). The cultural view. In B. R. Clark (Ed.), *Perspectives in higher education* (pp. 165–198). Berkeley: University of California Press.

Becher, T. (1987a). *British higher education*. London: Allen & Unwin.

Becher, T. (1987b). The disciplinary shaping of the profession. In B. R. Clark (Ed.), *The academic profession* (pp. 271–303). Berkeley: University of California Press.

Becher, T. (1989). *Academic tribes and territories: Intellectual enquiry and the cultures of disciplines*. Milton Keynes, England: SRHE and Open University Press.

Berger, P. L., & Luckmann, T. (1967). *The social construction of reality* (3d ed.). Garden City, NY: Anchor Books.

Beyer, J. M. (1978). Editorial policies and practices among leading journals in four scientific fields. *Sociological Quarterly, 19,* 68–88.

Beyer, J. M. (1981). Ideologies, values, and decision-making in organizations. In P. Nystrom & W. H. Starbuck (Eds.), *Handbook of organizational design* (Vol. 2, pp. 166–197). London: Oxford University Press.

Beyer, J. M., & Lodahl, T. M. (1976). A comparative study of patterns of influence in United States and English universities. *Administrative Science Quarterly, 21,* 104–129.

Beyer, J. M., & Lutze, S. (1992). The ethical nexus: Organizations, values, and decision making. In C. Conrad (Ed.), *The ethical nexus: Communication, values, and organizational decisions* (pp. 23–45). Norwood, NJ: Asley Publishers.

Biggart, N. (1977). The creative-destructive process of organizational change: The case of the post office. *Administrative Science Quarterly, 22,* 410–420.

Bridges, A., & Hartman, H. (1975). Pedagogy by the oppressed. *Review of Radical Political Economics, 6*(4), 75–79.

Cameron, K. S., & Ettington, D. R. (1988). The conceptual foundations of organizational culture. In J. C. Smart (Ed.), *Higher education: Handbook of theory and research* (Vol. 4, pp. 356–396). New York: Agathon Press.

Chaffee, E. E., & Tierney, W. G. (1988). *Collegiate culture and leadership strategies*. New York: American Council on Education/Macmillan.

Clark, B. R. (1983). *The higher education system*. Berkeley: University of California Press.

Clark, B. R. (1992). [Originally published in 1970]. *The distinctive college*. New Brunswick, NJ: Transaction Publishers.

Clark, G. A. (1990). Organizational structure, leadership strategies, and organizational systems in a recognized community college: A case study. Ph.D. dissertation, University of Texas at Austin.

Cohen, M. D., & March, J. G. (1976). Decisions, presidents, and status. In J. G. March

& J. P. Olsen (Eds.), *Ambiguity and choice in organizations* (pp. 174–205). Bergen, Norway: Universitetsforlaget.

Cohen, M. D., March, J. G., & Olsen, J. P. (1972). A garbage can model of organizational choice. *Administrative Science Quarterly, 17*, 1–25.

Cousins, R. B. (1994). Ruminations on Professor Mowday's "Reflections on editing AMS." *Journal of Management Inquiry, 3*, 99–102.

Crane, D. (1972). *Invisible colleges.* Chicago: University of Chicago Press.

CTE is 20! (1993). *Teaching Network, 15*, 4. Center for Teaching Effectiveness, University of Texas at Austin.

Ferguson, H. (1936). *Modern man: His belief and behavior.* New York: Knopf.

Geertz, C. (1973). *The interpretation of cultures.* New York: Basic Books.

Gumport, P. J. (1991). The research imperative. In W. G. Tierney (Ed.), *Culture and ideology in higher education: Advancing a critical agenda* (pp. 87–105). New York: Praeger.

Hagstrom, W. O. (1965). *The scientific community.* New York: Basic Books.

Hofstede, G. (1993). Cultural constraints in management theories. *Academy of Management Executive, 7*, 81–94.

House, R. J. (1977). A 1976 theory of charismatic leadership. In J. G. Hunt & L. L. Larson (Eds.), *Leadership: The cutting edge* (pp. 189–273). Carbondale: Southern Illinois University Press.

Kanter, R. M. (1977). *Men and women of the corporation.* New York: Basic Books.

Kempner, K. (1991). Understanding cultural conflict. In W. G. Tierney (Ed.), *Culture and ideology in higher education: Advancing a critical agenda* (pp. 129–150). New York: Praeger.

Kilbourne, L. M., & O'Leary-Kelly, A. M. (1994). A reevaluation of equity theory: The influence of culture. *Journal of Management Inquiry, 3*, 177–188.

Kimberly, J. R. (1980). Initiation, innovation, and institutionalization in the creation process. In J. R. Kimberly & R. H. Miles & Associates (Eds.), *The organizational life cycle: Issues in the creation, transformation, and decline of organizations* (pp. 18–43). San Francisco: Jossey-Bass.

Kotter, J. P., & Heskett, J. L. (1992). *Corporate culture and performance.* New York: Free Press.

Kuhn, T. (1970). *The structure of scientific revolutions.* Chicago: University of Chicago Press.

Langton, N., & Pfeffer, J. (1992). Paying the professor: Source of salary variations in academic labor markets. *American Sociological Review, 59*, 236–256.

Latham, G. P., Winters, D. C., & Locke, E. A. (1994). Cognitive and motivational efforts of participation: A mediator study. *Journal of Organizational Behavior, 15*, 49–63.

Leach, E. (1968). Ritual. In *International encyclopedia of the social sciences* (Vol. 13, pp. 520–526). New York: Macmillan.

Lockwood, G. (1987). The management of universities. In T. Becher (Ed.), *British higher education* (pp. 87–106). London: Allen & Unwin.

Lodahl, J. B., & Gordon, G. (1972). The structure of scientific fields and the functioning of university graduate departments. *American Sociological Review, 37*, 57–72.

Lodahl, J. B., & Gordon, G. (1973a). Differences between physical and social sciences in university graduate departments. *Research in Higher Education, 1*, 191.

Lodahl, J. B., & Gordon, G. (1973b). Funding the sciences in university departments. *Educational Record, 54*(1), 74–82.

Lodahl, T. M., & Mitchell, S. M. (1980). Drift in the development of innovative organizations. In J. R. Kimberly & R. H. Miles & Associates (Eds.), *The organizational life cycle: Issues in the creation, transformation, and decline of organizations* (pp. 184–207). San Francisco: Jossey-Bass.

Lott, B. (1985). The devaluation of women's competence. *Journal of Social Issues, 41,* 43–60.

Making the Grades. (1994, June 5). *New York Times,* 16.

Martin, J. (1992). *Cultures in organizations: Three perspectives.* New York: Oxford University Press.

Martin, J. (1994). The organization of exclusion: Institutionalization of sex inequality, gendered faculty jobs, and gendered knowledge in organizational theory and research. *Organization, 1*(2), 401–431.

MBA Handbook. (1993–1994). Stanford Graduate School of Business.

McCain, B. E., O'Reilly, C., & Pfeffer, J. (1983). The effects of departmental demography on turnover: The case of a university. *Academy of Management Journal, 26,* 626–641.

McClelland, D. C. (1961). *The achieving society.* Princeton, NJ: Van Nostrand.

McClelland, D. C. (1971). *Motivational trends in society.* Morristown, NJ: General Learning Press.

Merton, R. K. (1976). *Sociological ambivalence and other essays.* New York: Free Press.

Meyer, J. W., & Rowan, B. (1977). Institutionalized organizations: Formal structure, myth, and ceremony. *American Journal of Sociology, 83,* 340–361.

Nisbet, R. A. (1971). *The degradation of the academic dogma: The university in America.* New York: Basic Books.

Ortner, D. (1984). *How humans adapt: A biocultural odyssey.* Washington, DC: Smithsonian Institution.

Ortner, S. B. (1984). Theory in anthropology since the sixties. *Comparative Studies in Society and History, 26,* 126–166.

Pfeffer, J. (1985). Organizational demography: Implications for management. *California Management Review, 23,* 67–81.

Putnam, L. L., & Pacanowsky, M. E. (Eds.). (1983). *Communications and organizations.* Beverly Hills, CA: Sage.

Reibstein, L., with King, P., Rosenberg, D., & Biddle, N. A. (1994, June 13). Give me an A, or give me death. *Newsweek,* 62.

Rhoades, G., & Slaughter, S. (1991). The public interest and professional labor: Research universities. In W. G. Tierney (Ed.), *Culture and ideology in higher education: Advancing a critical agenda* (pp. 187–216). New York: Praeger.

Richardson, R. C., Jr. (1971). Comment. *Journal of Higher Education, 42,* 516–519.

Roueche, J. E., Baker, G. A., & Rose, R. R. (1989). *Shared vision: The open door college.* Washington, DC: Community College Press.

Salancik, G. R., & Pfeffer, J. (1974). The bases and use of power in organizational decision-making: The case of a university. *Administrative Science Quarterly, 19*(4), 453–473.

Salancik, G. R., Staw, B. M., & Pondy, L. R. (1980). Administrative turnover as a response to unmanaged organization interdependence. *Administrative Science Quarterly, 23,* 422–437.

Schein, E. H. (1985). *Organizational culture and leadership.* San Francisco: Jossey-Bass.

Schermerhorn, J. R., Jr., Hunt, J. G., & Osborn, R. N. (1994). *Managing organizational behavior* (5th ed.). New York: Wiley.

Scott, W. R. (1987). *Organizations: Rational, natural, and open systems* (2d ed.). Englewood Cliffs, NJ: Prentice-Hall.

Shils, E. (1975). *Center and periphery: Essays in macrosociology.* Chicago: University of Chicago Press.

Slaughter, S. (1991). The "official" ideology of higher education: Ironies and inconsistencies. In W. G. Tierney (Ed.), *Culture and ideology in higher education: Advancing a critical agenda* (pp. 59–85). New York: Praeger.

Sonnenfeld, J. (1988). *The hero's farewell: What happens when CEO's retire.* New York: Oxford University Press.

Sowell, T. (1994, February 14). Power without responsibility. *Forbes,* 85.

Tierney, W. G. (1991a). Academic work and institutional culture: Constructing knowledge. *Review of Higher Education, 14,* 199–215.

Tierney, W. G. (Ed.). (1991b). *Culture and ideology in higher education: Advancing a critical agenda.* New York: Praeger.

Tierney, W. G. (1991c). Ideology and identity in postsecondary institutions. In W. G. Tierney (Ed.), *Culture and ideology in higher education: Advancing a critical agenda* (pp. 35–57). New York: Praeger.

Trice, H. M. (1993). *Occupational subcultures in the workplace.* Ithaca, NY: ILR Press.

Trice, H. M., & Beyer, J. M. (1984). Studying organizational cultures through rites and ceremonials. *Academy of Management Review, 9*(4), 653–659.

Trice, H. M., & Beyer, J. M. (1991). Cultural leadership in organizations. *Organization Science, 2,* 149–169.

Trice, H. M., & Beyer, J. M. (1993). *The cultures of work organizations.* Englewood Cliffs, NJ: Prentice-Hall.

Van Maanen, J. (1984). Doing new things in old ways. In J. L. Bess (Ed.), *College and university organization: Insights from the behavioral sciences.* New York: New York University Press.

Van Maanen, J., & Barley, S. R. (1984). Occupational communities: Culture and control in organizations. *Research in Organizational Behavior, 6,* 287–365.

Weick, K. E. (1976). Educational organizations as loosely coupled systems. *Administrative Science Quarterly, 21,* 1–19.

10 Organization Design and Job Characteristics

DOUGLAS T. HALL AND
MAX H. BAZERMAN

The role of teaching in colleges and universities has changed dramatically over the last century. Until the late nineteenth century, teaching dominated universities. Then research was added to the functions of the university (Bess, 1982). Subsequently, in the twentieth century research came to dominate faculty activities in most academic organizations. Scholarly excellence was seen as the route to international acclaim, for both the organization and the individual faculty member.

In the 1990s, however, universities have become increasingly concerned about quality and responsiveness, as they struggle to adapt to the realities of a very competitive environment. In a shift back from research as the favored route to academic excellence, the new domain for competition is the classroom and the curriculum. Not only can universities and colleges ill afford to tolerate poor teaching; they are being pushed to demand excellence in the classroom.

Although many organization design researchers work in universities, they rarely consider the organization design of their own organizations. This chapter deals with how aspects of a university's design affect faculty

The helpful comments of our colleagues Linda Argote (Carnegie-Mellon University), Philip Friedman (Bentley College), John Hennessey (University of Vermont), Paul Lawrence (Harvard Business School), and David Schoorman (Purdue University) are gratefully acknowledged.

motivation to teach. By examining how the "macro" area of organization design affects the "micro" area of motivation, this chapter seeks to (1) expand the knowledge base concerning the interaction between multiple levels of organizational analysis, (2) help university designers create systems that will increase faculty motivation to teach, and (3) help faculty better understand that organization and suggest innovative changes.

In Chapter 4, Deci, Kasser, and Ryan proposed that teaching is naturally an intrinsically rewarding activity. These authors suggest that a crucial goal for universities should be to prevent organizational factors from negatively affecting this intrinsic motivation. In agreement with this position, we propose that the intrinsic motivation of that faculty member is a cost-free input that universities cannot afford to waste. Consequently, we propose that as we begin to consider how to design an organization, primary attention needs to be given to avoiding the use of extrinsic motivators that will be perceived as controlling and to searching for external factors that will enhance faculty feelings of competence.

Organization (University) Design

Rather than trying to provide a review of the organization design literature in this section,[1] we outline one framework that may be useful in identifying alternative ways in which universities can change organizational variables to increase faculty motivation. The basic assumption of most organization design theories is that an organization is an open system existing in an environment, from which it must obtain "inputs" (resources, raw materials, students, information, and so forth) for "processing" (e.g., generating learning for students) and to which it must export "outputs" (e.g., selling products, placing graduates, disseminating research findings). And as the environment changes over time, the organization must adapt and transform itself. If the system does not adapt to a changing environment, over time it will die (Parsons, 1960; Handy, 1994).

Jay Galbraith (1977, 1994) argues that organizations that successfully adapt to their environments do so by creating alignment (or congruence) among five strategic systemic variables: (1) strategic tasks, (2) structure, (3) information and decision process, (4) reward systems, and (5) people. These organization design elements represent what has been dubbed his "star" model. The notion of congruence implies that there may be no best way to design an organization but that certain combinations of these five strategic variables (task, structure, and so on) may fit together more effectively than others. For example, for a very unpredictable, uncertain task activity, a decentralized structure, giving decision-making discretion to the individual performing the task, may be more effective than a more centralized structure in which decisions are made at higher levels. Congruence implies that for a given set of goals certain patterns of task, structure, information technology, people, and rewards will fit more effectively than others. The choice of a given strategic variable is *contingent* upon the nature of the other strategic variables that are already in place.

We have selected the Galbraith model for our analysis because its elements are well suited to intervention (i.e., they are changeable) and because they deal especially well with issues of cross-functional (lateral or horizontal) coordination, which are critical tasks in an academic organization. So, with apologies to Mintzberg, Pfeffer, the population ecologists, Wheatley, and other theorists, we will pursue our "theory of the practice" with Galbraith.

Galbraith implicitly suggests that goal selection precedes design selection or change. We believe, however, that decisions concerning goals and designs should be, and in fact *are,* made simultaneously. This is especially true in an academic organization, which is highly decentralized and in which responsibility for decision making is quite diffused, so that goals emerge as action is taken. Goals are never truly "set" in a definitive way, and work on goals is never a purely rational process. There is a *negotiated* rationality to goal issues in organizations (Neale & Bazerman, 1991), especially in colleges and universities. In fact, much of the work of organizational leadership consists of confronting goal issues, through processes such as strategic planning, total quality management, and reengineering. Perspectives such as these require that organizations examine the design cost and benefits of pursuing a certain set of goals.

Goals often emerge through a confluence of forces (decisions needing to be made, people with personal agendas, resources that are available, and so on), with many of the attendant biases one might expect (Bazerman, 1994; March & Olsen, 1976; Wheatley, 1992). In fact, more apparent to an observer than a clear set of goals may be a sense of *strategic direction.*

Goal determination is the most overlooked area of organization planning by the academic literature, strategic planners, and university administrators. Universities often claim to have a balanced emphasis on teaching, research, and community service. When we look at reward behavior (tenure decisions, for example), however, we often find "biased behavior." Our position is that university decision makers need to evaluate and communicate more honestly what it is that they want to achieve. We argue that university effectiveness can be best achieved by simultaneously identifying the goals of the university and designing (in terms of Galbraith's five strategic variables) the best organization to achieve these goals.

Organization Design Strategies

A central concept in the study of organization design is uncertainty (Duncan, 1971; Wheatley, 1992). Galbraith (1973, 1977) argues that the greater the uncertainty of a task, the greater is the amount of information which must be processed to perform that task effectively. Traditionally, Galbraith argues, organizations have reduced uncertainty and achieved coordination through three mechanisms: (1) rules and programs, (2) hierarchy, and (3) goals or targets.

These mechanisms are central elements of a traditional bureaucratic administrative structure (Weber, 1947). Using these three coordinating elements can produce fairly "tight coupling" (interdependence), a quality not commonly seen in most universities. Indeed, as March and Olsen (1976) have shown, universities are loosely coupled systems in which decisions result from a "garbage can" mixture of problems seeking solutions, solutions looking for problems, participants who come and go, and choice opportunities (defined as "occasions when an organization is expected to produce behavior that can be called a decision" by March and Olsen, 1976, p. 27). In this type of system, rules are minimized, hierarchy is at a minimum (only three or four levels typically exist between junior faculty members and the president), and goals are highly ambiguous and debatable.

Although we believe that March and Olsen have overstated the role of randomness in universities, especially in the contemporary resource-constrained environment, which calls for more coordinated sharing of resources, we do believe that academic organizations are unique. Perhaps the "truth" is closer to Wheatley's (1992) notion of an underlying order in the apparent chaos of organizational phenomena. However, the process for reaching this order, we think, is compatible with the March and Olsen approach. Our focus here is on providing rational design advice to help to design universities to cope with coordination problems in an era of increasing teaching importance. (In fact, we would argue that coordination is far more important—and now more common—around teaching and curricular issues than around research activities.)

What alternatives, then, are available for university coordination? Galbraith (1977) argues that there are two basic design approaches: (1) reduce the need for information processing, and (2) increase the organization's capacity for processing information. The first strategy can be pursued by either creating slack resources (higher budgets, looser deadlines, buffer inventories, and so forth) or creating self-contained tasks (i.e., organizing by output categories, such as academic programs, rather than by inputs, such as functional departments).

The second approach, increasing the capacity to process information, can be attained in two ways: developing vertical information systems (e.g., targets, plans, budgets, periodic feedback reports, and technology-based systems, such as E-mail and voice mail), and creating lateral relationships (i.e., informal links across different functional areas). Examples of lateral relations include liaison roles (such as joint appointments), interdepartmental task forces, teams, integrating roles, managerial linking roles, and matrix structures.

Design Strategies and Teaching Motivation

How do these design strategies apply to a university and to a faculty teaching motivation? Let us start with the premise that the ingenious feature of university design in the past has been its ability to organize the unorganizable: university faculty members. Professors are distinguishable in our society by their inordinately high levels of the need for autonomy. They also have high needs for achievement, recognition, and security. Much faculty motivation is provided by rewards that satisfy these needs. The environmental climate conducive to satisfying these needs is what is called "academic freedom."

Thus, given this type of person as the major line operator (deliverer of service) in the system, universities have generally opted for the design strategy of "information reduction." Higher education in the past had seen conditions of relatively high degrees of slack (especially in the 1960s and 1970s), and institutions have been organized into relatively self-contained task units (schools or departments). Universities have not been known for their high information-processing capacities (vertical information systems or lateral relations).

In the 1990s, however, there has been a major change in the design model for universities: a drastic reduction of slack resources and a resulting decrease in uncertainty. That is, with less favorable demographics and smaller applicant pools and declining enrollments, budgets have become tighter and tuition increases less tenable. Consequently, universities have been pushed to become more competitive, often through a strong push for system integration and total quality management. To maintain equilibrium, other parts of the system must adjust, or performance will decline. In the pages that follow, we examine design alternatives for compensating for slack resources in the creation of teaching systems: more self-contained tasks, vertical information systems, and better lateral relations. In short, we will argue that factors in the context of the organization's design (e.g., job design, customer-related goals, and peer influence) may be becoming more important than individual needs in driving faculty motivation to teach.

Case Examples: Higher and Lower Motivation to Teach

To elaborate further on these organization design concepts as they affect motivation to teach, case examples might be helpful. We examine one university organization known for high motivation to teach and one known for low motivation to teach, electing from a universe with which we are familiar, schools of business. We use each element in the Galbraith design model (goals, tasks, structure, etc.) to analyze the faculty members' context for motivation in each university.

A Higher Motivation to Teach

One business school known to have highly motivated teachers is the Harvard Business School (HBS). HBS is nationally known for the quality of its teaching and the quality of its graduate business programs (master of business administration, or MBA, programs). Harvard is generally ranked highly in most surveys of MBA programs. The performance and career success of its graduates have been similarly successful. There may be disagreement on the definition of teaching quality, but there is little disagreement that HBS has it. Further, in an effort to maintain this leadership, Harvard is currently engaged in a highly publicized review of its MBA curriculum. We start with the first element in the Galbraith model, goals.

Goals

Having clear goals means that uncertainty about fundamental strategic choices is low. Getting clear about goals is one of the most powerful ways an organization can reduce uncertainty, as goal clarity allows the organization to focus limited resources on its most important objectives. At HBS, teaching is a primary goal. Harvard has a doctoral program, but, in our opinion, doctoral education is treated as a second-class activity. (In fact, it has been the object of external and internal concern.) Harvard does not have an undergraduate business program. It does have an extensive array of executive programs. Teaching quality is the number one goal.

One of the most powerful ways that other business schools have started the improvement of their MBA and undergraduate curricula, in fact, has been simply to raise the priority of teaching quality as a formal goal. In view of the great freedom that academics have in their daily activities, simply increasing the priority of teaching and reducing faculty members' uncertainty about the value of teaching can provide powerful focus and energy for improving teaching. We would argue that one of the most important underlying features of successful change efforts in this area has been changing the business school's *culture* regarding the value of good teaching.

Tasks

Related to this MBA teaching goal, faculty activities are closely geared to teaching and are organized as self-contained tasks. As Galbraith's model shows, this reduces uncertainty by reducing the need for information processing (e.g., inter-course, interdepartmental, interschool communication). Core courses are run by committees of the faculty who teach sections of those respective courses. Standardized course outlines, books, case materials, and exercises are often used. It is not unusual for a course committee to spend several hours each week reviewing and preparing for that week's classes. Team preparation may extend to developing a common set of questions to be used throughout the case discussion. Common evaluation activities (e.g., a common final case) are often used. External activities, such as a limited amount of consulting, are valued for increasing the teaching ability of faculty members. Uncertainty-reducing slack resources, such as support for case development, teaching assistants, time off for new course development, financial support for visiting lecturers, and so on, are used generously to support excellence in the classroom.

(Of course, this creation of self-contained tasks reduces the need for information processing on routine activities, but it can also interfere with integration across units when it is needed for nonroutine activities, such as curriculum revision and other major changes. During these nonroutine periods, tasks need to be made more interdependent, and this is a counter-cultural activity in many academic organizations.)

Structure

Organization structure appears related to teaching activity as well. Academic structure is primarily based on functional specialization (departments such as finance or marketing). However, a program or course committee (a self-contained task unit) can also constitute an equally strong unit in the school. The power of a program or a course committee chairperson to structure the amount and nature of committee time, to vary the degree of course structure, to evaluate other faculty, and, in general, to shape the education offerings can be considerable. As relatively self-contained units, both programs and departments reduce the need for information processing.

Information Systems

Information and decision processes are well developed in relation to teaching. Because teaching is such a central activity, the decision processes for revising the curriculum and individual courses are complex, time consuming, and carefully controlled by the administration, as can be seen currently in the long, deliberate process by which the MBA curriculum is being changed. This rich exchange of information for integration is necessary in view of the nonroutine, highly uncertain nature of what environment is saying the new curricula should be. This is a case where, in Galbraith's organization design strategies, there is a clear need to increase the system's capacity to process information. Thus new electronic information technology, such as E-mail, networks, bulletin boards, and group decision software, can be invaluable in promoting faculty information flow and learning regarding teaching and curricular innovation.

Rewards

It is the reward system that most clearly reflects Harvard's stress on teaching quality. It is strongly aligned, as Galbraith would advocate, with the goals, tasks, and structures that are designed to motivate good teaching. Promotion and tenure are highly dependent on teaching and course development excellence; research excellence is desirable but not always seen as essential. This is counter to the reward system in most other high-quality business schools. Informal rewards (esteem from students and faculty colleagues) are also associated with teaching excellence: "Stars" are those who shine in the classroom, not necessarily in print.

People

There is also a strong fit between the type of faculty who are attracted to and recruited by HBS and the primary teaching goals, tasks, structures, and rewards of the organization, per the Galbraith model. In fact, the faculty at HBS are both a cause and an effect of the strong teaching orientation. Faculty are selected largely on the basis of their teaching and course development motivation and skills, and these skills are further refined and rewarded over time. Students are attracted on the basis of teaching quality, and their expectations for teaching excellence are high; they also pay unusually high tuition and therefore feel that they have every right to expect classroom quality. Because HBS is highly selective, its students are exceptionally bright and well motivated, which provides excellent "raw material" and intrinsic motivation for the teacher.

A Lower Motivation to Teach

Another excellent business school with comparatively lower motivation to teach is the Graduate School of Industrial Administration at Carnegie-Mellon University. Like Harvard, Carnegie is also an elite school and highly rated, but it is not known for high faculty motivation to teach. Why is teaching motivation apparently lower at Carnegie? The answer lies in Galbraith's main input to organization design: *goals*. Carnegie's primary goal is research, in particular, high-quality research. This goal fits with the nature of *people* (students and faculty) who are attracted to Carnegie-Mellon. The school produces excellent graduates because it enrolls excellent students who are self-motivated. The faculty's impact on the student's learning processes comes from the former's intellectual gifts (content) rather than their teaching skills (process). When academicians think of education at Carnegie, it is common to think of the production of research-oriented doctoral students, rather than businesslike MBAs.

At Carnegie the other design elements in the Galbraith model are noticeably aligned with basic research and theory building. Concerning *tasks*, new faculty are advised that research comes first and that teaching is lower-priority activity. Faculty often work independently on their own courses.

Regarding *structure*, there is no formal course committee structure, only a loose area structure. Furthermore, there are no formal departments that would "reduce interdisciplinary research." Power is based on one's stature in the research arena. *Rewards* (promotion and tenure) are primarily based on the publication of high-quality, high-impact research and theory. Poor teaching does not disqualify one from tenure, except in extreme situations. In fact, through a form of reverse snobbery, low course evaluations may be seen as a sign that one is intellectually demanding and not about to compromise one's standards to satisfy students.

Information technology is geared to research activities (faculty research seminars, assistance with grant proposals, highly developed research-oriented computer systems, and strong contacts between Carnegie scholars and researchers at other institutions). Information technology geared toward teaching (classroom observation and feedback by senior colleagues, a course evaluation system strongly tied to the promotion and tenure systems) is not highly developed at Carnegie.

Finally, as we said before, people are selected and developed to fit with this style of organization: brilliant faculty who accommodate students while they write to satisfy colleagues, and students who adapt to a system in which teaching is not viewed as primary by their eminent faculty. (Although there certainly are dedicated teachers at Carnegie who devote a great deal of time and support to students, these arguments apply to modal behaviors at the respective institutions.)

Thus the basic organization design elements at Carnegie-Mellon are, like Harvard's, well aligned with one another, but the alignment is aimed more in the direction of research and scholarly excellence than teaching. In recent years teaching has become more important at Carnegie-Mellon, and our suspicion is that, over time, the differences we have described between the two schools will decrease.

Improving Organization Design and Teaching Motivation

In the light of these examples and the organization design model, let us consider some of the complex issues involved in attempting to influence faculty motivation to teach, again using the five elements in Galbraith's "star" model of organization theory.

Goals

The first issue, which becomes obvious in comparing Carnegie-Mellon with Harvard, is the problem of goal conflict. Although most schools claim a balanced emphasis in research and teaching, teaching excellence requires trade-offs on other dimensions of university effectiveness. An organization that primarily attempts to maximize teaching quality will not be equally outstanding on research or community service because it will commit more of its critical resources to teaching. Emphasizing teaching leads a business school to run the risk of becoming a local (as opposed to cosmopolitan) institution, defining its own internal reality for members. This localism can, in turn, insulate a school from changes in the profession it serves, which can hinder its long-term teaching effectiveness. Research performs an adaptive function for the organization; an organization that downplays research does run the risk of obsolescence even in nonresearch activities. At issue is the clarity, balance, and salience of the twin goals, as well as the choice of the goals themselves.

Curriculum Revision

One of the most powerful mechanisms for responding to the competitive pressures on academic organizations is the review of the curriculum in relation to the basic goals of the organization and the expectations of its student customers. This has been done in recent years in the context of quality improvements, utilizing lateral relations structures such as interdepartmental curriculum task forces and design teams. Such a process provides clear feedback to the faculty and reduces uncertainty about the expectations and needs of the students. This provides a much clearer image to the faculty about the educational goals they should be working toward and thus eliminates much of the traditional discipline-based conflict about what "should" be included in the core curriculum. The first author headed up such a curriculum task force recently and was impressed to see how this direct "link to the customer" got the faculty all working in the same direction, with little of the traditional "turf battles" he had experienced in previous curriculum revisions.

Tasks

Regarding the task activities of teaching, with tightened resources we may see higher teaching loads, larger class sizes, more stress on basic, core courses and fewer electives (which provide more intrinsic rewards for faculty), and more demanding students. What we may have is a vicious cycle with increasing task (quantity) demands on faculty and decreasing rewards. This may result in less faculty effort and involvement per course and thus lower-quality teaching. In turn, this may produce more student protests and demand for quality, making the focus of faculty's work life even less intrinsically motivating. One result could be formal, negotiated agreements between administrators, faculty, and students on teaching activities that can be quantified: class size, number of office hours per week, limits on graded assignments, limits on outside consulting, and so on. Finally, optional faculty activities that contribute to the students' quality of life (participation in social events, counseling and advising, independent study courses being available for informal discussion) may also decrease and, in turn, become the subject of negotiated, quantified requirements.

Impact of Student Culture

One factor that could mitigate these quality-threatening effects on scarce resources is the student culture. The norms, values, and informal rewards provided by the student culture can have a strong effect on faculty attitudes and, in fact, on the faculty culture. A student body that expects quality teaching and is prepared to contribute to classroom activities increases the intrinsic rewards associated with teaching. This increased participation, combined with the resulting increase in faculty intrinsic motivation, can substantially increase the quality of instruction.

We can begin by communicating to the student body the potential effects they can have on teaching effectiveness. Second, we can increase the likelihood of the development of a strong student culture by physically creating meeting places for students and emotionally and financially supporting the development of student organizations. The more attention a dean devotes to student organizations, for example, the more power those organizations will have. Finally, we can bring the teaching and the culture issues to the attention of student organizations.

Release Time for Course Development

A critical task in teaching is innovation. Getting a sabbatical for funded research projects is common. Yet time to develop a new set of courses is rare. Why? Perhaps course development is considered by our educational system as a standard part of a faculty member's job. This task, however, when competing with day-to-day internal (teaching meetings) and external (conferences, consulting) activities, often gets limited attention. We need to increase the saliency of innovations in teaching. Making funded release time available provides extrinsic rewards and information (signals) that can increase the intrinsic motivation from course development.

Structure

Organization structure can have a subtle but pervasive effect on faculty motivation to teach. Two of the most common structural forms in a university are functional (departmental) form and the more self-contained program structure (analogous to a "product" structure in a business organization). Although the departmental form dominates in the university, the program form may be more favorable to teaching.

In the program form, faculty are grouped in terms of the program in which they teach (e.g., specific degree programs, professional programs, executive programs). The program faculty would be a team, drawing on all the academic disciplines necessary to deliver that program.

Our hypothesis is that motivation to teach is higher in a program structure than in a departmental structure, since program faculty identify more with the ultimate product of the program: fully educated and prepared students.

In general, though, the academic department is stronger than the program unit. It is the department that typically controls faculty hiring and tenure decisions and has primary influence over compensation increases. In most schools, courses are initiated, offered, and staffed through the departments, although we are seeing more cross-departmental courses. (For example, at Boston University, general management courses, such as "The Global Manager and Consulting Skills," which had been listed under departmental names, are now listed under CD names, for Cross-Disciplinary.)

There is a need to find ways to obtain greater balance between the power of the department and the power of the teaching program, to give more priority to teaching and curricular matters. Structures that give more staffing power to programs would help them provide the faculty who work best with their students. (Some faculty's talents are best suited for particular programs and levels of students.) Some ways of shifting power toward the program can include recruiting strong program administrators, rotating strong faculty into program administration roles, giving programs direct hiring authority, and giving programs budgetary resources to provide resources to departments and faculty to engage in teaching improvement activities.

As one example, at Boston University the School of Management has created the position of faculty director for its three major teaching programs (undergraduate, MBA, and DBA). The faculty director works as a peer with the assistant dean for the program, leading curriculum improvement initiatives and serving as the "champion" for the program within the faculty of the school.

Most academicians have been socialized to believe in a traditional hierarchy. As Galbraith's model shows, various forms of lateral relations can increase the university's information-processing capacity. For example, the Harvard Business School and the Wharton School at the University of Pennsylvania have used a matrix organization, whereby each faculty member reports directly to directors of the programs in which they teach and research, as well as to their functional (e.g., accounting) department chairpersons. This creates an integration mechanism and vehicle for communication across both programs and functions. Obviously, these benefits do not come without costs, such as conflict, complexity, and so on (see Davis & Lawrence, 1977, for comprehensive discussion). Alternately, universities can consider less consuming methods of increasing interactions across functional academic departments. This might include interdepartmental committees, interdepartmental task forces for special problems, joint appointments for key faculty members, or simply organizing teaching symposia of general interest to the faculty. As slack resources diminish and the need for information processing increases, new forms of lateral relations will have to be developed.

People

Student Demographics

Composites of both students and faculties appear to be changing since the 1980s. Demographic changes have decreased the number of recent high school graduates entering universities and increased the number of older, more mature students. Another change is that more students will become self-supporting (through part-time or full-time jobs) as tuition and the cost of living increase. Thus, even though student motivation may be high, the amount of time and energy the student has available for schoolwork may decrease. The changing student mix will require that faculty be more responsive to the needs of more assertive, mature students.

Faculty Demographics

The second people-oriented issue emerging in many universities is the changing demographics of the faculty. With the postwar baby boom members now coming into tenured positions in their thirties and forties, we face the prospect of large numbers of faculty in a thirty-year, full-rank career plateau, with the concomitant risk of a frustrated tertiary faculty and a bored, if threatened, tenured group. A number of remedial and development activities are called for in light of these changes.

Tenure Decisions.   Many universities are currently facing the problem of an overtenured faculty. In addition to the perceived necessity to reward (tenure) hardworking assistant professors, we potentially face a situation in which "new blood" and intrinsically motivated faculty may become a rare commodity in the future. We argue that a tenure decision can no longer be viewed simply as a reward but must now meet the condition of improving the predicted effectiveness of the university in the long run. To do this, we need more research on the best predictors of productivity of tenured faculty.

Matching Faculty and Tasks.   The scenario of "deadwood" faculty being punished as the goals of the university change is a very common story. For example, when a university increases its emphasis on research, we often find the established teaching faculty no longer rewarded. Rather than view these individuals as the wrong people for the job, a more appropriate question to ask might be: What role can such individuals play under the revised goal profile? Typically, these individuals can perform many tasks that are needed in the new research-dominated organization (e.g., course coordinators). We believe that matching the existing people to the appropriate tasks is an underutilized strategy in academia today.

Another favorable trend for faculty motivation in the future is the prospect of "new blood" in the faculty ranks. One way this is happening is through programs of early retirement for senior faculty, which permit an infusion of new junior faculty. Another factor operating here is the increased employment of non-tenure-track faculty, often practitioners from the fields in which students in a particular school are being trained. In business schools, for example, we are seeing more former executives in the faculty, engaging in teaching as a second career. As careers in the future become less linear and more protean or flexible, we will see more diversity of experience, in addition to more racial, ethnic, and international diversity, in the faculty ranks (Mirvis & Hall, 1994).

Faculty Development.   Related to the "training" activity under the "people" component of the Galbraith model, we would stress the longer-term issue of faculty development. As faculty recruiting has slowed at many schools, and as more faculty enter midcareer, with tenure, development of current faculty may be a more realistic strategy than selection of new faculty. Many schools have instituted faculty development workshops on a variety of topics, such as how to use certain teaching methods (e.g., case teaching, experiential teaching), how to deal with difficult students (e.g., cheating, sexual attraction/harassment), and how to get through various career and life crises (e.g., tenure, juggling work and home roles).

New faculty development roles can also give more focus on faculty learning. For example, Boston University's School of Management has created the position of master teacher, filled by a gifted educator, whose assignment is to share his or her craft skills with colleagues. Boston University has also used the position of associate dean for faculty development to give more focus to this area (although the scope of this role was wider than teaching). Publications such as the *Journal of Management Education* and books such as Schuster, Wheeler, and Associates' *Enhancing Faculty Careers* (1990) have also helped to establish a literature to facilitate this faculty learning process.

Another way in which the "people" side of the academic organization is changing is in the greater use of teams for teaching and learning. As has industry, academe has found that self-managed teams are a powerful way to get "closer to the customer" and make big improvements in quality and responsiveness. This team element in academic design shows up in two ways. First, learning about teams and learning team skills have become major components of the curriculum in many schools of business and management (e.g., Barnett, 1990). Even business schools such as Harvard, which have always had strong cultural norms of individual achievement and competition, have been moving toward a stress on cooperation and team learning.

The second way teams are showing up increasingly in the design of the academic organization is as a delivery mechanism. Increasingly, as we move toward more integrative, interdisciplinary courses, it becomes essential to employ interdepartmental teaching teams to deliver these new courses. These teams are used for the course design as well as the teaching process.

Doing more faculty work in teams means we need to find new ways to account for faculty workloads and to evaluate and reward teaching quality. For example, it usually takes more time to do a team-taught course, yet most university accounting systems give faculty *less* course credit for a team course rather than more. (For example, if two people jointly teach a course, it takes each one half as much time, so the workload accounting thinking goes.) We need to find creative ways to provide the benefits to students of multiple faculty perspectives in a course, within the current resource limitations.

Outplacement.   Another common scenario concerns the ostracized faculty member who wishes to leave the university but, without the administration's support, lacks the contacts for successful outplacement. This is often a situation in which both the administration and the faculty member desire outplacement but are unable to cooperate in the effort to bring it about. We believe that universities need to consider assistance programs that support rather than hinder such outplacement. Finally, Astin and others (1974) have even suggested the development of career (financial) insurance that provides faculty members with financial backup if they wish to attempt a midcareer change. Such financial assistance would last for an amount of time which the transaction would reasonably take.

Rewards

What rewards are available to motivate midcareer faculty toward excellence in teaching? Money, promotion, chair professorships, and the like will be less available in the future. What can be done? As with others in this volume, we would argue that this reduction of extrinsic reward may have the silver lining of forcing administrators to develop more of the potential intrinsic rewards in teaching. Three rewards conditions (also discussed in other chapters) seem necessary to the development of intrinsic motivation.

Maintaining Faculty-Perceived Control

A crucial determinant of intrinsic motivation to teach is perceived control over the task of teaching (see Chap. 4 in this volume). Consequently, we believe that academic institutions should make sure that teaching remains enjoyable and that faculty members are not led to be so concerned with other factors (extrinsic motivators) that the fun (intrinsic motivation) of teaching is reduced or eliminated (see Chap. 5 in this volume).

Establishing Clear Customer Feedback

Clear feedback on performance is another vastly underrated, intrinsic motivational method in most universities today. More feedback is coming now from students (on teaching), but much more feedback is needed from department chairpersons and deans on the quality of a person's research, teaching, and service to the school. Perhaps the biggest deficiency in customer feedback is feedback from employees.

Differentiated Roles

Still another option beyond the two conditions listed above, is to have a clearly differentiated reward system with a differentiated faculty. It is possible to have certain faculty whose primary role is teaching and others whose main responsibility is conducting research. By giving visibility and recognition to teaching faculty, status distinctions can be minimized. With this structure, people who love to teach are not diverted by the notion that the only route to rewards is a long publication list, and excellent teachers are rewarded directly for teaching: It is not just an activity that comes "out of the faculty's hides."

Information Systems

Several issues of information flow have strong effects on faculty teaching motivation. Let us examine inputs and outputs of teaching activity.

Information Inputs

On the input side, the process by which teaching assignments are made is critical. If a professor is told what he or she will teach, without consultation or discussion, two demotivators could be present: (1) There may be a poor match between the courses taught and the teacher's skills and interests, and (2) the nonparticipative process may reduce the instructor's commitment, perceived control, and intrinsic motivation in the courses taught. Some attempt to involve faculty in the course selection process, either by individual consultation or by group decision, is extremely useful in building faculty commitment to the course schedule. We argue strongly that faculty should be included in administrative decisions that directly affect them. This is particularly true as universities attempt to increase capacity for information processing through the increased use of budgets and other formal planning and control systems. For example, more management-by-objectives (MBO) performance-appraisal systems are now seen frequently in academic organizations. The more these systems are developed and implemented with high faculty involvement and participation, the more effective they can be as motivators.

Information Outputs

On the output side (Nadler & Tushman, 1991), feedback from information has a critical effect on the instructor's self-esteem and motivation. One type of feedback is the formal information from the course evaluation system. There is little question, however, that current course evaluation systems are extremely naive and unsophisticated in their design and underutilized in practice. The other type of feedback which is potent is the general reputation of the professor within the student culture. This may have more impact on the newer faculty, as more experienced instructors come to accept their reputations, perhaps with rationalizations if their ratings were low ("I'm very demanding in my courses"). Here, too, administrators have been slow in recognizing the motivational value of this type of information flow.

Information Technology

Another form of information system which is having great impact on teaching motivation and productivity is technology-based systems. Classroom-based electronic mail, bulletin boards, and pedagogical software make it much easier for a faculty member to communicate immediately with all members of a class. With such an information system, assignments can be made or quickly modified electronically, students can turn in their written work electronically, they can address questions to the instructor and get timely replies in writing, among the many applications of this technology. Classroom seating charts and student profiles (with pictures) can be made available to the instructor, via CD-ROM technology, along with a convenient spreadsheet program to track student performance data, compute running descriptive statistics on class performance, and maintain notes on class participation and individual student issues.

Not only does this information technology make for faster and more accurate communication between students and faculty and for easier and more accurate administrative data work by the faculty member, but the technology heightens the faculty's (and students') intrinsic rewards in the teaching process. Faculty who have used the CD-ROM technology for student profile data, for example, report that they learn student names much faster and find they can tailor comments in class to the background of particular students. The technology makes for a much more personal contact between the faculty member and the students.

Research on electronic information systems indicates that they are, in fact, powerful facilitators of learning (Sproull & Kiesler, 1992). By easing and promoting general inquiry (e.g., with general questions such as, "Does anyone know anything about topic x that they might share?"), they make the knowledge and experience of large numbers of people immediately available to an individual.

In a similar vein, Wheatley (1992) has shown how new structures such as these information systems can also facilitate relationships which, in turn, can promote learning. In this way, what appears to be chaos in the environment can be made more sensible through a self-directed discovery process. When a faculty member experiences students learning independently this way and getting "turned on" by their own insights, the result is strong intrinsic motivation all around.

Management School in the 1990s

Teaching is receiving greater attention in management schools in the mid-1990s than at any time in the past. Part of the reason for this attention has been the competitiveness between management schools which has been fueled by the increased popularity of surveys of the management community. Most notable have been the Business Week surveys. In 1988, 1990, and 1992, these surveys rated Northwestern's Kellogg Graduate School of Management the top business school in the country. Although many management scholars questioned the validity of these surveys, they have had a tremendous effect on business schools. Resources and student applications have flowed to the schools that did well in the surveys—showing the potency of the reward systems and information technology elements in the Galbraith design model.

What explains Kellogg's success?[2] Kellogg is a research-oriented business school with many leading research departments. Yet the overall motivation to teach is unusually high. Research is the primary criterion for the awarding of tenure. However, faculty seem highly motivated to teach well. Success in teaching makes faculty happy. In fact, the overwhelming mood of Kellogg is highly positive. Students, staff, and faculty like being at Kellogg, and for the faculty, liking Kellogg creates the desire to provide excellence in teaching. This excellence is not created by highly structured coordination of courses. In contrast, faculty are encouraged to create their courses as they see fit. We would argue that this freedom, coupled with an environment that encourages excellence, creates the intrinsic motivation to excel in the classroom.

Thus, in terms of the Galbraith model, there is a good fit between the five elements of the organization's design. The goals of the organization reflect a strong value for teaching. The people are faculty who are oriented toward teaching and students who show appreciation for good teaching. The information system provides excellent, fast feedback on teaching (e.g., ratings are publicly posted), and there are rewards (status, awards) for good teaching. The task of teaching provides autonomy in curriculum and course design so that faculty can integrate their research interests with their teaching. And the structure of the school is autonomous vis-à-vis the university, so that the dean and the faculty can effectively control their own faculty hiring and tenure process and can "fine-tune" the alignment among the five design elements.

In many business schools the changes have been extrinsic and sometimes more cosmetic than substantive. Our fear is that we have increased attention to the teaching function in the short run but have not made fundamental changes in the total system (i.e., the five Galbraith elements) which would empower the faculty through intrinsic motivation. Many faculty seem to have developed a greater concern for their own teacher evaluations than for being a good educator. At one prestigious school with an increased focus on teaching coupled with concern for grade inflation, a decision was made to limit the percentage of A's. One professor argued that these new events would lead to an increase in professors providing cookies and pizza on teacher evaluation days. Clearly, this is not the sign of an intrinsic desire to improve the educational product. What is needed is the hard work of changing all five elements of the organization design of a school to bring them into better alignment with a goal of excellent teaching.

As management schools head to the second half of the decade, short-term pressures will exist for excellence in teaching, whereas long-term pressures will exist for status through excellence in research. Making a static decision on which is more important is not the answer. Rather, successful management schools will develop the appropriate design to manage this dynamic tension. As we look back over the Galbraith framework, many specific issues have changed over the last ten years. However, the direction that this model provides for developing an integrated and contingent framework for motivating faculty remains useful.

Summary

We have attempted to show how the five elements of the Galbraith "star" model of organization design can be usefully applied to the analysis of the functioning of an academic unit (i.e., a business school) to help understand the level of faculty motivation to teach within that unit. In the example of the Harvard Business School, we have discussed how great clarity on the goal of good teaching, combined with a tight interconnection among tasks, structure, people, information technology, and reward systems, leads to an extremely high teaching motivation—and teaching excellence. In our other example, the Graduate School of Industrial Administration at Carnegie-Mellon University, we can see how faculty uncertainty about the value of teaching, coupled with a clearly high value for research, permeates the basic organization design and is associated with lower motivation to teach.

We also discussed the current process of curriculum redesign, which is being driven by environmental uncertainty regarding future student enrollments and thus financial resources. Organization design strategies that have been effective for business schools in the past—those that have reduced the need for information processing, such as creation of slack resources and creation of self-contained units—are now less available. It is now becoming more necessary to cope with environmental demands by increasing the capacity of the school to process information. The necessary strategies here are better vertical information systems and creation of lateral relations and other integrative devices. Two of the more frequent examples of these strategies in action are interdisciplinary teaching and curriculum development, more team teaching and learning. While these approaches are an adaptive response to the external environment, they are tasks that do not come naturally to very independent-minded university faculty. (In fact, a colleague once compared the process of leadership with faculty to "herding cats.")

Because creating these new alignments in the total system of the school organization is not a natural act for faculty, it is clear that before we can create better environments for student learning, we must find good ways to promote faculty learning. These changes in the overall system represented by the Galbraith model amount to a fundamental culture change for an academic organization. It is very clear that these faculty "cats" will not be herded—it is necessary to design systems in which they will make their own decisions to head in the direction of excellent teaching.

Notes

1. Other organization design models, such as the McKinsey 7S model or Wheatley's (1992) "new science" theory, or the Nadler and Tushman (1991) congruence model would also be relevant here, but we find Galbraith's to be especially relevant to universities, because of its explicit inclusion of reward systems and information technology, which are amenable to intervention.

2. One of the authors is on Kellogg's faculty, and the other author is a past faculty member and department chairperson at Kellogg. Thus the authors have the benefit of an inside perspective and the disadvantage of potential biases associated with inside information.

References

Astin, A. W., Comstock, C., Epperson, D. C., Greeley, A. M., Katz, S., & Kauffman, J. F. (1974). *Faculty development in a time of retrenchment.* New Rochelle, NY: Change Magazine.

Barnett, C. K. (1990). The Michigan global agenda for research and teaching in the 1990s. *Human Resource Management, 29,* 5–26.

Bazerman, M. H. (1994). *Judgment in managerial decision making* (3d ed.). New York: Wiley.

Bess, J. L. (1982). *University organization: A matrix analysis of the academic professions.* New York: Sciences Press.

Davis, S. M., & Lawrence, P. R. (1977). *Matrix.* Reading, MA: Addison-Wesley.

Duncan, R. B. (1971). Characteristics of organizational environments and perceived environmental uncertainty. *Administrative Science Quarterly, 17,* 313–327.

Galbraith, J. R. (1973). *Designing complex organizations.* Reading, MA: Addison-Wesley.

Galbraith, J. R. (1977). *Organization design.* Reading, MA: Addison-Wesley.

Galbraith, J. R. (1994). *Competing with flexible lateral organizations* (2d ed.). Reading, MA: Addison-Wesley.

Hall, D. T., & Bazerman, M. H. (1982). Organization design and faculty motivation to teach. In J. L. Bess (Ed.), *New directions for teaching and learning: Motivating professors to teach effectively* (No. 10, pp. 71–83). San Francisco: Jossey Bass.

Handy, C. (1994). *The age of unreason.* Boston: Harvard Business School Press.

March, J. G., & Olsen, J. P. (1976). *Ambiguity and choice in organizations.* Bergen, Norway: Universitetsforlaget.

Mirvis, P. H., & Hall, D. T. (1994). Psychological success and the boundaryless career. *Journal of Organizational Behavior, 15,* 365–380.

Nadler, D. A., & Tushman, M. (1991). A congruence model for diagnosing organizational behavior. In D. A. Kolb, I. M. Rubin, & J. S. Osland (Eds.), *The organizational behavior reader* (pp. 544–561). Englewood Cliffs, NJ: Prentice-Hall.

Neale, M. A., & Bazerman, M. H. (1991). *Cognition and rationality in negotiation.* New York: Free Press.

Parsons, T. (1960). *Structure and process in modern societies.* New York: Free Press.

Schuster, J. H., Wheeler, D. W., & Associates. (1990). *Enhancing faculty careers: Strategies for development and renewal.* San Francisco: Jossey-Bass.

Sproull, L., & Kiesler, S. (1992). *Connections: New ways of working in the networked organization.* Cambridge: MIT Press.

Weber, M. (1947). *The theory of social and economic organization.* (A. M. Henderson & T. Parsons, Trans. & Eds.). New York: Oxford University Press.

Wheatley, M. J. (1992). *Leadership and the new science: Learning about organization from an orderly universe.* San Francisco: Berrett-Koehler.

11

Technology and Teaching Motivation

DIANE M. DUNLAP

The rapid advance of technology is permanently changing the conditions of faculty teaching. The advance is on many fronts. The consequences of participating or not participating in that advance are not always obvious. Even for people familiar with developments, it is difficult to determine how and where a particular technology potentially affects faculty teaching conditions for the better, where it potentially does harm, and where today's promises will remain unfulfilled and will ultimately not affect faculty teaching at all. What is predictable is that faculty motivation to teach will be influenced in some way, just as all lives and all organizations are being influenced.

In a recent survey of participants in the Pew Higher Education Round-table discussions (1995) held at 160 higher education institutions across forty-four states, 84 percent of respondents named "more effective use of technology in teaching and learning" as the most important issue facing higher education today. Sixty-two percent named "becoming a more learn-ing-centered or student-centered institution" as the second most highly ranked issue, and 54 percent named addressing the "nature, balance, and rewards of faculty work" as the third highest issue of concern. Taken to-gether, these three concerns point directly at technology and faculty moti-vation to teach as the heart of the future in academe.

Questions about technology and faculty motivation emerge in the already complex organizational and societal context that surrounds university teaching. Teaching is only one role of the complex faculty position, and it is not always the role for which faculty are promoted or rewarded (Blackburn & Lawrence, 1995; Kerlin & Dunlap, 1993; Glover, 1993; Hammond et al., 1992). Faculty motivation to teach is influenced by the changing context of society and higher education; by how roles in the academic profession are enacted within particular higher education institutions; by arguments and subtleties in basic concepts and learning theories which frame each academic discipline and subdiscipline; by the characteristics, skills, and enthusiasm of each individual instructor; by the characteristics, skills, and enthusiasm of each individual student; by the governance, evaluations, and reward systems for teaching in each institution; and by resources available for faculty development and training in new areas (Dooris & Fairweather, 1994; Faseyitan & Hirschbuhl, 1992; Eble, 1983: Morrill and Spees, 1982).

There is also ambiguity about technology itself. The recent history of technological inventions applied to education is one of more promises made than fulfilled and of subtle and not so subtle negative consequences of using seemingly innocuous technological inventions in teaching (Norman, 1993). People have been promising that technology will revolutionize teaching at least since the mid-1960s (Green & Gilbert, 1995; American Chemical Society, 1995). Any teacher has ample historical evidence to be skeptical about a promise, for example, that a computer-based information search can be equal to or better than personal use of a research library; or that an on-line interactive exchange between students and teacher can replace teaching in a good university classroom; or that electronic texts can elicit the same responses as books. However, it would also be a waste of good teaching tools and Luddite shortsightedness to assume that all new technology has no useful application to the art of university teaching. Technology now shapes the contexts of teaching, and faculty cannot afford to ignore the consequences.

Deciding if a particular technology has a negative or positive influence on faculty motivation to teach depends on understanding at least four interrelated factors: (1) new developments in today's technology; (2) the personal theory we use to understand faculty motivation to teach; (3) the theory used to construct individual understanding of teaching and learning; and (4) how technology and faculty motivation to teach interact with specific departmental, university, and societal conditions that surround and influence teaching. This chapter addresses these factors.

Today's Technology: Computers, Communications, and Content

There are at least three separate but interrelated trends in technology which impact faculty teaching: developments in computer and multimedia hardware and software, expansion of electronic communication networks, and changes in how content is structured, recorded, and transferred.

Computers

Technological development in computer hardware has progressed from big, expensive machines that are accessible to only a few people to much smaller, much less expensive machines that are more accessible. These new personal computers have power equal to or greater than that of earlier computers and are more readily available through schools, libraries, and home purchase.

The new computers have the processing capacity to handle everything from the large data sets required for some types of research to specific teaching tasks previously done by hand or typewriter. Many faculty have already incorporated into their classroom teaching such computer uses as electronic mail, interactive video, on-line conferencing, local area computer nets, electronic "black" boards, and computerized overhead projection (Wilkins & Nantz, 1995; Denk et al., 1994; Kumar et al., 1994; Gresham, 1994; Kendall & Oaks, 1992; Stahl & Johnson, 1990). The availability of on-line courses, computer conferencing for instruction, and telecourses is increasing (Goodwin, Miklich, & Overall, 1993; Torres et al., 1992). Production of and experimentation with uses of interactive videodisk technology in the classroom is also increasing (Olson et al., 1992).

Several formerly separate technologies are merging. Audiographics, for example, is the merger of microcomputer graphics, telephone communications systems, and in-person teaching strategies which allows the teacher to create visual images that can be sent and stored on computers at remote sites. These images can be viewed without the teacher, or the teacher and remote-site participants can connect many remote sites simultaneously via telephone lines and modem and can interact in ways very similar to the traditional in-person classroom (Frederickson, 1990). Costs are similar to those of hiring a faculty teacher for a traditional course to teach at each site. Faculty attitudes toward the use of audiographic techniques have been reported as positive when sufficient training and technical support are provided.

Computer technology is also moving to compatible platforms in hardware and software, thus increasing ease of use. Teaching stations ("electronic classrooms") can be equipped with multiple forms of technology which faculty can learn to use as part of regular classroom presentations (Anderson & Cichochi, 1993; Janda, 1989). Electronic environments have been created for clinical teaching settings as well, including architectural design studios and teaching in the health professions (Billings et al., 1994; Learn, 1994; Haist et al., 1993; Demao & Saltzberg, 1992; Groesbeck, 1992; Money, 1992). Videoteleconferencing use is also increasing (Billings et al., 1994; Kendall & Oaks, 1992).

Software systems for word processing, data bases, spreadsheets, and graphic systems are becoming more sophisticated as well as easier to learn and use. Relatively easy-to-use "point and click" software is available for word processing, searching of on-line bibliographies, group work in classes, participation in electronic group discussions, participation in individual or group simulation activities, use of synchronous and asynchronous data exchange systems, and so forth.

The combined impact of these trends in hardware and software is that it is more likely that a faculty member can have ready access to technology for teaching which is easier and faster to use than in the past. University students are even more likely than faculty to have had similar or greater access to new technology prior to coming to the faculty member's course or program. However, the ways in which many of today's students learn, through passive viewing of television and through the nonreflective, split-second experiential responses of video games, are different. The intrusion of passive technology and high-speed imagery challenges the human capacity for reflective thinking. The combination also challenges the traditional one-way lecture mode as a successful learning modality.

Expansion of Communication Networks

Rapidly expanding electronic communication networks are also changing higher education (Lincoln, 1992). What started as a small astronomy research project tying together the separate computers of a few scientists has now become the "net"—what Stoll and others call an uncontrollable and ungovernable "communications juggernaut" (Stoll, 1995; Norman, 1993). There is a wide proliferation of electronic hookups linking individual computers, libraries, data bases, electronic mail systems (E-mail), and "home page" addresses of anyone who wants to communicate with others. Communications software packages and commercial access providers have created relatively simple ways for even the most technologically inept to have home-based access to on-line services of libraries, to leave E-mail messages for friends and colleagues around the world, and to join in like-interest group discussions that erase many of the historical effects of boundaries of time and physical distance.

All of these connecting devices have potential uses in teaching. Computer-based communications tools are powerful new ways to enter the many worlds of information and knowledge. Lincoln (1992) and others have argued that this relatively easy and private access to world knowledge is changing work and communication patterns for higher education faculty (Gresham, 1994; Farber, 1992; Mensching & Mensching, 1989). Many institutions have begun to issue free E-mail addresses to faculty and students and to provide free access to communication networks. Many faculty have begun to use E-mail and group E-mail (listservs) as an integral part of course-related communications and group projects outside the classroom. Whether the worldwide connection of people interested in common topics is called the "invisible college," the "virtual university," or "cyberspace," the change is immense and is viewed as a dramatic extension of collegial and teaching networks by most regular participants (Wolcott, 1993).

Promises for the future are even farther reaching. The technology for interactive simulations exists today and opens potential for teaching and learning that exceeds simple game playing (for one current fictional example of a potential future world changed by interactive simulation, see Neal Stephenson's *The Diamond Age,* 1995).

Content

Content is also changing, both in format and quantity, as well as in the ways in which we can learn it and teach it. Negroponte (1995), Norman (1993), and others have argued that the sheer mass of data available today has changed how we think about information. It has also changed how we access the data. Humans have been developing artifacts to extend our cognitive powers from the time of counting on our fingers and using sticks to kill (see also Zuboff, 1988). Alphabets and written language are examples of cognitive artifacts that allow humans to transfer knowledge from the brain to where it can be seen by those who can read. Pens, pencils, paper, and books help us organize, calculate, and remember more than we might remember on our own. Use of cognitive artifacts also frames our perceptions. Norman (1993) has argued persuasively that many mechanized artifacts, such as computers and electronic communication networks, are of a different order of cognition than the inventions of writing and reading. There is a difference between surface representation, where what you see is what you get, and internal representation, where some part of the information is internal to the cognitive artifact and is not visible to the user. An example is a hand-held calculator; the numbers and functions can be punched in and an answer will appear, but it is not obvious to the eye what the calculator did to select the answer. Computers and electronic communication nets are other examples of an internal representation. Norman argues that internal representations do not always assist humans in becoming more agile learners or teachers. He also argues that many forms of advanced technology affect more than our ability to work in and understand large amounts of information. They affect how we think and how we are motivated to learn. Learners and teachers can be helped, hindered, and manipulated by the way in which knowledge is represented in machine systems.

Another way in which content is changing is how we transfer knowledge to one another. In human history, we have moved from oral transmission of information and knowledge to the addition of written text. Now we have added the ability to transmit and record audio and video text as well. Negroponte (1995) argues that our ability to digitize and transmit all of these forms of transfer has created a "digitized" society in which some forms of cognition and some forms of learning are made more possible and others very difficult. A digitized set of data which cannot be seen or fully conceptualized is limited by a searcher's ability to identify and properly locate the specific data that he or she desires out of an untold number of bits of data (Shirato, 1992). One only needs to recall "browsing" around an identified book on a university library shelf to know that not all searchers know specifically what they seek. The inability to name in advance what one wants to know limits the ability to pull specific data bits out of an invisible digitized environment.

Technology and Faculty Motivation to Teach

So, how do all these changes in computer hardware and software, electronic communications networks, and expansion of content and content forms influence faculty motivation to teach? How we answer this question depends on our understanding of technological choices, and also depends on our beliefs about motivation and teaching and about individual, institutional, and societal capacity to help us make good technology choices for the future. This volume offers many theories of motivation to teach and many different ways of looking at the act of teaching and learning. I have chosen several of these theories to build the matrix in table 11.1. I use cells of this matrix to demonstrate how one might describe, categorize, and critique particular forms of technology and how they might influence faculty motivation to teach in a particular classroom. The reader can insert a more preferred motivation or teaching theory in the matrix. My goal is to demonstrate one schema for examination of today's technology and its potential effects on faculty motivation to teach, regardless of which motivation or teaching theory is used. The matrix, then, provides an opportunity to examine the interaction of teaching elements with motivational components in the context of the new and developing technologies noted earlier.

The vertical axis of the matrix is composed of elements of motivation theory. Walker and Quinn (1995) identified five elements that exist in all leading theories of human motivation. They argue that human motivation is seen at its highest when (1) people feel competent, (2) people have sufficient autonomy, (3) they set worthwhile goals, (4) they get appropriate and immediate feedback on progress, and (5) they are affirmed by others. Walker and Symons (Chap. 1 in this volume) argue that these five themes are interdependent, minimum elements of a self-renewing motivational system. I have added Csikszentmihalyi's (1990) optimal experience theory, or "flow," to this list (see also Chap. 5 in this volume). Csikszentmihalyi's optimal experience theory contains Walker and Quinn's minimal elements. Instead of focusing on what minimal conditions are needed for motivation to occur, however, Csikszentmihalyi examines what is needed for a "flow" experience to happen. I have added Csikszentmihalyi's term to the matrix in order to capture the transformative aspect of teaching which many describe as the ultimate goal of teaching and learning (Chap. 5 in this volume; Weimer & Lenze, 1991; Eble, 1983). These motivational elements (competence, autonomy, goals, feedback, affirmation, flow) constitute the vertical, motivational axis of the matrix.

The horizontal axis reflects the components of the teaching act, which can be organized in accordance with the sequence in which they are employed by faculty: for example, what happens for faculty to prepare for the teaching event, what happens in the event itself, what happens to evaluate the event, and what rewards or punishments follow from each stage. Teaching functions can also be sorted by instructional planning and objectives, decision making about appropriate knowledge and practices to be used, faculty attitudes about teaching the subject and the students, faculty understanding of presentation skills and setting a supportive context for motivated individual and group learning, and decisions about appropriate evaluation techniques and processes.

Teaching has also been described as the personal caring of the univer-

Table 11.1   The Interaction of Motivational Elements and Components in Teaching

		COMPONENTS OF TEACHING				
	Attitudes	Knowledge of Subject	Planning	Teaching Skills	Environment	Evaluation
MOTIVATIONAL ELEMENTS						
Competence	Cell 1					
Autonomy						
Goals						
Feedback						
Affirmation						
Flow				Cell 2		

sity community (Pelikan, 1992). From Newman's description of a university as a "place of teaching" to the Socratic method of teaching as common inquiry, teaching has been characterized as a powerful expression of community between teacher and students (Newman, 1852/1985). According to Csikszentmihalyi, the real task of a professor is to enable the learner to enjoy learning. Teaching may be about the transmission of information, but it is more deeply about the transmission of meaning.

Each part of the teaching act also includes the development of knowledge, skills, and conceptual understanding by the faculty member, which then must be transformed into teaching modalities that are successful in producing learning for students (Berlak & Berlak, 1981). The act of teaching includes complex purposive behaviors that have been historically under the primary control of the individual faculty member. Teaching is not a simple act, regardless of how it is examined.

Most discussions of teaching include attention to attitudes about self, students, and teaching; knowledge of subject matter; planning and preparation for the teaching event; appropriate use of varied teaching skills; ability to maintain a positive learning environment; and ongoing evaluation as an integral component of teaching (Guardo & Rivinius, 1995; Guskin, 1994b; Joyce & Weil, 1986; Romiszowski, 1984). These are the components of teaching which form the horizontal axis of the matrix.

Each cell of the matrix represents one point where technology can be discussed as it affects that element of motivation and that component of teaching. Two selected cells are used as illustrations.

Competence and Attitudes (Cell 1)

Having a sense of competence to learn or teach is directly related to having a positive attitude about using new technology in teaching. A reduced sense of competence in learning technology has been frequently reported by faculty who have little or no prior experience in the use of computers or other complex electronic technology (Mitra, 1994; Todd, 1993; Torres et al., 1992). Frequently reported sources of diminished competence are unfamiliarity with hardware and software, confusion about how to cope with print text and electronic text, philosophical or operational conflicts with the instructor's prior choices of instructional methods, and lack of knowledge about what is available and what is needed for an appropriate electronic teaching facility (Klem & Moran, 1992).

Terry and Geske (1990) described four distinct groups of faculty, in terms of prior experience with technology: "programmers," "processors," "pre-processors," and "non-users." The level of prior experience influences how the task of learning a new innovation will affect sense of competence. Programmers, for example, are heavy computer users who personalize their computer systems to meet their own individual needs and who have already used computing extensively in their teaching. These faculty are less likely to feel threatened by the introduction of another innovation. Processors, on the other hand, use the computer to process information, as a tool to replace a previous method, and as a tool in the classroom. They are likely to learn and use new processing methods readily, but they have more difficulty with other uses of computers or other technology in the classroom. Pre-processors see the value of computing and are motivated to learn more about it but may be stopped by not knowing how to proceed or by feeling embarrassed about displaying ignorance. Non-users, those who do not use the computer for teaching or other work, are the most likely to feel threatened when faced with a new electronic innovation.

Terry and Geske also reported that most faculty in their study adopted new computer uses that simply replaced past methods that were slower or more cumbersome. This makes sense in terms of prior experience influencing a sense of competence. When a new use can readily be seen to improve an old use, it is more likely that it will be adopted and less likely that a sense of competence will be threatened. Faseyitan and Hirschbuhl (1992) also found that the underlying technological orientation of the faculty member's discipline, a personal sense of computer self-efficacy, and basic computer utility beliefs and attitudes influence a sense of competence with technology.

Attitudes of resistance are likely to form when faculty feel incompetent or believe that they do not have a learning setting free from challenge to their authority or competence (Farber, 1992; Weimer, 1991; Eble, 1983). Many barriers to faculty learning and practicing a new electronic skill exist. First, learning how to use a new technique and learning to use it appropriately take time. Many faculty experience cost and time constraints in learning new computer skills (Denk et al., 1994; Dooris & Fairweather, 1994; Torres et al., 1992; Layne & Forester, 1991). Stahl and Johnson (1990) reported that it took faculty five times longer to prepare an illustrated lecture than a normal one.

Second, a faculty member typically teaching alone may have difficulty finding a safe, readily available forum for learning about using technology in teaching. The college or university classroom has traditionally been a private space where what occurs is between the faculty member and the students. The faculty member has had almost complete autonomous control over the processes, content, and assessment of the classroom experience. Peer exchange about teaching has not been widespread. In fact, in a recent issue of the *Teaching Professor* (July 1987), 42 percent of 1,680 faculty at fourteen institutions that represent the many types of higher education institutions in the United States reported that they had never discussed teaching with their colleagues. Faculty culture generally does not support peer exchange about teaching, in or out of the classroom.

Third, teachers have traditionally occupied a position of power in the classroom, where they are expected to know their subject and how to teach it. They are defined as the learned experts and are expected to do a good job of managing the classroom learning experience; in Weimer's words (1990), "if they do not . . . they have far to fall." Fear of failing at a task that one is supposed to understand at an expert level may be a barrier to learning to use new technology in teaching.

There are additional barriers to adoption of technology. Hammond et al. (1992) and others have documented other attitudinal, disciplinary, training, and budgetary barriers to the adoption of new technology in teaching (Lowther & Sullivan, 1994; Rakhonen et al., 1993; Todd, 1993; Layne & Forester, 1991). Problems with courseware, lack of institutional support, and lack of immediate access to a friendly colleague who is perceived as knowing about computing have also been reported (Herling, 1994; Mergendoller, 1994; Farber, 1992; Terry & Geske, 1990). In several studies, faculty have reported lack of recognition for teaching as a barrier to improvement (Burton, 1993).

Overcoming these barriers in order to increase a sense of competence with technology and to improve attitudes about technology in teaching can be as simple as providing sufficient information for faculty to make good decisions about appropriate tools for teaching. Personal ownership of a computer and access to training in which mistakes can be made and corrected without fear of ridicule are reported to make the biggest difference in overcoming faculty resistance to technology (Rowe, 1993; Hurd, 1986).

A sense of competence may also be diminished or threatened because of the expansion of knowledge available and because of the ability of many people to get new knowledge outside the university classroom. A faculty member who may have felt competent in command of subject matter and in habitual teaching patterns may feel that sense of competence threatened by the rapid expansion of knowledge that may not be included in traditional journals and books and by student insistence on new teaching forms.

The rapid rise of new forms of technology adds an additional peculiarity to faculty-perceived sense of competence in the classroom. With technology, it is more likely that the students entering the classroom will know as much or more about the new technology with which the faculty member is experimenting than the faculty member knows. Wide generational differences come into existence when the rate of innovation is fast, and when much of the innovation happens first at the level of games for children to play. Children of the 1980s have typically been exposed to computer technology in their schools and homes and at the local video arcade. When they come to a university classroom, they are likely to have had more extensive experiences with various types of technological innovation than the faculty teacher, who was born earlier. Word processing is a good example of this generational difference. When most faculty practicing today wrote their theses or dissertations, it was done with manual or electric typewriters. If the project was done before 1980 at a typical research university, it was also probably done with carbon paper and multiple paper copies on which "erasures" could not be made. Today's university students typically have widespread access to word processing for the first freshman papers. This change occurred in less than a decade.

When students know more than the teacher about a specific technology, or are likely to be more comfortable in using technology generally, their knowledge may cause the teacher to feel less competent. The faculty sense of having full command of the context in which one is teaching may be threatened. Recent research findings that students typically view technology more favorably than do faculty support this argument (Goodwin, Miklich, & Overall, 1993). Many faculty members are not used to a classroom setting in which some or all of the students may know more than the faculty member about an aspect of the classroom. This can lessen the likelihood that the teacher will try something new with which she or he has little or no prior experience. No one likes to fail at something in front of people who already know how to do the task successfully.

Faculty attitudes about teaching make the critical difference in whether experimentation with new technology reduces faculty sense of competence. If faculty believe that the teaching act is fundamentally an act of dialogic learning in which the teacher may be learning along with the students, faculty failure at a task, and faculty responses to failure, can be seen as one more teaching tool instead of a threatening failure (Ross, Cornett, & McCutcheon, 1992; Chickering & Gamson, 1991; Schön, 1983, 1987). "Failure" at a task becomes another way to teach learning. The faculty teacher can incorporate practice at a task into the teaching of the task and can maintain a high sense of competence as a learner. A sense of competence can be derived from expertise in content and teaching modalities, as well as from expertise in the use of new technology. Experimentation in teaching, and both success and failure at the experiment, can be used to model expertise as a learner as well as a teacher, content knower, and technology user.

Other methods to improve faculty attitudes about technology and to overcome initial ignorance and lack of experience with an innovation are the creation of safe places to learn before bringing the new learning into the classroom. Faculty forums, newsletters, training centers, library trainers, and individual peer consultants have all been reported as successful methods that reinforce faculty sense of competence and autonomy (Shirato, 1992; Karjala, 1991; Malena, 1990; Maynard, 1990; Mensching & Mensching, 1989). Faculty need to be certain that the technology will improve student learning, that they will know how to use the technology appropriately when the time arrives to use it, and that all necessary equipment will be available, ready to use, and in good working order (Spotts & Bowman, 1993). Nothing more quickly reduces faculty sense of competence and develops negative attitudes about technology in teaching than spending considerable time preparing a class experience that is dependent on a specific form of technology and then arriving at the teaching site and discovering that the needed equipment is not there or is the wrong kind or is broken, or, for some unexplainable reason, just won't work when it is needed. At that moment, even the most motivated faculty member will be grateful for old lecture notes that are known by heart and can be delivered by the time-tested technology of mental recall and verbal telling. A sense of competence in classroom and nonclassroom choices about technology is critical to the formation of positive faculty attitudes about new technology.

Flow and Teaching Skills (Cell 2)

Flow has been described as deep, spontaneous involvement with the task at hand, whereby the person experiences complete immersion with the experience (see Chap. 5 in this volume). Among the characteristics of an optimal flow experience are high intensity of interaction, a dynamic balance of challenge and skill, a sense of direct engagement, use of appropriate tools, and few distractions to the experience.

High Intensity of Interaction

The first characteristic of a flow experience is high intensity of interaction. This can be experienced in teaching as the intimacy that comes from close communion with students around a beloved subject. To date, most teaching experiences that achieve any form of high-intensity flow have been in person. Technology allows for asynchronous teaching but at the potential risk of reduced intimacy with students. Another aspect of high intensity is the experienced power of a personal exchange around a subject of common interest. That power often comes in the free form of emergent dialog that is impossible to duplicate in asynchronous form. Like good jazz or performance improvisation with an audience, you have to be there to experience the power and high intensity of free exchange.

Intimacy, power, and high intensity in teaching can cause withholding behaviors because the experience is too intense or feels too exposed to surrounding behavioral norms. Technology has the potential to liberate the teaching-learning exchange, thus increasing the experienced intimacy and power of the event. In Freirian terms, the control of the all-powerful teacher and the all-powerful knowledge institution can be reduced if the learned has freer access to knowledge without going through the teacher or the institution. Where learners are empowered to guide their own learning, they may lose some of the intimacy and power of personal exchange with the institution-affiliated faculty teacher, but they gain freedom and autonomy in the search for knowledge.

Technology also has the potential, in feminist pedagogical terms, of expanding and transforming the capacity of the individual student to "speak" in ways that do not require face-to-face confrontation (Maher & Tetreault, 1995). Current theorists argue that the differential power relationships embedded in the traditional faculty-student relationship reduce "voice" for both female faculty and students. In other words, if the arguments for equalizing power relationships in faculty-student interactions are persuasive, then indirect, on-line, anonymous contacts may have the potential for making faculty and students feel safe in challenging "authority."

High-intensity teaching requires sufficient time, space, autonomy, and commitment. It also requires a willingness on the part of the teacher to be fully immersed in the subjective experience. This may be initially more difficult when new tools and techniques must be mastered. However, those tools and techniques may also be the way to more flow experiences. For example, it may be difficult to learn how to use a large electronic data base as part of a lecture format, but once learned and practiced, the ability to move quickly to multiple displays of answers to impromptu student questions can be energizing.

Dynamic, Appropriate Balance of Challenge and Skills

A second aspect of a flow experience is the creation and sustaining of a dynamic and appropriate level of challenge, whereby skills and challenges are at equilibration. The fact that Csikszentmihalyi and his colleagues underscore the need for dynamic tension between challenge and skill takes us back to the earlier discussion of a sense of competence as essential to the formation of positive faculty attitudes toward the uses of technology in teaching. Faculty need multiple opportunities to experiment with technology in order to gain sufficient skills to try new teaching challenges.

What one faculty member considers appropriate balance will be different from what another teacher considers appropriate. Teaching has always had different meanings to different people. For some faculty, it is the heart and soul of their professional life. For others, it is a necessary nuisance that allows the core of professional life to focus on research or clinical practice. For some, it is primarily about the transfer of knowledge from the faculty to the student whereby lack of student learning is not necessarily the same thing as poor teaching. For others, teaching is an act of social-psychological empowerment which transfers knowledge but, more important, empowers the learner to use knowledge independent of the teacher. Faculty beliefs about teaching will influence perception of optimum challenge and will determine the motivation to develop new teaching skills.

Direct Engagement

A third aspect of flow experiences is a sense of direct engagement. Many faculty have been most motivated by in-person exchanges with motivated students. What happens to this sense of personal connection to the subject and to the students if the students are not present in the same place and at the same time as the instructor? What happens if there is little direct feedback to the teacher from the students about the learning experience?

Feedback on teaching is essential for a sense of direct engagement in a flow teaching experience. There are many potential sources of feedback to the faculty member: self, students, peers (in a home department, on campus in a different department, at a professional conference, on-line, and so on), and others (such as library staff, teaching center staff, other trainers, on-line forums and discussion groups, administrators, accreditation teams, other external evaluators).

The form of feedback most frequently used for faculty teaching is the faculty member's own assessment and that of the students at the end of a course. Although these traditional forms of feedback help with some aspects of teaching with technology, they may not provide the improvement experience needed when attempts to use technology are not successful (e.g., the teacher tries a new technology and it fails, the teacher knows it failed, and the student evaluations report failure). If these are the only forms of feedback used, the teacher may not be encouraged to try new things in the classroom or to continue on with a failed experiment until it succeeds. Feedback through working with colleagues can be very important in helping the faculty teacher overcome the limitations of student evaluations and in helping expand teacher understanding of alternative teaching strategies (Wahlstrom & Selfe, 1994; Terry & Geske, 1990). It may be difficult for the individual faculty member to find a supportive forum for discussion of successes and failures, but where it is found, results are quite positive (Cochran-Smith, 1991). It is ironic that one of the best forms of useful feedback on technology and teaching today is through technology itself—through national electronic linking of faculty who exchange experiences and teaching techniques using new technologies (Selby et al., 1994).

A perceived loss of active involvement with students can be a consequence of the use of technology for teaching (Billings et al., 1994; Newbold, 1993; Kendall & Oaks, 1992). Many faculty value the personal interactions between themselves and students; if faculty believe that this interaction will be lessened or significantly changed by the use of distance options in technology, they will be less likely to try them. If they receive negative feedback from students about changes in interaction patterns, they may be less likely to continue to use distance techniques.

Many faculty have also historically resisted learning about innovations from library staff, teaching center staff, other off-campus trainers, administrators, accreditation team members, and other external evaluators (Shirato, 1992; Weimer, 1990). Although there are examples of successful training interventions with library staff, graduate teaching assistants, teaching teams, and so forth, the primary mode of university teaching has continued to be one faculty person working alone on each course (Fifield & Peifer, 1994; Wetzel, 1993; Groesbeck, 1992; Maynard, 1990). The source of much of the resistance is a conceptualization by the faculty teacher that the teaching act is a solo event and that other staff or students do not have contributions to make to that event. Feedback and a sense of direct engagement may need to come from other people who also engage in or support the teaching-learning interaction in a future where faculty and students may not have as much direct contact.

Recent research findings in many disciplines indicate that direct student contact can be reduced and learning outcomes simultaneously improved when technology is used appropriately to expand student learning (Mitchell, 1995; Scheponik, 1995; Reiger & Rees, 1993; Malinconico, 1992; Wright & Lickorish, 1989). Learning in community is likely to continue as a natural human behavior; community will be formed in ways that extend beyond the classroom, as they always have (Oldenburg, 1989). With the advent of such technology as electronic mail, a supportive learning community of power and intimacy can form even between strangers who only know one another by their anonymous interactions around a subject of common interest. Technology does not always decrease a sense of direct engagement with others.

Appropriate Tools

The fourth aspect of a flow teaching experience is use of appropriate tools that aid but do not distract from teaching. There is no question that more tools exist for today's teacher through advances in technology; there is also little question that these tools, with insufficient support or practice in learning how to use them, can distract from teaching.

Even with low faculty skills in technology, students with access to networked personal computers can engage in independent learning and accumulation of knowledge and data. They can work with peer or college groups that may or may not be part of the teacher's class. They can identify simulations and case studies that may not have been identified by the teacher, and they can use their independent knowledge to build an understanding of skills and concepts in the subject area which is not necessarily constrained or guided by the understanding and requirements of the teacher. These are appropriate tools for learning but may be distracting or confusing or threatening to a teacher who does not have and utilize the same skills.

Books are a familiar technology. Gutenberg's invention of the printing press was made in a world where few people knew how to read and fewer wrote. Neither books nor literacy were realities in the daily lives of most people. Now, both books and literacy are the very stuff of campus life. Computers and electronic communications may be less familiar to many faculty, but they are increasingly the stuff of society life. They are, therefore, increasingly the stuff of classroom life and demand understanding and skill for appropriate utilization.

Absence of Distractions

The fifth and final aspect of a flow teaching experience is the absence of distractions or disruptions. Again, that requires faculty to be familiar and comfortable with the use of technology in teaching in order to preclude personal distraction from interfering with the teaching experience.

Any university teacher is familiar with the kinds of distractions or disruptions which can come from student lack of comprehension or inability to concentrate; from inadequate or nonfunctional equipment or classroom space; from insufficient departmental or institutional support for uses of technology; and from inconvenient hours, too long hours, too large classes, too short a class time, lack of job security, inadequate pay, disconnected reward schemas, and so on. Although distractions are not limited to technology, neither are they helped by problems with technology in teaching. In today's busy and fragmented society, the greatest teaching skill may be to create and hold a teaching-learning space that is free from distraction or disruption of any kind.

Conclusions

As a result of technology, neither universities nor teaching will be the same. Technology is not a neutral agent in teaching, as it is not neutral in shaping the future of society. It would be easy to view today's new technology as just more toys in a series of instructional toys and gadgets that promise more than they deliver. That would be a critical error (Gilbert, 1995). What is different about technology today is that it enables a rapidly expanding global network of learners/users to seek and use knowledge outside the confines of geographic space or institutional sponsorship.

In two persuasive *Change* articles, Alan Guskin (1994a, 1994b) argued that colleges and universities today face their most significant crisis in more than forty years. He documents the "double-edged sword of costs," a situation in which the expenses of many institutions are too high for available revenues and costs are growing beyond the capability or willingness of the pubic to pay for access to university knowledge and credentials. Guskin names public demand for reduction of costs, documentation of learning outcomes, and the use of new information technologies as the three major forces that will alter colleges and universities whether we like it or not. He concludes that faculty must change how they work, how they conceptualize teaching, and how they measure and accommodate student learning. This change must occur because the circumstances of university teaching have changed and because economic and political circumstances are also pressuring institutions to change.

Changes in society potentially restrict diverse values and social structures to a mechanistic and experiential orientation. Much current writing about technology in teaching, for instance, is heavily influenced by behavioralist information-processing motivation theory—to the exclusion of intrinsic theories that allow for inner motivation of teacher or students, for commitment and autonomous learning modalities, or for understanding of flow experiences. An expanded understanding of extrinsic and intrinsic motivation theory is an important prerequisite for predicting high-quality output in all organizations (Handy, 1995). It is also an important prerequisite for expanding our understanding of learnable intelligence (Perkins, 1995).

What exists today is not always a good predictor of tomorrow. Hammer and Champy (1993) have argued that the fundamental error that most of us commit when we look at technology is to view it through the lens of existing processes. This applies to teaching in higher education as well. Even if faculty choose not to change, the context that surrounds university teaching is changing, as are the students who come to the teaching experience. Technology, in all its forms, permeates our society so completely that university teaching cannot escape its consequences.

The real power of the advance of technology is not just that technology can make old teaching techniques work better but that it enables individuals and organizations to break old rules and create new ways of working. Classrooms, laboratories, seminars, libraries, and all other locations of learning exist in a new environment that offers both positive and negative possibilities for higher education teaching. Boundaries are more permeable: Classrooms, subjects to be taught and learned, and teachers and learners themselves now exist in a much more real global classroom.

Faculty cannot ignore the advance of technology. Faculty form beliefs from experiences with colleagues, students, administrators, and university rules and norms, and these beliefs affect motivation to teach with new technology (Blackburn & Lawrence, 1995). Technology can improve or sustain faculty motivation to teach when appropriately applied. In the words of one gifted teacher, "the human teacher will not be replaced by technology, but the human teacher may be replaced by the human teacher who knows how to use technology" (Barna, 1995). An openness to technology and to new learning by the teacher can provide the role model needed by students for tomorrow's technological society and can also lead to the reinvigoration of one's own intellectual life.

References

American Chemical Society. (1995). Information: How the revolution is transforming chemistry. Special issue of *Chemical and Engineering News, 73*(3).

Anderson, J. A., & Cichochi, R. R. (1993, January). Educational technology equipped classrooms: Re-design based on faculty feedback. Paper given at the Annual Convention of the Association for Educational Communication and Technology, New Orleans.

Barna, E. (1995). Languages and technology at Middlebury. *Liberal Education, 81*(3), 16–21.

Berlak, A., & Berlak, H. (1981). *Dilemmas of schooling: Teaching and social change.* London: Methuen.

Billings, D., et al. (1994). Faculty perceptions of teaching on television: One school's experience. *Journal of Professional Nursing, 10*(5), 307–312.

Blackburn, R. T., & Lawrence, J. H. (1995). *Faculty at work: Motivation, expectation, satisfaction.* Baltimore: Johns Hopkins University Press.

Burton, V. (1993). Teaching historians with databases. *History Microcomputer Review, 9*(1), 9–17.

Chickering, A. W., & Gamson, Z. (1991). *Seven principles for good practices in undergraduate education.* New Directions in Teaching and Learning, 47. San Francisco: Jossey-Bass.

Cochran-Smith, M. (1991). Learning to teach against the grain. *Harvard Educational Review, 61*(3), 279–310.

Csikszentmihalyi, M. (1990). *Flow: The psychology of optimal experiences.* New York: Harper & Row.

Demao, J., & Saltzberg, S. (1992). Making the transition from the traditional to the electronic design studio. *Interactive Learning International, 8*(4), 297–310.

Denk, J., et al. (1994). Not yet comfortable in the classroom: A study of academic computing at three land-grant universities. *Journal of Educational Technology Systems, 22*(1), 39–55.

Dooris, M. J., & Fairweather, J. S. (1994). Structure and culture in faculty work: Implications for technology transfer. *Review of Higher Education, 17*(2), 161–177.

Eble, K. (1983). *The aims of college teaching.* San Francisco: Jossey-Bass.

Farber, E. I. (1992). Teachers as learners: The application of BI. In L. Shirato (Ed.), *Working with faculty in the new electronic library.* Ann Arbor: Pierian Press.

Faseyitan, S. O., & Hirschbuhl, J. (1992). Computers in university instruction: What are the significant variables that influence adoption? *Interactive Learning International, 8*(3), 185–194.

Fifield, S., & Peifer, R. (1994). Enhancing lecture presentations in introductory biology with computer-based multimedia. *Journal of College Science Teaching, 23*(4), 235–239.

Frederickson, S. (1990, March). Audiographics for distance education: An alternative technology. Paper presented at the annual conference of the Alaska Association for Computers in Education, Juneau.

Gilbert, S. W. (1995). The technology "revolution." *Change, 27*(2), 6–7.

Glover, H. (1993). The tenure survey: Expectations for research, technology, and service. *Journal of Education for Business, 69*(2), 89–93.

Goodwin, B. N., Miklich, B. A., & Overall, J. V. (1993). Perceptions and attitudes of faculty and students in two distance learning modes of delivery: Online computer and telecourses. Paper presented at the Symposium for the Marketing of Higher Education, Orlando.

Green, K. C., & Eastman, S. (1994). *Campus computing 1993: The USC national survey of desktop computing in higher education.* Los Angeles: University of Southern California Press.

Green, K. C., & Gilbert, S. W. (1995). Great expectations: Content, communications, productivity, and the role of information technology in higher education. *Change, 27*(2), 8–18.

Gresham, J. L. (1994). From invisible college to cyberspace college: Computer conferencing and the transformation of informal scholarly communications networks. *Interpersonal Computing and Technology Journal, 2*(4), 37–52.

Groesbeck, M. A. (1992). Integrating electronic information sources into an undergraduate course on immunology: Successful librarian-faculty cooperation. In L. Shirato (Ed.), *Working with faculty in the new electronic library.* Ann Arbor: Pierian Press.

Guardo, C. J., & Rivinius, S. (1995). Save before closing: Bringing technology to the liberal arts. *Liberal Education, 81*(3), 22–27.

Guskin, A. E. (1994a). Reducing student costs and enhancing student learning: The university challenge of the 1990s, Part I, Restructuring the administration. *Change, 26*(4), 23–29.

Guskin, A. E. (1994b). Reducing student costs and enhancing student learning, Part II, Restructuring the role of faculty. *Change, 26*(5), 16–25.

Haist, S. A., et al. (1993). Teaching in a physical diagnosis course: Identifying faculty characteristics and motivational factors. *Teaching and Learning in Medicine, 5*(2), 72–76.

Hammer, M., & Champy, J. (1993). *Reengineering the corporation.* New York: Harper-Collins.

Hammond, N., et al. (1992). Blocks to the effective use of information technology in higher education. *Computers and Education, 18*(1–3), 155–162.

Handy, C. (1995). Trust and the virtual organization. *Harvard Business Review, 73*(3), 40–48.

Harasim, L., Hiltz, R., Teles, L., & Turoff, M. (1995). *Learning networks: A field guide to teaching and learning online.* Cambridge: MIT Press.

Herling, T. J. (1994). Resistance to the adoption of computer communication technology by communication faculty. Paper presented at the annual meeting of the Association for Education in Journalism and Mass Communication, Atlanta.

Hurd, S. J. (1986). Survey of computer use in economics and business studies. *Economics, 22*(95), 120–127.

Janda, K. (1989, August 31–September 3). Teaching American government in an electronic classroom. Paper presented at the annual meeting of the American Political Science Association, Atlanta.

Joyce, B., & Weil, M. (1986). *Models of teaching.* Englewood Cliffs, NJ: Prentice-Hall.

Karjala, H. E. (1991). Putting research to work in the music classroom. *Music Education Journal, 77*(9), 44–49.

Kendall, J. R., & Oaks, M. (1992). Evaluation of perceived teaching effectiveness: Course delivery via interactive video technology versus traditional classroom methods. *Journal of Continuing Higher Education, 40*(3), 2–12.

Kerlin, S. P., & Dunlap, D. M. (1993). For richer, for poorer: Faculty morale in periods of austerity and retrenchment. *Journal of Higher Education, 64*(3), 346–377.

Klem, E., & Moran, C. (1992). Teachers in a strange LANd: Learning to teach in a networked writing classroom. *Computers and Composition, 9*(3), 5–22.

Kubey, R., & Csikszentmihalyi, M. (1990). *Television and the quality of life: How viewing shapes everyday experience.* Hillsdale, NJ: Erlbaum.

Kulik, C.-L. C., & Kulik, J. A. (1991). Effectiveness of computer-based instruction: An updated analysis. *Computers in Human Behavior, 7*(1–2), 75–94.

Kumar, D. D., et al. (1994, March 26–29). A survey of interactive video use in science teacher education in Ohio. Paper presented at the annual meeting of the National Association for Research in Science Teaching, Anaheim.

Landow, G. (Ed.). (1994). *Hyper/text/theory.* Baltimore: Johns Hopkins University Press.

Laurillard, D. (1993). *Rethinking university teaching: A framework for the effective use of educational technology.* London: Routledge.

Layne, R. G., & Forester, G. (1991, May 19–22). The cutting edge: Sharpening faculty skills in a changing world. Speech presented at the National Institute for Staff and Organizational Development Conference on Teaching Excellence, Austin, TX.

Learn, C. D. (1994). Distance learning: Issues and applications for nontraditional programs. *American Journal of Pharmaceutical Education, 58*(4), 406–410.

Lincoln, Y. S. (1992, October 28–November 1). Virtual community and invisible colleges: Alterations in faculty scholarly networks and professional self-image. Paper presented at the annual meeting of the Association for the Study of Higher Education, Minneapolis.

Lowther, D. L., & Sullivan, H. J. (1994). Teacher and technologist beliefs about educational technology. *Educational Technology Research and Development, 42*(4), 73–87.

Maher, F. A., & Tetreault, M. T. (1995). *The feminist classroom: An inside look at how professors and students are transforming higher education for a diverse society.* New York: Basic Books.

Malena, R. F. (Ed.). (1990). *Vision '90: The Maricopa Community College Journal of Teaching and Learning, 2*(1–2), 1–73.

Malinconico, S. M. (1992). What librarians need to know to survive in an age of technology. *Journal of Education for Library and Information Science, 33*(3), 226–240.

Maynard, J. E. (1990). A case study of faculty attitudes toward library instruction: The Citadel experience. *Reference Science Review, 18*(2), 67–76.

McKeachie, W. J. (1990). Research on college teaching: The historical background. *Journal of Educational Psychology, 82*(2), 189–200.

Mensching, G. E., & Mensching, T. B. (Eds.). (1989). *Coping with information illiteracy: Bibliographic instruction for the information age.* Ann Arbor, MI: Pierian Press.

Mergendoller, J. R. (1994). *The Utah educational technology initiative: Evaluation update.* Salt Lake City: Utah Educational Technology Initiative. Available through ERIC, ED370534.

Mitchell, W. (1995). *City of bits: Space, place, and the infobahn.* Cambridge: MIT Press.

Mitra, A. (1994). "Instructor-Effect" in determining effectiveness and attitude towards technology-assisted teaching: Report on a case study. *Journal of Instruction Delivery Systems, 8*(3), 15–21.

Money, S. M. (1992). What is teaching effectiveness? A survey of student and teacher perceptions of teacher effectiveness. Technical report available through ERIC, ED351056.

Morrill, P. H., & Spees, E. R. (1982). *The academic profession: Teaching in higher education.* New York: Human Sciences Press.

Negroponte, N. (1995). *Being digital.* Cambridge: MIT Press.

Newbold, W. (1993, April 1–3). Strategies for computer-based distance writing courses. Paper presented at the Conference on College Composition and Communication, San Diego. Available through ERIC, ED377476.

Newman, J. H., Cardinal. (1985). *The idea of a university defined and illustrated.* (Edited with introduction and notes by I. T. Ken). Oxford: Clarendon. (Original work published 1852).

Norman, D. A. (1993). *Things that make us smart: Defending human attributes in the age of the machine.* Reading, MA: Addison-Wesley.

Oldenburg, R. (1989). *The great good place.* New York: Paragon House.

Olson, M. A., Muyshens, L., & Busby, N. C. (1992). Attitudes toward videodisc technology in the Dallas County Community College District. Technical report available through ERIC, ED354953.

Pascarella, E. T., & Terenzini, P. T. (1991). *How college affects students: Findings and insights from twenty years of research.* San Francisco: Jossey-Bass.

Pelikan, J. (1992). *The idea of the university: A reexamination.* New Haven: Yale University Press.

Perkins, D. (1995). *Outsmarting IQ: The energizing science of learnable intelligence.* New York: Simon & Schuster.

Perry, R. P. (1991). Perceived control in college students: Implications for instruction in higher education. In J. C. Smart (Ed.), *Higher education: Handbook of theory and research* (Vol. 7, pp. 1–56). New York: Agathon Press.

The Pew Higher Education Roundtable Survey. (1995). Published in The Landscape, *Change, 27*(4), 41–44.

Rakhonen, C. J., McFerron, J. R., Bowher, L. H., Lynch, D. M., & Krusec, M. (1993). Communication among music faculty, department chairs, and deans in American higher education. Technical report available through ERIC, ED366268.

Reiger, R. C., & Rees, R. T. (1993). Teachers and motivation: A demographic study. *Technology and Higher Education, 113*(3), 482–483.

Romiszowski, A. J. (1984). *Producing instructional systems: Lesson planning for individualized and group learning activities.* New York: Kogen Page.

Ross, W., Cornett, J. W., & McCutcheon, G. (1992). Teacher personal theorizing and research on curriculum and teaching. In W. Ross, J. W. Cornett, & G. McCutcheon (Eds.), *Teacher personal theorizing: Connecting curriculum practice, theory, and research.* Albany: State University of New York Press.

Rowe, H. A. H. (Ed.). (1993). *Learning with personal computers: Issue, observations, and perspectives.* Victoria: Australian Council for Educational Research.

Scheponik, P. (1995, February/March). Interactive multimedia: Challenge, change, and choice. *Community College Journal*, 20–25.

Schön, D. A. (1983). *The reflective practitioner.* San Francisco: Jossey-Bass.

Schön, D. A. (1987). *Educating the reflective practitioner.* San Francisco: Jossey-Bass.

Selby, L., et al. (1994). Teachers' perceptions of learning with information technology in mathematics and science education: A report on Project Prometheus. *Journal of Computing in Teacher Education*, 10(3), 24–30.

Shirato, L. (Ed.). (1992). *Working with faculty in the new electronic library.* Ann Arbor: Pierian Press.

Spotts, T. H., & Bowman, M. (1993). Increasing faculty use of instructional technology: Barriers and incentives. *Educational Media International*, 30(4), 199–204.

Stahl, W. A., & Johnson, B. (1990). Evaluating the electronic blackboard. Technical paper written for the Canadian International Development Agency project "A Design Model for a Computerizing University."

Stephenson, N. (1995). *The diamond age.* New York: Bantam.

Stoll, C. (1995). *Silicon snake oil.* New York: Doubleday.

Teaching Professor. (1987). 1(7), 2–3.

Terry, J. L., & Geske, J. (1990, August 1–4). A case study for evaluating the diffusion of computing technology in teaching undergraduates by a faculty in journalism and mass communications program. Paper presented at the annual meeting of the Association for Education in Journalism and Mass Communication, Minneapolis.

Todd, N. I. (1993, January 13–17). Faculty concerns as gateways to teacher competency with computer technologies. Paper presented at the convention of the Association for Educational Communications and Technology, New Orleans.

Torres, R., et al. (1992). Examining computer conferencing as a technique for enhancing personnel development activities. Final report for year two of a three-year interdisciplinary study. Available through Ohio State University.

Wahlstrom, B. J., & Selfe, C. L. (1994). A view from the bridge: English departments piloting among the shoals of computer use. *ADE Bulletin*, 109, 35–45.

Walker, C. J., & Quinn, J. (1995). Supporting instructional vitality: Some practical implications of theory and research. In R. Menges and M. Weimer (Eds.), *Colleges and the climate for teaching.* San Francisco: Jossey-Bass.

Weimer, M. (1990). *Improving college teaching: Strategies for developing instruction effectiveness.* San Francisco: Jossey-Bass.

Weimer, M., & Lenze, L. F. (1991). Instructional interventions: A review of the literature on efforts to improve instruction. In J. C. Smart (Ed.), *Higher education: Handbook of theory and research* (Vol. 7). New York: Agathon Press.

Wetzel, K. (1993). Teacher educators' uses of computers in teaching. *Journal of Technology and Teacher Education*, 1(4), 335–352.

Wilkins, M. L., & Nantz, K. (1995). Faculty use of electronic communications before and after a LAN installation: A three-year analysis. *Journal of End User Computing*, 7(1), 4–11.

Wolcott, L. L. (1993). Faculty planning for distance teaching. *American Journal of Distance Education*, 7(1), 26–36.

Wright, P., & Lickorish, A. (1989). The influence of discourse structure on display and navigation in hypertexts. In N. Williams & P. Holt (Eds.), *Computers and writing: Models and tools.* Norwood, NJ: Ablex Publishing.

Zuboff, S. (1988). *In the age of the smart machine: The future of work and power.* New York: Basic Books.

12 Leadership and Faculty Motivation

J. G. HUNT AND ARJA ROPO

Very early in this book, motivation was defined as the conditions and processes that activate, direct, and sustain behavior. For us, this definition is appropriate both because of the organizational emphasis in Part Four and because it captures our broad-ranging conception of motivation, which we label "systems motivation." As we show in this chapter, our systems motivation approach embeds leadership and teaching within a wide range of individual and organizational conditions, which we term "capabilities" (and define later). Our approach also emphasizes the process that operates across time as these capabilities are played out in a specific and increasingly significant motivational context.

The motivational context that we use to illustrate our approach and its application is that of the initiation and development of a new and very different curriculum concentration in a master's program in a school of business administration. That new thrust focuses on

- interdependent efforts among several administrators and faculty members;

The authors wish to acknowledge various kinds of assistance from their colleagues Alex Stewart and Carlton Whitehead and to thank Robert Hooijberg at Rutgers University for his helpful comments.

- individual and organizational leadership and numerous other motivational aspects that go beyond those for teaching single courses;
- utilization of these aspects as motivational "action levers" to facilitate the concentration's developmental process across several semesters; and
- emphasis on teaching, which is influenced by development of the concentration and which itself influences the concentration's development.

It is evident from the above that our motivational context lodges motivation to teach within the broader question of how the motivation for a new curriculum concentration can be activated, directed, and maintained across time and among numerous faculty and administrators. Always important, this question has become even more crucial in today's "downsizing" climate, in which, as with many other kinds of organizations, an increasing number of colleges and universities are being asked to do more with less. That is, they are being asked to launch and sustain new initiatives at the same time that many traditional rewards such as increased pay are less available. Furthermore, there are many cases in which institutional reward systems are tilted toward research and publication with less weight given to curriculum initiatives, even as these initiatives are assuming increasing importance. Such a "more with less" setting is nicely captured in an industrial context by Stewart's (1989) term "running hot," and it is in such a running hot context that we examine our systems motivation approach. First, however, we selectively review literature linking motivation and various aspects of leadership to serve as a takeoff point for our treatment, which involves an extended scenario. Before we discuss the unfolding of the scenario, it is initially important to note that the concentration involved development of new courses or transformation of previous courses. Second, the concentration also made possible a course infrastructure not otherwise available (e.g., faculty and student tours of outstanding entrepreneurial organizations and lunch with their founders). Finally, the concentration and courses received much more than usual external attention.

As we shall see, characteristics such as these had a substantial impact on course teaching motivation. In turn, the perceived initial quality of the course teaching (as influenced by student teaching evaluations, among other things) influenced the concentration's development and later teaching motivation.

Review of the Literature

In preparing this review, we judged five aspects of the leadership and motivational literature to be particularly relevant for our systems motivation emphasis: (1) exchange; (2) transformational; (3) relational; (4) systems embeddedness; and (5) process.

Exchange Aspects

Leadership exchange theory focuses on leader-follower exchange relationships (see Bass, 1990; Yukl, 1994). For example, a department head praises a faculty member for doing a good job chairing a committee. In exchange, the faculty member reciprocates with good committee work in the future, the Chair reciprocates, and so forth.

These exchanges take numerous forms. In one form the leader provides various social rewards (e.g., praise) or punishments in exchange for or contingent upon job performance (Podsakoff, Todor, Grover, & Huber, 1984). This perspective is related to the behavior modification motivational approach discussed in Chapter 6 by Nord. In the related path-goal leadership theory (Evans, 1970; Georgopolis, Mahoney, & Jones, 1957; House, 1971), the leader clarifies follower paths to desired rewards, and the followers reciprocate by increased motivation to perform. In the leader-member exchange theory (e.g., Graen & Cashman, 1975), across time, leaders classify followers into in-groups and out-groups and treat in-group members more favorably; in exchange, followers are motivated to do numerous things to enhance the leader's role. Jacobs (1970) uses a somewhat similar exchange approach, in which followers provide leaders with extra status and esteem in exchange for the leader's unique contribution to their goals. Finally, Hollander (e.g., Hollander, 1978; Hollander & Offerman, 1992) perhaps has gone the furthest in emphasizing such exchange relationships in work, over many years, stressing the extreme importance of the follower in truly understanding leadership.

Transformational Aspects

The depth and nature of the leader-follower exchange relationship have been extended in transformational and related charismatic leadership approaches (e.g., Bass, 1990; Bryman, 1992; Burns, 1978; Hollander & Offerman, 1992; House, 1977; House & Shamir, 1993; Sashkin & Rosenbach, 1993). In these approaches, leaders use traditional, transactional leadership, such as performance (stability-oriented)–contingent rewards and punishments, and followers reciprocate through acceptable performance.

To encourage followers to exchange performance beyond expectations or exert extraordinary effort, leaders engage in transformational leadership, emphasizing such behavior as visionary and charismatic leadership, intellectual stimulation, and individualized consideration.

Some, such as House and Shamir (1993) and Shamir, House, and Arthur (1993), have argued that such exchanges can involve transformation of follower needs, values, preferences, and aspirations from individual self-interests to collective interests. These leaders go far beyond the call of duty and focus on a deeply felt sense of mission. Accompanying such transformation is the imparting or strengthening of follower self-efficacy, emphasized throughout this book as important in its own right. Such leadership can also transform organizations or subunits by infusing ideological values and moral purpose, as demonstrated in many small religion-oriented institutions.

Relational Aspects

Closely related to the literature on exchange is the relational literature, which moves beyond leader-subordinate exchanges to relations with individuals and groups wherever they are located. This diverse literature involves work ranging from sociometric and social network approaches (cf. Bass, 1990; Coglisher & Schriesheim, 1994) to extensions of traditional exchange approaches (e.g., Graen & Uhl-Bein, 1993), multidimensional scaling thrusts (e.g., Salancik, Calder, Rowland, Leblebici, & Conway, 1975). Lateral, as well as vertical, one-way and reciprocal relations are emphasized (cf. Osborn, Hunt, & Jauch, 1980; Sayles, 1965). Especially important for our purposes is representational leadership, which involves networking and related notions throughout the organization (e.g., Baliga & Hunt, 1988). Ropo (1989) also has argued that representational leadership helps tie together transactional and transformational leadership behaviors.

Systems Embeddedness and Process Aspects

The previous notions lead quite naturally to systems of organizational embeddedness and process aspects of leadership and motivation. Systems embeddedness emphasizes relational aspects as a part of a total organization system (e.g., Hunt, 1991; Hunt & Ropo, 1995; Likert, 1967; Melcher, 1977; Osborn, Hunt, & Jauch, 1980) such that their meaning can best be interpreted by considering other variables, internal and external to the system. It also is important to consider exchange and relational notions as a process, as argued by Hollander and Offerman (1992), Graen and Cashman (1975), and others.

Even with such process arguments, only a very small portion of the leadership and motivational literature actually focuses on process (Hunt, 1991; Pettigrew, 1990). Typically, the literature deals with cross-sectional or static studies emphasizing a narrow set of relationships at a single point in time. Even the relatively small number of "comparative statics" studies examine relations at two or more separate time periods but do not consider the path between the periods. For that, some kind of processual analysis is necessary.

If static studies are snapshots and comparative statics studies are a series of snapshots, then processual analysis is a motion picture (Hunt, 1991). Processual analysis reflects time in terms of such aspects as pace, rhythm, timing of actions, and the like. When we teach a course, we may be concerned about whether to cover the material rapidly or slowly (pace); allowing enough time on portions of a major project assignment so that momentum can be established and maintained (rhythm); and when to cover various topics or when to come across as forceful versus relaxed (timing of actions).

Our systems motivation perspective focuses on the above notions as we analyze the unfolding of the new management concentration. That is, our perspective emphasizes exchanges and relations across time, within the context of a wide range of individual and organizational capabilities, in which an important part of the individual capabilities is composed of transformational, transactional, and representational leadership.

The New Management Concentration Scenario

The anonymous but real scenario is that of a management department in a college of business administration in a large, comprehensive public university. For the last several years the business community, and indeed society at large, have become increasingly disenchanted with business school offerings, especially at the master's degree level. Periodically, articles appear arguing that curricula must become more globalized and people oriented, with a stronger hands-on thrust, if the United States is to remain competitive or, indeed, to regain its lost competitiveness (cf. Byrne, 1993).

All these external pressures have been felt by the business school in question and caused its dean recently to appoint a committee to recommend changes in the current master's program. The committee has been laboring diligently but has not quite completed its recommendations. In the meantime, the management department has set up a globalized, hands-on concentration, based largely on the transformation of some courses currently listed in the catalogue.

The idea for the concentration came from a newly hired assistant professor in combination with the department head. Both hoped not only that the transformed courses and their packaging within a new management concentration would become successful in their own right but also that the new concentration would serve as a key part of the revised collegewide master's program. However, for these hopes to materialize, faculty, students, and potential employers needed to view these new courses as an integrated concentration, consistent with the broader master's program, and not simply as a series of separate management courses. Achieving such breadth and integration called for a comprehensive emphasis consistent with our systems motivation approach.

Because of cutbacks in state support, there was no provision for released time, additional clerical help, and so forth. Yet there was a need for extensive advertising and promotion as well as establishment of a student organization to impart the concentration's spirit. These activities were carried out by the assistant professor along with two other faculty members who taught in the concentration. Although there was "moral support" from other departmental faculty, the college's tenure and promotion system gave little weight to the kind of teaching-oriented activities just mentioned.

At the same time, the new assistant professor was under pressure to do research and publish to meet his tenure clock. Furthermore, one of the other two faculty members teaching in the concentration faced similar concerns if he was to be promoted to full professor. Finally, there was very little merit raise money available from the state even if a faculty member did an exemplary job in any area. Both of these faculty, and especially the assistant professor, were strongly torn between being completely caught up in the excitement of developing and teaching in the new concentration and the realities of the bureaucratic system with its narrow focus and restricted resources.

One of the traditional approaches emphasizing individual leadership and its relationship to individual motivation to teach at a given time might be used to analyze this scenario. However, the previous discussion and our systems motivation approach encourage us to (1) think in terms not only of individual teaching but of developing a new curriculum concentration within which teaching and numerous other individual and organizational systems capabilities are embedded; and (2) focus on the path these curriculum concentration capabilities take across time, as opposed to simply examining them at one or two time periods. As previously indicated, this is a processual as opposed to a static or comparative statics approach. The components and dynamics of such an approach will become clearer as we provide additional information with respect to the scenario.

Systems Motivation Explication and Application to the Scenario

We start our treatment by referring to table 12.1. The table shows two broad sets of what we referred to earlier as "capabilities"—individual and organizational. We use *individual capabilities* here to mean relevant individual's behaviors, competencies, and basic orientations toward self, work, and new concepts and ideas. The term *organizational capabilities* refers to the organization's shared orientation toward new concepts and ideas, planned or emergent ways of operating, strategies and policies, and concrete organizational actions and responses across time (Ropo & Hunt, 1994). The categorization of items within these categories is based on our judgment of the primary source from which the item in question emanates. For example, we classified strategy as emanating primarily from the organization (or subunit), whereas leadership emanates primarily from various individual sources including the dean, Chair, and various faculty members. Items that we included as a part of individual and organizational capabilities are summarized in the table, where they are further broken down into elements, dimensions, and (in some cases) subdimensions.

Individual capabilities include two *elements*: leadership behavior, and orientation and feeling of efficacy toward new ideas and concepts. Each of these elements, in turn, contains more specific items termed *dimensions*—transformational, transactional, and representational leadership, and three dimensions under the orientation and feeling of efficacy element. Similarly, the table shows organizational capability to be broken down into the four elements of strategy, structure, human resources, and concentration performance assessment. As previously mentioned, the table also shows that some elements include not only dimensions but even more specific subdimensions. For example, one of the dimensions of the human resources element is faculty constellation and communication, which includes the seven subdimensions (a) through (g).

We derived the individual and organizational capabilities and their dimensions and subdimensions (modified to fit our teaching and curriculum context) essentially from three sources: the organizational and strategy literature (e.g., Daft, 1989; Osborn, Hunt, & Jauch, 1980; Quinn, Mintzberg, & James, 1988); our knowledge of the previously described scenario for the new management concentration; and some conceptually similar com-

Table 12.1   Summary of Systems Motivation Individual and Organizational Capabilities for Management Concentration Scenario

---

1. **Individual capabilities:** Relevant individual's behaviors, competencies, and basic orientations toward self, work, and new concepts and ideas.
      element a. Leadership behavior: Dean's, associate dean's, department Chairs', individual faculty members', students' behaviors
         dimensions (1) Transformational
               (2) Transactional
               (3) Representational
      element b. Orientation and feeling of efficacy toward new ideas and concepts
         dimensions (1) Openness and feeling of efficacy toward contributing to college/department
               (2) Openness and feeling of efficacy toward teaching and course and student success
               (3) Openness and feeling of efficacy toward new curricula and this concentration in particular
2. **Organizational capabilities:** Organization's shared orientation toward new concepts and ideas, planned or emergent ways of operating, strategies/policies, and concrete organizational actions and responses across time.
      element a. Strategy at college and department levels
         dimensions (1) Teaching/research emphasis and linkages with each other at college and department levels
               (2) Mission statement or vision
               (3) Objectives
               (4) Efforts to encourage teaching innovation
               (5) Efforts to encourage joint teaching and research among colleagues
      element b. Structure
         dimensions (1) Formalized departments vs. loose groupings of faculty into interest areas
               (2) Centralization of decision making within college and department
               (3) Hierarchical vs. collegial emphasis in developmental issues and decision making at college and department levels
      element c. Human resources
         dimension (1) Faculty constellation and communication
           subdimensions (a) Age variation
                    (b) Proportion of tenured/nontenured
                    (c) Faculty career stages
                    (d) Area of specialization
                    (e) Common faculty interests

Table 12.1   (cont.)

	(f)	Number of joint projects
	(g)	Type and intensity of faculty interaction/communication
dimension	(2)	Student ability, interest, maturity, numbers, activities, etc.
dimension	(3)	Human resource management policies/practices
subdimensions	(a)	Faculty recruitment
	(b)	Faculty development
	(c)	Reward system
	(d)	Concentration performance
element	d.	Concentration performance assessment

ponents derived from a grounded theory or qualitative study of leadership and change (see Hunt & Ropo, 1995; Ropo, 1989; Ropo & Hunt, 1994, in press). Note that we see the specific items as more illustrative than comprehensive.

Before elaborating on the capabilities and their elements with their more specific dimensions and subdimensions in table 12.1, it is important to reiterate the differences between a traditional approach and our approach. In a traditional approach, these capabilities and their more specific subparts would be divided into independent and dependent variables, with motivation to develop the curriculum concentration (or something similar) as a dependent variable. The approach might examine the separate or combined motivation of each of the three faculty most involved in the concentration, and it might go further by considering intervening or moderating variables.

The basic difference between this traditional treatment and our processual systems motivation approach is our emphasis on the process and on viewing the important components (capabilities, elements, dimensions, subdimensions) in holistic configurations, rather than as a series of separate independent and dependent variables. The components in question are seen as exerting a supportive or countervailing force in reinforcing or restraining development of the curriculum across time. We conceptualize intensity of this force as the motivational aspect of our systems motivation approach. That is, teaching motivation, as well as motivation for other activities, emerges from various possible combinations of these two sets of capabilities.

Based on the previous discussion, we now develop the various components in table 12.1 in greater detail. We first do this statically, and then we show how our systems motivation perspective involving them would operate processually, across time, in the context of the new management curriculum concentration scenario introduced earlier.

Individual Capabilities

Leadership

The overall role of leadership here is its use as one of several "action levers" to help develop and sustain the new curriculum. Consistent with our earlier review, we conceptualize leadership in terms of transformational, transactional, and representational aspects. Transformational leadership involves visionary and related behaviors to move those involved beyond current thinking and performance to help transform the curriculum. It is engaged in by relevant participants in the new concentration, regardless of their formal status, and does not necessarily involve charisma. Thus, it involves visionary, transformationally oriented behaviors taken by the department Chair, dean, or even the involved faculty members to transform the initial idea into the reality of a viable concentration.

Transactional leadership focuses on behavior from the relevant participants involving traditional exchange relationships designed to maintain stability to accompany the transformationally oriented behavior (cf. Hunt, 1991; Yukl, 1994). In the scenario, for example, this would mean that the department Chair not only would extol the vision of the new concentration to the dean but would follow through with the departmental secretary to schedule a meeting to work through some additional details on the concentration (a transactional leadership behavior).

Representational leadership, as mentioned previously, involves networking kinds of behavior (cf. Sayles, 1993) which, among other things, help link together the transformational and transactional behavior (cf. Ropo & Hunt, 1994; Ropo, 1989). For example, the department Chair might spend time trying to influence other department Chairs and outside businesspeople to help move the concentration forward. Again, although we have used the department Chair as an example, such leadership actions would not be restricted to formally assigned administrators but would be assessed for all relevant actors in the system. In other words, as we have argued earlier, we would be considering the leadership process, wherever it occurred.

Orientation and Feeling of Efficacy toward New Ideas and Concepts

Table 12.1 shows this as an additional individual capability element, together with some related dimensions and subdimensions judged by us to be particularly important in the scenario. The new ideas and concepts orientation notion essentially is self-explanatory. However, our assumption is that in addition to an orientation toward new ideas, there needs to be a feeling of efficacy toward such ideas. Much like this book's other treatments, we consider efficacy to be a feeling of competence and effectiveness or a sense of mastery over the environment (cf. Bandura, 1991). Each of the dimensions in 1.b. of table 12.1 focuses on different but related aspects of openness and efficacy which we believe to be important in moving the concentration forward. Of these, item 1.b.(2) in the table, with its emphasis on teaching, is the most direct link between this book's emphasis on teaching well and development of the new curriculum concentration.

Openness and feeling of efficacy would be examined not only for the key participants but also for relevant others, since their orientation and feeling of efficacy could help or hinder the concentration's development. Orientations of department Chairs outside management also would need to be considered. Our general assumption is that the degree of openness and feeling of efficacy concerning new ideas can have a substantial impact on the motivation of the system in developing the concentration across time.

Organizational Capabilities

The organizational capabilities in table 12.1 are strategy, structure, human resources and performance feedback from the curriculum concentration. Keeping in mind our earlier organizational capabilities definition, the argument is that these, in combination with the individual capabilities, exert positive and negative forces concerning the concentration's development across time.

Strategy

It is important to recognize that the strategy we are considering here is focused on the college and department level rather than on the university as a whole. We assess the dimensions 2.a.(1)–(5) in table 12.1 to be especially relevant for our curriculum scenario. Each of the dimensions in question can encourage or discourage teaching and curriculum initiatives such as the new management concentration.

Structure

Our use of structure here essentially focuses on the degree of separateness or autonomy of departments vis-à-vis the college. At one extreme, a department would be virtually freestanding with its own budget and other resources. At the other extreme, a department would be closely tied to the college, would not possess its own budget, and would have very few resources independent of other units within the college. In the first case, the department could establish a curriculum concentration virtually independent of the college. In the second case, it would be so heavily dependent on the college and other departments that it could not develop a concentration without them. Dimensions 2.b.(1)–(3) were chosen to be reflective of those extremes, and the system involving the concentration was partway between these extremes but closer to the second extreme than the first. Thus, successful development of the concentration could not be done independently of participants outside the department.

Human Resources and Human Resource Policies and Practices

These dimensions and subdimensions essentially focus on human resource aspects that could help or hinder the motivational forces involved in the concentration's development across time. For example, the organization (subunit) may emphasize faculty members who are freely interacting with one another; working on numerous joint projects; being hired with specializations consistent with those covered in the concentration; and, in terms of career, past the tenure anxiety of new faculty. If so, there is likely to be a generally more positive climate of support for the new concentration than from a faculty with a less open constellation. Similarly, human resource policies could function to help or hinder systems motivation forces, as we show in our subsequent analysis.

Concentration Performance Assessment

We also have included concentration performance assessment as a kind of organizational capability. Essentially this is an overall assessment of how well the concentration is currently progressing. The progression is influenced by the overall force (or systems motivation) of the capabilities operating in combination across time. At the same time, the concentration performance assessment has a reciprocal impact on the motivational force. For example, if the concentration is progressing well, leadership behavior, openness toward new ideas, teaching of the individual courses, and the like tend to respond positively.

From Description to Application of the Processual Systems Motivation Framework

Here, we apply our systems motivation framework to the scenario and deal with the approach processually and holistically. Figure 12.1 shows this emphasis diagrammatically, and we use it as the basis for our discussion. The figure is based on intensity of systems motivation forces on the y-axis and time on the x-axis. As previously indicated, this intensity can be

Fig. 12.1   Processual Systems Motivation Archetypes and Tracks

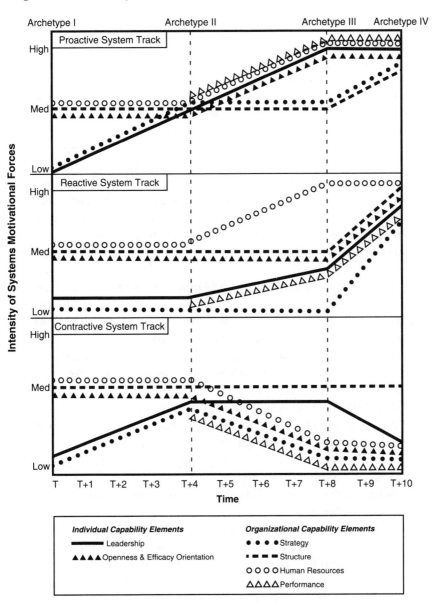

thought of as the force or energy involved in each of the two individual elements and the four organizational elements across the hypothetical time periods (T, T + 1, etc.), where the time periods could be years, quarters, months, and so on.

The intensity concept is consistent with the activation, direction, and sustainment notions mentioned earlier and set forth in many traditional motivation theories. It is beyond this chapter's scope to discuss measurement of the intensity in detail, but we can say that the nature of the various activities involved in the dimensions and subdimensions can be categorized by level, frequency, and direction, and the categories can be combined more or less quantitatively to provide a rough idea of the overall intensity of forces. For example, transformational leadership behaviors can be categorized, their level (strong to weak) assessed, and their frequency and direction (supporting or not supporting the concentration development) assessed and ultimately combined with assessments of other dimensions and subdimensions to provide a rough assessment of force intensity.

The figure shows three hypothetical processual paths—proactive, reactive, and contractive—each made up of the two individual and four organizational elements in differing patterns across various time periods. As we elaborate below, there is an initial pattern of elements at time T, called archetype I. After that, new archetypes (II, III, and IV) are identified at those periods (T + 4, T + 8, T + 10) when a major turning point takes place in one or more of the elements.

Consistent with the organizational literature, we describe the interplay of the six individual and organizational processual elements as "configurational." Miller and Friesen (1984) conceive of configurations as composed of tightly interdependent and mutually supportive elements, such that the importance of each element can best be understood by making reference to the whole configuration—a holistic or systems notion as opposed to an individual variable thrust.

Each of the archetypes in figure 12.1 represents a specific configurational pattern of elements at a given point in time. Borrowing from some notions set forth by Greenwood and Hinings (1988, 1993) and Hinings and Greenwood (1988), and building on some of our related work (e.g., Hunt & Ropo, 1995; Ropo & Hunt, 1994), we use the term *systems track* to refer to the processual path connecting the archetypes across time. Put another way, the systems tracks may be seen as maps of the extent to which a system moves from the constraining assumptions of a given archetype and assumes the characteristics of an alternative one (cf. Greenwood & Hinings, 1988). By tracing those prototypical tracks in a college or university, we can understand better why faculty may or may not be motivated to teach.

Figure 12.1 shows archetype I to be the same for proactive, reactive, and contractive systems tracks. However, the processual path or track from archetype I to archetypes II, III, and IV is quite different for each of these. The differing shapes of the systems tracks illustrate their overall configurational nature across time. In addition, starting with archetype III, the differences in the archetypes become particularly noticeable.

Let us elaborate on the previous discussion. The proactive systems track indicates a smoothly progressing and increasing intensity of systems motivation across time. Anticipatory efforts are made primarily ahead of anticipated counterforces, and there is strongly increasing intensity of systems motivation forces across time. The reactive track indicates a lag in some of the elements and then a reactive "catching up," so that systems motivational forces intensity at archetype IV is high. The contractive track indicates a temporary increase in archetype II that declines substantially at archetype IV.

Note that archetypes are formed when there are one or more jolts to the system from external or internal events or both. For example, a sharp cutback in university support would provide an external jolt, and the replacement of the management department Chair might provide an internal jolt. Such external and internal events cause a turning point toward something new or different in a systems track and move the elements composing the track toward a new archetype at a given time, as shown at several places in the figure. It also is possible that the "new" archetype essentially will end up virtually the same as the previous one, if the elements move back as they were before the jolt. Note finally that, in the absence of an abrupt jolt, the elements will tend to be in rough equilibrium and will continue to move relatively smoothly together, configurationally across time, maintaining the previous archetype.

There are some similarities between the archetypes and tracks used here and the stages and phases reported in the small-group literature (e.g., Bales & Strodtbeck, 1951; Tuckman, 1965) and in the organizational life cycle literature (e.g., Baliga & Hunt, 1988; Hunt, 1991; Quinn & Cameron, 1983). The various archetypes here might be considered as roughly comparable to the stages or phases discussed in these literatures in that they form breaks and turns in a process. However, unlike phases or stages, they do not necessarily vary in a consistent pattern. While, say, the forming stage precedes the storming stage in small-group research, given kinds of archetypes do not necessarily precede others, one does not have to go through one kind of archetype to move to another, and there is no pre-specified number of archetypes through which the process must move. Furthermore, the amount of time between archetypes may vary considerably from one to another.

Returning to our systems motivation framework, as previously mentioned, we start with the same archetype for the proactive, reactive, and contractive systems tracks. We also assume the same jolt to the system occurring at the same time for each of the tracks. The differences in the tracks and archetypes, then, are a function of the way the various elements come together as a response to the jolt. In addition, one could compare systems tracks in different settings where there would be differences in the time periods, number of archetypes, and specific aspects composing each element. Such a comparison would serve a different purpose than the present one, which looks at three illustrative systems tracks within the single management concentration across the same time periods.

Given the previous discussion, we now analyze in more detail our example scenario involving the new management concentration. The figure shows that at archetype I, the leadership behavior and strategy elements are low in systems motivation intensity while the orientation and feeling of efficacy toward new ideas and concepts, as well as the structure and human resources elements, are medium in systems motivation intensity. The concentration performance assessment element is currently unknown, since the concentration has just started. Essentially, the above points reflect:

- *Leadership behavior element.* Leadership passivity from the dean and an encouraging but wait-and-see set of transformational, transactional, and representational behaviors from the department Chair, who encourages the new assistant professor and others directly involved with the concentration but cautions against overextension.
- *Orientation and efficacy element.* Medium overall intensity in orientation toward new ideas, based on openness and a feeling of efficacy toward new ideas among those in the department and especially the new assistant professor and the others directly involved with teaching in the concentration, but counterbalanced by a substantially lower intensity level by those outside the department.
- *Strategy element.* Low overall strategy intensity based on some general effort to promote curriculum and teaching openness in the department and considerably less effort at the college level.

- *Structure element.* Medium overall structure motivational forces intensity based on a rough balance between departmental autonomy and centralized college decision making and hierarchical emphasis concerning the concentration.
- *Human resources element.* Medium intensity of human resources motivational forces based on human resource characteristics generally favorable toward curriculum and teaching openness at the department level and less so at the college level.
- *Concentration performance assessment.* An unknown level of performance, since the concentration has just started.

Proactive Systems Track

In this track, the department Chair's leadership behavior intensity increases sharply at archetype II after the initial teaching of two of the concentration's courses and an initial attempt to start a student organization to focus on the concentration. The Chair's leadership increases as partial compensation for feedback about mediocre course evaluations from one of the classes (although the other one received very positive ratings) and in response to feedback concerning the small student turnout at the initial meeting to start the student organization. At the same time, the dean, though interested in the concentration, is concerned about the mixed ratings in the courses and the small number of students at the initial meeting. Therefore, his intensity of leadership behavior for the concentration, though higher than before, is still relatively low—hence, the overall medium level of leadership behavior intensity at archetype II. Overall, orientation and feeling of efficacy toward new ideas essentially remains at the same medium level as before, influenced to a large extent by the responses concerning the mixed teaching evaluations.

Along with the above, various aspects of strategy as they relate to the concentration have increased noticeably in terms of such things as a formally prepared and widely distributed write-up of the concentration, its role vis-à-vis departmental and college mission and objectives, and so on. Thus the strategy element moves from a low to a medium intensity at archetype II. Similarly, concentration performance assessment moves from unknown to medium in the minds of the department Chair, those involved with the concentration, and others in the department.

The remaining elements essentially remain at roughly the same level of motivational intensity in the movement from archetype I to II. We see, then, a modest overall upward trend in the track from time T to archetype II at T + 4.

In terms of archetype III, leadership in the proactive track moves from medium to high as the assistant professor and the other concentration faculty members hold a series of meetings successfully pushing the concentration, and the Chair, associate dean, and dean all aggressively support the new curriculum. At the same time, the student association begins to increase substantially in membership and activities undertaken. The overall orientation and feeling of efficacy toward new ideas increases as faculty in and outside the department notice the concentration's momentum and as feedback concerning teaching ratings within and across the courses in the concentration is strongly positive. Overall strategy and structure remain essentially unchanged. In terms of human resources, the department Chair has increased the intensity by utilizing the perceived momentum of the concentration and negotiating for a new position largely on the strength of his arguments about the concentration's contributions to the department, college, and university. Finally, concentration performance is now assessed as high by most of the key people at the department and college level; this assessment reinforces the motivational intensity of the previously mentioned capabilities.

Turning now to archetype IV, there is strong lobbying behind the scenes for acceptance of the report of the MBA committee with the management concentration as one of its showpieces. This effort leads to the report's acceptance by the college's graduate faculty and is reflected in the increased motivational intensity of the strategy and structure elements. The high intensity of leadership previously exhibited both has helped here and has been reinforced. The previous positive teaching evaluations have continued, both reinforcing other aspects of openness and efficacy and themselves being reinforced by such aspects. Those involved with the concentration, particularly the assistant professor, especially reflect this mutually beneficial phenomenon. The management department is successful in hiring a new person whom the departmental members expect to be helpful in continuing the new concentration's impetus and to teach well, especially in the new concentration. Finally, as before, concentration performance continues to be assessed as high, and that reinforces other components.

Overall, the proactive systems track is an example of what was earlier termed "running hot"—getting increasingly more out of a limited set of resources. The track displays an increasingly favorable motivational intensity across time and in reaction to such earlier system jolts as acceptance of the new MBA program. In other words, the systems motivation force impelling the concentration forward is very strong; indeed, it probably is strong enough to overcome all but the most powerful counterforces. The force also can be expected to reinforce future motivation toward effective teaching in the concentration's courses, which in turn can be expected to increase overall momentum. The attempt now should be made to continue to monitor the system and anticipate ongoing jolts to the system so that appropriate steps can be taken to keep the momentum going. Obviously, these steps must consider the relationships among the kinds of components just discussed.

Reactive Systems Track

Turning now to the reactive systems track in figure 12.1, we see that archetype II is essentially the same as archetype I despite the fact that the jolts were the same as those in the proactive track, where the intensity of three of the elements increased. In this reactive systems track, the department Chair's reaction to the mixed course evaluations and low student attendance at the initial student organization meeting is a continued wait and see, in contrast to his compensatory leadership in the proactive track. The dean's leadership behavior is the same as in the proactive track, so the overall leadership intensity remains low. The concentration's faculty members' reaction to the mixed feedback concerning teaching evaluation is no more positive than in the proactive track.

The strategy element remains essentially the same as before, as those involved with the concentration basically are advised by the Chair to hold back on such items as concentration write-ups until there are more positive and consistent student evaluations of the concentration's courses. Based on the other elements, assessment of concentration performance moves from unknown to low but hopeful.

Moving to archetype III, for the reactive systems track, we see a compensatory increase in leadership intensity from low to high and an increase in human resource element intensity from medium to high. There is also an increase in concentration performance assessment from low to medium. Here, as in the proactive track, there is a compensatory increase in leadership intensity at both the department and college level, and there is a strong push from the concentration's faculty even though teaching ratings indicate the faculty are not as strong overall as in the proactive track. Further, in contrast to the proactive track, the student association does not display strong growth, partially because of the relatively less positive course teaching evaluation. At the same time, overall orientation and feeling of efficacy toward new ideas is not as strong as in the proactive track, again influenced by the mixed teaching evaluation feedback that has spread across the department. Even so, the department Chair is able to negotiate a new position. In summary, there is forward movement for leadership, human resources, and concentration performance assessment but not for orientation and efficacy toward new ideas, strategy, or structure.

In contrast, at archetype IV, all elements in the reactive systems track display a high level of systems motivation intensity. The same activities as in the proactive track take place and have a positive effect strong enough to push the negative track into an overall highly positive motivational intensity. The reactive track differs from the proactive track in that some of its elements and dimensions lagged earlier; however, they have now caught up, and there is an overall high intensity configuration (positive teaching evaluations are a case in point). As with the proactive track, maintenance of such a high intensity of motivation calls for vigilance across the various systems components, especially in terms of teaching evaluation feedback.

Contractive Systems Track

As contrasted with the other systems tracks, the contractive track ends up worse off at archetype IV than at archetype I. Interestingly, at archetype II the contractive track is actually better off than the reactive track (its leadership and strategy intensities are higher and are roughly the same as in the proactive track).

It is in the movement from archetype II to archetype III that a decline starts in the contractive systems track. Leadership behavior remains at a medium level of intensity, as does structure. Orientation toward new ideas/self-efficacy, strategy, human resources, and overall concentration performance intensities drop. Even though the concentration faculty members hold meetings, the Chair, associate dean, and dean retain their previous medium intensity level of leadership. The student association drops off in attendance and enthusiasm, and the Chair fails at negotiating a new position. Those outside the department begin to feel less enthusiastic about the concentration than before as they tire of hearing about it, as they see that the Chair was not able to get a new position, and as feedback spreads that concentration teaching ratings have not been very high. In addition, people within the department begin to get caught up in this perceived loss of momentum; their new ideas orientation/efficacy intensity drops, and teaching ratings are seen as a problem. Concentration performance is assessed as low and not getting noticeably better.

Finally, in moving from archetype III to IV, the strong lobbying is not successful in obtaining faculty acceptance of the MBA committee recommendations, and the recommendations are rejected. There is an overall feeling of malaise and status quo which engulfs the concentration, since it was a centerpiece of the MBA committee recommendations. In turn, over-all leadership intensity drops, new ideas orientation and feeling of efficacy gets even lower, partially because teaching has not improved (reinforced by earlier lower ratings and perceived lack of support), the overall college strategy of openness drops even lower, structure intensity remains medium, human resources intensity remains low, and concentration per-formance is assessed as even lower than before.

Overall, there is low systems motivation. Although the concentration probably is not beyond salvaging, given our systems orientation, we would predict that no single compensatory action would be sufficient, and it may be very difficult indeed to reverse the contractive systems track. Teaching well is likely to be particularly difficult because of all the negativity. The new assistant professor is likely to be especially demoralized by all these occurrences.

Use of Action Levers in the Systems Motivation Framework

Here, we address the "So what?" question running implicitly through this chapter by returning to the new curriculum scenario and illustrating the use of various action levers to maintain a currently desirable archetype and de-velop a proactive systems track. We emphasize this relatively straightfor-ward illustration, in some detail, to convey the essence of the kinds of thinking and actions which would be needed to deal with other, more dif-ficult situations (e.g., an undesirable archetype or a contractive track).

Dealing with a Desirable Archetype

The currently desirable archetype is assessed, by those involved, as one where all or most of the relevant elements, dimensions, and subdimensions have come together in a pattern reflecting an overall positive motivational force. In the context of the current new management curriculum concen-tration, the important individual capability elements and dimensions are

1. leadership behavior; and
2. a strong feeling of openness and efficacy concerning the new curricu-lum and the development and teaching of its courses.

The important organizational capabilities are

1. a strong strategy of openness and organizational support;
2. a structure encouraging freedom and autonomy in support of the new curriculum and courses;

3. a human resource emphasis toward faculty, and students supportive of the kind of new curriculum and course ideas involved here; and

4. positive overall concentration performance assessment.

Note that this archetype reflects both high individual and organizational capabilities and sets the stage for a proactive systems track. Note also that each of the previously mentioned elements, dimensions, and subdimensions is considered as a potential action lever. The question of interest is as follows: "Given this desirable current archetype, what action levers can be used to proactively maintain it or avoid its becoming less desirable?"

Here, we assume the concentration team (the three faculty members and the department Chair) is most interested in maintaining this archetype. Consistent with our systems motivation approach, the team members first need to recognize that emphasis on any one lever influences all the levers (this is the earlier-mentioned holistic, or configurational, notion). For example, if building membership in a new student organization to help with the concentration is directly emphasized, this may have indirect consequences in terms of negative responses from other faculty advisors as their own organizations' memberships drop off, or student course performance may decrease because of effort spent on the new organization, and the like.

Bearing in mind this configurational caveat, the team members can think in terms of the ability to influence the two individual and four organizational levers (with their more specific dimensions and subdimensions). They also need to make a judgment concerning the relative motivational intensity of each of the levers. Given these considerations, leadership enters here as a key lever. The question is, How much does transformational, transactional, and representational behavior need to be used, and who needs to provide the behavior?

We stated earlier that transformational behavior essentially is used to impart a vision and encourage extraordinary performance. Transactional behavior is utilized to take care of mundane, day-to-day details. Finally, representational behavior is used to provide linkages between transactional and transformational leadership and help link these with relevant individuals or groups outside the unit. We speculate that there should be an initial strong emphasis on transformational leadership and an increasing emphasis on transactional leadership across time, as the concentration develops. Representational leadership is likely to be important throughout, to maintain necessary resources and support. The department Chair or dean should probably play a major role in these, but if that does not occur, the other team members will need to emphasize the behaviors.

In terms of new idea orientation and efficacy, including course teaching, the team members themselves have a major direct impact on this individual lever. The organizational levers are far less directly under their control. Team members need primarily to assess these accurately and to work with the department Chair and dean to try to maintain or even increase their intensity.

Constant awareness and sensitivity concerning the previously mentioned levers are necessary to proactively maintain this archetype in the absence of jolts to the system. Of course there will be jolts where there is a turning point in one or more of the elements. It is here that one tries to use one or more action levers to compensate for or reinforce changes in the others. For example, we argued earlier that a positive jolt occurred when a new concentration faculty member was hired. Although this was generally very favorable for the new concentration, one would still need to be concerned about leadership changes to deal with such things as orientation and direction of the new member and interaction with those in other departments not receiving an additional position. In addition, the openness and efficacy lever would need to be considered in terms of teaching and the role of the new member in the concentration, and the like.

The considerations discussed above should maintain the original archetype. They also should provide a generally proactive track in the sense that it would continue to provide the motivational force to move the curriculum concentration forward.

Dealing with Other Kinds of Archetypes

The other kinds of archetypes can take different forms, from a currently undesirable one with low individual and organizational capabilities to those where either the individual or the organizational capabilities are low. The accompanying tracks can also range from proactive to contractive. Without going into detail, in our judgment, the general action lever notions indicated for the illustrative desirable archetype would apply, but the specifics almost certainly would be more difficult to implement than for the desirable archetype.

Summary and Additional Considerations

We have developed a motivational approach that ties together a number of individual and organizational capabilities processually across time. The approach has been applied to the development of an innovative, new management curriculum concentration and has embedded course teaching within it. The new concentration was part of changes in a master's in business administration program designed to respond to concerns articulated by businesspeople and influential media. These concerns, among other things, argued for a much heavier hands-on, skills-oriented, and global emphasis in the hope of ultimately having an impact on the competitiveness of U.S. organizations. At the same time, as these external environmental pressures were operating, the support base within the university and its colleges and departments was declining, especially so in the business school and management department within which the new concentration was developed. Accompanying this declining support base was a reward system emphasizing research, teaching to a lesser extent, and the development of new concentrations to an even lesser extent.

This combination of pressure for innovation in the face of declining resources and a skewed reward system provided us with an example of an ongoing system that we used to illustrate the development and application of our systems motivation approach within which teaching in the concentration was embedded. We used a series of what were termed *archetypes* and *systems tracks* to illustrate the approach. We argued that the positive, proactive systems track was an illustration of "running hot," where the combination of individual and organizational capabilities moved the concentration aggressively ahead despite the recent history of declining resources.

We also illustrated two other systems tracks—a reactive one, where the concentration moved ahead but with a lag, and a contractive one, where after an initial slight move ahead there was a negative jolt to the system and the concentration's momentum was reversed and slipped into a decline that, if not arrested, could lead to its ultimate demise. Finally, we briefly discussed the use of action levers to keep the system moving proactively, and we elaborated on the use of transformational, transactional, and representational leadership behavior.

Application to Individual Teaching

Our management concentration example applied the systems motivation approach to explain motivation of an entire system as opposed to a single individual. As such, it extended the notion of exchange, relational, or double interact notions (this time in terms of systems as opposed to individual aspects) mentioned earlier. We have argued implicitly and explicitly throughout that the management curriculum concentration example was a particularly appropriate one to illustrate this systems approach, and we looked at teaching within the context of the new concentration's development across time. Treated in this way, teaching was only one (albeit an important one) of numerous aspects that were discussed.

Of course, the systems motivation perspective, instead of considering the development of a new concentration as its focal point, could focus on motivation of an individual faculty member to teach well in a traditional setting. Indeed, one could examine the new assistant professor's motivation to teach well in such a setting. Here, one would focus on the configurational patterns or archetypes of appropriate individual and organizational capabilities as these played out in tracks across one or more courses. For example, say that the assistant professor taught a two-hundred-student undergraduate class and a doctoral seminar with ten students. We would consider those individual and organizational capability aspects thought to be a part of the professor's motivation to teach the two courses. Individual capability elements would include the leadership of the department Chair and possibly other faculty particularly knowledgeable about teaching, and perhaps the content of the courses. In addition, commitment of other faculty to undergraduate and doctoral-level teaching would likely be among those individual capabilities particularly important to the assistant professor. Relevant organizational capability elements might include such strategy dimensions as relative teaching and research emphases and emphasis on teaching innovation and such human resource management policy aspects as the reward system and opportunities for faculty development to enhance teaching.

Additional individual and organizational capability aspects could be obtained through interviews and from the literature. Then the individual and organizational capabilities, however determined, would be analyzed in a fashion similar to our analysis of the management concentration example. The key, as before, is to examine the capabilities and their subparts in question across long enough time periods to allow us to map the process. Then, depending on the nature of the systems track, one would focus on various action levers, determine which ones to emphasize most strongly, and decide who would be involved. That issue is a complicated one that goes beyond the scope of this chapter. However, the systems motivation approach developed here is one way of providing the processual analysis preceding the use of such action levers.

Extensions of the Systems Motivation Perspective

We think the systems motivation perspective can make both methodological and substantive contributions to future understanding. Methodologically, it suggests that one can examine not only different aspects of motivation but other phenomena as well. A series of carefully selected case studies can be utilized with the underlying configurational and arche-type/systems track notions in mind as a way of focusing on the questions of interest. Then a form of grounded theory, a notion originally discussed by Glaser and Strauss (1967) and elaborated recently by Glaser (1992), can be used to derive the kinds of capabilities and elements discussed in this chapter.

Such a project would be quite involved and, because of its temporal aspects, probably would take a relatively long time to conduct. Originally, in our hypothetical management concentration, we deduced the elements and their subparts from the literature, our experience, and some of our other work (Hunt & Ropo, 1995; Ropo & Hunt, 1994), using a form of grounded theory. For the case studies, however, elements now would be derived from the data (see, e.g., Eisenhardt, 1989; Fox-Wolfgramm, Boal, & Hunt, 1994; Glaser and Strauss, 1967). From such data and appropriate data analysis methods, it is possible to begin to build preliminary processual theories relating to questions of interest. Alternatively or supplementally, it also is possible to use a much more nomothetic or objectivist methodology, such as structural equation modeling, which in some ways picks up on the holistic emphasis in this chapter (cf. Hunt, 1991).

If we think in terms of an objectivist/subjectivist continuum, such as that suggested by Morgan and Smircich (1980) or Hunt (1991), we would locate our overall perspective closer to the middle or "hologram, cybernetics, brain" position. For us, this allows holistic, nonlinear, up-close types of thinking which may be addressed using a range of methodologies that are consistent with underlying philosophy of science assumptions. For readers of the postmodernist persuasion (cf. Hassard & Parker, 1993; Venkatesh, 1989), our approach would likely partially embrace it, while still retaining some objectivist or modernist assumptions.

Regardless, in our opinion, a holistic processual way of thinking, such as was illustrated in this chapter, is likely to become increasingly important in addressing the more and more complex behavioral concerns of teaching, higher education, and society in general.

References

Bales, R. F., & Strodtbeck, F. L. (1951). Phases in group problem-solving. *Journal of Abnormal and Social Psychology, 46,* 485–495.
Baliga, B. R., & Hunt, J. G. (1988). An organizational life cycle approach to leadership.

In J. G. Hunt, B. R. Baliga, H. P. Dachler, & C. A. Schriesheim (Eds.), *Emerging leadership vistas* (pp. 129–149). Lexington, MA: Lexington Books.

Bandura, A. (1991). Social cognitive theory. *Organizational Behavior and Human Decision Processes, 50,* 248–287.

Bass, B. M. (1990). *Bass and Stodgill's handbook of leadership: Theory, research, and managerial implications* (3d ed.). New York: Free Press.

Bryman, A. (1992). *Charisma and leadership in organizations.* London: Sage.

Burns, J. M. (1978). *Leadership.* New York: Harper & Row.

Byrne, J. A. (1993). *A business week guide: The best schools* (3d ed.). New York: McGraw-Hill.

Coglisher, C. C., & Schriesheim, C. A. (1994). Social network analysis of leader-member relations for examining the impact of dyadic structures on workgroup interactions. Paper delivered before the Southern Management Association, New Orleans.

Daft, R. L. (1989). *Organization theory and design.* St. Paul, MN: West.

Eisenhardt, K. M. (1989). Building theories from case study research. *Academy of Management Review, 14,* 532–550.

Evans, M. G. (1970). The effects of supervisory behavior on the path-goal relationship. *Organizational Behavior and Human Performance, 5,* 277–298.

Fox-Wolfgramm, S. J., Boal, K. B., & Hunt, J. G. (1994). A dynamic, configurational study of strategic issue processing and adaptation. Unpublished manuscript, College of Business Administration, Texas Tech University, Lubbock.

Georgopolis, B. S., Mahoney, G. M., & Jones, N. W. (1957). A path-goal approach to productivity. *Journal of Applied Psychology, 41,* 345–353.

Glaser, B. G. (1992). *Basics of grounded theory analysis.* Mill Valley, CA: Sociology Press.

Glaser, B. G., & Strauss, A. L. (1967). *The discovery of grounded theory: Strategies for qualitative research.* New York: Aldine.

Graen, G. B., & Cashman, J. F. (1975). A role-making model of leadership in formal organizations. In J. G. Hunt & L. L. Larson (Eds.), *Leadership frontiers* (pp. 143–166). Kent, OH: Kent State University Press.

Graen, G. B., & Uhl-Bien, M. (1993). Development of leader-member exchange (LMX) as a relationship-based approach to leadership. Unpublished manuscript, University of Cincinnati, Cincinnati, OH.

Greenwood, R., & Hinings, C. R. (1988). Organizational design types, tracks, and the dynamics of strategic change. *Organization Studies, 9,* 293–316.

Greenwood, R., & Hinings, C. R. (1993). Understanding strategic change: The contribution of archetypes. *Academy of Management Journal, 36,* 1052–1081.

Hassard, J., & Parker, M. (1993). *Postmodernism and organizations.* Newbury Park, CA: Sage.

Hinings, C. R., & Greenwood, R. (1988). *The dynamics of strategic change.* Oxford: Basil Blackwell.

Hollander, E. P. (1978). *Leadership dynamics.* New York: Free Press.

Hollander, E. P., & Offerman, L. R. (1992). Leadership in organizations: Relationships in transition. *American Psychologist, 45,* 179–189.

House, R. J. (1971). A path goal theory of leader effectiveness. *Administrative Science Quarterly, 16*(3), 321–338.

House, R. J. (1977). A 1976 theory of charismatic leadership. In J. G. Hunt & L. L. Larson (Eds.), *Leadership: The cutting edge* (pp. 189–207). Carbondale: Southern Illinois University Press.

House, R. J., & Shamir, B. (1993). Toward the integration of transformational, charismatic, and visionary theories. In M. M. Chemers & R. Ayman (Eds.), *Leadership theory and research: Perspectives and directions* (pp. 81–107). San Diego: Academic Press.

Hunt, J. G. (1991). *Leadership: A new synthesis.* Newbury Park, CA: Sage.

Hunt, J. G., & Ropo, A. (1995). Multi-level leadership: Grounded theory and mainstream theory applied to the case of General Motors. *Leadership Quarterly, 6,* 375–412.

Jacobs, T. O. (1970). *Leadership and exchange in formal organizations.* Alexandria, VA: Human Resources Research Organization.

Likert, R. (1967). *The human organization.* New York: McGraw-Hill.

Melcher, A. J. (1977). Leadership models and research approaches. In J. G. Hunt & L. L. Larson (Eds.), *Leadership: The cutting edge* (pp. 94–108). Carbondale: Southern Illinois University Press.

Miller, D., & Friesen, P. (1984). *Organizations: A quantum view.* Englewood Cliffs, NJ: Prentice-Hall.

Morgan, G., & Smircich, L. (1980). The case for qualitative research. *Academy of Management Review, 5,* 491–500.

Osborn, R. N., Hunt, J. G., & Jauch, L. R. (1980). *Organization theory: An integrated approach.* New York: Wiley.

Pettigrew, A. M. (1990). Longitudinal field research on change: Theory and practice. *Organization Science, 1,* 267–292.

Podsakoff, P. M., Todor, W. D., Grover, R. A., & Huber, V. L. (1984). Situational moderators of leader reward and punishment behavior: Fact or fiction? *Organizational Behavior and Human Performance, 34,* 21–63.

Quinn, J. B., Mintzberg, H., & James, R. M. (1988). *The strategy process.* Englewood Cliffs, NJ: Prentice-Hall.

Quinn, R. E., & Cameron, K. S. (1983). Organizational life cycles and shifting criteria of effectiveness: Some preliminary evidence. *Management Science, 29,* 33–51.

Ropo, A. (1989). *Leadership and organizational change.* Acta Universitatis Tamperensis ser. A/vol. 280. Tampere, Finland: University of Tampere. (Available from University Microfilms).

Ropo, A., & Hunt, J. G. (1994). Leadership and organizational change: Development of a processual grounded theory. Unpublished manuscript, College of Business Administration, Texas Tech University, Lubbock.

Ropo, A., & Hunt, J. G. (in press). Entrepreneurship processes as virtuous and vicious spirals in a changing opportunity structure: A paradoxical perspective. *Entrepreneurship Theory and Practice.*

Salancik, G. R., Calder, B. J., Rowland, K. M., Leblebici, H., & Conway, M. (1975). Leadership as an outcome of social structure and process: A multidimensional analysis. In J. G. Hunt and L. L. Larson (Eds.), *Leadership frontiers* (pp. 81–101). Kent, OH: Kent State University Press.

Sashkin, M., & Rosenbach, W. E. (1993). A new leadership paradigm. In W. E. Rosenbach & R. L. Taylor (Eds.), *Contemporary issues in leadership* (3d ed., pp. 87–108). Boulder, CO: Westview Press.

Sayles, L. R. (1965). *Managerial behavior: Administration in complex organizations.* New York: McGraw-Hill.

Sayles, L. R. (1993). *The working leader.* New York: Free Press.

Shamir, B., House, R. J., & Arthur, M. B. (1993). The motivational effects of charismatic leadership: A self-concept based theory. *Organization Science, 4,* 1–17.

Stewart, A. (1989). *Team entrepreneurship.* Newbury Park, CA: Sage.

Tuckman, D. W. (1965). Developmental sequence in small groups. *Psychological Bulletin, 63,* 384–399.

Venkatesh, A. (1989, February). Modernity and postmodernity: A synthesis or antithesis? Paper presented at American Marketing Association Educators' Conference, Miami, FL.

Weick, K. E., & Bougan, M. G. (1986). Organizations as cognitive maps. In H. P. Sims Jr. & D. A. Gioia (Eds.), *The thinking organization* (pp. 102–135). San Francisco: Jossey-Bass.

Yukl, G. A. (1994). *Leadership in organizations* (3d ed.). Englewood Cliffs, NJ: Prentice-Hall.

13 Student Diversity: Challenge and Potential for Faculty Motivation

DARYL G. SMITH

Few would doubt that the issue of diversity is one of contemporary higher education's dominant themes. Fundamental to the vast literature on the topic is the role of faculty in educating an increasingly diverse student body. The problem as defined in the literature suggests a potential conflict between an aging faculty relatively uncommitted to teaching faced with a much more heterogeneous student body, less well prepared and less able to engage higher education's expectations (Astin, 1993: Baldwin & Blackburn, 1981; Carnegie Foundation, 1989).

In light of the increasing concern about teaching in higher education and the growing necessity for institutions to demonstrate effectiveness, this purported tension between faculty and student profiles does not bode well for students, for institutions, and for faculty motivation. Indeed, it would be very easy to suggest, and many authors do, that the issue of student diversity is in tension with the campus need to engage and improve teaching. Moreover, there is considerable literature on diversity which focuses attention on the need for fundamental changes in faculty—both in composition and in behavior—and the implication that faculty pose a considerable obstacle in efforts to achieve the goals of diversity.

At the present time, the presumed tension between student diversity and teaching is based, in part, on the traditional ways in which the issues are framed (Smith, 1989). All too often both the faculty and students are used as the explanation for the problem. Each group—faculty and students—is used to explain the problem of "the other"; that is, the students are underprepared and the faculty do not care about teaching. It is important to note that many of these issues, including student preparation, the lack of concern about teaching, and ineffective advising systems, have been issues for years. The changing student bodies on our campuses may highlight the problems, but the issues predate the current demographics.

Nevertheless, it is the thesis of this chapter that contrary to much of the literature, student diversity and issues of diversity have the potential to create conditions that enhance both teaching effectiveness and the motivation of faculty to teach. Moreover, there is evidence that on many campuses this process has already begun.

A broad look at several literatures—on motivation (including Chap. 1 in this volume), on the motivation to teach, and, interestingly, on motivations to learn (the student literature)—suggests some general characteristics necessary to enhance motivation. Motivation is highest when an individual feels competent to succeed, has sufficient autonomy, can set worthwhile goals that have meaning and importance, and receives regular feedback and when efforts are affirmed and are embedded in an affiliative environment (Bandura, 1982; Deci & Ryan, 1991). As Bess said, "motivation is enhanced by the provision of opportunities for individuals to demonstrate their competence in work that has meaning and is related to institutional outcomes bearing on values important to society" (Bess, 1982, p. 24).

If these notions are true, the conditions for motivation have not been strong for many years—arguably, for decades. The issue of student diversity has simply highlighted the disjuncture between traditional sources of faculty motivation and institutional characteristics.

This chapter focuses both on a conceptual approach to the topic of student diversity and its relationship to faculty motivation and on the potential for creating conditions that enhance both student and faculty responses. By framing the tension between student diversity and faculty motivation solely in terms of conflicting profiles between the two groups, the issues become highly oversimplified, even stereotyped. Rather, it is important to begin to examine the concept of student diversity, look at the context of campus environments in which these issues are being addressed, and examine more carefully the conditions and attitudes of the faculty.

Student Diversity and Faculty Motivation

Dimensions of Diversity

The term *diversity* is often discussed rather broadly. In reality the concept has developed in rather complex ways to reveal a number of dimensions that frame the issue of diversity with different emphases and with different implications for teaching and learning. The conceptual framework for understanding the concept of diversity, as presented in figure 13.1, has emerged over time and is grounded in the evolution of campus discourse about the topic. What each dimension highlights, however, is that diversity raises the stakes concerning teaching and calls for fundamental shifts in thinking about the classroom, the role of the faculty, and the very subject matter under consideration. It is from this perspective that one sees the ways in which diversity both challenges and provides opportunities for faculty and teaching. The framework outlined makes the challenges to faculty apparent.

Figure 13.1 depicts each of the four dimensions to be considered. The first dimension has to do with *representation*. This dimension emanates from a particular focus on those who have been traditionally underrepresented in higher education and includes certain underrepresented persons of color, and in some areas Euro-American women. It is often the starting point for a discussion of diversity, although in too many cases it is also presumed to be the ending point as well. In the literature, issues of representation focus not just on students but on all areas of the institution including faculty, staff, and trustees. When conversations occur about the changing demographics and the need to respond to these changes, the focus is most often on this representational dimension. From a policy perspective, affirmative action programs are directed to this dimension of increasing the representation of those from historically underrepresented groups from a perspective of overcoming injustice and increasing equity.

These efforts, combined with other economic and social changes, have resulted in students who are quite unlike their counterparts in the 1950s and early 1960s. The student body in higher education today is 53 percent women, 43 percent over twenty-five, 43 percent attending part-time, and about 20 percent students of color along with increasing numbers of first-generation college students and students for whom English is not a first language (Curtis & Herrington, 1992; NCES, 1990). Diversity of students and their varied backgrounds are certainly more characteristic of most campuses, from two-year community colleges to research universities, than ever before, though there is general agreement that on many cam-

Fig. 13.1   Dimensions of Diversity

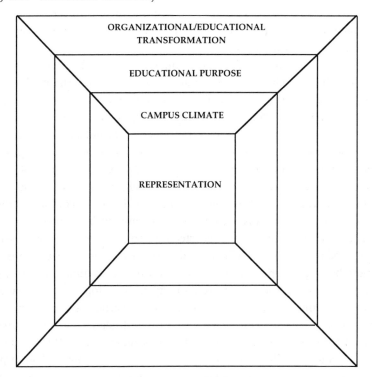

puses equity has not been achieved. The days of a student body that is predominantly white, male, and eighteen to twenty-two years old are gone
and with them easy statements about what students want, why they are in
college, and what they need to succeed. It would appear, then, that institutional and classroom practices that have remained largely unchanged for
years are coming under scrutiny as students question or, by their presence,
cause questions to be raised. And even if students don't challenge, concerns about attrition and retention are calling attention to the need to develop more effective approaches. Faculty comfort and competence is challenged as students question all dimensions of their education from new
perspectives. Faculty comfort is also challenged as the demands to increase
representation at all levels appear to suggest that representation is more
important than quality. Thus, diversity in this dimension is often perceived, inappropriately, to suggest a conflict between quality and equality.
Although essential to an understanding of diversity, this dimension of rep-

resentation is not sufficient, for it fails to engage directly other issues related to diversity and fails to make explicit the direct connection between demographics and quality, demographics and excellence, and demographics and quality of campus life.

A second dimension of diversity concerns issues related to *climate*—campus climate and classroom climate. Much has been written about the ways in which institutions and classes are "chilly" for those who are different (e.g., Hall & Sandler, 1982; Institute, 1991; Smith, 1989). Here, issues of diversity impact not only underrepresented racial and ethnic groups and Euro-American women in such areas as math and science but also groups which, though not underrepresented, may also experience hostility, discrimination, and barriers on campus, including gays, lesbians, Jewish students, and students with physical challenges. Issues of conflict, harassment, intolerance, and discrimination emerge under this dimension.

The curriculum has been suggested as a possible place for addressing the second dimension, the climate and responses to intolerance, because of a more broadly accepted notion that education will facilitate understanding and thus intergroup relations. As incidents of intolerance and harassment occur, the curriculum and the classroom, particularly in general education, are seen as vehicles for response and change (Cannon, 1990; Auletta & Jones, 1994; Osajima, 1991; Weinstein & Obear, 1992). Such efforts are aimed at the large parts of populations which have lived in primarily segregated and homogeneous communities with little contact with persons of color and at those who may be perpetuating the intolerance. Increasingly, there is recognition that most persons from the society have had little contact with persons from other racial and ethnic groups or socioeconomic backgrounds. Many campus requirements concerning issues of race, ethnicity, and gender reflect the use of the curriculum as a response to this second dimension of diversity.

This second dimension has implications for the classroom because it focuses not just on who is there but on the atmosphere in which learning takes place and the opportunities to engage the educational process. For the classroom, particularly one in which the faculty member is attempting to have a discussion, the challenge can be formidable. Many faculty have not been prepared to deal with emotion in their academic sanctuary. As Margaret Wilkerson so aptly describes: "Some faculty fear they will be unable to handle the inevitable conflict, anger, frustration, and confusion of their students, as well as their own fear, anger or feelings of guilt. 'I am not prepared to be a social worker,' they cry: 'I am a scholar and teacher!'" (Wilkerson, 1992, p. 59). Campuses have also found themselves immersed in "difficult dialogues," which are often rancorous, contentious, and accusatory (Weinstein & Obear, 1992). Thus, this is not always a comfortable response or domain for faculty except for those faculty whose area of expertise is closely connected to issues of race, class, and gender.

The third dimension has to do with *educational purpose and the curriculum*. From the beginning, part of the discussion about diversity has focused on an inclusive curriculum for "the new students." The challenge for many faculty has been the fact that, in higher education, the curriculum has rarely been thought of as serving psychological needs of students in terms of self-esteem and role modeling. Rather, the curriculum—what is important to know and do—has emerged in part from the disciplines and from prevailing notions about what an education ought to provide. Although this chapter does not permit an in-depth analysis of the relationship between student characteristics and curricular development (an analysis that occurs in more detail in Garcia & Smith, 1996), it is important to note that, to some degree, student characteristics *do* connect to patterns of learning and culture. Moreover, student characteristics can also prompt tests of the validity of what is taught—that is, the content. Nevertheless, an analysis of the curriculum which relies on the first dimension of diversity, representation, will often reveal a misunderstanding about the nature of curriculum development in higher education in which the curriculum and representation are largely unrelated. Through all of this, faculty find themselves in unfamiliar territory in which the assumption is made that the demographics of the student body ought to impact the curriculum. For faculty, whose understanding has been that the discipline, not the student, defined the curriculum, the new justifications for curricular change seem irrelevant or, worse, politically inspired. This dimension challenges faculty preparation and expertise in the development, evaluation, and creation of the new curriculum. Not only have few students been educated to live in a pluralistic society and world, but few faculty have had any academic background in these areas as well. This dimension thus challenges faculty in areas closest to the core of an important competence— their intellectual and disciplinary expertise.

The fourth dimension, *transformation*, focuses on the institutional and educational changes that can occur as discussions of diversity require rethinking practice, policy, and philosophy. As campuses have begun to engage the curricular and educational questions, faculty find themselves deeply immersed in a host of questions about the purpose of the curriculum, philosophies about teaching and learning, questions about assessing institutional accountability and excellence, changing views on the legitimacy of traditional institutional practices such as grading on the curve, and general calls for fundamental transformation. Traditional indicators of excellence such as standardized testing or publishing in certain journals or being prepared at certain kinds of graduate schools are being scrutinized. Here again, faculty time is required and expertise is called into question. As many have suggested, faculty have little background in the fundamental educational questions being discussed, and these topics have traditionally not been made a part of faculty reward structures (Bess, 1982). Moreover, rethinking fundamental questions challenges long-standing assumptions about excellence, knowledge, and practice (Scott & Aubrey, 1993; Bruffee, 1993; Bensimon, 1993; Tierney, 1993; Minnich, 1990; Harding, 1991; hooks, 1989).

These four dimensions are central to conceptually understanding the role of diversity and student diversity on matters related to the faculty. At the heart of the topic of diversity is the issue of representation, and most particularly, student representation. This dimension has a fundamental relationship to each of the other dimensions. Nevertheless, each of the four dimensions includes different groups and perspectives, and each focuses on expanding domains of the institution. On most campuses today, conversations about diversity usually involve all these dimensions and often simultaneously. Faculty, then, may find themselves facing a wide array of issues related to the emerging "new majority" which seems to press for greater individualization of learning in environments where class size grows and faculty ranks thin. Students are more apt to challenge the curriculum, the climate, the purpose, and the effectiveness of what is being taught, how it is being taught, and who teaches. Each, in its own way, challenges the elements essential to faculty motivation—competence, feedback, and autonomy.

The Campus

The issues related to diversity are played out in an institutional context that adds tension and difficulty for all concerned. Each dimension has implications for resources, not only monetary but time and space as well. These demands occur at a time when institutions face scrutiny and strain concerning resource allocations and accountability. For many public institutions, enrollments are increasing but public funding is not. On independent campuses, the pressure to limit tuition increases grows while expenditures also mount. Thus, most campuses are faced with extraordinary tension about budgets commonly entailing salary freezes and program cuts.

In addition, institutional accountability and the need to demonstrate effectiveness are subjecting higher education to continuing examination and the need to justify resources. Relative lack of success in graduating students of color combined with growing numbers of incidents on campus surrounding race, gender, and sexuality are eroding public trust and creating a climate that is often volatile, strained, and competitive. Large classes, longer times to graduation, increased use of part-time faculty, and eliminating part-time faculty who have often staffed additional sections are exacerbating the climate for teaching within the context of calls to improve teaching and learning—calls that come from all quarters including research universities such as Stanford and Harvard (Halpern, 1994).

Faculty are being asked to do more with less at a time when experimentation and risk are less likely to be satisfying or even politically viable given the scrutiny that departments and programs feel. Rather than enhancing environments for collaboration and discussion, many find themselves fighting battles to retain existing positions, resources, and programs. Thus, the context in which the complex discussions of diversity occur is not at all supportive of the fundamental issues being raised through the dimensions of diversity.

The Faculty

As expressed in the literature, the tension between a more diverse student body and faculty motivation is impacted not only by the complexity of the topic and institutional conditions but also by the nature of the composition of the faculty and by the nature of the profession.

The American professoriate is, on average, aging, and its composition grows less and less like the composition of its student bodies. Recent studies depict a faculty, half of whom are close to fifty, who have been comfortable at their institutions for more than twenty years, and who are largely white, male, and middle class (Baldwin & Blackburn, 1981; El-Khawas, 1991; NCES, 1990). The significance of age is based on interpretations of common wisdom and some research evidence suggesting that faculty interest in teaching decreases with age. It is also based on the classical assumption that faculty impatience with "the young" increases as they age (Astin, 1993). Moreover, the profession and the reward system of higher education are traditionally oriented to the discipline and its content, to publication and research, and to a rather conservative view of change in academic programs. This scenario, while open to question, paints a picture of faculty who are less interested and capable in areas under discussion today—changing curricula, changing pedagogies, advising, classroom and campus climate (Astin, Korn, & Dey, 1991).

Although more needs to be known about faculty as teachers, we do know that traditional pedagogical practices, such as the lecture, reflect faculty comfort with traditional approaches to learning in a context, unfortunately, in which students have much more divergent approaches to learning (Ellner & Barnes, 1983). Indeed, some have suggested that faculty "learning styles" are dominated by more abstract conceptual ways of thinking at the same time that the diversity of student learning styles is growing. In an environment where many more learners no longer match the style of the teacher, there is less reinforcement for the faculty members' efforts and thus real potential for the reduction of faculty and student motivation. Fundamental to this dynamic is that faculty feelings of competence in teaching are likely to erode. It is important here to note that this dynamic has existed for decades, as students have always brought different learning styles to the classroom. The difference is that institutions were more willing to tolerate and even encourage dropouts who did not "fit" and to label those students less able. Today, the profile of those who drop out is under greater scrutiny, and the social costs of having little diversity among graduates—and in as many fields as possible—are better understood. Using prevailing modes of thinking and teaching as filters to "weed out" those who didn't seem to fit is now seen as too costly. The future of the society and the various fields of study will require that talent not be wasted in ways that were once considered acceptable. As to the impact on a "typical" faculty member, the potential for discouragement, dissatisfaction, and a lack of motivation is evident, too often leading to disengagement (Carnegie Foundation, 1989).

This picture, though painted with an admittedly broad brush, describes a considerable challenge to issues of diversity. In general, a climate not very conducive to the most motivating conditions for faculty prevails. Indeed, the current scene is one of quite problematic conditions from the point of not only the faculty but also students and the institution as a whole.

Potential to Enhance Motivation

This rather bleak picture reflects limited understandings about the relationship between diversity and the curriculum, outdated views about student preparation and excellence, and problematic assumptions about faculty. Using the conceptual framework outlined in the beginning of this chapter, we can look at a number of developments that are occurring which have the potential to address institutional concerns about quality and accountability while at the same time tapping rather than threatening faculty motivation.

For many years, the discussion about diversity focused on the issue of representation and often focused on the ways in which characteristics of students were primarily at issue—whether students attended colleges and universities and whether they succeeded. There is now an expanding literature that describes issues related not only to preparation and background characteristics but also to institutional responsibility for educational outcomes. Partly in response to issues generated by the first two dimensions of representation and climate, the dialogs about diversity have moved more forcefully into the third dimension of diversity related to educational mission. Here the question of diversity meets the more traditional role of faculty. But rather than being framed simply in terms of representation, it is now more often being reframed from an educational perspective. It is in the context of asking questions about the purpose of education today that diversity is addressed in terms of educational mission and educating students for a vastly more diverse society and a more interconnected world. That is, educating students for pluralism in the society and the world is now as important as educating students for an increasingly technological society and world was some years ago (and continues to be). From that construction, educational discussions can occur which address the institution's role in education and the educational needs of all students in ways that build on faculty roles and expertise (Levine & Cureton, 1992; Carnegie Foundation, 1992).

Indeed, on many campuses across the country, college faculty and administrators are including in strategic plans and revised mission statements the goal of educating all students to live in a pluralistic society and world. These discussions have led to considerable efforts to rethink the content of the curriculum to engage issues of diversity in the society and world, issues related to the climate on campus, and to respond to the needs of all students to know more about populations different from themselves (Butler & Walter, 1991; Levine & Cureton, 1992; Schmitz, 1992).

This dimension of diversity encompasses all students and, in some ways, focuses increased attention on those students who have little experience with the other dimensions of diversity (Gaff, 1992). Today about 20 percent of campuses have a requirement for a course addressing race and gender, and about 46 percent require a course in world civilizations (Carnegie Foundation, 1992). Increasingly, at the institutional level, campuses are beginning to ask about their own success in educating all students using grades, retention rates, and graduation rates as indicators of institutional success. Moreover, as the needs of the curriculum shift to incorporate new areas of expertise, there is increased demand for faculty who have such expertise and who often come from backgrounds different from those of traditional faculty. Out of the educational demands, the call for a more diversified faculty moves beyond representational issues to substantive calls for new perspectives for both the curriculum itself and for broader issues of educational policy and practice. This has also reinvigorated discussions about the role of the classroom, about teaching, about learning, and about advising. Although this perspective can still be confined to the domain of general education and curricular content, increasingly it is penetrating the disciplines as learned societies and disciplinary associations engage the new scholarship that has been growing over the last thirty years primarily through ethnic studies and women's studies.

Prompted by the recognition that educating all students for a diverse society ought to be an important part of the educational mission of many campuses and universities, scholars, foundations, and organizations have launched major efforts to support the kind of institutional transformation that might be necessary. Central to these efforts has been a focus on curriculum transformation centered in the scholarly and intellectual issues being engaged in the disciplines, in a variety of interdisciplinary research communities, and in the critiques of traditional paradigms of scholarship, which are growing in both number and respectability (AAC&U, 1995; Butler & Walter, 1991; Lincoln, 1985; McIntosh, 1990; Minnich, 1990; Harding, 1991; hooks, 1989). Although some of the literature is still framed in such a way as to make a direct correspondence between a changing student body and the curriculum, many now see that regardless of the student composition, new knowledge and new perspectives need to be added if scholarship is to be enhanced and if the curriculum is to serve the goals of society and the institution.

These projects are being led by faculty and designed to build on faculty culture and strengths—indeed, designed to enhance and sustain faculty motivation. Recent studies suggest that many current efforts have intentionally or intuitively tapped into the need to increase and sustain faculty motivation. Most projects, and particularly those that are successful, are designed to invite voluntary faculty participation and to provide support through release time and stipends for faculty to create time to engage the intellectual and pedagogical aspects of diversity. By focusing on the academic aspects of the curriculum, these projects are focusing on areas in which faculty do feel competent—their disciplines. By providing release time for intellectual activities, these efforts are building on the strengths faculty bring. Issues of pedagogy are often embedded in the content discussions and often build on faculty leaders who have had some success and expertise in these areas.

The emerging literature provides some evidence that faculty rejuvenation is occurring, scholarly communities within and among disciplines are being created among faculty, and interdisciplinary projects are emerging. In addition, there is evidence that younger faculty and faculty who come from diverse backgrounds often find themselves being appreciated as internal resources for other faculty. Moreover, the existence of stipends and release time, though often modest, suggests that the activity is valued and deserving of attention. Campuses have also built in time for research projects related to diversity and have encouraged faculty-student collaboration in research and bibliographic development. Although research on the topic is still thin, available indicators suggest that successful efforts invite faculty to participate in ways that build competence from strength, reward participation, and build a stronger community among faculty, between faculty and students and, sometimes, between academic and student affairs personnel—something that has been lacking for years (El-Khawas, 1993).

In this conceptualization of the relationship between diversity and curriculum, faculty often find themselves more at home because changes within the disciplines have always been part of the role of scholar and teacher. New developments in virtually all fields prompt faculty members who wish to stay current to stay engaged.

Classroom and Pedagogy

There is less evidence that faculty roles in the classroom have changed quite as much, and the challenges to the classroom certainly represent a powerful threat to faculty motivation for teaching. Nevertheless, the urgency of issues of diversity simply highlights the concerns and now offers both support and incentive for change (Auletta & Jones, 1994). With many curriculum projects, faculty are being invited to participate in discussions about pedagogy which address diversity in learning, collaborative approaches, classroom climate, the potential of emotion to assist students in engaging the subject matter even as it represents real risks, and the use of classroom assessment. Although the tension over dealing with emotion remains, the potential for improved teaching and learning is also highlighted. Classroom research, a technique for providing nonthreatening and immediate feedback to faculty on student learning (Angelo & Cross, 1993), has provided a vehicle for faculty to learn more about student learning, to get feedback on the class, and to engage students in the process of learning more directly. There is now some evidence that the use of these assessment methodologies, which give feedback to faculty and require participation of students, tends to increase both faculty and student motivation (Fairweather, 1993).

In addition, numbers of projects have been developed which focus on collaborative learning; these engage students and faculty in new learning communities that build on faculty strengths while creating new ones (Bruffee, 1993). Moreover, there is evidence that significant numbers of faculty, especially older faculty, are participating in these projects. With increased student engagement, the diversity of student backgrounds and perspectives has the potential to add a liveliness and involvement that are absolutely reinforcing to faculty who have become accustomed to seeing lack of interest and involvement on the faces of their students. These approaches are also more likely to include material on the diversity of learning styles, cultural values, and goals for attending college which more readily describes students today (Border & Chism, 1992). From the point of view of good learning theory, these insights and developments have made positive contributions to our understanding of students and learning and are long overdue. The questions are being reformulated to ask about the ways in which institutions, classrooms, and teaching approaches can respond to the individual as well as to group differences among students (Claxton & Murrell, 1987; Entwistle, 1981).

Student Preparation and Excellence

The presence of remedial classes in response to large dropout rates continues to symbolize the notion that diversity and excellence are in conflict. The potential of engaging issues of diversity to prompt transformation of traditional assumptions and practices is probably most powerfully seen in the evidence concerning reframing and transforming approaches to issues of student preparation and success. There is growing evidence that traditional remedial approaches to underpreparation are not effective and that campus practices must change. Increasing efforts are oriented toward involving students in a highly challenging and supportive environment, particularly in math, science, and engineering, where the lack of student success has been a great concern (Bonsangue, 1994; Treismann, 1985; Jackson, 1989). The number of such projects is growing all over the country with a focus on excellence, high expectations, support, peer teaching, and belief in the students' capacity to succeed. Seeing success, particularly with students from diverse backgrounds, reinforces the idea that attending to issues of diversity can and will create potential for all students by reconsidering traditional practices and approaches to teaching and learning. Most powerful of all has been the faculty motivation that comes from success—from students succeeding in rigorous courses designed to challenge.

Implications

What is quite evident is the way in which faculty interest in teaching is being tapped by these issues and the way in which successful programs focusing on educational and intellectual issues engage faculty. These efforts build on the belief that faculty do care about teaching and that disinterest and disengagement have been a function in part of lack of success and lack of feelings of competence. Indeed, contrary to the kinds of prevailing myths and interpretations of research findings about faculty, reliable evidence for years has suggested that a significant percentage of faculty care about teaching and prefer teaching over research. Although research faculties do tend to express lower primary commitment to teaching and younger faculty, women, and faculty of color express stronger commitments to teaching, the vast majority of faculty do value teaching (Astin, Korn, & Dey, 1991; Carnegie Foundation, 1989; Blackburn, Lawrence, Bieber, & Trautvetter, 1991). Recent research on senior faculty suggests that in this group, even at research universities, there is an increasing, not *declining,* commitment to teaching (El-Khawas, 1991).

Moreover, faculty over the years have expressed strong support for issues of social justice. Thus, although faculty as a whole have tended to be quite conservative about academic matters, changes in student diversity combined with the potential for increased success in teaching reveal conditions for increased faculty motivation.

In addition, faculty may be discovering a community that has all too often been absent. These more collaborative environments provide support, ideas, and a stronger sense of connection to the institution. Again, despite the argument that the faculty role is highly individualistic and that faculty enjoy isolation, there is considerable evidence that such conditions negatively impact faculty morale and motivation (Austin, Rice, Splete, & Assoc., 1991; Palmer, 1993; Shulman, 1993).

The conditions for increasing motivation—a sense of competence, feedback, autonomy, significance, and meaning in an affiliative and rewarding environment—so often framed as being antithetical to issues of diversity, are coming into place and represent a significant potential for higher education and faculty.

Organizational Conditions

This discussion is intended to reframe the conversation toward realizing the potential—indeed, the imperative—of diversity. Isolated projects and faculty development approaches are not sufficient, however. Numerous institutional and cultural factors continue to limit the impact of the changes being discussed. In the literature about needed changes in higher education, in general, and transformation related to diversity, in particular, five topics are frequently identified as most salient. None of these is uniquely tied to discussions about diversity. Indeed, as stated in the beginning of this chapter, issues of diversity often serve to highlight long-standing issues, and the solutions and initiatives taken will more often than not serve to highlight principles of good practice and sound theory.

1. *The reward structure.* Boyer's *Scholarship Reconsidered* (1990) has framed alternative ways to reconceptualize teaching and scholarship to give faculty credit for involvement in knowledge development and transmission that also will enhance teaching and learning. The changes proposed, however, tap into fundamental issues of institutional values, assessment of excellence, politics, and prestige. That is to say, a discussion about the reward structure requires engagement with complex and deep-seated values that will not be altered easily. For example, although many more outlets exist now for faculty to write and speak about issues related to pedagogy, it is not always clear that campus review committees are competent or interested in evaluating anything but publications in the most traditional journals and presses. Moreover, the use of conventional student evaluations of teaching, while very important in the process of changing reward structures to increase attention to teaching, has also come into question as faculty find students' reactions to the introduction of controversial material sometimes negative and reflected in student evaluations. For younger, untenured faculty and for faculty who bring widely differing perspectives to the classroom, student evaluations of teaching can be quite threatening (Sandler, 1991). In addition, faculty who bring diverse backgrounds to the campus often find much larger amounts of time spent on committees, in advising, and in mentoring students. This reality is often not acknowledged in review processes that evaluate productivity in terms of numbers of articles and books. The available literature suggests the use of more qualitative approaches to the evaluation of both teaching and scholarship, the use of

faculty professional development agreements, and institutional responses that differentiate faculty requirements depending on an individual's stage and on factors in the institution. Altering the reward
structures will require a much more thorough and comprehensive review of these kinds of issues; such changes will be necessary in order to
validate the amount of time and effort faculty will need to invest in cut-
ting-edge educational issues over the next decade.

2. *Class size and faculty loads.* At many universities, traditional large lecture classes, the use of graduate students as teaching assistants, and the
use of part-time instructors whose contracts do not include time for advising and working with students individually run counter to some of
the conditions for student learning and motivation. Although it is clear
that a variety of approaches to settings for learning can be both efficient
and effective, increasing the full-time enrollment (FTE) and decreasing
personal contact is conducive neither to learning nor to faculty satisfaction. Motivation is weakened both because it does not appear that institutional practice really supports the rhetoric about the need for good
teaching and because such structures make the barriers between faculty
and students all the more difficult. Transformation of the kind being
discussed requires engagement, time, and reinforcement for the risks
being taken.

3. *Long-term commitments.* Some of the changes that have occurred have
been greatly facilitated by the presence of outside funds, sometimes
from public agencies and sometimes from private foundations. There is
evidence that some of the change has generated genuine enthusiasm
and increased morale related to the curriculum, to teaching and scholarship, but it is not clear that campuses have committed the resources
to continue these efforts once outside funding sources end. Moreover,
because many graduate programs still neither provide course work relevant to new forms of scholarship nor introduce graduate students, as
teaching assistants, to alternative forms of teaching, many younger faculty will continue to need further development on the campus. In addition, sources of support and dialog among faculty about how to engage
these important but sensitive issues will require institutionalized vehicles for collaboration—resources that tend to be reduced in times of
fiscal crisis.

4. *Diversification of the faculty.* Ultimately, a community of faculty who
themselves bring diverse perspectives to scholarship and the curriculum, combined with structures to facilitate collaboration, will facilitate

the development of ongoing internal resources for discussion as new issues emerge. A more diverse faculty will reduce the burden on the few that are on campuses at present and will bring stronger views on the ways in which teaching, learning, and campus practices can be improved. Currently, diversifying faculty on most campuses is proceeding slowly, if at all. While the pipeline is used as a continued reason for failures in this area, there is still little awareness about the barriers and biases for hiring faculty already in the pipeline. These barriers reflect the same roadblocks to increasing diversity in the faculty which they present to continued efforts to increase diversity among students.

5. *The need for strong leadership.* These issues are complex, volatile, and fundamental. Virtually every scholar engaged in the study of diversity in higher education, in addition to those studying higher education in general, notes the increasing need for strong and effective leadership. Based on the dimensions of diversity outlined in the beginning of this chapter, it appears that calls for new forms of leadership which engage communities, ideas, and issues will increase in importance. Student voices for change will become stronger. There will be increasing pressure from those outside and inside the institution to change and to change quickly. Yet the conditions for effective change require opportunities to take risks and to collaborate and to involve broad segments of the faculty. Negotiating competing demands and attention to educational values and goals will continue to require skilled leadership. Campus leaders will be required to be educators, not just managers or politicians—developing the capacity to involve varieties of perspectives in difficult dialogs on campus regarding academic freedom, free speech, harassment, campus climate, affirmative action, all in the context of educating students for a much more complex and diverse society.

If crisis produces opportunities for change which might not otherwise be considered, higher education is in—or at least entering—such a situation. Blaming students or faculty in traditional ways will only serve to enhance faculty disengagement and student hostility. Through careful development of the ways in which issues are framed and through deeper understanding of the already existing potential in both faculty and student demographics, there is significant potential for revitalization of faculty motivation centering on involvement, feedback, support, clear focus on the task, and opportunities for success. Many scholars and practitioners have pointed to this period as both an opportunity and an imperative for fundamental rethinking of the functions and practices of higher education. The values and concepts associated with diversity are at the center of that imperative. Like other periods of fundamental change in the history of higher education, this one engages both social and intellectual transformation in response to conditions of the society and the world and within education itself. It is clear that by engaging these issues in ways that enhance the educational and intellectual missions of colleges and universities, there is increased opportunity for excellence and quality in a time of public scrutiny and limited resources.

References

Anderson, J. A., & Adams, M. (1992). Acknowledging the learning styles of diverse student populations: Implications for instructional design. In L. Border & N. V. N. Chism (Eds.), *Teaching for diversity* (pp. 19–33). New Directions for Teaching and Learning 49. San Francisco: Jossey-Bass.

Angelo, T., & Cross, P. (1993). *Classroom assessment techniques.* San Francisco: Jossey-Bass.

Association of American Colleges and Universities (AAC&U). (1995). American pluralism, American commitment, and the college curriculum. Washington, DC: AAC&U.

Astin, A. W., Korn, W. S., & Dey, E. L. (1991). *The American college teacher.* Los Angeles: UCLA, Higher Education Research Institute.

Astin, H. S. (1993). Responsive faculty or responding to student needs. In M. Weimer (Ed.), *Faculty as teachers: Taking stock of what we know* (pp. 5–8). State College, PA: National Center for Teaching, Learning, and Assessment.

Auletta, G. S., & Jones, T. (1994). Unmeshing the myths of racism. In D. Halpern (Ed.), *Changing college classrooms* (pp. 165–174). San Francisco: Jossey-Bass.

Austin, A. E., Rice, R. E., Splete, A. P., & Associates. (1991). *A good place to work.* Washington, DC: Council of Independent Colleges.

Baldwin, R. G., & Blackburn, R. T. (1981). The academic career as a developmental process. *Journal of Higher Education, 52*(6), 598–614.

Bandura, A. (1982). Self-efficacy mechanism in human agency. *American Psychologist, 37,* 122–147.

Bensimon, E. (1993). The development of culturally responsive faculty. In M. Weimer (Ed.), *Faculty as teachers: Taking stock of what we know* (pp. 17–20). State College, PA: National Center for Teaching, Learning, and Assessment.

Bess, J. (1982). *University organization.* New York: Human Sciences Press.

Blackburn, R. T., Lawrence, J. H., Bieber, J. P., & Trautvetter, L. (1991). Faculty at work: Focus on teaching. *Research in Higher Education, 32*(4), 363–381.

Bonsangue, M. (1994). An efficacy study of the calculus workshop model. *Research in Collegiate Mathematics, 4,* 1–19.

Border, L., & Chism, N. V. N. (Eds.). (1992). *Teaching for diversity.* New Directions for Teaching and Learning 49. San Francisco: Jossey-Bass.

Boyer, E. L. (1990). *Scholarship reconsidered: Priorities of the professoriate.* Princeton: Carnegie Foundation for the Advancement of Teaching.

Bruffee, K. A. (1993). *Collaborative learning.* Baltimore: Johns Hopkins University Press.

Butler, J., & Walter, J. (Eds.). (1991). *Transforming the curriculum*. Albany: State University of New York Press.

Cannon, L. W. (1990). Fostering positive race, class, and gender dynamics in the classroom. *Women's Studies Quarterly, 18*(1, 2), 126–134.

Carnegie Foundation for the Advancement of Teaching. (1989). *The condition of the professoriate: Attitudes and trends, 1989*. Princeton: Princeton University Press.

Carnegie Foundation for the Advancement of Teaching. (1992). Signs of a changing curriculum. *Change, 24*(1), 49–52.

Claxton, S. C., & Murrell, P. H. (1987). *Learning styles: Implications for improving educational practice*. ASHE-ERIC Report No. 4. Washington, DC: George Washington University Press.

Curtis, M. S., & Herrington, A. J. (1992). Diversity in required writing courses. In M. Adams (Ed.), *Promoting diversity in college classrooms: Innovative responses for the curriculum, faculty, and institutions*. New Directions for Teaching and Learning 52. San Francisco: Jossey-Bass.

Deci, E. L., & Ryan, R. M. (1991). A motivational approach to self: Integration in personality. In R. Diensbier (Ed.), *Nebraska symposium on motivation* (Vol. 38). Lincoln: University of Nebraska Press.

El-Khawas, E. (1991). Senior faculty in academe: Active, committed to the teaching role. *ACE Research Brief, 2*(5).

El-Khawas, E. (1993). Shared or solitary labor? Overcoming the individualistic culture of academe. In M. Weimer (Ed.), *Faculty as teachers: Taking stock of what we know* (pp. 41–43). State College, PA: National Center for Teaching, Learning, and Assessment.

Ellner, C. L., & Barnes, C. P. (1983). *Studies of college teaching*. Lexington, MA: Lexington Books.

Entwistle, N. (1981). *Styles of learning and teaching*. New York: Wiley.

Fairweather, J. (1993). Faculty rewards reconsidered: The nature of the tradeoffs. *Change, 25*(4), 44–47.

Gaff, J. (1992). Beyond politics: The educational issues inherent in multicultural education. *Change, 24*(1), 30–35.

Garcia, M., & Smith, D. (1996). Reflecting inclusiveness in the college curriculum. In L. Rendon & R. Hope (Eds.), *Educating the new majority*. San Francisco: Jossey-Bass.

Hall, R. M., & Sandler, B. M. (1982). *The classroom climate: A chilly one for women*. Washington, DC: Association of American Colleges.

Halpern, D. F. (Ed.). (1994). *Changing college classrooms*. San Francisco: Jossey-Bass.

Harding, S. (1991). *Whose science? Whose knowledge? Thinking from women's lives*. Ithaca, NY: Cornell University Press.

hooks, b. (1989). *Talking back: Thinking feminist, thinking black*. Boston: South End Press.

Institute for the Study of Social Change. (1991). *The diversity project: Final report*. Berkeley: University of California.

Jackson, A. (1989). Minorities in mathematics: A focus on excellence, not remediation. *American Educator, 22*–27.

Levine, A., & Cureton, J. (1992). The quiet revolution: Eleven facts about multiculturalism and the curriculum. *Change, 24*(1), 24–29.

Lincoln, Y. (Ed.). (1985). *Organizational theory and inquiry: The paradigm revolution*. Beverly Hills: Sage.

McIntosh, P. (1990). Curricular revision: The new knowledge for a new age. In C. Pearson, D. Shavlik, & J. G. Touchton (Eds.), *Educating the majority* (pp. 400–412). New York: Macmillan.

Minnich, E. K. (1990). *Transforming knowledge.* Philadelphia: Temple University Press.

National Center for Educational Statistics (NCES). (1990). *Digest for education statistics.* Washington, DC: U.S. Department of Education, pp. 91–660.

Osajima, K. (1991). Challenges to teaching about racism: Breaking the silence. *Teaching Education, 4*(1), 145–152.

Palmer, P. (1993). Good talk about good teaching. *Change, 25*(6), 8–13.

Sandler, B. R. (1991). Women faculty at work in the classroom, or, why it still hurts to be a woman in labor. *Communication Education, 40,* 6–15.

Schmitz, B. (1992). Cultural pluralism and core curricula. In M. Adams (Ed.), *Promoting diversity in college classrooms: Innovative responses for the curriculum, faculty, and institutions* (pp. 61–69). New Directions for Teaching and Learning 52. San Francisco: Jossey-Bass.

Scott, D. K., & Aubrey, S. M. (1993). Transforming scholarship. *Change, 25*(4), 38–43.

Shulman, L. S. (1993). Teaching as community property: Putting an end to pedagogical solitude. *Change, 25*(6), 6–7.

Smith, D. (1989). *The challenge of diversity: Involvement or alienation in the academy.* ASHE-ERIC Report No. 5. Washington, DC: George Washington University.

Tierney, W. (1993). *Building communities of difference: Higher education in the 21st century.* Westport, CT: Greenwood Press.

Treismann, U. (1985). A study of the mathematics performance of black students at the University of California, Berkeley. Unpublished doctoral dissertation, University of California, Berkeley.

Weinstein, G., & Obear, K. (1992). Bias issues in the classroom: Encounters with the teaching self. In M. Adams (Ed.), *Promoting diversity in college classrooms: Innovative responses for the curriculum, faculty, and institutions* (pp. 39–52). New Directions for Teaching and Learning 52. San Francisco: Jossey-Bass.

Wilkerson, M. B. (1992). Beyond the graveyard: Engaging faculty involvement. *Change, 24*(1), 59–63.

14 Assessment and Evaluation Techniques

STEPHEN A. STUMPF AND
VIOLINA P. RINDOVA

Is a scoreboard a motivator? To some, keeping score is essential to knowing one's relative position in life. Their motivation stems from an inner desire to win. They will find a way, sometimes any way, to achieve a higher score. To others, evaluation is a control and influence tool. If you do not measure something, you cannot manage people to improve it. You need accurate measures of performance to assess goal accomplishment. If people are not meeting their goals, it is up to the manager to identify corrective action and motivate others to try harder. To still others, assessments are just another form of feedback, not all that much different from the feedback one gets from the task itself or self-appraisals. The feedback may be perceived as positive, negative, or just interesting. It may be ignored, or it may be used to modify goals, modify behaviors, or modify the measures used to define the behavior. The assessment remains feedback independent of what is done with the information by the person being evaluated.

How do academics view assessment and evaluation (A&E) information on their teaching performance: as a scoreboard, as a tool for administrator influence and control, or as feedback that may be positive, negative, or just interesting? Or are they indifferent to such information, not responding to

The authors wish to thank Joel DeLuca and Toni Riccardi for their insightful comments about performance appraisal systems and how they might be improved by "rounded appraisal."

it one way or another? Do faculty members want to know how their teaching performance is evaluated and how to improve it? Or are faculty members indifferent to becoming master teachers because their institution's A&E and reward systems value grant getting, research, and publishing more highly than teaching effectiveness?

In order to use A&E techniques to motivate faculty members, such indifference, when it exists, must be transformed into personal interest. This suggests that feedback to faculty must be judiciously designed so that it both meets organizational needs for assessing achievement of institutional goals and simultaneously addresses individual and probably idiosyncratic needs for rewards that sustain or enhance one's motivation to teach. We examine this premise throughout the chapter by first reflecting on the role of evaluation in higher education and then exploring several assumptions about A&E and conducting a brief review of motivation/evaluation theories and sources of feedback. We then identify several A&E myths and suggest a research agenda to improve our understanding of faculty motivation to teach.

Evaluation in Higher Education

In higher education, evaluation is a common, daily activity that academics do with respect to others. What other profession is responsible for evaluating so many people's performances so frequently? Evaluation activities consume a significant proportion of one's teaching responsibilities. It requires that one set standards of performance, provide opportunities for others to perform, identify or create measures of performance, and then critically apply the measurement methods to the behaviors to arrive at an evaluation.

With so much time spent in the role of expert evaluator, it is not surprising that some faculty members question the validity and reliability of the assessment techniques that are used to evaluate *their* performance. A common criticism of teaching evaluation is, "How could someone else [read students, the chairperson, a peer teaching a different course, a more junior peer, a more senior peer who is out of touch with the contemporary theories] using standardized measures and methods or observing a small portion of what I do make an accurate and useful evaluation of my performance? I am unique in what I do. I am the expert." If you accept this as a representative faculty member reaction to teaching evaluations, then the motivational potential of many A&E methods is severely limited.

What if you do not accept the above description as representative of faculty members at your institution. Then your A&E methods are motivational, right? Research strongly suggests the opposite. DeLuca and Riccardi (1993) reviewed the performance appraisal literature as it related to a group of professionals: public accountants. Findings of researchers and practitioners who have investigated performance evaluation based mainly on supervisor appraisals do not provide much hope for the motivational potential of A&E methods. Quotes reported by DeLuca and Riccardi (p. 10) include:

- "The traditional top down approach to performance appraisal is anachronistic, passé, and obsolete."
- "The performance appraisal system is the biggest inhibitor to continuing improvement in any organization."
- "Performance appraisal is the Achilles' heel of our profession."
- "An American Society of Personnel Administrators survey concluded that less than 10% of companies have reasonable successful performance appraisal programs."
- "Study after study has shown that the typical performance ratings done by a superior tend to be suspect."

We argue that an A&E system centered around the individual, not the supervisor, will have the highest motivating potential in academic settings. This idea is substantiated by recent developments (see DeLuca & Riccardi, 1993). More important, it reflects the central role of the individual faculty member in the teaching process, with its ambiguous goals, undefined outcomes, and nonstandardized technology. Unless the A&E techniques used recognize the importance of unique individual contributions in making teaching effective, they are not likely to motivate the desired behaviors.

A key factor in understanding the extent to which A&E techniques motivate faculty members to teach is the faculty member's acceptance of the assessment information as valid and representative feedback. For A&E techniques to have a positive motivational potential, they must also be perceived by the assessees as having value—either directly or in an instrumental way through the technique's value to others whose opinions and actions the assessee values. The value of the feedback received may be based on its perceived objectivity and accuracy as determined by validation research and statistical analyses. Or its value may be based on the faith one has in the integrity and observational skills of the evaluator(s). Without a perceived value, the information provided is likely to be ignored, treated as noise, or viewed as misinformation. There may be a faculty member response to such feedback, but it is not likely to be one that inspires efforts to improve in future teaching activities.

What leads faculty members to accept A&E information as valid and representative feedback when its source is from others often believed to be less expert than themselves? A substantial amount has been theorized, researched, and written about with respect to motivation and performance evaluation. We now review select knowledge accumulated in this area as it relates to the use of A&E techniques as motivators to teach in order to derive some guidance for faculty administrators and a research agenda for the field.

Motivation and Evaluation Theories

A Historical Perspective

Motivation and A&E techniques have roots within two different social science domains. Motivational research evolves from diverse philosophical and psychological assumptions about human behavior. It deals with a fundamental question—what stimulates people to do what they do—having a basic understanding of people as the cornerstone of the inquiry. The A&E studies stem from an applied, instrumental approach to improving human performance in organizations. An instrumental role was assigned to individuals, with the focus of effort on measurement of their behaviors, rather than understanding the source or cause of the behavior.

While motivational researchers attempted to find the cause of behaviors, their assessment methods counterparts took an interest in behavioral and business outcomes. The legacy of this early distinction is still present in the design of most performance evaluation systems in use today. Although the administrative focus may be less pronounced in academic settings owing to the unusual and distinctive governance or authority structure, the temptation to measure and count outcomes persists. For example, teaching effectiveness is often measured by the number of students who perceived the instructor as "presenting course materials in an organized fashion" or "showing interest in students" or "grading fairly." As a result, the effectiveness of assessments and evaluations for motivational purposes, rather than administrative purposes, remains questionable.

Most A&E approaches treat individuals in organizations as objects of evaluation and the administrative representatives of an institution as an authoritative source of correct judgments. Consider the following assumptions that underlie such an approach:

- External appraisals are more valid than internal ones because people tend to overrate their own effectiveness.

- Appraisals are based on standardized information that ensures comparability and objectivity.
- Appraisals measure outcomes relative to clearly defined goals and performance standards.
- People derive value from knowing how well they fulfill organizational expectations because organizations control future outcomes that individuals value.

Although these assumptions are pervasive in many A&E approaches, they are disconnected from the realities of work situations, and they ignore the links between evaluative information and motivation. These assumptions are even more damaging to the motivating potential of A&E techniques for academics. Academics (and other highly educated professionals) often perceive themselves as experts, value academic/professional freedom, and have considerable autonomy in setting their own goals, priorities, and rewards.

In order to understand how A&E techniques affect human motivation in organizations, three points of reference should be considered—the individual, the organization, and the profession. Performance looks different from each of these perspectives, and so do evaluation systems in terms of their purpose, design, effectiveness, and appropriateness. Although A&E techniques have their greatest motivational or demotivational effects at the individual level, the organization and profession provide a structural and normative context for their use.

We do not attempt to reconcile the contradictions inherent in these three perspectives herein. Rather, we argue from the point of view of the faculty member—the object of the evaluation process in its traditional form. Through this choice we hope to minimize the external evaluator bias in evaluation research of academic settings (Centra, 1979; Doyle, 1983; Miller, 1987; Seldin, 1989).

Research on performance feedback in organizations has evolved from early management appraisal and job quality approaches (Hackman & Lawler, 1971; Katz & Kahn, 1978; Turner & Lawrence, 1965; Larson, 1984) to an understanding of feedback as an individual resource and mechanism of self-regulation (Ashford & Cummings, 1983; Ashford, 1986, 1989; Lord & Hanges, 1987; Morrison & Bies, 1991; Klein, 1989; Taylor, Fisher, & Ilgen, 1984). This latter research stream is rooted in information-processing and symbolic interactionism theories. It examines how people make use of the information available at the work place and derive value from that information.

The idea that people do value performance information is not new. Most theories of motivation use information as an explanatory component of human behavior. It has been suggested that "the motivational effect of knowledge of results is one of the best established findings in the research literature" (Locke, 1968, p. 324), but just how knowledge of results is communicated, by whom, and to whom greatly alter the nature of the motivation that follows the feedback. Various relationships exist between types of feedback and motivating mechanisms, which form "motivation-evaluation linkages." In the following section we examine some of these possible relationships to uncover how the A&E process can increase faculty motivation to teach.

Motivation-Evaluation Linkages

Intrinsic motivation theories view information as a motivating factor that facilitates an internal perceived locus of causality and perceived competence. This "causal competence" belief (i.e., "I'm the reason why I am competent") enhances intrinsic motivation for tasks in which the feedback is positive. Negative information is demotivating, as it reduces one's sense of competence (Deci & Ryan, 1985).

An activity is intrinsically motivating to the degree that it provides challenge and yields positive feedback. Complexity, novelty, and unpredictability are characteristics of an activity which allow it to challenge one continuously. Teaching is likely to be rich in each of these characteristics. Quite often teaching shifts from "a flow experience" of the absorption and effortless action of optimal challenge (Csikszentmihalyi, 1990) to anxiety associated with an overwhelming task. According to intrinsic motivation theories, teaching evaluations that enhance the perceptions of competence both increase intrinsic motivation and make the activity itself more enjoyable.

Equity theories of motivation posit performance feedback as central to the perceptions of justice in the organization (Folger, 1977; Folger & Konovsky, 1989). Equity theory augments the intrinsic motivation view with a social comparison dimension. According to equity theorists, people value rewards not only because they satisfy needs, but also because the rewards recognize relative contributions. Equity and justice theories suggest that evaluations will have a greater value to the assessee if the feedback involves a two-way communication process, is rich in details, is open, and shows respect for the individual's contributions. No specific mention is made about how an assessee's motivation varies as a function of the feedback being positive versus negative.

Expectancy theory proposes that performance information triggers the motivational process by helping the assessee develop estimates of the probabilities that actions lead to desired outcomes, which in turn lead to desired rewards (Vroom, 1964). Expectancy theory has been criticized as an overly rational representation of human behavior. Nevertheless, it establishes a link between work motivation and subjective cognitive constructs, such as expectancies and instrumentalities. Expectancy theory suggests that the value of an assessment increases (i.e., the assessee will exhibit more effort toward a goal) when the information provided (1) clarifies performance-outcome contingencies, (2) pertains to specific behaviors, and (3) reduces uncertainty about desired outcomes. Associated with each of these cognitions should be a change in performance effort.

The cognitive approaches to motivation have led to other theories of evaluation-motivation linkages. For example, motivation, feedback, and goals form a dominant construct triad in social learning theory (Bandura, 1977, 1986) and control theory (Miller, Galanter, & Pribrum, 1960; Carver & Scheier, 1981; Lord & Hanges, 1987).

Social learning theory postulates two cognitive mechanisms of motivation. One mechanism operates through the exercise of forethought by representing desired future consequences symbolically. These expectations can be thought of as instrumentalities, after Vroom (1964). The second major source of cognitive motivation derives from internal standards and self-evaluative reactions to one's performances. It concerns expectations about personal mastery or self-efficacy, that is, the personal judgment of one's confidence that he or she can execute specific behaviors (Bandura, 1977).

Self-efficacy mediates the process of translation of knowledge and abilities into skilled performance. Self-efficacy has been shown to influence (1) goal level and goal commitment (Locke, Frederick, Lee, & Bobko, 1984; Taylor, Fisher, & Ilgen, 1984); (2) the initial choice of activities and coping efforts while engaged in a task (Lent, Brown, & Larkin, 1987; Stumpf, Brief, & Hartman, 1987); (3) the interpretation of feedback; (4) emotional reactions; and (5) persistence. Some evidence suggests that the predictive validity of self-efficacy for performance of complex tasks can be weaker than for performance of simple tasks (Stumpf, Brief, & Hartman, 1987; Taylor, Fisher, & Ilgen, 1984).

Control theory elaborates on the cognitive mechanism through which goals, or referent standards and feedback, jointly determine motivation. Control theories imply that goal-feedback discrepancies are the crucial determinants of motivation and behavior. If the goal-feedback discrepancy triggers motivation, then any aspect of goals for which specific feedback is not available eventually will be underemphasized. Similarly, aspects of feedback for which there are no clear goals will be hard to interpret and have minimal impact on motivation.

The application of cognitive theories of motivation to behavior in the work setting has produced a fundamental shift in the understanding of performance feedback, namely the individual resource perspective. The refreshing vigor of the individual resource perspective on feedback is that it focuses on active feedback-seeking behaviors that goal-oriented, motivated, and self-regulating individuals exhibit. Secondly, these theories offer a dynamic view of motivation based on the interdependence of a person and the environment, which considers several perspectives, including organizational and professional viewpoints. These interpretations bring to the traditional evaluation context a longer-term, individual growth role for feedback. They shift the focus from organizational control to individual development and learning through activities and assessment. Support for this alternative approach to motivation rests in the structure of goals and rewards in academia, the work orientations of faculty members as expressive rather than instrumental (Goldthorpe, Lockwood, Bechoffer, & Platt, 1969), and faculty member personal characteristics such as self-esteem and self-focus. We believe that an individual resource perspective holds the greatest potential for enhancing faculty motivation to teach.

Based on the belief that academic independence and professionalism (autonomy, creativity, commitment to learning, novelty, and discovery) are dominant job context factors for faculty, we propose that the impact of assessment practices on teaching motivation be evaluated within an analytic framework centered around the individual. It derives from the cognitive theories discussed above. Control theory, for example, considers the individuals' concepts of self as the highest-order standards from which they derive subordinate goals and standards. This framework is particularly important in the context of evaluation and assessment techniques, for in order to measure something, one has to determine what is to be measured and establish standards of performance for comparison purposes. This raises the question: Which are the relevant standards, and who provides the assessment?

Sources of Feedback

We presented different motivational theories and their implications for individual evaluation, trying to expand the notion of what is relevant to the assessee. We overview below several evaluation practices, again with a view to expand the limits of the traditional performance appraisal process.

Who are the relevant and appropriate evaluators of faculty teaching effectiveness? Numerous studies have investigated the sources of assessments along with their relative contributions in administrative decisions. Seldin (1989) reports on the factors that administrators consider in evaluating overall faculty performance, as well as the sources of information that colleges use to evaluate teaching performance. He has found that the department Chair remains the predominant source of information in faculty evaluation. The systematic use of student ratings has risen significantly, so that ratings have become the second most frequent source of data (only a fraction of a point behind the department Chair input). Classroom visits by colleagues have gained significantly, despite problems with the lack of standardized procedures for them.

The implications of Seldin's study involve the importance of using multiple sources of data and understanding the relative weights assigned to the sources of data by the institution. We are concerned with how faculty members evaluate, use, and incorporate assessment information in their subsequent motivation to teach. What is the developmental effect of feedback as it affects self-perceptions, professional learning, and commitment to teach? The answers would vary substantially depending on which motivational theory one prefers and the perceived positive, negative, and interesting elements of the feedback.

Siagian (1983) found that student evaluative feedback did not have any significant impact on the perception of teachers regarding their teaching performance, nor did it correlate with self-ratings. This is a common finding in the literature across many different schools and faculties. In addition, self-ratings frequently correlate marginally with external evaluative sources and are often viewed as biased.

Evaluation writers and researchers in academic settings frequently agree that the literature in the field of faculty evaluations—and particularly student ratings—must go beyond the measurement questions that have dominated the literature. Student evaluations of faculty need to be considered within the complex configuration of faculty-student-administrator interactions (Manicas & Secord, 1983; Theall & Franklin, 1989, 1990).

A second concern comes from research on feedback in organizations. In an exploratory study of the sources of feedback, Greller and Herold (1975) found that feedback is received or perceived from five sources: self, task, supervisor, co-workers, organization. They concluded that feedback can be meaningfully thought of as emanating from different sources and that

Table 14.1   Motivation-Evaluation Linkages by Source of Feedback

	SOURCES OF FEEDBACK			
MOTIVATION THEORIES	Faculty Member	Teaching Process	Peers' Evaluations	Administrative Appraisal
Intrinsic Motivation	Competence enhancement	Most important motivating factor	Not relevant	Motivation reduction
Equity & Justice Theories	Comparison between own output and others'	Not relevant	Adjustment of comparisons	Perception of procedural justice
Expectancy Theory	Source of valences	Not relevant	Not relevant	Source of instrumentalities
Social Learning Theory	Self-efficacy enhancement	Self-efficacy enhancement	Vicarious learning	Vicarious learning
Control Theory	Continuous monitoring to adjust referents and behavior	Immediate feedback	Additional feedback	Adjustment of referents and behavior, if accepted

these sources differ in the degree of informativeness. Hanser and Muchinsky (1978) replicated the Greller and Herold study with a sample of 387 faculty members. They obtained similar results: The formal organization and the supervisor in their study were reported to provide less useful information. These results seem to indicate that sources identified as intrinsic, or psychologically closer to the individual, are seen as providing more useful information than those sources identified as external, or psychologically distant. What makes something "psychologically closer" may vary based on one's interest in the work itself and organizational/professional values and rewards. Table 14.1 summarizes the motivation-evaluation linkages by source of feedback.

Uncovering Motivation-Evaluation Myths

For A&E techniques to generate valid and representative feedback that has motivational potential, they need to be grounded in realities that are shared by faculty members, their institutions, and the profession. Yet most A&E techniques are designed from an organizational (performance appraisal) rather than an individual (useful feedback) perspective. In this section we expose several myths underlying such approaches and propose more realistic views that could replace them.

The following myths seem to be alive and well in many work organizations, including academic institutions. To the extent that these myths are left unchallenged, the motivational potential of the feedback generated by the assessment system will remain severely limited.

Myth: A&E techniques involve a rational process.
Reality: A&E techniques involve a human process.

Human beings are complex, have many agendas, and frequently attempt to be rational. But they also make judgments and behave in ways that are subject to group pressures, personal egos, and emotion. Such judgments may not be perceived as rational by those being judged. It is because of this "less than rational" human process that feedback on performance is rarely perceived as being completely accurate—particularly when it is negative with regard to something that the assessee knows much more about than the assessor.

Myth: A&E techniques can be designed to be objective.
Reality: A&E techniques cannot remove subjectivity.

Even when measures of performance are objective, the choice of those measures, as well as the use of one measure over others, is subjective. To make matters worse, the interpretation of an objective measure—by the assessee and the assessor—is likely to be different.

Myth: A&E techniques have a motivational potential because people want to know where they truly stand so as to improve future performance.
Reality: A&E techniques have conflicting motivational value; they motivate when they enhance competence and learning, but they demotivate when they shake self-esteem.

There is significant evidence that we do not want to know how we are actually doing unless we are doing well. People tend to overrate their own contribution to performance. It seems that almost everyone has a need to feel that they are at least average. This leads to the 80/30 phenomena: 80 percent of us believe that we are in the upper 30 percent of performers. Our above-average performance is important to our self-esteem, which is closely tied to performance motivation. Given the lack of clear performance standards in teaching (Centra, 1979), A&E techniques can emphasize opportunities for improvement and deemphasize current flaws.

Myth: A&E techniques can provide independent evaluations of performance from different sources of observation.
Reality: A&E techniques cannot provide independent observations but should involve multiple sources of information.

Teaching behaviors are intended to accomplish many goals—some of which are not known to some evaluators, others of which might be inconsistent with respect to some evaluators. Students evaluate teaching against their perceived learning and enjoyment of the process. Peers evaluate teaching against the knowledge available in the field and how well they perceive it as being represented to the learners. Department chairpersons rate teaching performance based on student feedback, grade distributions, the absence of student complaints, the thoroughness of syllabi, and so on. Other evaluators may see still other aspects of teaching performance. Since the teaching behavior does not separate these facets of performance, nor do observers see only one aspect of performance at a time, there is not likely to be much independence in the judgments of different raters.

Unearthing these myths for scrutiny allows us to consider the motivational aspects of A&E systems apart from the ways in which such systems are used in organizations today. Faculty members that are committed to becoming master teachers are likely to respond favorably to evaluative feedback that (1) reflects a human system perspective (as opposed to a rational system view), (2) acknowledges its subjectivity, (3) is presented in the context of 80 percent of one's behavior being evaluated in the top 30 percent of performance, and (4) is based on many raters from different perspectives that are not held out to be independent. It is also likely that some faculty members will be threatened by such a system as it will involve valuable time, expose their values, and identify how their performances are not meeting the needs of all relevant constituencies. To be successful, the design of A&E techniques must creatively address these anxieties.

A Research Agenda

The proposed demythologization of the evaluation and assessment processes in academia to enhance their motivational potential is consistent with recent developments in the field of organizational behavior. Several research streams have presented a changing view of the roles of individuals in organizations. A new question being asked is "How do individuals deal with organizations?" rather than only asking, "How do organizations deal with people?" Self-management, self-leadership, and self-assessment are a few examples of an employee empowerment approach to the work environment (Ashford, 1986, 1989; Brief & Aldag, 1981; Manz & Sims, 1980).

Thinking about important organizational results as individual achievements coincides with the way individuals think about results. It follows that more individual-centered organizational solutions serve the organization as well, since they contribute to the overall organizational performance. Trading institutional control for self-management can be particularly beneficial in universities where faculties are not well disposed to being managed and zealously guard their autonomy and right to participate in major decisions affecting their organizations (Mintzberg, 1979).

In the context of the academic profession and the teaching activity in particular, organizational achievement is possible only through distinct individual and even individualistic accomplishments. Given the ambiguity and multiplicity of goals in the academic setting, the individual performance of the faculty members is not only measured against some standards but directly affects the level of these standards. The paramount importance of the individual faculty member in the teaching activity—from its definition, through its design and execution, to its evaluation—should be reflected in the formal evaluation and assessment system. This is a necessary condition for the latter to be a source of motivation and valued feedback, geared toward individual development. Performance appraisal and evaluation techniques historically have formed the core of organizational control systems. Consequently, they are a critical part of initiating a more individual-oriented work environment.

A new design agenda in organizations suggests a new research agenda for evaluation and assessment techniques research. An important step will be made if old assumptions are abandoned and pervasive myths are substituted with insights from a rich body of research in feedback and performance appraisal. Next, knowledge about evaluation-motivation linkages should guide design choices. Given the multiple and conflicting effects of feedback on motivation, understanding of these linkages will help administrators to walk the fine line between the positive stimulation and debilitating frustration that performance feedback can yield.

However, designing A&E systems requires more detailed analysis of specific aspects of the evaluation process. Who should provide information and who should communicate it? What information—about outcomes or about behaviors—how often, in what context? These are just a few of the salient questions to be answered. Possibly more important is the challenge of integrating choices along each dimension into a cohesive A&E system that talks to the individual faculty member, rather than about him or her. Current research seems more positioned to provide ideas about the parts rather than the whole.

Highlighting the importance of individual measures and reference standards constitutes only a part of the reevaluation of our A&E techniques. The question of how to design more individualized systems is equally important. The design process involves several decision points:

- How to combine subjective input with institutional standards
- How to standardize performance information and preserve its meaningfulness as individual feedback
- How to measure the effectiveness of this different evaluation approach —in terms of increased motivation, developmental effects, and performance data for the reward systems

How to design such A&E systems remains an interesting and promising question with many answers. Our purpose is to increase the awareness of the trade-offs in the process and to suggest a gestalt shift that might be required on behalf of academic administrators to arrive at more motivating A&E approaches.

In order to include more subjective input, both assessors and assessees should provide reference standards and information for evaluations. For example, specific ratings might ask the respondent to anchor the evaluation in something familiar to the instructor via metaphor or analogy. Learning that several students felt that they were "treading water" rather than working toward an agreed-upon goal adds texture to an agreement rating of "3" out of "5" on the statement "Graded assignments were clearly presented." A process that solicits more subjective input requires a more human, less than rational approach. Such an approach allows for greater diversity and more novelty. It supposes more involvement of the assessors with the evaluation process. The high return on this much higher effort is increased faculty receptiveness toward such feedback and a more motivated effort to incorporate it in teaching practices.

More subjectivity in assessment techniques means more individual flavor in place of role definitions and abstract standards. It means more credibility of the feedback message and more dialogue, as well as more understanding. This poses a big challenge to the assessors' initiative to obtain and communicate meaningful, specific, and essentially individual feedback. Since more subjective appraisals are less likely to be perceived as tied to rewards and promotion, they are more likely to fulfill their informational function and developmental function.

More variety of sources of information and criteria means more participants in the evaluation process and more interaction among them. Diversity always poses the problem of integration and blending. To resolve it, evaluators have to employ more comprehensive approaches that include a combination of measures, such as cognitive measures—learning and subsequent students' performance; behavioral—the attributes of "the good teacher"; and affective measures such as satisfaction and students' involvement. In addition, they have to seek to appraise discrete behaviors (acts) as well as patterns of behavior (teaching); short-term performance (teaching a course); and long-term performance (teaching as an aspect of an academic career).

Finally, current A&E techniques infrequently include "live," holistic measures of the teaching process. This omission, rooted in their administrative purposes and usage, actually undermines the measurement adequacy. Teaching is a dynamic, interactive, live process that certainly transcends the items on student rating sheets. The role model effect of the classroom interaction is an example of a completely different set of measurement categories for teaching performance. Unfortunately, this approach to A&E techniques seems absent from both academic reality and research agendas.

Summary

To use organizationally designed assessment and evaluation techniques to motivate faculty members to teach more effectively is a difficult task. The many roles that faculty members assume within their institution and profession often place teaching performance secondary in importance. The expert role assumed by most faculty members, the difficulty in observing teaching performance by administrators, and the wide variety of preferences held by the students create a complex context in which to evaluate teaching effectiveness. Our challenge is to expose this complexity, move away from "one size fits all" evaluation models, and link faculty member preferences for feedback and rewards to the organizational A&E system.

From a systems view, it may be easier to give faculty members more of what they want which is consistent with what the institution wants than it is to change faculty members to want what they do not want but which the institution wants. A key to future institutional success may be in knowing what it wants and then selecting appropriate faculty members to perform accordingly, rather than try to design an A&E system to motivate people to do things they have little interest in doing.

References

Ashford, S. J. (1986). Feedback-seeking in individual adaptation: A resource perspective. *Academy of Management Journal, 29,* 465–487.

Ashford, S. J. (1989). Self-assessments in organizations: A literature review and integrative model. In B. M. Staw and L. L. Cummings (Eds.), *Research in organizational behavior* (Vol. 11, pp. 133–174). Greenwich, CT: JAI Press.

Ashford, S. J., & Cummings, L. (1983). Feedback as an individual resource: Personal strategies of creating information. *Organizational Behavior and Human Performance, 32,* 370–398.

Bandura, A. (1977). Self-efficacy: Toward a unifying theory of behavioral change. *Psychological Review, 84,* 191–215.

Bandura, A. (1986). *Social foundations of thought and action: A social-cognitive view.* Englewood Cliffs, NJ: Prentice-Hall.

Brief, A., & Aldag, R. (1981). The "self" in work organizations: A conceptual review. *Academy of Management Review, 6,* 75–88.

Carver, C., & Scheier, M. (1981). *Attention and self-regulation: A control theory approach to human behavior.* New York: Springer-Verlag.

Centra, J. A. (1979). *Determining faculty effectiveness: Assessing teaching, research, and service for personnel decisions and improvement.* San Francisco: Jossey-Bass.

Csikszentmihalyi, M. (1990). *Flow: The psychology of optimal experience.* New York: HarperCollins.

Deci, E. L., & Ryan, R. M. (1985). *Intrinsic motivation and self-determination in human behavior.* New York: Plenum Press.

DeLuca, J. M., & Riccardi, T. (1993). Rounded appraisal: Prerequisite for sustained organizational excellence. Evergreen Business Group, Philadelphia.

Doyle, K. O. (1983). *Evaluating teaching.* Lexington, MA: D. C. Heath.

Folger, R. (1977). Distributive and procedural justice: Combined impact of "voice" and improvement on experienced inequality. *Journal of Personality and Social Psychology, 35,* 108–119.

Folger, R., & Konovsky, M. (1989). Effects of procedural and distributive justice on reactions to pay raise decisions. *Academy of Management Journal, 32,* 115–130.

Goldthorpe, J., Lockwood, H., Bechoffer, F., & Platt, S. (1969). *The affluent worker in the class structure.* Cambridge: Cambridge University Press.

Greller, M., & Herold, D. (1975). Sources of feedback: A preliminary investigation. *Organizational Behavior and Human Performance, 13,* 244–256.

Hackman, R., & Lawler, E. (1971). Employee reactions to job characteristics. *Journal of Applied Psychology, 55,* 259–286.

Hanser, G., & Muchinsky, P. (1978). Work as an information environment. *Organizational Behavior and Human Performance, 21,* 47–60.

Katz, D., & Kahn, R. (1978). *The social psychology of organizations.* New York: Wiley.

Klein, H. (1989). An integrated control theory model of work motivation. *Academy of Management Review, 14,* 150–172.

Larson, J. (1984). The performance feedback process: A preliminary model. *Organizational Behavior and Human Performance, 33,* 42–76.

Lent, R. W., Brown, S. D., & Larkin, K. C. (1987). Comparison of three theoretically derived variables in predicting career and academic behavior: Self-efficacy, interest congruence, and consequence thinking. *Journal of Counseling Psychology, 34,* 293–298.

Locke, E. A. (1968). Motivational effects of knowledge of results: Knowledge or goal setting. *Journal of Applied Psychology, 51,* 324–329.

Locke, E. A., Frederick, E., Lee, C., & Bobko, P. (1984). Effect of self-efficacy, goals, and task strategies on task performance. *Journal of Applied Psychology, 69,* 241–251.

Lord, R., & Hanges, P. (1987). A control systems model of organizational motivation: Theoretical development and applied implications. *Behavioral Science, 32,* 161–178.

Manicas, P. T., & Secord, P. F. (1983). Implications for psychology of the new philosophy of science. *American Psychologist, 38,* 399–413.

Manz, C., & Sims, H. (1980). Self-management as a substitute for leadership: A social learning perspective. *Academy of Management Review, 6,* 361–367.

Miller, G., Galanter, E., & Pribrum, K. (1960). *Plans and structure of behavior.* New York: Holt, Rinehart & Winston.

Miller, R. I. (1987). *Evaluating policy for promotion and tenure.* San Francisco: Jossey-Bass.

Mintzberg, H. (1979). *The structuring of organizations.* Englewood Cliffs, NJ: Prentice-Hall.

Mitchell, T. R., & Gist, M. E. (1991). Self-efficacy: A theoretical analysis of its determinants and malleability. *Academy of Management Review, 17,* 183–211.

Morrison, E., & Bies, R. (1991). Impression management in the feedback-seeking process: A literature review and research agenda. *Academy of Management Review, 16,* 522–541.

Seldin, P. (1989). How colleges evaluate professors. *AAHE Bulletin, 41,* 3–7.

Siagian, E. (1983). The impact of student evaluative feedback on the perception of the teaching faculty at Andrews University. Unpublished doctoral dissertation, Andrews University.

Stumpf, S. A., Brief, A. P., & Hartman, K. (1987). Self-efficacy expectations and coping with career events. *Journal of Vocational Behavior, 31,* 91–108.

Taylor, M., Fisher, C., & Ilgen, D. (1984). Individuals' reactions to performance feedback in organizations: A control theory perspective. *Research in Personnel and Human Resource Management, 3,* 81–124.

Theall, M., & Franklin, J. (1989). Two different worlds: Research and practice in faculty evaluation. *Instructional Evaluation, 10,* 10–19.

Theall, M., & Franklin, J. (1990). Student ratings in the context of complex evaluation systems. In M. Theall & J. Franklin (Eds.), *Student ratings of instruction: Issues for improving practice.* San Francisco: Jossey-Bass.

Turner, A. N., & Lawrence, P. R. (1965). *Industrial jobs and the worker.* Boston: Harvard Graduate School of Business Administration.

Vroom, V. (1964). *Work and motivation.* New York: Wiley.

V Systemwide Conditions

15 The Influence of Faculty Backgrounds on the Motivation to Teach

JOSEPH M. STETAR AND
MARTIN J. FINKELSTEIN

Who are the college teachers? And does who they are affect their motivation to teach? Over the past generation, the demographics of the college teaching force have changed in a variety of absolute terms; and perhaps even more saliently, they have changed relative to the characteristics and demographics of the student bodies they teach. In this chapter, we begin by charting the changing demographics of college faculties in the context of changing student demographics and how those changes appear to impact the centrality of the academic role in the life of the contemporary professoriate. We then pose and seek to respond to two general questions: (1) How are these changes affecting the key variables that current theories have identified as the arbiters of motivation? (2) What might this mean for efforts to enhance faculty motivation to teach?

Background

The last four decades has witnessed the enormous numerical expansion of the academic profession from about 150,000 faculty in the mid-1940s to more than 600,000 in the mid-1970s and more than 800,000—nearly 500,000 of whom were full-time—in the late 1980s (Ladd & Lipset, 1975; NCES, 1991). This enormous numerical expansion of the academic profession has been associated with only a modest diversification in the traditional demographic characteristics of socioeconomic status, religious background, gender, race, age, and ethnicity.[1]

In at least two respects, however, the pace of diversification has equaled that of growth. First, there is the area of faculty appointments, including various part-time and term options. From 1960 to 1982, there was a three-fold increase in the number of adjuncts used nationally, from 82,000 to 220,000 (Bowen & Schuster, 1986). In 1992 the National Center for Educational Statistics reported that a full 40 percent of the total instructional staff were part-time and at least 10 percent were on term appointments. Both part-time and term categories of appointments are increasing—to the point where nontenure trackers represented approximately one-third of all new faculty appointments in 1981 (Annual Report on Economic Status, 1992).

Second, there is the matter of where college teachers practice, that is, their institutional location. In 1969 nearly half of all college faculty were concentrated at universities; by 1980 barely one-third were (Finkelstein & Schuster, 1992). By the 1980s the vast majority of faculty were spread over the rapidly growing community college sector, now claiming nearly one-quarter of the total, and the comprehensive public college and university sectors (NCES, 1991). Not only have faculty broadened where they call home, but they have come increasingly to "stay put" once arrived, largely, to be sure, as a result of the decline of the academic job market in most fields. Thus, even if not by choice, faculty have increasingly become "homebodies."

The experience of American college students, who constitute a major component of the "working conditions" in higher education, represents a stark contrast. Unlike their teachers, students have changed dramatically in the past twenty-five years in terms of gender, age, and ethnicity. Moreover, as the costs of higher education escalate, many students pursue their education on a part-time basis or attempt to work full-time while pursuing a full-time course of study.

What do the constants and changes in faculty demographics mean for their teaching and how they approach work with students, especially in light of the dramatic diversification of the student body? We turn first to a more detailed review of the faculty demographics in the context of the changing student in American higher education.

Changes in Demographic and Social Background of the Professoriate

Twenty years ago in their study of American academics, Ladd and Lipset drew upon the Carnegie Commission's 1969 Survey of Student and Faculty

Opinion and their own 1972 supplementary survey to describe a professoriate which, in the years since World War II, had grown in size from about 150,000 to more than 600,000 faculty members. With that growth had come changes in the social, religious, and ethnic origins of faculty. For example, the barriers limiting opportunities for male Catholics and Jews to secure a college education—let alone a faculty appointment—in the first half of the twentieth century began to crumble after 1945. Blacks and women did not fare as well, as they have been afforded marginal opportunities for higher education and professorial posts for most of this century (Ladd & Lipset, 1975).[2]

Who are the faculty that teach in our colleges and universities? What do we know about their social demography? How has the professoriate changed over the past twenty years? Demographic changes are examined from three basic perspectives:

1. Social origins of faculty as evidenced by such factors as parental education and occupation and religious origins
2. Race and gender of faculty
3. Current demographic status as evidenced by such factors as professorial salaries, age, and political orientation

Parental Education and Occupation

In examining the social backgrounds of faculty, Ladd and Lipset described a professoriate in the late 1960s with a strong middle-class bias: the sons and occasional daughters of professionals, managers, and business persons (Ladd & Lipset, 1975). Although we will see that there has been some modest diversification of faculty with respect to religious origins in recent decades, their socioeconomic roots, at least to the extent that they are reflected in the educational levels of their fathers as illustrated in figure 15.1, are remarkable with respect to how slowly the profile has changed over the last twenty years (Ladd & Lipset, 1975; NCES, 1987; Astin, Korn, & Dey, 1991).

The relatively high educational level of the fathers of professors is matched by an occupational level that is skewed to the educational, professional, or managerial fields. As table 15.1 illustrates, the occupation of the fathers of professors changed little in the period from the late 1960s to the mid-1980s. In 1969, 57 percent of the faculty were the offspring of fathers whose occupations placed them securely in the professional, managerial, or business categories; in 1984 the comparable figure was 58.4 percent (NCES, 1987; Ladd & Lipset, 1975). Although the socioeconomic

Fig. 15.1   Father's Education

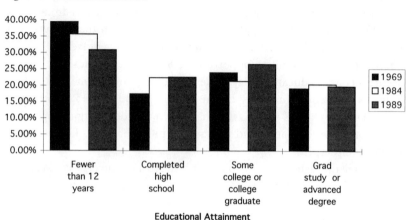

Educational Attainment

backgrounds of students changed significantly in the seventies and eighties to reflect a more pluralistic society, it is evident that those of faculty remained highly consistent.

Ladd and Lipset did not report on the educational attainment of mothers, but the strong middle-class bias in the ranks of the professoriate is further illuminated by the realization that the mothers of professors are substantially more educated than the fathers (table 15.2) at other than the graduate and advanced degree levels. And, even at the advanced degree level, the mothers of professors show signs of closing the gap (NCES, 1987; Astin, Korn, & Dey, 1991).

Not only are faculty being drawn from the highest education cohorts in society, but they are also marrying or forming highly committed relationships in that stratum. Faculty responding to the 1989 Higher Education Research Institute (HERI) Faculty Survey, 76 percent of whom indicated they were currently married, reported that 19.3 percent of their spouses or partners had graduated from college. A staggering 49.6 percent of their spouses or partners had attended a graduate or professional school or had attained an advanced degree (Astin, Korn, & Dey, 1991). These figures are up somewhat from those reported in the 1984 National Faculty Survey, which requested data regarding only spouses rather than spouses or partners. Nevertheless, those data reported 18.8 percent of all faculty spouses were college graduates and 43.1 percent had attended graduate or professional school or attained an advanced degree (NCES, 1987). Faculty not only come in disproportionate numbers from highly educated families;

Table 15.1   Father's Occupation

	1969	1984
College or university teaching	4%	5%
Other teaching	3	4
Other professional work	14	14
Managerial and administrative	16	15
Business owner	20	20
Farm owner	10	NA
Clerical and sales	8	8
Skilled wage worker	16	21
Semiskilled or unskilled wage work	8	11
Armed forces	NA	2

Table 15.2   Parental Education of Faculty, 1984 and 1989

Parental Education	Father 1984	Mother 1984	Father 1989	Mother 1989
Fewer than 12 years	35.7%	27.4%	30.9%	25.4%
Completed high school	22.4	31.3	22.6	33.0
Some college or college graduate	21.4	31.2	26.6	31.1
Graduate study or advanced degree	20.5	10.0	19.9	10.3

they are also forming households with equally highly educated spouses or partners.

Religious Origins of Faculty

The past forty years have seen a very modest diversification of faculty away from their solid Protestant roots of the 1960s, when two out of three faculty members nationally were Protestant (fig. 15.2). For Catholics, the somewhat enhanced opportunities to join the ranks of the professoriate in the decades since 1960 were the dividend of the expansion of education opportunities in earlier decades. Catholics, a predominantly immigrant, working-class group in the early half of the twentieth century, found few opportunities for higher education in the decidedly middle- and upper-middle-class enclaves of the nation's public and private colleges and universities in the pre–World War II era. And with only limited opportunities to secure a college education, Catholics were effectively shut out of faculty posts at non-Catholic institutions. Led by the Jesuits and a desire to provide socioeconomic mobility for their constituency rather than by any strong evangelical impulse, Catholics built a substantial national network of colleges and universities in the first half of this century. For example, enrollment in Catholic colleges and universities rose from 32,000 in 1916 to 162,000 in 1940 (Levine, 1986). It was this expansion of Catholic higher education which laid the basis for the increased opportunities—but perhaps discretely and still very circumscribed today at the most prestigious private institutions—for Catholics to join the nation's professoriate.

For Jewish males, the restrictive admission quotas that severely limited their higher educational opportunities in the decades between the two world wars began to collapse after 1945. However, throughout the 1920s and 1930s many of our most prestigious institutions embraced informal, if not systematic, efforts to restrict severely the number of Jewish students. Unlike Catholics, who sought to build a separate but equal system of higher education, Jews addressed access barriers through sustained and highly successful efforts to fight discrimination while diversifying and democratizing higher education. The proletariat College of the City of New York (CCNY) became the Jewish version of Catholic higher education, perhaps at a somewhat higher standard, as its enrollment grew from 3,000 in 1930 to 24,000 in 1940. As early as World War I, nearly four out of five CCNY students were Jewish (Levine, 1986).[3]

It was efforts such as these leading to the democratization of higher education which provided the foundation for the modest diversification of faculty with respect to religious origins in the decades after World War II. Ladd and Lipset point to a 1955 study suggesting that more than two-thirds of all social scientists described their religious background as Protestant. Fourteen years later, in 1969, data from the Carnegie Study found that proportion reduced significantly to 51 percent. These figures on social scientists notwithstanding, as figure 15.2 illustrates, the religious origins of all faculty in 1969 and 1984 were still decidedly Protestant, while there has been a modest increase in the percentage of Catholics from 18 to 21 percent and declines in the percentage of Protestants from 66 to 62 and of Jews from 9 to 8 percent (Ladd & Lipset, 1975).

When these figures are contrasted with those of the general population, it is evident the American professoriate is, in relation to the population, very much disproportionately Protestant and Jewish. For example, in 1985 Catholics constituted 28 percent of the population, Protestants 57 percent,

Fig. 15.2   Religious Origins of Faculty

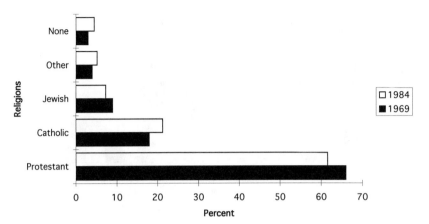

and Jews 2 percent (*Statistical Abstract,* 1993). While the social and religious origins of faculty help us to understand socioeconomic status, they
also tend to reflect other values (cf. Murray, 1971). However, if we are to
understand better the changes that have occurred in recent decades, we
must also look more closely at changes in gender and racial composition of
faculty.

Racial and Gender Composition of Faculty

While the faculty has become somewhat more diverse with respect to
religious origins, there has been an appreciable, albeit still disappointing,
rate of change in the racial and gender makeup of the professoriate. As figure 15.3 illustrates, a professoriate in 1969 which was 95 percent white and
81 percent male has in twenty years slowly altered its complexion and profile so that by 1989 it was 88.5 percent white and 30.3 percent female
(Ladd & Lipset, 1975; Carter & Wilson, 1993). If looked at in the context
of a faculty that was virtually universally white and male for the last 150
years, the changes in the last two decades have been significant, and given
the pipeline—the number of new hires that are female—and the changing
national demographics of our nation, they suggest that big changes are
imminent.

Although the racial and gender makeup of the professoriate shows signs
of diversification, current contrasts between the composition of the faculty
and the students they teach are pronounced. Women make up nearly 50
percent of all college students, but female faculty members constitute only

Fig. 15.3   Faculty by Race and Gender

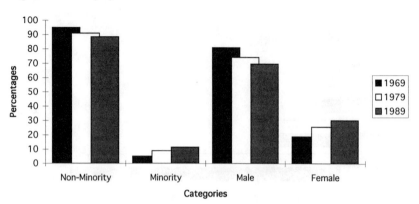

approximately 30 percent of the professoriate. While minorities account for nearly 18 percent of all the freshmen entering higher education in the fall of 1992, minority faculty members hover around the 11 to 12 percent figure.

Changing Income of Current Academics

Total mean income from all sources of full-time faculty in the fall of 1987 ranged from $32,740 at liberal arts colleges to $74,732 at private research institutions. The overall mean income for all full-time faculty in 1987 was $48,701, with institutional sources (i.e., basic salary and other institutional income) constituting 88.35 percent of the faculty members' total income. Institutional sources of funds constitute 83.53 percent of the mean income for faculty members at private research universities, 89.5 percent at public research universities, and 92.7 percent of faculty income at liberal arts institutions. As figure 15.4 illustrates, faculty as a whole are supplementing their institutional sources of income rather modestly (NCES, 1991). However, there have been wide swings in academic salaries over the past two decades. For example, in the 1970s the average faculty salaries in the United States fell by approximately 20 percent in real terms, whereas in the 1980s it rose by about 16 percent in real terms (Ehrenberg, 1991; cf. Budd, 1994).

Although this would suggest some loss of ground, economists remind us that it is often useful to look at faculty salaries within the context of other fields. In his look at doctoral study and employment choices, Ronald Ehrenberg contrasted the average nine-month starting salaries of new Ph.D., assistant professor economists with the average starting salary of

Fig. 15.4   Mean Income for Full-Time Faculty, Fall 1987

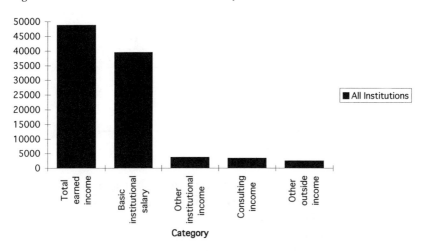

MBAs with nontechnical undergraduate degrees. He also compared the nine-month median starting salaries for new assistant professors of mathematics with the average starting salary of graduates with master's degrees in engineering.

Ehrenberg reports that substantial short-term swings were evident throughout the 1970s and 1980s with respect to the salaries of new assistant professor economists and new MBAs. However, the overall data suggest that the ratio between the starting salaries of the two positions has tended to remain relatively stable when looked at over the last two decades. In 1970, for example, the salary ratio of new assistant professor economists to MBAs was .95, in 1977 it was .92, and in 1980 it was .91, and, despite some fluctuation in the MBA boom years of the 1980s, it had settled back to .91 in 1988 (Ehrenberg, 1991; cf. Hansen, 1986).

When comparing the salaries of new assistant professor economists with the average starting salaries of lawyers across eight cities (unweighted) in non-patent-law firms, similar results emerged. In 1974 the salary ratio of new assistant professor economists to new lawyers was .90, in 1984 it was .87, and in 1988 it was again at .90. To the extent academic economists are willing to compare their starting salaries with those of new MBAs and attorneys in non-patent-law firms, the data suggest a high degree of long-term constancy. Similar trends exist with respect to salary comparisons of new assistant professors in mathematics and new master's level engineers. Although faculty overall lost economic ground in the sev-

Table 15.3 Faculty Spouses' Income, 1988

Academic Rank of Married Faculty	Percentage Whose Spouses Earned $30,000 or More in 1988
Professor	25.5%
Associate Professor	26.0%
Assistant Professor	24.4%

enties which they still have not recovered, the problems, as Ehrenberg suggests, may not be as severe at the starting level, where institutions are forced to compete more directly for talent.

Equally, if not more, important than average starting salaries or average faculty earning may be the limited opportunities for earning growth over the life of the academic career. In virtually all academic fields, salary compression between the junior and senior ranks over the past twenty years (Annual Report on Economic Status, 1994) has been and remains severe, especially when contrasted with other professions. With few exceptions the salary ratio of full professors to new assistant professors is less than two to one (i.e., the typical full professor earns less than twice as much as new assistant professor colleagues); the situation is quite different in other professions. Ehrenberg points out, for example, in law it is quite common for partners to earn four to six times as much as starting attorneys (Ehrenberg, 1991). This salary compression may well influence the attractiveness of an academic career for recent college graduates considering graduate or professional school options, but it may also impact the satisfaction an aging senior faculty feels with its economic status.[4]

Moreover, with senior faculty less inclined to leave their institutions because of stronger institutional and community ties or fewer opportunities, colleges and universities have felt less pressure to adjust salaries of senior faculty in response to tightening labor market conditions. These conditions suggest that the salary compression between ranks will continue and perhaps exacerbate as institutions compete for talent at the junior ranks.

While the decline in real wages in the 1970s and recovery in the 1980s coupled with the trend to maintain competitive *starting* salaries perpetuated the severe salary compression that has shaped the economic condition of the professoriate and perhaps diminished somewhat the attractiveness of an academic career, these same trends may also have diminished its eco-

Table 15.4   Aging of Faculty

Age of Faculty	1969	1989
60 and older	7.44%	11.70%
50–59	15.92	28.50
40–49	27.26	36.20
30–39	34.82	21.40
<30	14.56	2.20

nomic centrality to the family. Faculty, as previously pointed out, tend to have partners with extraordinarily high educational levels, and these levels tend to be reflected in earnings. Although income data are available only for faculty spouses—not partners—the figures are impressive. In 1983, 21.9 percent of faculty spouses had annual earnings of $25,000 or more; in 1988, 26.8 percent of spouses reported annual incomes in excess of $30,000.[5] There was little variation among ranks; table 15.3 illustrates that the percentage of spouses of assistant and associate professors earning $30,000 or more was virtually identical to that for full professors. Given the generally younger age of spouses of assistant and associate professors and the tendency to have their peak earning years still ahead, it seems reasonable to conclude that spousal earnings will continue to provide a substantial if not greater percentage of the family income and reduce the importance of the academic career in the family economic structure.[6]

Aging of Faculty

Contemporary faculty as a cohort are, as table 15.4 suggests, considerably older than the faculty who staffed American colleges and universities in the late 1960s (Ladd & Lipset, 1975; Astin, Korn, & Dey, 1991). The number of faculty aged sixty and above as well as those in the fifty to fifty-nine range has risen appreciably, whereas those in the thirty to thirty-nine age range as well as those below thirty have dramatically declined. In looking at these figures it is important to keep in mind that we are looking at the same people hired in the 1960s and 1970s who are advancing in age.

On the basis of the 1969 Carnegie study, Ladd and Lipset described a faculty whose age cleavage (23% over fifty years of age; 49% under forty) formed the basis for some sharp differences with respect to conservatism and liberalism leanings. For example, the protests and demands for greater student roles in university decisions which rocked the 1960s garnered considerably more support among younger rather than older faculty. Twenty years later the situation is different, as faculty over fifty outnumber those under forty by nearly two to one.

Changes in Political Leanings of Faculty

The demographic changes in faculty have also been accompanied by shifts in their political leanings. Looking at a relatively young professoriate in the late 1960s (nearly 50% were under the age of forty, whereas in the late 1980s only 23.6% of faculty fell into that category) and the findings of Ladd and Lipset that faculty political views tend to moderate with age, we should see a faculty becoming *relatively* more conservative (Ladd & Lipset, 1975). However, the National Center for Educational Statistics surveys on faculty in 1984 and 1988 suggest little drift to the right. As table 15.5 indicates, even though the categories used to report faculty political orientations were altered for the 1988 report, faculty were, as a whole, more left of center in 1988 than they were in 1984 or 1969. Although some of these findings may reflect changes in methods of data collection, the evidence suggests that faculty remain slightly to decidedly left of center. Students, however, at least as evidenced by the 1992 freshmen survey, are decidedly more centrist than their professors (Carter & Wilson, 1993; NCES, 1987, 1991). While there clearly have been changes in the demographic makeup of the professoriate in recent decades, the changes in the students they teach have been much more pronounced.

Students and Faculty: The Axis of Difference

In her important study of undergraduate cultures, Helen Horowitz describes the enormous changes in undergraduate values and culture which began in the 1970s and continue virtually unabated. It is far too parochial to think of this change merely in terms of enrollment figures, although they certainly were significant. In 1979 almost 11.7 million students were enrolled in American colleges and universities, 42 percent more than the 8 million a decade earlier. By 1992, total enrollment in higher education approached 14.5 million, and it is expected to cross the 16 million mark early in the next century.

The changes in our students were qualitative as well as quantitative. In describing the changes in the nature of American undergraduates, Horowitz reminds us that by the late 1970s the traditional definitions of undergraduate students were badly dated. By 1979 half of our undergraduates held jobs, and more than 40 percent went to some classes in the evening. Only about one-third of the undergraduates lived in residence

Table 15.5   Political Leanings of Faculty and Students, Selected Years (%)

| | Faculty | | | Freshmen |
	1969	1984	1988	1992
Far left				2.3
Left	5.1	5.8		
Liberal	35.7	33.8	24.6	24.4
Moderately liberal			31.0	
Middle of the road	27.5	26.6	16.5	53.0
Moderately conservative	25.6	29.6	21.2	19.0
Conservative			6.7	
Strongly conservative	5.68	4.2		1.3

halls or fraternity or sorority houses; a greater number lived on their own in apartments, rooming homes, or houses. Twenty-eight percent lived with their parents or relatives (Horowitz, 1987).

Undergraduates today are actively engaged in a variety of pursuits, with higher education merely one of them and, in many instances, seemingly not the most important. Faculty are teaching undergraduates with a substantially different value system than they themselves had as undergraduates. In a study supported, in part, by the Pew Charitable Trusts, the New Jersey Institute for Collegiate Teaching and Learning (NJICTL) surveyed more than eighteen hundred undergraduates at New Jersey colleges and universities in the spring of 1993, the results of which reveal the competing pressures for students' time and attention and the limited interaction between students and faculty outside the classroom.

As table 15.6 indicates, on average, New Jersey students generally spend as much time each week working as they do in class (15 hours), and the median study and preparation time weekly is eight hours. These findings come at a time when the research on students and colleges widely recognizes the importance of viewing the learning environment in a much larger context than mere faculty-student interactions in the classroom:

> The weight of evidence indicates that the links between involvement and change tend to be specific [e.g., intellectual development is influenced by classroom involvement, changes in values linked to peers], the greatest impact may stem from the student's total level of campus engagement, particularly when academic, interpersonal and extracurricular involvements are mutually sup-

Table 15.6   "How Many Hours a Week Do You Spend . . .?" (*n* = 1,890)

Activity	Range	Mean	Median	Mode
Working at a job	0–52	14.7	15.0	0
Attending classes	1–70	15.3	15.0	15.0
Studying alone in library	0–50	2.7	1.0	0
Studying alone where you live	0–64	9.2	7.0	10.0
Studying in a group outside class	0–71	1.3	0	0
Participating in student organization activities	0–50	1.8	0	0
Participating in recreational activities	0–81	6.1	4.0	0

portive and relevant to a particular educational outcome. (Pascarella & Terenzini, 1992, p. 626)

Students, as table 15.6 also illustrates, spend little or no time participating in student organization activities. For many New Jersey students their collegiate experience is one of sandwiching in very modest study time between attending class and working.

Thus, at a time when it is widely acknowledged that the educational impact of a college's faculty is enhanced as contacts with students extend beyond the classroom to informal, nonclassroom settings, student-faculty contact appears to be rather minimal. The same Pew/NJICTL data suggest (table 15.7) that student-faculty discussions are limited.

As both faculty and students are pulled away from central academic commitments, real questions arise about what can be expected outside the classroom. Indeed, class time may become all the more important as the only common ground. Alternately, the traditional limitations we all understand about the classroom and traditional teaching may lead us to seek to transcend time and space constraints via increased use of technology. The "virtual classroom" may be a possibility, but its attainment may be yet another area of generational conflict between students and faculty and between technologically sophisticated faculty (often the younger academics) and their less conversant colleagues. Educational technology is a two-edged sword. It has the potential to redefine the teaching role, but it also has the potential to disrupt the routine and consistency of the workplace, a disruption that if too extreme or too rapid could exacerbate the tendency of a significant number of faculty to place their institutional role on the further periphery of their professional lives.

Table 15.7   "How Often Have You Talked to Faculty in
Their Offices This Semester?"

Frequency	Number of Respondents	Percentage
Never	361	19.0
1 or 2 times	725	38.2
3 or 4 times	442	28.3
5 or more times	342	18.0
No response	28	1.5
Total	1,898	100

Demographic Gulf between Faculty and Students

Faculty have historically resembled their students in socioeconomic profile to an extraordinary degree: Both constituencies tapped the upper middle and upper classes of American society after the Civil War. That surface resemblance has always hidden very real normative or cultural differences between faculty and their students (Veysey, 1965)—the faculty focused then on character building and their role *in loco parentis,* and the students simply seeking the credentials and connections to make their way in the occupational world. What we are currently witnessing, a historical first, is the superimposition of the demographic cleavages upon already real intraclass cultural gaps. This demographic "gap" has implications at three levels: behavioral, intellectual, and societal.

From a behavioral perspective, the gap may express itself in different repertoires between faculty and students which create strangeness and discomfort in their interaction. From an intellectual perspective, the gap may manifest itself as divergence in views between faculty and students on the curriculum—what should be studied and historical relative homogeneity of the disciplines. From the societal perspective, the gap may express itself in varieties of tribalism wherein students isolate themselves from faculty and vice versa.

The common thread here is that the adjustment of both faculty and students to their institutional roles may require more deliberate and sustained institutional intervention than ever before. And part of that adjustment may need to address the legitimacy of the roles assigned faculty—in the very different eyes of their new students.

Thus it may be that the socioeconomic, racial/ethnic, and class differences between faculty and students are greater than ever before in this century. Institutions will need to attend more explicitly to the socialization of both groups to their institutional roles. The aging of both groups, however, affords a terrific opportunity for connection. The question is how to make this connection educationally effective.

Centrality of Faculty Academic Role and Institutional Commitments: Centrifugal and Centripetal Forces

The opportunities and motivations for faculty and students to focus their energies on teaching and learning and the satisfactions each derive from those endeavors are closely tied to the centrality of the academic role in their lives and the strength of their institutional commitments. The centrifugal forces pulling faculty and students away from their academic roles and institutional commitments are significant. In looking at large and complex organizations in our society beset with fragmentation and inconsistency, William Bergquist (1993) poses a fundamental question: "Can the center hold?" Colleges and universities are also asking this same question.

The historical development of the academic profession in America has largely been one perceived to be characterized by the increased centrality of the academic role in the life of its incumbents, centrality in terms of role preemptiveness (e.g., the carryover into family and personal life) and exclusivity (i.e., excluding other careers both concurrent and future). By the early twentieth century, choosing academic work meant nothing less than an exclusive lifetime choice. And that choice was, as the demographics suggest, largely reserved for young men from the more affluent, educated stratum of American Protestantism.

The increasing centrality of the academic role, so pronounced in the early decades of this century, appears to have peaked for the majority of faculty, and institutional participation, especially the attachments for teaching and instruction—always a bit nebulous for academics—may now have to be looked at from varied perspectives. Is the academic role declining in centrality for faculty? To what extent have changes in the institutional context of universities contributed to or limited the affective investment that faculty place upon their broad academic role? If the centrality of the academic role and especially the instructional role is declining in importance, how might this affect faculty interest and motivations with respect to the most central of institutional commitments—teaching?

There are, as Antti Kauppi (1992) suggests, important contextualities or intersections between working life and working institutions, intersections that are marked by periods of presence and absence, of fading away, and the shading or marking of boundaries. This is certainly characteristic of the academic profession, and faculty, like others, tend to place a premium on routine and consistency in the workplace. That is, faculty are inclined to think and act in certain contexts that influence and organize the institutions in which they work. For example, to the degree faculty perceive that their success as academics will be measured by their standing in the discipline rather than through the fulfillment of institutional roles, the more they will tend to influence and organize the university along lines that help them to meet that standard.

William Faunce and Robert Dubin (1975) take the intersections between working life and working institutions a bit further. When classifying the relationship of people to their work and nonwork situations, they look at two basic dimensions: assignment and adjustment. The *assignment dimension* refers to the fit between the individual's personality and the behavioral characteristics (e.g., specialized knowledge, responsibility, autonomy) required to perform successfully. The *adjustment dimension* concerns itself with how the individual negotiates the requirements of the institutional environment in which he or she works. For faculty, as with others, there is a constant ebb and flow between the two dimensions throughout a career as the level of adjustment between personality and the demands of the profession, discipline, and institutional setting changes.

Changes in the professional competencies a faculty member is expected to exhibit can lead to changes in self-esteem, career aspirations, and the composition of professional and personal networks. Similarly, changes in the institutional setting may precipitate a greater interest in adjusting or may lead to a greater sense of withdrawal and the marking of boundaries. The key conundrum for Faunce and Dubin was the difficulty of dealing with the problem of fostering motivation for self-investment and for identifying meaningful rewards in an organizational setting. For colleges and universities the question is similar. Teaching basically falls within the assignment dimension for academics, but it is only one of the activities in that dimension competing for a faculty member's time and energy.

The assignment of teaching as an institutional responsibility does little to ensure that individual faculty will invest heavily in the activity. In addition, faculty are increasingly confronted by students who view higher education in an exchange rather than use-value model. That is, students persevere in their studies based upon a belief that they will be able to "exchange" their time and effort in a course for a good grade and their credentials—a degree for a job. In the use-value model students remain interested in the content of their studies and make an effort to derive benefit in the applicability of their studies to working life (Parjanen, 1993). As higher education has democratized in the twentieth century, the "exchange" value has gained the ascendancy. Therefore, any decision by faculty to invest heavily in their teaching role is very much related to the adjustment dimension, that is, how faculty negotiate their changing role, the changing norms of their institutions, and the demographics of students within those institutions (cf. Dubin, 1979).

As we watch faculty negotiate the changes in their roles and the norms of the institutions in which they work, there are two basic factors that must be considered: (1) to what extent has the academic role and its corollary of institutional commitment remained central to the academic profession in an era during which the number of academics has mushroomed, and (2) how have rapidly changing student demographics and the increasing exchange value of education impacted the motivation of this greatly expanded professoriate to teach?

To what extent have we witnessed and are we witnessing a decline in the professor's *role preemptiveness?* For the large and growing contingent of part-timers (and temporary full-timers), their teaching (institutional) appointments are, of necessity, less central to their own long-term career prospects and to their personal/family economies than a full-time permanent position. So too for those, including full-timers, who as previously indicated are finding an increasing share of their family incomes derived from noninstitutional sources, including their own outside employment as well as the employment of a spouse or partner. This will become especially significant among entering faculty cohorts who are increasingly female and whose spouses or partners are typically well-educated males.

Moreover, the swelling of faculty ranks in the nonuniversity sector and outside the traditionally "academic" liberal arts in favor of vocational and professional fields of practice means a new academic majority will emerge among precisely those groups of faculty who have historically been less engaged in the traditional intellectual life of the disciplines and less active in research and publication (as historically have been part-timers and temporary full-timers in the aggregate).

Together, these trends suggest a professoriate characterized in the aggregate as less engaged in the life of their institutions as well as in the life of their academic disciplines. These trends that suggest a decline in the centrality of the academic role and the centrality of institutional commitment have been reinforced, at least from the institutional perspective, by a reward system that has devalued institutional activities such as teaching and service and focused faculty energies and attentions on extrainstitutional connections, especially to academic disciplines and professional associations.

As previously suggested, the experience of American college students roughly parallels that of their teachers, as evidenced by a noticeable decline in the centrality of the student role (its preemptiveness and exclusivity), as more students pursue their educations on a part-time basis or attempt to work full-time while pursuing a full course of study. There, however, the parallelism abruptly ends. American students, unlike their teachers, have changed dramatically in the past twenty-five years, in terms of gender, age, and ethnicity.

What do the changes in faculty demographics and the centrality of the academic role and institutional commitment mean for their teaching and how they work with students in light of the substantial diversification of the student body and a parallel decline in the centrality of the student role?

The Demography-Motivation Interface

In Chapter 1, "The Meaning of Human Motivation," Walker and Symons identify five themes encompassed within the eight current theories they discuss. They go on to conclude that human motivation is at its highest when people feel *competent,* have sufficient *autonomy,* set worthwhile *goals,* get *feedback* on performance, and are *affirmed* by others. The relation of the theories to these themes is depicted in table 15.8. Individual theories include some or most of theses themes, but no single theory includes or integrates all of them. Yet all of these elements would seem to be required to support as complex and creative an endeavor as college teaching.

What do the demographic changes we have identified mean for any, some, or all of these five key elements of the motivation to teach? We believe that at least three of the new demographic facts have direct and not altogether salutary implications for faculty motivation: the widening faculty-student demographic gap, the aging faculty, and the rise of the temporary part-time faculty.

The Faculty-Student Gap

The demographic portrait of a relatively unchanged and homogeneous faculty meeting an increasingly diverse student body translates most concretely into the contemporary "standoff" that seems to characterize many college classrooms. The available evidence suggests that the vast majority of faculty continue to "lecture"; barely one in seven makes substantial use of any alternatives, such as small-group work or computer-assisted in-

Table 15.8 Basic Themes/Elements of Current Motivation Theories

Motivation Theories	Competence/ Self-Efficacy	Autonomy	Worthwhile Goals	Feedback on Performance	Affirmation/ Reward
External Factors					
Learning and reward systems					x
Job design		x	x	x	
Goal setting			x	x	
Internal Factors					
Expectancy theory	x				
Self-efficacy theory	x				x
Mixed					
Optimal experience theory	x				
Self-determination theory		x		x	
Social motivation theories					x

struction (Thielens, 1987). Faculty continue to view "mastery of the discipline" as the primary goal of undergraduate education. There is little evidence of any substantial preparation either prior to or after in-service pedagogy (Finkelstein, 1995). Students, as we have seen, tend to be most interested in credentials and in meeting the minimum requirements for "getting by" in the course—the exchange value of education. This standoff has enormous implications for faculty motivation.

Many faculty are painfully aware that what worked for them in the past is no longer working. This lack of success has challenged the faculty's sense of competency and self-efficacy as teachers. Not only is the teaching competence of faculty being challenged, but their very socialization experience in graduate school which valorized disciplinary mastery as the ultimate goal of undergraduate education is under siege. This resounding, albeit silent, disaffirmation by students has led many senior faculty members to withdraw from teaching as no longer a significant source of professional satisfaction or, what is more disturbing, to be angry, in effect blaming their students for not appreciating what they, the faculty, have to offer.

An Aging Faculty

The aging of our college faculties shapes the motivation in at least two ways. First is the way in which age intersects with job design in the academic career. Academic jobs are designed to include a variety of activities—teaching, research, and service—but most instructional activities change little during the course of a career. Many faculty members teach the same courses year after year (to seemingly ever less appreciative students). Moreover, with the decline of the academic job market over the past generation, many faculty now make a career at a single institution, adding a sameness of setting to the sameness of activities. For many senior faculty who have been engaged in routine teaching assignments and who are relatively less involved in scholarship (as they are at all but the research universities), there is little sense of environmental challenge. Moreover, as some colleagues retire and new, junior faculty fresh from graduate school and schooled in the latest disciplinary frameworks enter, that sense of competence may be challenged on a second front, now by one's own colleagues. In addition, the seriousness of this challenge may be reinforced by institutional compensation and promotion policies that reward new entrants at the expense of their seniors (and this is especially true at that large group of comprehensive institutions that have moved over that past generation to "enhance quality" by developing a new and preeminent focus on research).

A Part-Time and Temporary Faculty

College faculties are increasingly part-time and temporary, especially in certain sectors (the community colleges and the small private colleges) as well as in certain fields (foreign languages, English composition, mathematics, and business). Although a contingent of such part-time temporary faculty includes individuals in the professions and business who are highly motivated to teach in their chosen fields,[7] many others face less ideal circumstances: teaching remedial, introductory, or off-campus courses assigned at the last moment, using someone else's syllabus (typically a full-timer's), giving someone else's examinations, being poorly compensated, and rarely encountering any full-time faculty (or for that matter, any students outside class). These individuals have neither the autonomy, the feedback, nor the affirmation to sustain their best efforts (Gappa & Leslie, 1993).

The Challenge of Enhancing and Sustaining Faculty Motivation

What is clear is that the new faculty-student demographic portrait may pose unprecedented challenges to that wellspring (no longer bottomless) of intrinsic (internal) motivation which has historically served as the platform for faculty work. How can higher education address these challenges to sustaining the "faculty's best effort"? The three most pressing needs to be addressed are (1) promoting a sense of competence and self-efficacy among both new and more seasoned teachers; (2) enhancing the feedback that faculty receive on their performance; and (3) promoting a climate of greater affirmation by students, colleagues, and the formal organizational reward system.

Promoting a Sense of Competence

Colleges and universities are already testing several approaches to promoting or renewing a sense of pedagogical competence among their faculties. These include programs that introduce faculty systematically to the learning needs and diverse learning styles of their students and which develop specific pedagogical skills (Eble & McKeachie, 1985). What is particularly encouraging and needed is the emergence of models of long-term sustained intervention, such as the Washington Center's "learning communities," wherein a single group of students register concurrently for an integrated set of courses taught by three or four faculty (Smith & Smith, 1993), or the Partners in Learning program developed by the late Joseph Katz and Mildred Henry (Katz & Henry, 1988), which pairs faculty with colleagues to engage in peer class visits and student interviewing. Both of these initiatives focus on bridging the distance between faculty and their students while developing a more reflective pedagogical conversation among colleagues.

Beyond focusing on current faculty, a number of our major graduate institutions are beginning to reformulate the preparation for teaching which apprentice scholars receive during their graduate training. Most recently, the Pew Charitable Trusts established the Consortium for the Preparation of Graduate Students as Teachers, involving Syracuse University, Ohio State, and the University of Washington, among others. The Association of American Colleges and Universities recently joined with the Council of Graduate Schools to sponsor a joint effort of graduate institutions and undergraduate colleges in a program entitled "Preparing Future College Faculty."

Enhancing Feedback on Performance

Student rating instruments may have become a fixture in American higher education (now in use in five out of six institutions), and there is considerable evidence of both their reliability and validity (Theall & Franklin, 1990; Centra, 1993), but the vast majority of faculty remain nonetheless uninformed about "good practices" in their use and find them less than helpful as sources of constructive, improvement-oriented feed-back on their teaching. In no small measure this is a function of how un-reflectively these programs have been implemented—mixing diagnostic and personnel uses of the data, minimizing follow-up by trained consul-tants, and all but eschewing the task of educating both faculty and admin-istration to their strengths and limitations. This evaluative effort needs to by systematized and carried forward as an important organizational re-sponse to the motivational imperative for feedback. The flurry of recent ac-tivity in the area of faculty evaluation suggests that institutions are in-creasingly recognizing these needs.

Beyond official organizational policy, faculty themselves are beginning to bring assessment for improvement into their own classrooms at the grass roots. The flowering of the classroom research movement, advanced by Patricia Cross and Tom Angelo (Angelo & Cross, 1993), reflects the deeply felt need on the part of faculty for generating constructive feedback on teaching which is directly anchored in their classroom practice. When provided with tested techniques for eliciting such feedback, techniques that are minimally invasive and improvement oriented (and that is pre-cisely what Cross and Angelo have done), many faculty jump at the chance. Institutions need to build directly on these basic motivations that are indeed self-sustaining (feedback–improvement–seeking more feed-back).

Promoting a Climate of Affirmation

Colleges and universities have a long way to go in promoting the affir-mation of their faculty's sense of competence and professional accomplish-ment. Such affirmation will require, in the first place, a recognition of the diverse skills, competencies, and professional goals of their faculties and a commitment to match as many of these as possible to the multidimen-sional character of faculty work and the multiple components of institu-tional mission (Stetar & Jemmott, 1991). The emergent movements to en-hance teaching and service and, more generally, to broaden our conception of scholarship beyond the reporting of new knowledge within the disci-pline (Boyer, 1990) represent an early recognition of this basic motiva-tional need. It will mean providing the institutional flexibility to allow fac-ulty to take on more congruent teaching or other assignments that provide appropriate challenges and make the best use of their competencies. Or in-stitutions may provide opportunities for off-campus assignments that will serve the same goal when possibilities do not exist at home—for example, faculty exchange, internship, and sabbatical programs (see, e.g., LaCelle-

Peterson & Finkelstein, 1993). Ultimately, of course, and with the help of the major disciplinary associations, it will mean opening up the campus reward system to recognize and indeed even celebrate such diversity.

Conclusion

Historically colleges have depended on the intrinsic motivation of faculty to teach, as working with students was considered to be its own reward. Decreasing centrality of the role and declining rewards for teaching, especially for senior faculty (as a consequence of salary compression), mean that faculty motivational problems will be accentuated. Institutions will need to address explicitly and think through approaches for motivating faculty which take into account instructional and organizational impediments. That means, in part, that institutions will need to think about designing and putting into place structures that provide durable incentives for faculty (and for students) to reengage in the work of teaching and learning—as it were, "against the odds." LaCelle-Peterson and Finkelstein (1993) have suggested a number of low-cost structural approaches to promoting involvement in teaching among midcareer and senior faculty. These include team teaching; the use of faculty committees to guide multisection courses (and "hammer out" common syllabi or course examinations); the use of course clustering and learning-community models, such as those developed at the Washington Center for Improving Undergraduate Educations and the New Jersey Institute for Collegiate Teaching and Learning (Smith & Smith, 1993).

What all these approaches have in common is a recognition that we need to build upon "naturally occurring" faculty incentives in more creative ways than heretofore. Moreover, among other things, those structures will need to build explicitly on what we are now learning is a critical "external" (albeit internalized) source of motivation for faculty: their colleagues. And this points us again to the "social" community concept as a key ingredient in the motivation of individualistic faculty in the new academic order.

Notes

1. Although the mean age has increased markedly as the large cohort hired in the late 1960s to staff higher education's expansion has grown older, the variance around that mean has probably decreased in what has become a positively skewed distribution.

2. More than sixty thousand professors responded to the Carnegie Commission's 1969 survey.

3. For an informative look at how Temple University and the University of Pennsylvania served their distinct urban constituencies in the first four decades of this century, see Angelo (1983, pp. 261–292).

4. In the most recent HERI Survey, approximately 45 percent of faculty characterized their salary and fringe benefits as satisfactory or very satisfactory (Astin, Korn, & Dey, 1991).

5. This figure—$30,000—represents approximately 70 percent of the mean institutional income ($43,027) of faculty in 1987 (NCES, 1991).

6. Results of a 1995 Lewis Harris & Associates survey indicated that married women who worked full-time in 1993 contributed a median 41 percent of the family's total income. That was up from 39 percent in 1987, and the percentage is expected to rise in the future. It is reasonable to expect that the percentage of income provided by the highly educated wives of academics would certainly be at the 41 percent figure, if not appreciably higher, further diminishing the centrality of the academic career to the family's economic status ("Women Are Becoming Equal Providers," *New York Times*, 11 May 1995).

7. Many part-timers indeed may have long records of service at the campuses on which they teach and may, in many cases, be anything but temporary in practice.

References

American freshmen: National norms for 1992. (1992). American Council on Education and UCLA Higher Education Research Institute.

Angelo, R. (1983). The social transformation of American higher education. In K. H. Jarausch (Ed.), *The transformation of higher learning, 1860–1930* (pp. 261–292). Chicago: University of Chicago Press.

Angelo, T., & Cross, K. P. (1993). *Classroom assessment techniques.* San Francisco: Jossey-Bass.

Annual report on the economic status of the profession, 1993–1994. (1994). *Academe, 80*(2), 5–89.

Astin, A., Korn, W., & Dey, E. (1991). *The American college teacher: National norms for the 1989–1990 HERI faculty survey.* Los Angeles: Higher Education Research Institute, University of California.

Bergquist, W. (1993). *The postmodern organization.* San Francisco: Jossey-Bass.

Bowen, H., & Schuster, J. (1986). *American professors.* New York: Oxford University Press.

Boyer, E. L. (1990). *Scholarship reconsidered: Priorities of the professoriate.* Princeton: Carnegie Foundation for the Advancement of Teaching.

Boyer, E. L. (1993). *Campus life.* Princeton: Carnegie Foundation for the Advancement of Teaching.

Budd, G. (1994). The motivation to teach at the college level. Unpublished manuscript, Seton Hall University, Higher Education Program.

Burke, D. (1988). *A new academic marketplace.* New York: Greenwood Press.

Carter, D., & Wilson, R. (1993). Minorities in higher education: 1992 annual status report. American Council on Education.

Centra, J. (1993). *Reflective faculty evaluation.* San Francisco: Jossey-Bass.

Dubin, R. (Ed.). (1976). *Handbook of work, organization, and society.* Chicago: Rand McNally College Publishing Company.

Dubin, R. (1979). Central life interests: Self-integrity in a complex world. *Pacific Socio-logical Review, 22*(4), 405–426.

Dubin, R., & Champoux, J. (1977). Central life interests and job satisfaction: Self-integrity in a complex world. *Organizational Behavior and Human Performance, 18,* 366–377.

Eble, K., & McKeachie, W. (1985). *Improving undergraduate education through faculty development.* San Francisco: Jossey-Bass.

Ehrenberg, R. (1991). Academic labor supply. In C. Clotfelter, R. Ehrenberg, M. Getz, & J. Siegfried (Eds.), *Economic challenges in higher education* (pp. 143–260). Chicago: University of Chicago Press.

Faunce, W. A., & Dubin, R. (1975). Individual investment in working and living. In L. E. Davis, A. Chernes, & Associates (Eds.), *The quality of working life: Vol. 1. Problems, prospects, and the state of the art* (pp. 299–316). New York: Free Press.

Finkelstein, M. (1995). College faculty as instructors. Paper presented at the National Educational Association Conference on Higher Education, Washington, DC.

Finkelstein, M., & Schuster, J. (1992). College and university faculty. In M. C. Alkin (Ed.), *Encyclopedia of Educational Research* (pp. 190–197). New York: Macmillan.

Gappa, J., & Leslie, D. (1993). *The invisible faculty.* San Francisco: Jossey-Bass.

Greeley, A. (1969). *From backwater to mainstream.* New York: McGraw-Hill.

Hansen, W. (1986). Changes in faculty salaries. In H. Bowen & J. Schuster (Eds.), *American professors* (pp. 80–112). New York: Oxford University Press.

Horowitz, H. (1987). *Campus life: Undergraduate cultures from the end of the eighteenth century to the present.* New York: Knopf.

Katz, J., & Henry, M. (1988). *Turning professors into teachers.* San Francisco: Jossey-Bass.

Kauppi, A. (1992). Towards transformative evaluation of training. In M. Parjanen (Ed.), *Legitimation in adult education* (pp. 31–50). Tampere, Finland: University of Tampere.

LaCelle-Peterson, M., & Finkelstein, M. (1993). Institutions matter: Campus teaching environments' impact on senior faculty. In M. Finkelstein & M. LaCelle-Peterson (Eds.), *Developing senior faculty as teachers* (pp. 21–32). New Directions in Teaching and Learning 55. San Francisco: Jossey-Bass.

Ladd, E. C., Jr., & Lipset, S. M. (1975). *The divided academy: Professors and politics.* New York: McGraw-Hill.

Levine, D. (1986). *The American college and the culture of aspiration, 1915–1940.* Ithaca, NY: Cornell University Press.

Murray, J. (1971). Catholic academicians and the intellectual subsociety hypothesis. In C. H. Anderson & J. D. Murray (Eds.), *The professors.* Cambridge, MA: Schenkman Publishing Co.

National Center for Educational Statistics (NCES). (1987). *1984 national survey of postsecondary faculty.* Washington, DC: U.S. Department of Education, Office of Educational Research and Improvement.

National Center for Educational Statistics (NCES). (1991). *1988 national survey of postsecondary faculty.* Washington, DC: U.S. Department of Education, Office of Educational Research and Improvement.

Parjanen, M. (1993). Values and responsiveness in adult higher education. In M. Parjanen (Ed.), *Values and policies in adult higher education* (pp. 31–50). Tampere, Finland: University of Tampere.

Parker, S. (1971). *The future of work and leisure.* London: MacGibbon & Kee.

Pascarella, E., & Terenzini, P. (1992). *How college affects students: Findings and insights from twenty years of research.* San Francisco: Jossey-Bass.

Report on the status of part-time faculty. (1992). *Academe, 78*(6), 39–44.

Seal, R. (1993). Interview with Parker Palmer. *Newsletter.* New Jersey Institute for Collegiate Teaching and Learning, South Orange, NJ.

Smith, B. L., & Smith, M. J. (1993). Revitalizing senior faculty through statewide efforts. In M. Finkelstein & M. LaCelle-Peterson (Eds.), *Developing senior faculty as teachers* (pp. 81–94). New Directions in Teaching and Learning 55. San Francisco: Jossey-Bass.

Stetar, J., & Jemmott, N. (1991). Fostering faculty: Institutional loyalty and professional rewards. *Review of Higher Education, 14*(2), 263–272.

Theall, M., & Franklin, J. (Eds.). (1990). *Student ratings of instruction.* New Directions in Teaching and Learning 43. San Francisco: Jossey-Bass.

Thielens, W. (1987). The disciplines and undergraduate lecturing. Paper presented at the annual meeting of the American Education Research Association, Washington, DC.

U.S. Department of Commerce, Bureau of the Census. (1993). *Statistical abstracts of the United States, 1993.* Lanham, MD: Bernam Press.

Veysey, L. (1965). *Emergence of the American university.* Chicago: University of Chicago Press.

16 Career Phases and Their Effect on Faculty Motivation

ROBERT T. BLACKBURN

The popular as well as the scholarly press increasingly calls attention to changes in adult development. Some speak of passages, others of seasons, and still others of cycles that adults are said inevitably to pass through— periods of flux and times of stability, phases of stress and those of relative serenity. To the extent that such time intervals do exist and change, it is reasonable to expect that the motivation to perform work roles also undergoes change in some predictable concordance with those time intervals. For example, according to one theory of motivation—expectancy theory[1] —individuals are induced to expend effort on the basis of their beliefs in their ability, their conviction that they will receive rewards for good performance, and their desire for the particular rewards that are available. Hence, the cycles or phases or seasons noted above might logically be associated with variations in the strength of each of the variables in this motivation equation. More particularly, expectancy theories of motivation thus might hypothetically provide insights as to whether career phases are connected with alterations in the motivation to teach.

However, as will be seen, such a model, although widely accepted as valid in other fields, has proved to be inadequate for the study of faculty. Hence, an alternative motivational model is needed which may better anticipate the existence of career phases in the motivation to teach. Presentation of such a model and its empirical testing represent a significant aim of this chapter.

Just as a theory of motivation can be used to understand fluctuations in teaching effort, so also is it important at the outset to identify a theoretical approach to the examination of career phases which can be connected to motivation theory. There is a career literature, of course, some of which constitutes a set of concepts for organizing a sequence of career events or, better, a theoretical model. Spilerman (1977), Stumpf (1981), and Super (1980) are worthy representative scholars of careers. Chickering and Havighurst (1981) and Austin (1987) use "career" as a construct in their examinations of part of higher education. Rosenfeld (1981, 1984) employs the concept of career in her studies of faculty mobility. The construct of "career" and its literature, however, are not helpful for investigating faculty phases vis-à-vis teaching, although some indicators of the construct predict scholarly productivity, especially that of "established scholar." For this role, past performance strongly relates to current performance. Unfortunately, in the case of teaching, there is no past performance measure. In addition, quality of teaching is not a function of career age or rating of one's graduate school.

It may seem pedantic to raise the question of whether or not career phases exist, since most academics will quickly give an affirmative answer. The question, however, is not simply a rhetorical one. Faculty speak of productive and dry periods, of exciting and dull classes. Moreover, structured academic life allows periodic renewal with its change of terms, courses offered, and students taught. Colleges and universities design leaves, different assignments, even the year itself—the "academic" year—to accommodate, precipitate, and facilitate changes. Theoretically, if there are clearly identifiable career phases for college professors, it should be possible to identify the conditions that explain and predict them. From a practical perspective, then, administrators could manipulate these conditions and find a way to alter an individual's institutional responsibilities during a phase when pedagogical motivations are low so as to maintain high teaching performance throughout the collective faculty. In addition, or alternatively, counseling might be able to change or mitigate low motivation periods. One could capitalize on particularly high motivation phases for the benefit of the individual and the college.

Surprisingly, little demonstrable evidence exists to support predictable phases for academics. I define a phase as a period of time over which a set of values and activities holds relatively constant. A phase is an indefinite interval whose duration is appreciably greater than moment to moment or day to day. It lasts at least a year, more often three to five years. A phase can be identified by plotting an individual's performance against time. The interval over which a performance level either increases (decreases) rather steadily or jumps (falls) rather abruptly and then holds constant constitutes a phase. A change of direction (increase or decrease) marks the onset of a new phase. A phase is like a stage as used by Levinson, Darrow, Klein, Levinson, and McKee (1978) in its being a distinctive and identifiable condition, one that conceivably could be otherwise. Phase differs from Levinson's stage in that it has no necessary developmental components nor chronological inevitability.

This chapter examines the literature for both direct and indirect evidence for the existence of faculty career phases. It first inspects the more general studies before it turns to more specific research on faculty careers. Although the literature suggests that there is ample evidence for career phases in other fields, the empirical evidence provides little or no support for faculty career phases. That is, contrary to expectation, there is no evidence for universalistic phases through which faculty move in the course of their careers. To be sure, faculty motivation waxes and wanes over the work years, but such fluctuation is idiosyncratic; that is, it is not predictable from phenomena common to the faculty work or career experience.

Given this rather anomalous finding, I turn next to an alternative theoretical explanation of faculty motivation which Janet Lawrence and I developed from motivational theories and then empirically tested. At the conclusion of the chapter, I draw warranted inferences from the findings of that research and conclude with a discussion and speculation of some consequences for faculty personnel policy and practice.

Direct Evidence for Phases

In this first section, I suggest that since there is firm evidence in higher education that faculty research performance varies with age (e.g., Bayer & Dutton, 1977), it is reasonable to assume that the motivation to produce those variations in performance also varies over time or with age (or both). As others in this book observe, there is a high correlation between motivation and performance. If it can be established, then, that these fluctuations in performance are regular and predictable, either by time or age, it can be further argued that there are similar perturbations in levels of fluctuations in motivation. As noted in the definition of phases above, such would be evidence of career phases for faculty. I discuss each of these surrogates for faculty motivation: fluctuations in performance over time, and fluctuations in performance with age.

A few studies report teaching performance over time. The research time span, however, is short, the longest being only three years (Felder & Blackburn, 1981). All studies demonstrate a stability over time. We can attribute observed fluctuations to measurement error. The one study that probes teaching over the better part of a career (Baldwin & Blackburn, 1981) contains some clues indicating that interest and concerns regarding teaching do change. The evidence, however, is anecdotal and not verified with performance indicators.

Some cross-sectional studies describe relationships between teaching performance and age. Centra and Linn (1976) show lower ratings for older faculty. Blackburn (1972) and Hitch (1980) find age distributions resembling a megaphone with its central axis being horizontal—more variance at older than at younger ages but with correlations near zero. None of these plots suggest career phases. Furthermore, one must have serious reservations about cross-sectional data, especially for trying to establish career phases in teaching.

The conclusion from direct evidence, then, is that there are no career phases in the motivation to teach. Of course, the absence of evidence does not prove the nonexistence of faculty career phases vis-à-vis motivation for teaching. Lacking a purposeful test of the proposition, however, one is reluctant to close the books. The assumptions made above remain open to challenge, and the data for rendering any decisive conclusion fall short of the quality one requires.

Indirect Evidence for Phases

An indirect approach to the problem is to examine evidence regarding the existence of career phases in the other academic roles. Faculty roles correlate (slightly) so that the appearance of phases in one could support an inference that they also exist in teaching (see, e.g., Feldman's [1989] summary of research on the relationship). For example, if evidence exists for phases in service or research role performance, it might be reasonable to conclude that there are also phases in the motivation to teach, provided the roles are correlated at a reasonably high rate.

Some faculty roles in higher education are related in a zero-sum manner. Thus, for example, time spent in teaching often takes away from research time. Accordingly, performance effectiveness in other roles (e.g., research) might be thought to be related to reduced teaching effectiveness, simply because of the required effort involved.[2] Recall that under an expectancy theory of motivation, effort expended is the operational definition of motivation. Hence, if we find that research effort fluctuates regularly, we can assume that teaching effort also so fluctuates—and so, by definition, would motivation.

However, we face difficulties in inferring phases in faculty motivation to teach well even if we do find evidence of phases in other roles if the inter-role correlations are low. The correlation studies between student-judged teaching effectiveness and different measures of faculty scholarly productivity tend to be positive (Feldman, 1987). However, they are not strong.

Second, the assumption that, say, increased research output results from an increased motivation to engage in research and that, in addition, a heightened research motivation ipso facto accompanies a lower motivation for teaching has no supporting evidence. One can teach less for periods of time (a phase) but be just as motivated to teach well as when teaching more hours.

Third, the productivity studies primarily deal with the publication output of faculty concentrated in research universities, institutions that house but a fraction of the six hundred thousand teaching faculty. Therefore, a statement asserting the existence of career phases in faculty motivation to teach is, at best, tentative.

One final cautionary note before turning to the evidence. A conclusion that the absence of evidence for the existence of career phases "proves" that they do not exist could be criticized as specious. For example, a life stage advocate can counter this concluding assertion by saying that the uncertainty today is nothing more than temporary ignorance, a hiatus soon to be filled by social-psychological researchers. The new findings will support the life stage position and allow accurate predictions to be made, the adherent life-stager would respond. Such a position parallels the one many physicists take with respect to the absence of an adequate theory accounting for the structure of matter. The missing link will be discovered or created tomorrow. Moreover, the devotee's position can take comfort from the existing evidence—as meager and as atheoretical as it is.

Having discussed the conceptual basis for understanding the potential direct and indirect evidence for phases, let us turn to the empirical evidence.

Studies

Studies on faculty participation in administrative duties (Willie & Stecklein, 1982) and governance (Mortimer, 1969) show an increase in this role with age. They do not, however, display any phases. As for consulting, Boyer and Lewis (1985) best review this literature but do not discuss phases. Two large-scale studies on faculty consulting have cross-sectional data. Lanning and Blackburn (1979) found a rise to a peak and then a decline toward retirement, with variation by discipline and degree of time given to consulting (four levels, including no consulting at all, a category composing about 50 percent of U.S. academics). Wenzel, Crawley, and Blackburn (1993) found insufficient evidence to support phase occurrences when using the National Study of Postsecondary Faculty 1988 data. In sum, the insubstantial evidence from the service role does not support a predictable existence of career phases.

Research

Both longitudinal (Pelz & Andrews, 1976; Cole, 1979) and cross-sectional (Bayer & Dutton, 1977; Blackburn, Behymer, & Hall, 1978) studies of faculty publications show career phases, at least in the natural and social sciences. Although there seem to be differences between disciplines (see especially Bayer & Dutton, 1977), and although there are some discrepancies between longitudinal and cross-sectional outcomes (particularly with mathematicians—see Cole, 1979; Allison & Stewart, 1974) and between studies using different dependent measures of scholarly productivity, career phases seem to appear—an early rise, a fall, another rise, and then a dropping off. Thus, using expectancy theory and the assumption of a zero-sum game, the motivation to engage in teaching will be reduced at certain stages in the faculty member's life. On the other hand, even with reduced time expended in teaching, faculty motivation to teach well could be maintained at a constant level, quite independent of the reduced number of teaching hours expended. As was the case with the research on the service role, the literature on the research role does not establish the existence of career phases for teaching.

Theoretical Predictions

Since it cannot be concluded from extant theory and the available empirical evidence presented above that phases exist, we need to seek an alternative theoretical framework to test for the existence of cyclical motivation for teaching. The theory presented next prognosticates individual shifts in a faculty member's motivation to replace her or his current priority role with increased effort to teach.

Below, I present a theoretical model for predicting faculty behavior, one based on alternative motivation theories that colleagues and I have developed. I then report a study of faculty in a variety of disciplines and institutional types which corroborates the model with data on the effort faculty give to the pedagogical role. Next, I discuss the discovered relationship between interest and effort with respect to their causal order. I conclude with a qualitative event history analysis of published semilongitudinal data from a group of retired social scientists and the inferences one draws regarding academics' predictable and cyclical academic interests.

The proposed theoretical framework integrates the research on faculty role performance and productivity with motivation theories.[3] We tapped both noncognitive and cognitive motivation theories. For the former we turned to Baltes and Brim (1983), Hall and Mansfield (1975), Levinson, Darrow, Klein, Levinson, and McKee (1978), Schaie (1983), Super et al. (1957), and Super (1980)—personality and career development theories; Atkinson (1977) and Staw (1983)—reinforcement theories; and Atkinson and Raynor (1974), Belenky, Clinchy, Goldberger, and Tarule (1986), Fausto-Sterling (1992), McClelland, Atkinson, Clark, and Lowell (1953), and McClelland (1961)—dispositional theories.

For the cognitive theories of motivation we turned to Maehr and Braskamp (1986), Vroom (1964), and Weiner (1985)—expectancy theory; Weiner (1985)—attribution theory; Bandura (1977, 1982), Bandura and Wood (1989), Gist and Mitchell (1992), and Weiner (1985)—efficacy theory; and Abelson and Levi (1985), Bargh and Pietromonaco (1976), Buss and Craik (1983), Cantor, Mischel, and Schwartz (1982), Carver and Scheier (1983), Gersick and Hackman (1990), Kihlstrom (1984), Langer (1989), Mitchell and Beach (1990), Nuttin (1984), Petty, Cacioppo, and Goldman (1981), Showers and Cantor (1985), and Staw (1983)—information-processing theories.

We derived the theoretical constructs representing properties of the individual and environment from the higher education literature. That is, our theoretical framework is higher education specific and drawn inductively from reported empirical research. Still, it has many parallels in the more general social science literature. On the other hand, cognitive motivation theories suggested the self- and social-knowledge categories that are the major new contributions of our theoretical framework. How faculty assess themselves (self-knowledge) and how they assess their workplace (social knowledge) become powerful predictors of behaviors and outcomes. These are clearly cognitive processes. It was also from the research evidence that we extrapolated the hypothetical paths through which different individual and situational factors may influence behavior and productivity from the cited motivation research. The theoretical framework models both immediate and future productivity as a result of ongoing interactions between individual faculty members and their work environments.

A Motivational Theoretical Framework for Faculty

The key premises underlying the theoretical framework follow.[4] First, organizations are achievement-laden environments in which the evaluation of workers' performance is ongoing. Second, workers use assessments of themselves and their social contexts to make meaningful decisions about their actions. However, not all decisions require the same level of detailed situation analysis. Third, experience over time leads individuals to modify their understanding of their work environment as well as their self-image. These changes can affect the subjective incentive value of different facets of work. Consequently, a worker's level of motivation and engagement in different activities can shift. Fourth, some types of self-referent thought and perceptions of the work environment are more enduring than others that change frequently on the basis of personal feedback and vicarious experience.

We base the ordering of the individual and environmental constructs within the theoretical framework on the results of empirical studies of faculty careers and cognitive motivation research. Specifically, we propose that *sociodemographic* characteristics exert direct effects on an individual's *career* and *self-knowledge*. We also propose that the *career* construct in our theoretical framework can mediate the impact of some *sociodemographic* characteristics on *self-knowledge*. Figure 16.1 contains illustrative indicators of the major constructs that we used.[5]

Sociological studies of social stratification and mobility demonstrating that individuals' access to career opportunities can vary depending on their ethnicity and sex support the first hypothesized paths. They are also supported by the psychological developmental theories suggesting that personal goals and commitments vary with age and by life course theories asserting that cohorts are socialized to different values and vary in expertise, depending on when they received their graduate preparation (Chubin, Porter, & Boeckman, 1981; Long, Allison, & McGinnis, 1979; Reskin, 1985). The possibility that *career* may mediate the effects of *sociodemographic* characteristics is suggested by the work of Allison and Stewart (1974) on the Matthew Effect. Specifically, they have demonstrated that individuals who are high achievers early on tend to continue to be high producers throughout their careers because they enjoy greater access to funds for their research. They conclude that the effects of age on role performance are mediated by this process of "accumulative advantage." We base the placement of *self-knowledge* ahead of *social knowledge* primarily on the results of cognitive motivation research. In most of the empirical

Fig. 16.1 Variables Used in Testing the Theoretical Framework

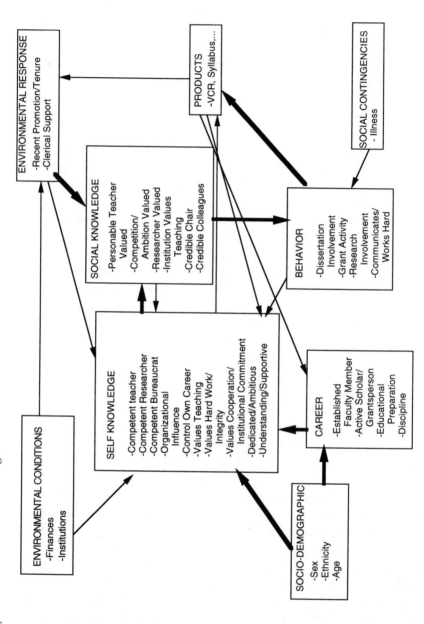

studies, the data suggest that individuals' understanding of themselves (e.g., their self-assessed competence, personality dispositions, and efficacy) predicts how they perceive their environments (e.g., norms, resources) more frequently than environmental perceptions predict this self-understanding (Kanfer & Ackerman, 1974; Wigfield & Braskamp, 1985).

We conceptualize *social knowledge* as the key link between self-referent thoughts, the other individual variables, and *behavior*. This construct owes its placement to the fact that *social knowledge* is influenced by both *self-knowledge* and *environmental response*. While performance feedback clearly affects perceptions of organizational priorities and individual competence, cognitive theories assume motivation is a function of both individual characteristics and perceptions of the environment. We therefore take this into account by showing that *behavior* is a result of the cumulative effects of *self-knowledge* directly as well as acting through *social knowledge*. (See the arrows in figure 16.1; the heavier ones indicate the stronger causal connections.)[6]

The environmental constructs in the theoretical framework have both direct and indirect effects on *behavior*. We assume that *social contingencies* exert direct effects because they typically place constraints on one's time and energy to engage in activities. We also assume that *environmental conditions* exert influence on *behavior* indirectly through faculty members' *social knowledge*. The normative context of an institution has pervasive effects on individuals within it. *Environmental conditions* affect faculty members' understanding of the standards of performance which predominate and the resources their institutions can make available (*social knowledge*). We believe that certain resources affect role performance to the extent that faculty know they exist, and therefore differences in this knowledge have the potential to affect *behavior*.

Environmental conditions also indirectly influence *social knowledge* through *environmental responses*. Standards of performance embedded in the institution's normative context in part shape direct feedback on performance. So, too, are decisions about requests for assistance with individuals' work. In effect, then, these *environmental responses* translate the more abstract shared understanding of an institution's goals into specific messages about organizational priorities and role expectations. This proposition reflects reinforcement principles of behaviorist psychology and socialization theory as well as social learning precepts that are central to cognitive motivation theories. We show the effects of feedback on *behavior* are mediated by *social knowledge* because research indicates that individuals will not necessarily interpret the same feedback in a similar fashion. Information is filtered through previous experiences, personal priorities, and competencies as well as the credibility one attributes to the source of the feedback.

We define *behavior* as the specific activities an individual engages in as well as the levels of effort expended. We take *products*, on the other hand, to be the specific outcomes achieved by individuals (for faculty in higher education, articles published, teaching awards received, grants and fellowships obtained, and so on). Because the framework is longitudinal, we indicate that *products* have effects on *self-knowledge* and *career.* We posit that levels of achievement in different activity areas can influence an individual's *self-knowledge* and *career.* (Again, in higher education, for example, grant acquisition to support one's research after a long period without funding may result in specific changes in the recipient's sense of efficacy.) These changes in *self-knowledge* can, in turn, affect her or his views of coworkers (*social knowledge*) and level of effort to research (*behavior*). Furthermore, performance at high levels of achievement over time can affect one's *career,* such as status within her or his occupation and specialization.

In this theoretical framework, *sociodemographic* variables include age, sex, and race. *Career* variables are career age, highest degree earned, rating of institution from which highest degree was earned, rank, and past publication performance. The *self-knowledge* variables are efficacy (sense of control, competence), interest in teaching or research, percentage of effort preferred to give to a role, and self-ascribed personality disposition for teaching or research. *Social knowledge* variables include beliefs among a faculty about their employing institution, such as the adequacy of laboratory and library holdings, grant support, department's commitment to research and teaching, morale, career success, perceived effort the institution expects to be given to a role, the norms of the specific workplace, and the characteristics of the discipline. *Behavior* is the time spent on various professional activities and represents the faculty member's decision about how to act. A *product* is the quantifiable outcome of behavior, say, a new syllabus of readings in the case of teaching, a VCR to accompany a lecture, or an annotated bibliography.

In our theoretical framework, we place the motivation variables in the *self-knowledge* category. Self-reported interest in research, preference for teaching over research, and percentage of time preferred to give to teaching (irrespective of actual time given or perceived institution preferred allocation, a *social knowledge* variable) each serve as measurable surrogates for motivation for teaching. We used them to predict actual percentage of their work effort they give to teaching. (See figure 16.1 for some of the motivation surrogates for teaching we used.) Those faculty who prefer to teach more than they do (other assignments and obligations limit time for teaching) or more than they believe is expected of them by their institution (or both) are judged to be more highly motivated toward teaching than those faculty who are lower on these dimensions. Our constructs do not imply that a faculty member teaching fewer hours is unmotivated toward teaching. Indeed, the individual may be highly motivated but is responding to other stimuli.

Recall that we did not construct our theoretical framework to predict motivations, nor did the tests of our theory have motivation as an outcome variable. What we have learned is that our theoretical framework successfully accounts for a significant percentage of the variance in effort given to teaching and that interest in (motivation for) teaching is a significant predictor.

We tested our theoretical framework on our national data base (National Center for Research to Improve Postsecondary Teaching and Learning survey, 1988) for both teaching behavior and research output (Blackburn, Lawrence, Bieber, & Trautvetter, 1991; Blackburn, Bieber, Lawrence, & Trautvetter, 1991; Blackburn & Lawrence, 1995; chaps. 4 and 5). Table 16.1 shows the regression outcomes for the percentage of effort faculty give to teaching in three institutional types and three disciplines, both categories selected to span the Carnegie classifications and disciplines within the humanities (English), natural sciences (chemistry), and social sciences (psychology).[7] The predictor variables are from the categories in our theoretical framework (see fig. 16.1).

As can be seen, the theoretical framework explains a high percentage of the variance, even a phenomenal amount for chemistry faculty in community colleges. We have a strong positive test of our theoretical framework. While commitment to teaching and interest in teaching are not especially strong predictors when all variables are in the equation, the percentage of time a faculty member prefers to give to teaching does predict in community colleges and comprehensive colleges and universities-I (but not in research universities-I—see Blackburn & Lawrence [1995] for a discussion). Surely this variable is another indicator of interest in teaching and becomes a significant predictor for faculty in all three institutional types when we aggregate the disciplines (see the row under combined R^2 row). The other important finding for the analysis here is the statistical significance of the predictor, perceived institutional preference for effort given to teaching.

Table 16.1 Summary of Regression Outcomes Predicting Percentage of Time Given to Teaching

	Community Colleges			Comprehensive-I's			Research-I's		
	English	Chemistry	Psychology	English	Chemistry	Psychology	English	Chemistry	Psychology
Sociodemographics									
Gender		*							
Career									
Career age		*							
Graduate school rating				*					
Rank		*		*					
Self-Knowledge									
Efficacy									
Interest in teaching		*							
% Preferred time for teaching	*	*		*	*	*			
Social Knowledge									
Perceived % time institution prefers	*			*		*			
Consensus and support		*							
Colleague commitment									
Percentage of Explained Variance	38	86	68	49	59	46	34	25	27
Percentage of Explained Variance When Disciplines are Combined		44			46			32	

Source: Blackburn, Lawrence, Bieber, & Trautvetter (1991). Reprinted with permission.
Note: The asterisks signify when the variable was significant at $p < .05$. All of the explained variance results are significant for the combined disciplines.

This faculty *social knowledge* variable also accounts for what fraction of their work effort faculty give to the teaching role.

What the theoretical framework also demonstrates which is relevant to the question being considered here is that faculty make decisions on what they will do (how they will behave) on their personal assessment of the external and internal environments and the environmental responses they believe they receive from their behaviors and what they produce. That is, faculty frequently cognitively reassess their *social knowledge*. Furthermore, that knowledge can differ for individuals even in a relatively small unit, to say nothing of variations that obtain across schools and colleges within a large university.

By way of illustration, were large institutional dollars suddenly allocated for rewarding good teaching, the environmental change would likely affect many faculty quite irrespective of their age or career stage.[8] In this case, were faculty at different career stages vis-à-vis interest in teaching, any existing cycle would be thrown out of phase by this environmental change. Consequently, we would be unable to predict on a phase basis who would change when. Or consider a social contingency—an illness or a family problem that greatly reduces available time or causes dysfunctional stress. The theoretical framework shows how this acts on behavior, including effort given to teaching. Here we have another case in which a cyclical pattern would be disrupted and lead to unpredictability of either apparent or real interest in teaching.

In short, sound theory leads to the conclusion that a pattern of life stages with respect to interest in teaching (or research, or service, or the like) should not be expected to be predictable. It appears as though personally meaningful, idiosyncratic events, not rational, long-range, discernible plans in accordance with anticipated career stages, have an appreciable influence on faculty careers, including changing motivation for teaching.

As an illustration, in a study of seventy-five retired male academic social scientists who provided career data, Blackburn and Havighurst (1979) found that career events profoundly affected career paths and career "success." Figure 16.2, taken from that article, displays some differences between very active (VA) and active (A) scholars and moderately active (MA) and inactive (I) scholars after retirement.

Figure 16.3 shows my inferences from these inquiries. It was an attempt to take career events all faculty pass through (the vertical lines) along with an adult development model and career events (Blackburn, 1985). Although different from the theoretical framework developed and tested

Fig. 16.2   Selected Career Events—VA's and A's versus MA's and I's

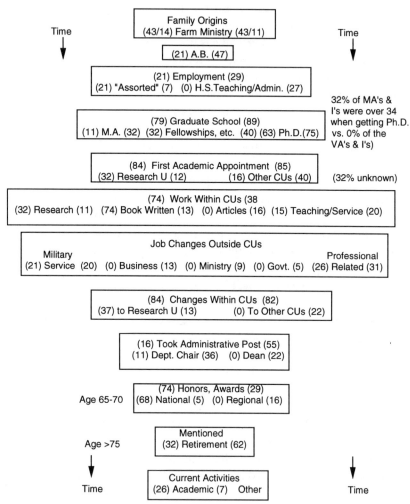

Source: After Blackburn and Havighurst (1979), p. 568. Used with kind permission of Kluwer Academic Publishers.

Note: Figure in parentheses on the left is percentage of VA's and A's mentioning event; figure in parentheses on the right is percentage of MA's and I's mentioning event.

above, it too leads to the same conclusion. One cannot predict when an individual will change her or his interest in teaching. That one can rationalize an individual's change after it has occurred is often possible, but post hoc rationalizations are not predictions.

Fig. 16.3 Transitional Period of Levinson et al. (1978) Overlaid on a Career Event Grid with Major Changes in Activities, New Ideas, Recognitions, and Accomplishments

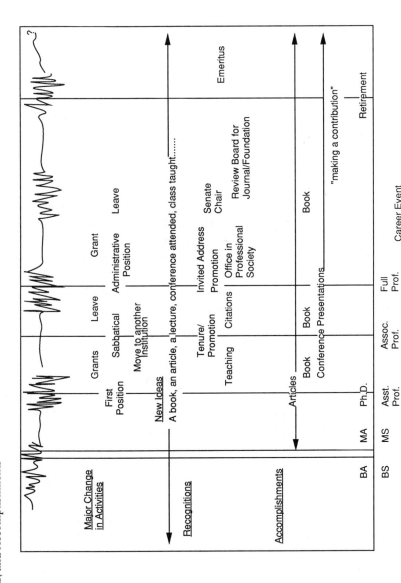

Source: After Blackburn and Havighurst (1979), p. 568. Used with kind permission of Teachers College Press.

Implications for Practice and Leadership

What do these findings suggest in a general way, and what do they add to practical knowledge? Quite frankly, probably not very much.

Our findings with respect to predicting percentage of work effort given to teaching showed that desired percentage of effort and perceived expected effort were consistently the strongest variables. The latter suggests that faculty would respond to awards given for excellence in teaching. Many institutions do recognize outstanding teachers in both public and private ways. The college or university may have an awards ceremony in which a number of faculty are publicly recognized—their pictures appear in the press, an honorarium accompanies a certificate or a plaque. Privately their merit raise might be greater that year. Faculty might also compete for support for preparing course materials, producing a videocassette as an instruction aid, and the like. There are a number of ways the message can be transmitted to faculty that quality teaching is honored and desired.

However, there can be a problem with these devices as motivation stimulators. They can too often become more of a political formality—the prizes have to be passed around even though the first winners are likely to be the ones who should receive the awards every year. There is also the more serious question as to whether or not external rewards are effective over time.

With regard to the predictor, percentage of time desired to give to teaching, what comes to mind is the developing concept of flexible scheduling, "flex time." Although most often designed to accommodate the daily schedules of workers who could better deal with their nonwork life by coming to the job earlier or staying later, or vice versa, or who would benefit from four ten-hour days rather than five eight-hour ones, this business practice suggests that there is more than one way an organization can accomplish its tasks and achieve its goals. True, changing schedules is not altering worker roles in the way that changing one's emphasis from research to teaching would be. Still, though not explored here, the literature on this topic might suggest innovations colleges and universities could adopt to allow faculty to exercise changed motivations when they arise.

In the case of a graduate department, courses essentially become owned by individual faculty. This situation already contains appreciable scheduling flexibility possibilities that should allow the professor who one day becomes excited about trying something new in her or his teaching to do so. On the other hand, if a department (say, English) has become solidified in its offerings (say, ordered by centuries), it becomes extraordinarily difficult for the existing organizational structure to integrate even a revolution in the discipline. The department simply tosses the novel materials into a newly created niche, and nothing really changes. English now has special courses in theory, but traditional research and pedagogy go about as usual.

Now let us examine the case of a faculty member who, for reasons unknown, has become motivated to spend more time than the typical norm of the unit in either the teaching or research role. Suppose also that neither the faculty member nor the Chair knows about this motivational change long enough in advance of next year's final schedule going to press (although this might be known a year in advance). In addition, suppose that the principal activities of the unit are in undergraduate education—say, a liberal arts college or a comprehensive college or university. What might be done?

The Chair and the curriculum committee lay out what existing courses need to be taught (e.g., general education offerings for the entire college; basic courses in major sequences; new courses that need to be created because of changes in the discipline). They make reasonable enrollment projections and calculate the number of sections needed. The matrix goes on a spreadsheet after a full department faculty meeting agrees upon alterations they make in the plan.

Faculty now sign on for their preferences—which courses, which term, which year. The Chair distributes the tallied results. Readily visible are faculty shortages for some courses and oversubscriptions for others. Faculty negotiate with their colleagues—trade A for B, double on C for a reduction in D. Some offer to overload in year two for a reduction in year three. Over the long run, the "workload" balances out. Faculty have an opportunity to alter their distribution of effort, to increase in some areas and decrease in others. Those who have some ideas about teaching they want to try out and who know that it is going to take more than an average amount of effort and time can do so.

This utopian setting has some assumptions faculty need to accept: all courses are equally valued, the creation of a needed new one gets extra credit, blocks of time for teaching or research are more effective than a standard pattern of exactly the same for all year after year. Birnbaum (1975) introduced flexible scheduling at the University of Wisconsin–Oshkosh, an ongoing plan that allows faculty to shift their efforts significantly from year to year and satisfy motivations that change from time to time. The above is a modification of his creative contribution.

These suggestions are not revolutionary for handling unpredictable changes in faculty motivation to teach. It is hoped that they can spark creative solutions for a local situation.

Notes

1. See the discussion of expectancy theories of motivation in Chapter 7 in this volume.

2. There is an implied assumption here that needs mentioning. One typically assumes that if the faculty member spent more time on his or her teaching, the quality would improve, that poor university teaching is the result of neglect, not skill. Hildebrand (1972) found otherwise. Faculty at the University of California–Davis who were judged by both students and faculty as the stars and the dregs spent equal amounts of time preparing for class. In addition, Choy (1969), Maslow and Zimmerman (1956), and Sherman and Blackburn (1975) provide evidence that student ratings of quality teaching are determined principally by the instructor's personality (e.g., being easily approachable, not distant), traits not readily changeable in adults and which may have no correlation with motivation to teach.

3. In this section, "we" is my colleague Janet H. Lawrence, a number of our Ph.D. research assistants, and myself. We constructed our theoretical framework after examining a number of theories. See Chapter 1 in this volume. See also chap. 1 in Blackburn and Lawrence (1995) for a full rationale for our theoretical framework.

4. With but slight modifications, I take this presentation of our theoretical framework directly from Blackburn and Lawrence (1995).

5. The constructs' indicators are also for research and service outcomes and not exclusively for the teaching role. In addition, the entries are illustrative rather than exhaustive examples of what we have used in our research investigations.

6. The absence of direct arrows from *sociodemographic* and *career* variables to *behaviors* does not mean that there are not correlations between some indicators of the construct and effort given to a role. Often there are, although typically not strong—for example, between sex and effort given to research. However, our theoretical framework posits that the effects of both *sociodemographics* and *career* are mediated by *self-knowledge,* as well as *demographics* being mediated by *career.* The research findings corroborate our procedure, as the regressions show the *sociodemographic* and *career* betas weakening and even becoming insignificant as *self-* and *social knowledge* variables are entered into the equation.

7. We have to use *behavior,* namely, percentage of effort given to teaching, since there are no accepted products for assessing teaching within our data set.

8. Evidence supports changes in productivity accompanying environmental changes. See, for example, National Science Board (1981, pp. 56–57) for the case of falling publications by U.S. mathematicians when federal support dropped precipitously.

References

Abelson, R. P., & Levi, A. (1985). Decision making and decision theory. In G. Lindzey & E. Aronsen (Eds.), *Handbook of social psychology* (pp. 231–309). New York: Random House.

Allison, P. D., & Stewart, J. A. (1974). Productivity differences among scientists: Evidence for accumulative advantage. *American Sociological Review, 39*(4), 596–606.

Atkinson, J. W. (1977). Motivation for achievement. In T. Blass (Ed.), *Personality variables* (pp. 25–108). Hillsdale, NJ: Erlbaum.

Atkinson, J. W., & Raynor, J. O. (Eds.). (1974). *Motivation and achievement*. Washington, DC: Hemisphere.

Austin, A. E. (1987, November). Career concept theory and its applicability to the study of faculty careers. Paper presented at the annual meeting of the Association for the Study of Higher Education, San Diego.

Baldwin, R. G., & Blackburn, R. T. (1981). The academic career as a developmental process: Implications for higher education. *Journal of Higher Education, 52*(6), 598–614.

Baltes, P. B., & Brim, O. G. (1983). *Life span and development and behavior.* New York: Academic Press.

Bandura, A. (1977). Self-efficacy: Toward a unifying theory of behavioral change. *Psychological Review, 84*(2), 191–215.

Bandura, A. (1982). Self-efficacy mechanism in human agency. *American Psychologist, 37*(2), 122–147.

Bandura, A., & Wood, R. E. (1989). Effect of perceived controllability and performance standards on self-regulation complex decision making. *Journal of Personality and Social Psychology, 56,* 805–814.

Bargh, J. A., & Pietromonaco, P. (1976). Automatic information processing and social perception: The influence of trait information present outside of conscious awareness on impression formation. *Journal of Personality and Social Psychology, 43,* 437–449.

Bayer, A. E., & Dutton, J. E. (1977). Career age and research-professional activities of academic scientists: Tests of alternative nonlinear models and some implications for higher education faculty policies. *Journal of Higher Education, 48*(3), 259–279.

Belenky, M. F., Clinchy, B. M., Goldberger, N. R., & Tarule, J. M. (1986). *Women's ways of knowing: The development of self, voice, and mind.* New York: Basic Books.

Birnbaum, R. (1975). Using the calendar for faculty development. *Educational Record, 56,* 226–230.

Blackburn, R. T. (1972). *Tenure: Aspects of job security on the changing campus.* Atlanta: Southern Regional Educational Board.

Blackburn, R. T. ((1985). Faculty career development: Theory and practice. In S. M. Clark & D. R. Lewis (Eds.), *Faculty vitality and institutional productivity* (pp. 55–85). New York: Columbia University, Teachers College Press.

Blackburn, R. T., Behymer, C. E., & Hall, D. E. (1978). Research note: Correlates of faculty publications. *Sociology of Education, 51*(2), 132–141.

Blackburn, R. T., Bieber, J. P., Lawrence, J. H., & Trautvetter, L. C. (1991). Faculty at work: Focus on research, scholarship, and service. *Research in Higher Education, 32*(4), 385–413.

Blackburn, R. T., & Havighurst, R. J. (1979). Career patterns of distinguished male social scientists. *Higher Education, 8,* 553–572.

Blackburn, R. T., & Lawrence, J. H. (1995). *Faculty at work: Motivation, expectation, satisfaction.* Baltimore: Johns Hopkins University Press.

Blackburn, R. T., Lawrence, J. H., Bieber, J. P., & Trautvetter, L. C. (1991). Faculty at work: Focus on teaching. *Research in Higher Education, 32*(4), 363–383.

Boyer, C. M., & Lewis, D. R. (1985). *And on the seventh day: Faculty consulting and supplemental income.* ASHE-ERIC Higher Education Report No. 3. Washington, DC: Association for the Study of Higher Education.

Buss, D. M., & Craik, K. H. (1983). The act frequency approach to personality. *Psychological Review, 90,* 105–126.

Cantor, N., Mischel, W., & Schwartz, J. (1982). A prototype analysis of psychological situations. *Cognitive Psychology, 14,* 45–77.

Carver, R. B., & Scheier, M. F. (1983). A control-theory approach to human behavior and implications for problems in self-management. *Advanced Cognitive Behavioral Research and Theory, 2,* 127–193.

Centra, J. A., & Linn, R. L. (1976). Student points of view in ratings of college instructions. *Education and Psychological Measurement, 36*(3), 693–703.

Chickering, A. W., & Havighurst, R. T. (1981). The life cycle. In A. W. Chickering & Associates (Eds.), *The modern American college* (pp. 16–50). San Francisco: Jossey-Bass.

Choy, C. (1969). The relationship of college teacher effectiveness to conceptual systems orientation and perceptual orientation. Unpublished Ph.D. dissertation, University of Northern Colorado, Greely.

Chubin, D., Porter, A. L., & Boeckman, M. (1981). Career patterns of scientists. *American Sociological Review, 46,* 488–496.

Cole, S. (1979). Age and scientific performance. *American Journal of Sociology, 84*(4), 958–977.

Fausto-Sterling, A. (1992). *Myths of gender: Biological theories about women and men* (2d ed.). New York: Basic Books.

Felder, N. L., & Blackburn, R. T. (1981). The course and the professor: The nature and stability of student judgments. Paper presented at the annual meeting of the American Educational Research Association, Los Angeles.

Feldman, K. A. (1987). Research productivity and scholarly accomplishment of college teachers as related to their instructional effectiveness: A review and exploration. *Research in Higher Education, 26*(3), 227–298.

Feldman, K. A. (1989). Instructional effectiveness of college teachers as judged by teachers themselves, current and former students, colleagues, administrators, and external (neutral) observers. *Research in Higher Education, 30*(2), 137–194.

Gersick, D. J. G., & Hackman, J. R. (1990). Habitual routines in task performing groups. *Organizational Behavior and Human Decision Processes, 47,* 65–97.

Gist, M., & Mitchell, T. (1992). Self-efficacy: A theoretical analysis of its determinants and malleability. *Academy of Management Review, 17*(2), 183–211.

Hall, D. T., & Mansfield, R. (1975). Relationships of age and seniority with career variables of engineers and scientists. *Journal of Applied Psychology, 60,* 202–210.

Hildebrand, M. (1972). How to recommend promotion for a mediocre teacher without actually lying. *Journal of Higher Education, 43*(1), 44–62.

Hitch, E. J. (1980). Similarity of student ratings for instructors and courses across time. Unpublished Ph.D. dissertation, University of Michigan, Ann Arbor.

Kanfer, R., & Ackerman, P. L. (1974). Motivation and cognitive abilities: An integrative/aptitude-treatment interaction approach to skill acquisition. *Journal of Applied Psychology,* 657–689.

Kihlstrom, J. F. (1984). The unconscious reconsidered. In K. S. Bowers & D. Meichenbaum (Eds.), *Unconscious processes: Several perspectives* (pp. 149–211). New York: Wiley.

Langer, E. G. (1989). Minding matters: The mindlessness, mindfulness theory of cognitive activity. In L. Berkowitz (Ed.), *Advances in experimental social psychology* (Vol. 22, pp. 137–173). New York: Academic Press.

Lanning, A. W., & Blackburn, R. T. (1979). Faculty consulting and the consultant. *Resources in Education, 14*(2), 24.

Levinson, D. J., Darrow, C. N., Klein, E. B., Levinson, M. H., & McKee, B. (1978). *The seasons of a man's life*. New York: Knopf.

Long, J. S., Allison, P. D., & McGinnis, R. (1979). Entrance into the academic career. *American Sociological Review, 44*, 816–831.

Maehr, M. L., & Braskamp, L. A. (1986). *The motivation factor: A theory of personal investment*. Lexington, MA: D. C. Heath.

Maslow, A. H., & Zimmerman, W. (1956). College teaching ability, activity, and personality. *Journal of Educational Psychology, 47*, 185–189.

McClelland, D. C. (1961). *The achieving society*. Princeton: Van Nostrand.

McClelland, D. C., Atkinson, J. W., Clark, R. A., & Lowell, E. L. (1953). *The achievement motive*. New York: Appleton-Century-Crofts.

Mitchell, T. R., & Beach, L. R. (1990). Do I love thee? Let me count: Towards an understanding of intuitive and automatic decision making. *Organizational Behavior and Human Decision Processes, 47*, 1–20.

Mortimer, K. P. (1969). Academic government at Berkeley: The academic senate. Unpublished Ph.D. dissertation, University of California, Berkeley.

National Science Board. (1981). *Science indicators, 1980*. Washington, DC: National Science Board, National Science Foundation.

Nuttin, J. R. (1984). *Motivation, planning, and action: A relational theory of behavioral dynamics*. Hillsdale, NJ: Erlbaum.

Pelz, D. C., & Andrews, F. M. (1976). *Scientists in organizations* (rev. ed.). New York: Wiley.

Petty, R. E., Cacioppo, J. T., & Goldman, R. (1981). Personal involvement as a determinant of argument based persuasion. *Journal of Personality and Social Psychology, 41*, 847–855.

Reskin, B. F. (1985). Aging and productivity: Careers and results. In S. M. Clark & D. R. Lewis (Eds.), *Faculty vitality and institutional productivity* (pp. 86–89). New York: Columbia University, Teachers College Press.

Rosenfeld, R. A. (1981). Academic men and women's career mobility. *Social Science Research, 10*, 337–363.

Rosenfeld, R. A. (1984). Academic career mobility for women and men psychologists. In V. B. Haas & C. C. Perrucci (Eds.), *Women in scientific and engineering professions* (pp. 89–127). Ann Arbor: University of Michigan Press.

Schaie, K. W. (1983). Age changes in adult intelligence. In D. S. Woodruff & J. E. Birren (Eds.), *Aging: Scientific perspectives and social issues* (pp. 137–148). Monterey, CA: Brooks/Cole.

Sherman, B. R., & Blackburn, R. T. (1975). Personal characteristics and teaching effectiveness of college faculty. *Journal of Educational Psychology, 67*(1), 124–131.

Showers, C., & Cantor, N. (1985). Social cognition: A look at motivated strategies. *American Review of Psychology, 36*, 275–305.

Spilerman, S. (1977). Careers, labor market structure, and socioeconomic achievement. *American Journal of Sociology, 83*(3), 551–593.

Staw, B. M. (1983). Motivation research versus the art of faculty management. *Review of Higher Education, 6*(4), 302–321.

Stumpf, S. (1981). Career roles, psychological success, and job attitudes. *Journal of Vocational Behavior, 19*(1), 98–112.

Super, D. E. (1980). A life-span, life-space approach to career development. *Journal of Vocational Behavior, 16*, 282–298.

Super, D. E., Crites, J., Hummerl, R., Moser, H., Overstreet, P., & Warnath, C. (1957). *Vocational development: A framework for research*. New York: Columbia University, Teachers College Press.

Vroom, V. H. (1964). *Work and motivation*. New York: Wiley.

Weiner, B. (1985). An attributional theory of achievement motivation and emotion. *Psychological Review, 92*(4), 548–573.

Wenzel, S. A., Crawley, S., & Blackburn, R. T. (1993, October). In partnership with industry: Business and engineering faculty. Paper presented at the annual meeting of the Association for the Study of Higher Education, Pittsburgh.

Wigfield, A., & Braskamp, L. A. (1985). Age and personal investment in work. *Advances in Motivation and Achievement, 4*, 297–331.

Willie, R., & Stecklein, J. E. (1982). A three-decade comparison of college faculty characteristics, satisfactions, activities, and attitudes. *Research in Higher Education, 16*(1), 81–93.

17 The Academic Marketplace and the Motivation to Teach

DOROTHY E. FINNEGAN

Scholars familiar with the literature on the academic labor market, if asked the one word that characterizes the operation of this phenomenon, would probably respond with *prestige, hierarchical, sponsorship,* or *ascription.* These responses reflect not only the most often cited state of our understanding but also the conceptual postures taken in much of the research on the topic and, unfortunately, the limited and exclusionary conclusions of most of our inquiries into the mechanisms of the academic labor market. Three decades of research have verified the entrance and exit processes by which the top-ranked research universities recruit and retain scholars who perform in accordance with their institutional imperative for professional productivity as well as the organizational variables that support or inhibit career advancement.

The academic labor market has traditionally been conceptualized as an employment-sorting mechanism, and as such, the literature shares several features. First, academic careers are perceived to be determined by a variety of forces outside the control of the individual seeking employment. The structure of organizations, the socioeconomic pressures of supply and demand, and normative—either functional or dysfunctional—social stratification mechanisms determine the individual's placement in the higher education system. Since these external forces prevail, the individual becomes insignificant. Second, therefore, individual aspirations, motivations, expectations, values, and beliefs concerning the professorial role and institutional affiliation have been neglected. Fundamentally, even though faculty have consistently indicated a preference for teaching over research (Carnegie Foundation, 1989), researchers seem to assume that all comers aspire to elite positions, which require an appropriate pedigree. The availability of positions coupled with ascribed status, factors that are both external to the individual, therefore sorts the wheat from the chaff. In the end, individual motivations to follow one particular route or another within academe have appeared to be inconsequential to analyses.

Third, few researchers have probed the dimension of time (see Bayer & Dutton, 1977). The labor market has greatly fluctuated in supply and demand throughout the past thirty-plus years. Yet, with our fixation on determinative forces, we have claimed positive effects in organizational prestige and on recruitment and retention mechanisms but have ignored the ramifications of change on and for individuals. All faculty do not necessarily share the same values, aspirations, and employment expectations at a given point in time; even within the same individual, needs modify over time (Baldwin & Blackburn, 1981). But then, once again, if the individual's response is of no concern, time and change do not matter. Finally, the majority of the research has well documented the academic labor market vis-à-vis faculty who are engaged in the research ethic and with its concomitant competition for prestige and rewards. Inquiry into the mechanisms that distribute and the factors that attract faculty to other sectors of higher education has been limited (see Dunham, 1969; McGee, 1971; Queval, 1990; Gamson, Finnegan, & Youn, 1991; Finnegan, 1992, 1993).

We have paid little attention to the relationship of teaching—the generic faculty attribute—to the operations of the academic labor market. Much of what we know about "teaching" faculty concerns their often limited professional products in comparison with those of the more "productive" research university faculty (Fulton & Trow, 1974; Long & McGinnis, 1981; Bailey, 1992) and the inverse relationship between productivity/rewards and the number of hours that faculty spend in the classroom (Fairweather, 1993). Indeed, the role that academic labor market processes and decisions play on faculty motivations to teach, both on individual and organizational levels, has been overlooked, as have been the career patterns of faculty engaged by research universities solely to teach (see Chronister, Baldwin, & Bailey, 1992).

As a result of the public's demand for accountability and economic value, scholars have begun to apply their research findings and "best practice" case studies to the recently recognized need to socialize junior university faculty to teaching and in pedagogical methods (Austin, 1992;

Boice, 1992; Austin, Brocato, & LaFleur, 1993) and to reinvigorate senior faculty (Finkelstein & LaCelle-Peterson, 1993). But these authors are concerned with teaching issues during employment—after recruitment.

In this chapter, I argue that we need to broaden the conceptual and locational boundaries of our research into the academic labor market. Specifically, I contend that academic labor market studies have been dominated and limited because of the fundamental conceptual framework employed, which assumes organizational determinism, sustains the prestige/competitive complex, and disregards potential interpretations related to other institutional sectors. I suggest that the labor market mechanisms are more than issues of prestige and supply and demand because individuals accept and reject just as institutions do. I propose that we consider the interrelationships between individuals and their institutions and develop person-environment interaction models (Pintrich, 1990). These models explore not only "cognitive and motivational beliefs and processes that individuals use to construct their interpretations of different situations, but also life tasks and social contexts that individuals confront that help shape their cognition, motivation and behavior" (Pintrich, 1990, p. 827). Careers are not merely the result of organizational structures or cultures but unfold as an individual makes one decision after another in connection with time, place, and personal values and beliefs. Careers also do not unfold in a vacuum but rather accrue from interactions with colleagues, administrators, students, and family; from involvement with personnel expectations, policies, and procedures; and in reaction to the external forces of the labor market.

Within this argument, I question not only the generalizability but also the serviceability of the most often cited academic labor market literature as well as newer scholarship, which under the guise of exposing the dysfunction of the system follows the traditional conceptual perspective. My purpose is to raise new questions about our understanding of the interrelationship between academic labor market mechanisms and the motivations that compel faculty to teach.

Traditional Academic Labor Market Research

Youn (1988b, 1992), sorting the major economic and sociological research by theoretical approach, has classified the literature into fixed coefficient; human capital; screening or queuing theory; institutional ascription; and structural perspectives. In the present review of the literature, I limit my framework to demographic and structural studies so as to evaluate the underlying perspectives of the traditional literature, add recent scholarship, and recognize neglected areas of research stemming from an accumulative effect from the dominant perspectives.

Demographic Studies

Projections related to supply and demand within the academic labor market not surprisingly and with great regularity accompany projections of significant changes in enrollment and thus in the need for faculty. After a variety of pessimistic studies conducted in the late 1950s and early 1960s (McGrath, 1959; Berelson, 1960; National Education Association, 1963), Allan Cartter (1965) initiated demographic analyses of the impending supply and demand for higher education to demonstrate that the reported slippage in the ratio of qualified (Ph.D., that is) faculty to the number of positions was unfounded. Then, the brisk transformations in the labor market for faculty between 1965 and the early 1980s compelled demographic researchers to explore even more sophisticated analyses. Brown (1967), for example, demonstrated that the market is balkanized with a variety of submarkets dependent on institutional size and disciplinary specialization. But the environment was so unstable that analytic priorities shifted rapidly.

By the early 1970s, the shift from high to low faculty demand produced new analyses of aggregated data in an effort to explain and project the extent of the downward turn in the academic labor market. Freeman (1971) argued his "cobweb" model of labor market behavior, advising graduate programs to be cognizant of the time lag between faculty demand and supply; if graduate faculty had anticipated the shifts in labor market demands, the output of Ph.D.'s might have been more rational. Cartter (1976) then combined fixed-coefficient and market-responsive models to advance further the projections of faculty supply and demand.

However elegant his combined model, Cartter assumed that placement of new faculty functioned as a prestige-delivery system for institutions as they lined up in a hierarchical procession. He assumed that an invisible hand sorted new doctorates into faculty positions through what Niland (1972) called the "trickle-down effect." *Quality* candidates are matched with *quality* institutions regardless of the supply and demand. Cartter (1976) demonstrated that this normative pattern permitted *lower-quality* institutions to hire *higher-quality* candidates in times of low demand and high supply. The presumption of a quality-descending queue has served as a basic postulate of most of the labor market research that has followed.

As supply increased and demand became less acute through the 1970s, the research shifted away from aggregate demographic projections and toward disciplinary supply and demand issues (Perrucci, O'Flaherty, & Marshall, 1983), including mobility and the rise and plight of the unemployed Ph.D.'s and part-time faculty. The focus on disciplinary exigencies continued until the mid-1980s, when researchers realized that the faculty was beginning to gray. Bowen and Schuster (1986), concerned with the current and future state of the American professoriate, reopened the dialogue about the national aggregate labor market. By piecing together various data, they projected a late-1990s market upswing owing to extensive retirements. Limited by aggregated academic labor market data, they recognized but could not forecast an accurate picture for what had become a very field- and subfield-specific labor market. Three years later, Bowen and Sosa (1989) forecasted an open market for faculty in arts and sciences by charting potential scenarios of supply and demand for the period 1997–2007 based on projected doctorates awarded within disciplinary area, retirement, and attrition patterns.

Both sets of researchers noted that the Carnegie-classified research I universities decreased their share of arts and sciences doctoral graduates between 1958 (81%) and 1987 (63%) as new graduate programs developed (Bowen & Schuster, 1986, p. 174; Bowen & Sosa, 1989, pp. 113–117). Cautioning against "exaggerat[ing] the correlations among institutional quality, quality of doctorate recipients, and institutional classification," they claim that a "possible implication of this shift is that the number of *exceptional* new Ph.D.'s being trained is indeed smaller in absolute terms—and smaller as a proportion of all new Ph.D.'s—than was the case in the 1960s and early 1970s" (Bowen & Sosa, 1989, p. 117; emphasis added). Implicitly, the "trickle-down effect" argument, then, permits the projection that as the labor market returns to the seller's advantage, less selective institutions will have a greater difficulty recruiting faculty or will suffer a reduction in quality by having to hire faculty of a lower caliber (Bowen & Schuster, 1986, pp. 171–174; Bowen & Sosa, 1989, p. 143). The authors assume that the input criteria for quality and selectivity in all doctoral programs are or should be based on potential for research and the output criteria should be measured by graduate placement into elite faculty research positions—normative criteria for departmental rankings.

Further, the presumption that candidates form a quality-descending queue and are dispersed into the labor market based on the degree of privilege ascribed to them by virtue of the prestige of their graduate program disregards individual career choice and drive. Individual career choices may be related to such variables as the candidate's field, family and educational background, professional aspirations, expectations, values, and activities as well as the attraction to the mission and values of the institutions in which they seek employment (Finnegan, 1992, 1993). Personal drive to accomplish the unexpected may allow some to achieve more than anticipated. Blackburn, Bieber, Lawrence, and Trautvetter (1991) have found recently that faculty who are graduates of nonresearch I universities are the highest publishers. "What this finding suggests is that if you have not graduated from an R-I and you are a voracious publisher, you can still be hired at an R-I institution" (p. 399). To assume a market comprising a fixed queue disregards the individual.

For a three- to four-year period in the mid-1960s, the number of new positions outnumbered the available faculty across all sectors, and less selective colleges hired some faculty with master's degrees (Dunham, 1969). The demand permitted many faculty to match their career aspirations and role expectations with a particular type of college and university. In my case study of comprehensive university faculty careers (1992, 1993), professors hired in the open pre-1972 market came from immigrant and working-class families and generally had been first-generation college students. These faculty deliberately chose to seek positions in this sector, valuing teaching above other activities. In addition, many were attracted to helping the type of students—generally first generation—served by these institutions.

By 1972, however, the academic labor market became a bust for faculty wanna-bes who sought positions in research universities and the more selective liberal arts colleges. Enrollments either stayed the same or diminished in these sectors. Community colleges, on the other hand, enjoyed tremendous enrollment growth, hiring almost one-half of the new faculty positions through the 1970s; the comprehensive colleges also expanded their faculty after enrolling 26 percent more students in 1976 than in 1970 (NCES, 1992, p. 219; Finnegan, 1992). The flood of candidates enabled many "less student-selective" institutions to become more faculty-selective, hiring almost exclusively faculty with doctorates, but only in liberal arts disciplines. Some sought additional prestige by recruiting liberal arts faculty who received doctorates from renowned programs, were research oriented, and had publishing track records (Muffo & Robinson, 1981; Finnegan, 1993).

Simultaneously, though, comprehensive colleges refocused and expanded their curricula to include occupational programs to respond to new student employment concerns. The labor market therefore favored the less plentiful faculty with preparation in applied areas, who in many cases had less impressive pedigrees, held master's degrees, and deliberately wanted to teach. Since 1982, after recognizing their inability to provide the support that the researcher-teachers needed, these universities appear again to be seeking faculty who emphasize teaching but who engage in research. The graduate programs from which the newer faculty originate have tended to be the newer doctoral programs that Bowen and Sosa (1989) and Bowen and Schuster (1986) noted. In general, these universities are having little difficulty attracting quality faculty who prefer a balanced professional life (Finnegan, 1992; Youn & Gamson, 1994).

The traditional presumption that quality and prestige derived from research productivity are synonymous once offered a blueprint for the pathways to career advantage and success, but it provided only a partial picture of the academic labor market. This conceptual position permitted negative evaluations of faculty who could not or would not compete within the research university system, and it simultaneously ignored alternative motivations and aspirations. As long as the labor market analyses concentrated on productivity in the aggregate, a seemingly impartial variable, the emphasis reflected society's positive upward mobility and individual achievement value. But the systemic advantage existed only for some; the scholarly emphasis on this "neutral" activity deterred treatment of additional structural issues, such as cumulative disadvantage arising from gender, ethnicity, and class membership. Scholars have begun to explore dysfunctional aspects of the labor market mechanisms.

Structural Studies

This genre within academic labor market research is concerned with institutional mechanisms that reflect larger societal issues and help to shape career outcomes. Career advantage and disadvantage, success, deficit, and failure are defined by and associated with the structural status quo, which has been viewed by scholars as either normative or inequitable depending upon their value perspective. As Youn noted, "structural perspectives [focus] on the larger structural and institutional mechanisms that *might cause* inequality among social positions" (1988b, p. 18; emphasis added).

A structural concept particularly apposite for the study of the professoriate is that of the dual labor market (Doeringer & Piore, 1971), which contends that institutional rules and procedures allocate positions in the internal markets within organizations (Kerr, 1954; Althauser, 1989), whereas competition within the workforce allocates positions in distinctive external labor markets—in this case, collegiate faculty. Internal labor markets segment the external competition according to the differential structural needs and values of the organizations within the labor market (Kalleberg & Sorensen, 1979). In other words, as Brown (1967) noted, we should expect that different institutional sectors—research, doctorate-granting, comprehensive, and so on—theoretically should segment the labor pool by virtue of their distinct missions and values. As a result, differential career lines or job histories form in relation to these organizational differences within a given occupation (Spilerman, 1977; Spenner, Otto, & Call, 1982). In and of themselves, these structural perspectives used to decipher labor market mechanisms represent no particular subjective predisposition, although when applied to research on the professoriate, researchers have argued diverse outcomes.

The Internal Market

Kalleberg and Sorensen (1979) differentiate between two major types of internal labor markets: one that is controlled by the firm with orderly promotions from within, and a second, a "craft occupation," in which recruitment into and employment within the internal market is controlled by the occupational group's members. Well documented are the mechanisms related to recruitment, retention, and rewards, which revolve around the buying and selling of prestige (Sorensen, 1989) and which systematize the internal academic "craft occupation" labor market of research universities. This internal research market is controlled to a large extent by the cosmopolitan (Gouldner, 1957, 1958) or discipline-oriented scholars, who define and control professional standards and affirmation through graduate teaching, journal editorships, professional association offices, consistent publications, and the peer review processes. Research universities and most doctorate-granting universities rely on an accrued collective professional judgment about comparative worth when they retain and promote an individual faculty member. Not only are instant peer evaluations sought in the affirmation process, but the cumulative record of successful peer evaluations that attend a publication record implicitly factor into the institutional investment of promotion and tenure.

Infrequently addressed, however, are the structural processes related to the first type of internal labor market, those that are "controlled by the firm," or what I call the *institutional-specific internal academic labor market*. Little is known about the institutional recruitment and retention policies and procedures of the colleges and universities that emphasize teaching and provide less support for faculty research activities. Even less is understood about the motivations of faculty who teach in less selective institutions, about faculty who are recruited specifically to teach within the "craft" or research internal market, and, for that matter, beyond their publication activities, about the values, beliefs, and motivations for teaching of the research elites (see Becher, 1989). Three major studies have documented trends in faculty personnel policy and practice in research universities over the past four decades. Although these studies have provided needed sociological analysis of one sector, the institutional-specific internal market awaits the same attention.

Caplow and McGee (1958), at the cusp of the expansion of the 1960s, furnished a baseline analysis of recruitment and retention processes in disciplinary departments in ten major universities. They declared the research internal market operations to be *collegial*; recruitment, mobility, and retention practices were informal, prestige based, and seated in personal contacts. They also found faculty who avoided voicing dissenting scholarly opinions for fear of negative personnel reprisals, retention and mobility processes that were dominated by productivity, and prejudice and hiring discrimination by religion, race, gender, and political affiliation. And they descried the incongruity between faculty job assignment (teaching) and the outcomes (research products) upon which success and failure are determined, and they lamented the reduction of local prestige for teaching at the expense of research demands.

By the mid-1970s, Smelser and Content (1980) found more rational and bureaucratic recruitment procedures within the University of California sociology department. The change, they claimed, resulted from the instability in the country's economic health, the emergence of affirmative action policies and new "political constituencies," ethnic- and gender-based organizations, and countermovements of "academically conservative" faculty (pp. 161–165). They predicted that recruitment strategies and procedures would become more time consuming and deliberate in the future because underrepresented applicants now had to be considered.

Finally, in 1988, Burke, relying on Caplow and McGee's framework, found more change in the research internal market. Although the market was more stable after several years of retrenchment and stagnation, certain subgroups had gained an advantage. Disciplinary and specialty segmentation in labor pools had increased. Religion and political affiliation were no longer employment factors, and substantially more women and minorities were not only in the labor pool but had also begun to fill positions at the assistant professor level (Burke, 1988, p. 30).

Burke found that most "collegial" recruiting norms had disappeared. Inbreeding and "silver-cording" (hiring one's own after an apprenticeship elsewhere) had faded, as had placement of new graduates by mentors.

Some norms, however, continue to predominate. Personal contacts now merely alert mentors of openings to ensure the best possible pool of candidates. Applicants become candidates through an appraisal of references (source and content) and research abilities (the quality of publications and dissertation); candidates become employees via a successful interview that includes a presentation of research results and the demonstration of potential for collegiality, of an ability to communicate, and of a commitment to teaching. The ultimate criteria, however, remain research experience and scholarship potential. The "relationship between the prestige of the Ph.D.-granting program and the prestige of the employing department has been found to be positive" (Burke, 1988, p. 65).

These three studies documented the structural properties of the recruitment processes into research university positions during an extended period in which the quest for research and its attendant prestige waxed, not only in the research university, but throughout the sectors. Additional focused research has disaggregated the same phenomenon to particular disciplines, confirming that within this internal market initial employment is more an effect of the prestige of a candidate's sponsorship, by either a mentor or the doctoral program, than the result of the individual's own achievement (Crane, 1970; Reskin, 1979; Long, Allison, & McGinnis, 1979; Thompson & Zumenta, 1985; McGinnis & Long, 1988; Youn, 1988a). Research-oriented "departments maximize prestige" and "are simply better situated to attract candidates who are motivated to do research and to hire the individuals they want" (Thompson & Zumenta, 1985, p. 132).

From recruitment, the leap to analyze workplace incentives, support, role requirements, rewards, and mobility was not far. Studies of structural factors that affect faculty achievement have favored the same internal market. As a result, the faculty activity receiving analytic preference has been productivity. Professional achievement has been tied to a structural cumulative advantage from mentorship and graduate department socialization (Crane, 1965; Reskin, 1977), predoctoral publication (Long, Allison, & McGinnis, 1979), the employing department (Blackburn, Behymer, & Hall, 1978; Long & McGinnis, 1981) or institution (Allison & Stewart, 1974; Kim, 1990), and collegial networks (Pelz & Andrews, 1976). Updating the 1969 productivity comparisons by sector which Fulton and Trow (1974) reported, Bailey (1992) has reconfirmed differentials in amount of publications, albeit increased levels of productivity across institutional type. Her work represents one of the few recent studies to analyze the professional accomplishments across institutional affiliation.

Even more rare are cross-sector studies that move beyond research productivity. In *The Academic Life: Small Worlds, Different Worlds* (1987), Clark employs an evolutionary structural framework discussing the work life of faculty across five Carnegie sectors. Although recognizing that faculty careers unfold differently owing to differential role requirements within particular types of institution, he posits that the segments compose a stratified hierarchy. Thus, the advancement of knowledge, and by extension, the faculty who perform the bulk of this activity and are employed at the top of the hierarchy, "propel the system" of the disciplines and higher education (p. 101). Research faculty have this power because they stand above the structural mechanisms of their institutions. "Teachers" at "lesser" institutions are subject to the whims of their administrators because to Clark they are without intellectual authority (p. 103). In the end, he argues that faculty at teaching institutions are at best disciples of the scholars and at worst victims of inadequate and inchoate institutional conditions.

Indeed, the faculty who write, who expand disciplinary knowledge, and who lead the professional associations propel the system and control disciplinary knowledge in general, but their careers and involvement with their institutions are based on particular types of social exchange mechanisms, which are prestige based and are fostered within that particular internal market. Entrance is based on ascription but sustained for mobility through achievement supported by the departments and institutions as careers progress (Sawyer, 1981).

Applying the current understanding of the mechanisms of the research internal market to institutions that promote teaching as their primary mission and whose distribution of resources primarily supports that mission disregards the probability that a second internal market exists within the contemporary higher education system, one that is controlled more by the institution than by the professionals "in the craft." From my own research, interest, and experience, many faculty within the second internal market are attracted to a different academic life than that required in a research university. Liberal arts college and comprehensive college and university faculty with whom I have spoken have explained to me that they are motivated to continue in their institution or sector by the type of students they encounter, the institutional community they find, the freedom to pursue eclectic research projects, and the institutional emphasis on teaching. These factors are essential components of their professional lives and are more important than smaller teaching loads, better pay, and the pressure to publish. These faculty all conduct research while managing four-course loads.

When teaching institutions are evaluated by applying research internal market processes, explicit and implicit judgments of worth and quality generally follow. Rather than determining the existence of and possible differences in a second internal market and then performing an internal evaluation (Bloom, 1956), based on criteria related to the way that this market operates, an external evaluation or sector comparison occurs. When evaluated by the criteria of the research internal market, teaching institutions will always have shortcomings. The question is not how faculty employed in teaching institutions or for teaching in a research institution stack up against their research-oriented colleagues but what personal motivations, values, and beliefs and institutional social exchange mechanisms drive these faculty members' careers and involvement in their institutions. But we have yet to ask these questions.

Market Inequity Studies

In addition to probing the influences of environmental, organizational, and disciplinary variables on the research internal market, the structural perspective has also fostered questioning inequities within the system. Merton (1968) introduced the Matthew Effect, exploring positive status attainment through his concept of cumulative advantage for those favored within the research internal labor market; subsequent scholars have probed the barriers that prohibit others from similar career success. The complexion of the faculty has not only changed over the past few decades, but the change is gathering speed (Lomperis, 1990). As of 1991, only 60 percent of the more than half million full-time faculty members are white males. Women command about 32 percent of the full-time faculty positions, whereas people of color constitute 12.6 percent (Minter, 1994; EEOC, 1991). Clearly, the documentation and subsequent demise of the old "collegial" patterns as well as the exposure of discriminatory practices have complemented affirmative action mandates to open the entry paths to the groves of the academy. Unfortunately, much of the market inequity research has continued to employ the traditional conceptual orientation, advocating implicitly the existence of one internal market, which is based on research and prestige. Although gender, ethnicity, and most recently class issues are being investigated, the questions rarely explore additional or alternative values and motivations for academic careers.

Gender, Ethnicity, and Class and the Academic Labor Market

Women academics have recognized and documented cumulative career disadvantage for three decades. Early studies of disparity documented constraints often peculiar to the employment of women as academics, such as role conflict, institutional marginality, and personal ambivalence (Bernard, 1964), nepotism (Dolan & Davis, 1960), disciplinary preference and availability (Office of Education, 1958), and myths such as career interruptions (Astin, 1969) and differential devotion of time (Johnson & Stafford, 1974, 1979; Stroeber & Questar, 1977). Explanations for salary gaps between men and women in academe soon followed (Bayer & Astin, 1968; LaSorte, 1971; Katz, 1973). Most of these disadvantages, however, were the result of informal habits of mind and practice resulting from normative social role designations.

Until the passage of the 1964 Civil Rights Act, disadvantage for minorities incorporated more deliberate disabilities. In eighteen southern states, de jure segregation proscribed equal education for African Americans on the collegiate level prior to 1936, when the civil rights cases began to challenge separate graduate education programs on a state-by-state basis. Until 1964, those southern (and many in other regions of the country) African American citizens who aspired to an undergraduate education were limited in choice to underfunded historically black colleges. For the minority faculty who taught in those institutions, participation in professional activities was severely limited. Research university libraries, archives, and laboratories as well as disciplinary associational meetings that were located in segregated states and locales were closed to their use and participation (Winston, 1971). Inadequate institutional financial support from the various states and access-oriented low tuition prevented comparative and competitive faculty salaries (Finnegan, 1991). In the North, where de facto segregation prevailed, few institutions employed those few African American faculty who had secured competitive disciplinary education.

In comparison, then, the disabilities that prevented equity in the academic labor market experienced by women since the 1960s have primarily been due to informal, albeit powerful, social norms, while for African Americans, the most prominent minority group in the labor pool until recently, the disabilities have been bolstered by legislative and judicial decisions. Regardless of the historical differences, the concepts explored in the maturing body of women's inequity studies have been adopted by the emerging research community of scholars who are addressing minority faculty issues.

Over the past thirty years, the variables tested have multiplied, and the concepts employed to demonstrate institutionalized discrimination have grown more sophisticated. The invisible curriculum both in the classroom (exclusive language and topics of study) and on campus (admissions quotas, campus social rules, residency requirements, and informal exclusion) has had a chilling effect on career aspirations and created structural barriers for females (Roby, 1972; Frazier & Sadker, 1973; Tobias & Weissbrod, 1980; Association of American Colleges, 1982) and for minorities (Rafky, 1972; McClelland & Auster, 1990). These formerly acceptable practices also served the latent function of inhibiting women and minorities in their pursuit of academic careers.

Apropos of labor market processes, employment access, reward differentials, and the institutional and professional barriers that prevent reward accumulation among women and minority academics have emerged as research concerns over the past decade. But these analyses of women and minority faculty members' achievement of positive status attainment have been circumscribed by the application and interpretation of those mechanisms essential for success within the internal research market. In productivity, for example, women have consistently been shown to produce less scholarship than their male colleagues (Cole & Cole, 1973; Hargens, McCann, & Reskin, 1978; Cole & Zuckerman, 1984; Bailey, 1992).

The nature of the socialization into the academic profession can either facilitate or impede the realization of a "successful" career. The choice of a graduate program and its faculty is the first crucial decision in the path toward an academic career. Although Blackburn, Bieber, Lawrence, & Trautvetter (1991) have demonstrated that the more prolific publishers are hailing from less selective programs, researchers have concluded that minority students have a less competitive edge in the prestige-related internal market because most attain their graduate degrees in non-research I institutions (Rafky, 1972; Mickelson & Oliver, 1991). Within their graduate programs, regardless of institutional type, role models and mentors for both women and minority graduate students are few in number (Berg & Ferber, 1983; Exum, Menges, Watkins, & Berglund, 1984; Sands, Parson, & Duane, 1991) and are pressed into too much institutional service, which takes further time away from their other professional activities (Clark & Corcoran, 1986). For these students, limited and differential interactions with cross-gender and cross-ethnic graduate faculty impede proper socialization (Holmstrom & Holmstrom, 1974; Hite, 1985; Turner & Thompson, 1993), but Holland (1993) has found a range of intensity and quality in the relationship between graduate advisors and African American doctoral students with more leaning toward the positive. Cumulative disadvantage may be decreasing with increased awareness of the historical deficits.

Just as all mentoring is not the same, certainly all career aspirations are not the same. Jensen (1982) suggests an acculturation model with three modal categories of career motivations among young women academics.

Women in one modality (reorientation) follow the traditional masculine commitment to their professional work, charting and regarding their careers as personal achievement rather than accidental opportunities. The second cluster (reaffirmation) combine the traditional demands of family with their professional careers and strive more to support other women colleagues rather than to gain professional prestige. Finally, in the third set (reconstitution), women are committed to teaching, to mentoring younger women, and to pursuing "frontier" specialties and ideas, even though colleagues think they are treating marginal topics. Jensen's modal categories demonstrate that the development of women faculty, during both graduate school and the first years of academic employment, is dependent upon a combination of the individual's aspirations, lifestyle preferences, personal and professional values, and the professional and personal relationships with graduate faculty and colleagues.

Jensen's typology could help to explain the tendency for women faculty to produce fewer publications than men (Bailey, 1992), a trait often linked to women's preference for teaching (Feldman, 1974; Centra, 1974). In the 1989 Carnegie survey of faculty attitudes,[1] men, when compared with women, reported more publications, a slightly higher preference for research, and less agreement that teaching effectiveness should carry more weight in tenure decisions (Bailey, 1992, app.). These differences may be related to cumulative disadvantage, to the missed opportunities within the professional socializing activities of graduate school, and to discrimination within recruitment and retention processes. Or they may be related to women's membership in Jensen's second and third modal groups, whose values are oriented toward relationships rather than professional competition. Since we tend to analyze only career variables peculiar to the internal research market, we assume that cumulative disadvantage, a normative structural trait, is the primary cause.

Moore claims that "the more lucrative, and the more status a particular field or occupation has, the less likely it is to have a high proportion of women in it" and that women "are usually clustered in the lower position and pay categories" (1987, p. 25). Clearly, women historically have gravitated to certain fields in academe, but they are gaining in representation among the faculty in most fields, are now earning one-third of the doctorates awarded, and are seeking academic employment more often than their male counterparts (Lomperis, 1990). Faculty report more affinity to teaching the further removed their institutional type is from the research university. The tendency for women to prefer teaching *may* be related at least in part to their larger representation in teaching institutions (NCES,

1993). Many may have deliberately chosen a career oriented toward teaching rather than research, even though this choice meant less prestige and lower pay.

To what extent, then, are the publication rates and attitudes about teaching associated more with institutional-specific role orientations and personal motivations and aspirations? Are these disparities purely a result of systemwide structural inequities, or might they possibly be related to the inappropriate comparisons by researchers of two internal markets? Without knowledge of how the genders and ethnic groups contrast *within* the particular sectors, which employ different proportions of men and women and of minority-majority members, the comparisons are virtually meaningless. Finally, in addition to or in spite of systemic discrimination, to what degree have women and minorities chosen to "cluster" in the traditional teaching institutions because of their own values and aspirations?

The newest structural writings to emerge on the academic labor market have been on class. Although Ladd and Lipset (1978) noted that faculty in more selective colleges tended to emerge from the higher classes and that one-quarter of the faculty originated from working-class families, class as a variable in labor market analyses has been neglected. In two essay anthologies, "working-class faculty" have discussed their experiences with academe demonstrating a revived interest in family roots. Ryan and Sackrey wanted to determine to what degree faculty, primarily men, from this class "experienced similar feelings of displacement or dissatisfaction, and perhaps most importantly, internalized conflict" as academics (1984, p. 6). Likewise, Tokarczyk and Fay (1993) let faculty women discuss issues of incongruent class values, of class-related barriers that have affected their aspirations and education choices, and of estrangement from family. Faculty-essayists raise questions about basic personal value sets that they maintain, wrestle with, or left behind when choosing a career.

In the comprehensive universities that I have studied, all but one of the faculty hired before 1972 came from working-class families, and many were born to immigrant parents; several of the those hired since 1982 came from the same class roots (Finnegan, 1992, 1993). These faculty deliberately chose teaching colleges because they wanted to teach; many specifically wanted to teach students who came from similar backgrounds. The aspirations of some "working-class faculty" may have been limited by lack of understanding of the mechanisms of the system. These same patterns emerge from among the voices of the faculty to whom Ryan and Sackrey (1984) and Tokarczyk and Fay (1993) provided a podium. Class could be an important variable in understanding the core values and motivations that draw and sustain people within the various tracks within academic careers.

Conclusion

The academic labor market research is remarkably silent on teaching. The research tends to address the requirements, norms, effects, and outcomes of labor market processes on faculty in the research institution sector. The sociological images generated in the literature as progeny of Merton's Matthew Effect (1968) direct attention to status attainment variables, such as prestige, privilege, rewards, position, and influence. These concepts constitute a *Weltanschauung* that expresses in- and out-group membership within a hierarchical lineage. An academic's worth is dependent initially upon the ascriptive status of the elder lineage and then reverts quickly to his or her achievements. And that achievement is defined by in-group appraisal and approval that translate into rewards: higher salary, accessible doors to obtain supplemental resources, bids to comment, speak, evaluate, and much more. Not surprising, these kinship patterns reflect our society's values.

In this conclusion, I argue three points. First, the traditional perspective that drives much of the labor market research is unproductive and limiting. Second, much of the newer research arises from the traditional structural approach and has adopted naively the orthodox status quo perspective. Third, an incongruity exists between public policy for higher education as an access system and the approaches we utilize in our investigations of the labor market.

The Traditional Perspective

The difficulty with approaching academic labor market processes with a lineal perspective is an implicit assumption that the value of descending quality attends the norms of recruitment, retention, and mobility as a natural escort. We then make no attempt to pursue alternative explanations for the values and motivations that faculty in teaching positions hold or experience. We rate faculty who pursue research as significantly more important, more liberated, more autonomy bearing, and more professional than those who primarily teach.

What occurs with this type of argument is that the professional efforts and worth of faculty are stereotyped according to institutional type.

Clearly, faculty play out their professional lives differently within the various sectors and are required, supported, and rewarded for different types of activities. Tuma and Grimes argue that "organizational and professional settings are as important as a person's role orientation in determining how the person performs professional and organizational roles." But the "patterns of associations between dimensions of role orientations or within organizations can vary widely . . . and depend on the structure of the organization and the structure of the profession" (1981, p. 187).

The faculty employed within the various sectors are not unidimensional professionals who fit such stereotypes. Within the various sectors, fluctuations in the labor market have permitted great variability in competitiveness. The shifts in supply and demand over the past thirty years have permitted institutions to hire for organizational aspirations, disregarding their missions and resources. Yet, simultaneously within these institutions, other faculty deliberately chose to follow a mission-congruent teaching role. Thus, to promote such a cliché that the various sectors produce or attract only a certain type of faculty is to ignore larger labor market issues. To assign degrees of quality to ascribed and achieved positions on a hierarchy is to ignore individual values, motivations, and abilities.

As Braxton has recently argued, "the role of institutional selectivity as an important index of academic quality or academic standards is well rooted in the academic folklore beliefs held by academics and the lay public alike" (1993, p. 657). He found, though, that faculty who teach in "more selective research universities do not tend to be any more rigorous than are their less-selective counterparts when a higher-order (critical thinking) level of understanding of course content required by examination questions is used as an index of academic rigor" (p. 669). Quality in research, or more accurately, success in the labor market processes, does not necessarily equate with quality in classroom practice.

The Structural Perspective

Recent structural analyses document systemic inequities that inhibit certain groups of faculty from succeeding within the normative structure. By demonstrating that the normative prestige-driven system discriminates against groups of faculty, the argument assumes our perception of the system has been accurate. In other words, the traditional labor market approach sees the glass half full, while the new structuralists see the glass as half empty.

By adopting the traditional philosophy as normative, many structuralists argue that ascriptive group membership, which is based on gender, ethnicity, and class, places them at a disadvantage to succeed in a closed system. To me, this argument follows an assimilationist perspective. Outgroups, as victims, want "into the system," rather than asking if different approaches to understanding the labor market might be undertaken. Or to return to my analogy, is the glass shaped right?

If two internal labor markets operate simultaneously within academe, as I am arguing, then we should be exploring their mechanisms and functions with similar vigor and without bias. To what degree do these other mechanisms and functions, assuming they differ, attract, motivate, and satisfy faculty across the sectors? If differential values accompany distinct ascribed-status groups seeking faculty positions, those values should be explored without compromise. Higher education has entered into a period of radical change as a result of increased participation by subgroups with emerging consciousness. To what degree do the values of these subgroups, assuming they differ, affect what occurs within faculty careers?

Access and the Academic Labor Market

As a system of advanced learning, we take great pride that almost all students who desire postsecondary education have access to some form of instruction. Yet, as evidenced above, we perpetuate a myth, as Braxton noted, that institutional type and the associated faculty differ in degree of quality. And, as if the assignation of status by sector is not enough, we differentiate additionally through the allocation of resources, whether tangible or not, both to institutions and to the faculty who are employed within the various institutions.

Rather than continue to foster a systemic model based on status attainment, should we not be more concerned with the attributes and properties of knowledge that we are communicating within the sectors and therefore with what we are producing or reproducing in our classrooms as a result of this perspective? "The field of knowledge, which some may have thought was relatively untouched by social relations, is in reality both the stage and the object of struggles between groups and social classes" (Tanguy, 1985, p. 21). At this point, we appear to support a state of knowledge about our own profession which sustains barriers, impels competition, and refuses to acknowledge a plurality of purpose. Our definitions of quality must be reconsidered.

The purpose of this chapter has been to review the existing literature on the academic labor market in light of motivating faculty to teach, the focus of this book. Scrutinized as a hierarchical sorting mechanism, the academic labor market research has advanced the values of prestige and hierarchy and the norms of competition, ascription, and achievement. This determinative perspective, although instructional about administrative and professional agencies, has neglected to take the individual's aspirations and values into account when considering labor market patterns. By employing the traditional structural perspective, recent scholars, leveling cumulative disadvantage criticism on the system, have absorbed the status quo rather than promoting a new approach. As long as we continue to limit our investigations to the prestige system with its affiliate variable, professional productivity, we restrict our interest in other elements of faculty life, such as the motivations related to teaching. By exclusively studying and thereby promoting the prestige-sorting mechanisms of the labor market as well as comparative rates of productivity across the sectors, we have disregarded, and often times dismissed, a significant portion of the profession who receive their primary intrinsic rewards from and are motivated by their interaction with and ability to engage students inside and outside the classroom. We have also inadvertently disregarded important value sets held by faculty within and across the sectors related to sharing knowledge and fostering new generations of educated citizens.

Note

1. Unfortunately, the Carnegie data are not disaggregated by ethnicity, so an equivalent argument cannot be made for minority faculty at this time. Although affirmative action programs have enabled more minority hiring, individuals experience negative or skeptical reactions to their abilities by colleagues (Banks, 1984). Women of color experience the double jeopardy of the combination of race and gender (Turner & Thompson, 1993). Minority faculty have predominated in historically black and Native American colleges and universities, many of which are either comprehensive institutions or two-year colleges and do not insist on publications. Thompson (1978) indicates that some African American faculty with opportunities to move to "white colleges" have chosen to stay at black colleges to assist black students. Without new data on the distribution of minority faculty in this new age of multiculturalism and an increasing number of minority doctorates, further conjecture is premature.

References

Allison, P. D., & Stewart, J. A. (1974). Productivity differences among scientists: Evidence for accumulative advantage. *American Sociological Review, 39,* 596–606.

Althauser, R. P. (1989). Internal labor markets. *Annual Review of Sociology, 15,* 143–161.

Association of American Colleges. (1982). *The classroom climate: A chilly one for women?* Washington, DC: Association of American Colleges, Project on the Status and Education of Women.

Astin, H. S. (1969). *The woman doctorate in America.* New York: Russell Sage.

Austin, A. E. (1992). Supporting the professor as teacher: The Lilly Teaching Fellows Program. *Review of Higher Education, 12,* 85–106.

Austin, A. E., Brocato, J. J., & LaFleur, M. (1993). Learning to teach: The socialization of university teachers. Paper presented at the annual meeting of the American Educational Research Association, Atlanta.

Bailey, T. G. (1992). Faculty research productivity. Paper presented at the annual meeting of the Association for the Study of Higher Education, Minneapolis.

Baldwin, R. G., & Blackburn, R. T. (1981). The academic career as a developmental process. *Journal of Higher Education, 52,* 598–614.

Banks, W. M. (1984). Afro-American scholars in the university: Roles and conflicts. *Behavioral Scientist, 27,* 325–338.

Bayer, A. E., & Astin, H. S. (1968). Sex differences in academic rank and salary among science doctorates in teaching. *Journal of Human Resources, 3,* 191–199.

Bayer, A. E., & Dutton, J. E. (1977). Career age and research-professional activities of academic scientists. *Journal of Higher Education, 68,* 259–282.

Becher, T. (1989). *Academic tribes and territories: Intellectual enquiry and the culture of disciplines.* Milton Keynes, England: SRHE and Open University Press.

Berelson, B. (1960). *Graduate education in the United States.* New York: McGraw-Hill.

Berg, H. M., & Ferber, M. A. (1983). Men and women graduate students: Who succeeds and why? *Journal of Higher Education, 54,* 629–648.

Bernard, J. (1964). *Academic women.* University Park: Pennsylvania State University Press.

Blackburn, R. T., Behymer, C. E., & Hall, D. E. (1978). Correlates of faculty publications. *Sociology of Education, 51,* 541–557.

Blackburn, R. T., Bieber, J. P., Lawrence, J. H., & Trautvetter, L. (1991). Faculty at work: Focus on research, scholarship, and service. *Research in Higher Education, 32,* 385–413.

Bloom, B. S. (Ed.). (1956). *Taxonomy of educational objectives: The classification of educational goals.* New York: Longmans, Green & Co.

Boice, R. (1992). *The new faculty member.* San Francisco: Jossey-Bass.

Bowen, H. R., & Schuster, J. H. (1986). *American professors: A national resource imperiled.* New York: Oxford University Press.

Bowen, W. G., & Sosa, J. A. (1989). *Prospects for faculty in the arts and sciences.* Princeton: Princeton University Press.

Braxton, J. M. (1993). Selectivity and rigor in research universities. *Journal of Higher Education, 64,* 657–675.

Brown, D. G. (1967). *The mobile professor.* Washington, DC: American Council on Education.

Burke, D. L. (1988). *A new academic marketplace.* Westport, CT: Greenwood Press.

Caplow, T., & McGee, R. J. (1958). *The academic marketplace.* New York: Basic Books.

Carnegie Foundation for the Advancement of Teaching. (1989). *The condition of the professoriate: Attitudes and trends, 1989.* Princeton: Carnegie Foundation for the Advancement of Teaching.

Cartter, A. M. (1965). A new look at the supply of college teachers. *Educational Record, 46,* 267–277.

Cartter, A. M. (1976). *Ph.D.'s and the academic labor market.* New York: McGraw-Hill.

Centra, J. (1974). *Women, men, and the doctorate.* Princeton: Educational Testing Service.

Chronister, J. L., Baldwin, R. G., & Bailey, T. (1992). Full-time non-tenure-track faculty: Current status, condition, and attitudes. *Review of Higher Education, 15,* 383–400.

Clark, B. R. (1987). *The academic life: Small worlds, different worlds.* Princeton: Carnegie Foundation for the Advancement of Teaching.

Clark, S. M., & Corcoran, M. (1986). Perspectives on the professional socialization of women faculty: A case of accumulative disadvantage? *Journal of Higher Education, 57,* 20–43.

Cole, J. R., & Cole, S. (1973). *Social stratification in science.* Chicago: University of Chicago Press.

Cole, J. R., & Zuckerman, H. (1984). The productivity puzzle: Persistence and change in patterns of publication of men and women scientists. In M. W. Steinkamps & M. L. Maehr (Eds.), *Advances in motivation and achievement.* Greenwich, CT: JAI Press.

Crane, D. (1965). Scientists at major and minor universities: A study of productivity and recognition. *American Sociological Review, 30,* 699–714.

Crane, D. (1970). The academic marketplace revisited: A study of faculty mobility using the Cartter ratings. *American Journal of Sociology, 7,* 953–956.

Doeringer, P. B., & Piore, M. J. (1971). *Internal labor markets and manpower analysis.* Lexington, MA: Heath Lexington Books.

Dolan, E. F., & Davis, M. P. (1960). Antinepotism rules in American colleges and universities: Their effects on the faculty employment of women. *Educational Record, 41,* 285–295.

Dunham, E. A. (1969). *Colleges of the forgotten Americans: A profile of state colleges and regional universities.* Carnegie Commission on Higher Education. New York: McGraw-Hill.

Equal Employment Opportunity Commission [EEOC]. (1991). *EEO-6 higher education staff information, 1991.* Washington, DC: Office of Education.

Exum, W. H., Menges, R. J., Watkins, B., & Berglund, P. (1984). Making it at the top: Women and minority faculty in the academic labor market. *American Behavioral Scientist, 27,* 301–324.

Fairweather, J. S. (1993). Academic values and faculty rewards. *Review of Higher Education, 17,* 43–68.

Feldman, S. D. (1974). *Escape from the doll's house: Women in graduate and professional school education.* New York: McGraw-Hill.

Finkelstein, M. J., & LaCelle-Peterson, M. W. (Eds.). (1993). *Developing senior faculty as teachers.* New Directions for Teaching and Learning 55. San Francisco: Jossey-Bass.

Finnegan, D. E. (1991). Opportunity knocked: The origins of contemporary comprehensive colleges and universities. Working paper #6. Boston: New England Resource Center for Higher Education, University of Massachusetts at Boston.

Finnegan, D. E. (1992). Academic career lines: A case study of faculty in two comprehensive universities. Ph.D. dissertation, Pennsylvania State University.

Finnegan, D. E. (1993). Segmentation in the academic labor market: Hiring cohorts in comprehensive universities. *Journal of Higher Education, 64,* 621–656.

Frazier, N., & Sadker, M. (1973). *Sexism in school and society.* New York: Harper & Row.

Freeman, R. (1971). *The market for college-trained manpower.* Cambridge: Harvard University Press.

Fulton, O., & Trow, M. (1974). Research activity in American higher education. *Sociology of Education, 47,* 29–73.

Gainen, J., & Boice, R. (Eds.). (1993). *Building a diverse faculty.* New Directions for Teaching and Learning 53. San Francisco: Jossey-Bass.

Gamson, Z. F., Finnegan, D. E., & Youn, T. I. K. (1991). Assessing faculty shortages in comprehensive universities. *Metropolitan universities: An international forum, 1*, 87–97.

Gouldner, A. W. (1957, 1958). Cosmopolitans and locals: Toward an analysis of latent social roles. *Administrative Science Quarterly, 2*, 281–306; *2*, 444–480.

Hargens, L. L., McCann, J. C., & Reskin, B. F. (1978). Productivity and reproductivity: Fertility and professional achievement among research scientists. *Social Forces, 57*, 154–163.

Heath, J. A., & Tuckman, H. P. (1989). The impact on labor markets of the relative growth of female doctorates. *Journal of Higher Education, 60*, 704–715.

Hite, L. M. (1985). Female doctoral students: Their perceptions and concerns. *Journal of College Student Personnel, 26*, 18–22.

Holland, J. W. (1993). Relationships between African American doctoral students and their major advisors. Paper presented at annual meeting of American Educational Research Association, Atlanta.

Holmstrom, E., & Holmstrom, R. (1974). The plight of the woman doctoral student. *American Educational Research Journal, 11*, 1–17.

Jensen, K. (1982). Women's work and academic culture. *Higher Education, 11*, 67–83.

Johnson, G. E., & Stafford, F. E. (1974). The earnings and promotion of women faculty. *American Economic Review, 64*, 888–903.

Johnson, G. E., & Stafford, F. E. (1979). Pecuniary rewards to men and women faculty. In D. R. Lewis & W. E. Becker Jr. (Eds.), *Academic rewards in higher education* (pp. 231–243). Cambridge, MA: Ballinger.

Kalleberg, A. L., & Sorensen, A. B. (1979). The sociology of labor markets. *American Review of Sociology, 5*, 351–379.

Katz, D. (1973). Faculty salaries, promotion, and productivity at a large university. *American Economic Review, 63*, 469–477.

Kerr, C. (1954). The balkanization of labor markets. In E. Wight Bakke, P. M. Hauser, G. L. Palmer, C. A. Myers, D. Yoder, & C. Kerr (Eds.), *Labor mobility and economic opportunity* (pp. 92–110). Cambridge: MIT Press.

Kim, S. (1990). A study of the advantage of organizational context on academic research productivity: The case of chemistry faculty. Ph.D. dissertation, University of Pittsburgh.

Ladd, E., & Lipset, S. (1978). *Survey of the American professoriate: Selected tabulations.* Storrs, CT: Social Science Data Center.

LaSorte, M. A. (1971). Academic salaries: Equal pay for equal work? *Journal of Higher Education, 42*, 265–278.

Lomperis, A. M. T. (1990). Are women changing the nature of the academic profession? *Journal of Higher Education, 6*, 643–677.

Long, J. S., Allison, P. D., & McGinnis, R. (1979). Entrance into the academic career. *American Sociological Review, 44*, 816–830.

Long, J. S., & McGinnis, R. (1981). Organizational context and scientific productivity. *American Sociological Review, 46*, 422–442.

McClelland, K. E., & Auster, C. J. (1990). Public platitudes and hidden tensions: Racial climates at predominantly white liberal arts colleges. *Journal of Higher Education, 61*, 607–642.

McGee, R. (1971). *Academic Janus: The private college and its faculty.* San Francisco: Jossey-Bass.

McGinnis, R., & Long, J. S. (1988). Entry into academia: Effects of stratification, geography, and ecology. In D. W. Breneman & T. I. K. Youn (Eds.), *Academic labor markets and careers*. New York: Falmer Press.

McGrath, E. J. (1959). *The graduate school and the decline of liberal education*. New York: Teachers College, Columbia University Press.

Merton, R. K. (1968). The Matthew effect in science. *Science, 159,* 55–63.

Mickelson, R. A., & Oliver, M. L. (1991). Making the short list: Black candidates and the faculty recruitment process. In P. G. Altbach & K. Lomotey (Eds.), *The racial crisis in American higher education* (pp. 149–166). Albany: State University of New York Press.

Minter, J. (1994, June). Personal communication.

Mommsen, K. G. (1974). Black Ph.D.s in the academic marketplace: Supply, demand, and price. *Journal of Higher Education, 45,* 253–267.

Moore, K. M. (1987). Women's access and opportunity in higher education: Toward the twenty-first century. *Comparative Education, 23,* 23–34.

Muffo, J. A., & Robinson, J. R. (1981). Early science career patterns of recent graduates from leading research universities. *Review of Higher Education, 5,* 1–13.

National Center for Education Statistics [NCES]. (1992). *Digest of education statistics, 1991*. Washington, DC: U.S. Department of Education.

National Center for Education Statistics [NCES]. (1993). *Digest of education statistics, 1992*. Washington, DC: U.S. Department of Education.

National Education Association. (1963). *Teacher supply and demand in colleges, universities, and junior colleges*. Washington, DC: National Education Association.

Niland, J. R. (1972). Allocation of Ph.D. manpower in the academic labor market. *Industrial Relations, 2,* 141–156.

Office of Education. (1958). *Statistics of higher education, 1955–1956: Faculty, students, and degrees*. Washington, DC: U.S. Government Printing Office.

Pelz, D. C., & Andrews, F. M. (Eds.). (1976). *Scientists in organizations: Productive climates for research and development*. Ann Arbor: Institute for Social Research.

Perrucci, R., O'Flaherty, K., & Marshall, H. (1983). Market conditions, productivity, and promotion among university faculty. *Research in Higher Education, 19,* 431–449.

Pintrich, P. R. (1990). Implications of psychological research on student learning and college teaching for teacher education. In W. R. Houston (Ed.), *Handbook of research on teacher education* (pp. 826–857). New York: Macmillan.

Queval, F. A. (1990). The evolution toward research orientation and capability in comprehensive universities: The California state system. Ph.D. dissertation, University of California, Los Angeles.

Rafky, D. M. (1972). The black scholar in the academic marketplace. *Teachers College Record, 74,* 225–260.

Reskin, B. F. (1977). Scientific productivity and the reward structure of science. *American Sociological Review, 42,* 491–504.

Reskin, B. F. (1979). Academic sponsorship and scientists' careers. *Sociology of Education, 52,* 129–146.

Roby, P. (1972). Structural and internalized barriers to women in higher education. In C. Safilios-Rothschild (Ed.), *Toward a sociology of women* (pp. 121–140). Lexington, MA: Xerox College Publishing.

Ryan, J., & Sackrey, C. (1984). *Strangers in paradise: Academics from the working class*. Boston: South End Press.

Sands, R. G., Parson, L. A., & Duane, J. (1991). Faculty mentoring faculty in a public university. *Journal of Higher Education, 62,* 174–193.

Sawyer, D. O. (1981). Institutional stratification and career mobility in academic markets. *Sociology of Education, 54,* 85–97.

Smelser, N., & Content, R. (1980). *The changing academic labor market.* Berkeley: University of California Press.

Sorensen, A. (1989). Academic careers and academic labor markets. Paper presented at the Ringberg Symposium, Max-Planck-Gesellschaft, Schloss Ringberg, Tegernsee, FRG.

Spenner, K. I., Otto, L. B., & Call, V. R. A. (1982). *Career lines and careers.* Lexington, MA: Lexington Books.

Spilerman, S. (1977). Careers, labor market structure, and socioeconomic achievement. *American Journal of Sociology, 83,* 551–593.

Stroeber, M. H., & Questar, A. O. (1977). The earnings and promotion of women faculty: Comment. *American Economic Review, 67,* 207–213.

Tanguy, L. (1985). Academic studies and technical education: New dimensions of an old struggle in the divisions of knowledge. *Sociology of Education, 58,* 20–33.

Thompson, D. (1978). Black college faculty and students: The nature of their interaction. In C. Willie & R. Edmonds (Eds.), *Black colleges in America: Challenge, development, and survival* (pp. 180–194). New York: Teachers College Press.

Thompson, F., & Zumenta, W. (1985). Hiring decisions in organized anarchies: More evidence on entrance into the academic career. *Review of Higher Education, 8,* 123–138.

Tobias, S., & Weissbrod, C. (1980). Anxiety and mathematics: An update. *Harvard Educational Review, 50,* 63–70.

Tokarczyk, M. M., & Fay, E. A. (1993). *Working-class women in the academy: Laborers in the knowledge factory.* Amherst: University of Massachusetts Press.

Tuma, N. B., & Grimes, A. J. (1981). A comparison of models of role orientations of professionals in a research-oriented university. *Administrative Science Quarterly, 26,* 187–206.

Turner, C. S. V., & Thompson, J. R. (1993). Socializing women doctoral students: Minority and majority experiences. *Review of Higher Education, 16,* 355–370.

Winston, M. (1971). Through the back door: Academic racism and the Negro scholar in historical perspective. *Daedalus, 100*(3), 678–719.

Youn, T. I. K. (1988a). Patterns of institutional self-recruitment of young Ph.D.s: Effects of academic markets on career mobility. *Research in Higher Education, 29,* 195–218.

Youn, T. I. K. (1988b). Studies of academic markets and careers: An historical review. In D. W. Breneman & T. I. K. Youn (Eds.), *Academic labor markets and careers* (pp. 8–27). New York: Falmer Press.

Youn, T. I. K. (1992). The sociology of academic careers and academic labor markets. *Research in Labor Economics, 13,* Greenwich, CT: JAI Press.

Youn, T. I. K., & Gamson, Z. F. (1994). Organizational responses to the labor market: A study of faculty searches in comprehensive colleges and universities. *Higher Education, 28,* 189–205.

18 Public Policy and Faculty Motivation

JACK H. SCHUSTER

The higher education community has begun to pay more attention in recent years to restoring greater balance between emphases on teaching and research. This currently takes the form of an intensification of efforts to rehabilitate teaching, for teaching is widely perceived to have suffered serious neglect over the past two decades as circumstances inspired (and permitted) many campuses to demand greater research productivity from their faculties. There are numerous levers at the campus level for determining how teaching occurs and how much and by whom, but this chapter explores whether and to what extent *public* policy plays a role in shaping the conduct of teaching. Accordingly, the questions this chapter seeks to answer are: Does public policy impinge significantly on the ways in which campuses determine how teaching is conducted and rewarded? In what ways do public policy and teaching activities intersect? How consequential are the effects?[1]

At the outset it is important to define what is meant by public policy. For present purposes public policy means the domain of governmental activity, or, more precisely, the actions taken by legislative and executive bodies, as well as by regulatory and advisory bodies, which influence higher education. A short list of examples would include a state legislature and its committees and subcommittees that are responsible for authorizing policies and appropriating funds for higher education, a state department of finance, a statewide coordinating council for higher education, and so on.

This exercise develops the thesis that public policy, as distinguished from institutional policy, does not often directly address the way in which teaching takes place. Even less does public policy directly affect the motivation to teach. However, in recent years, as policy makers have intensified pressures on campuses to pay greater attention to teaching, public policy measures have been exerting increasing influence on teaching. These pressures can be thought of as contributing to an "extrinsic motivation" to upgrade teaching effectiveness. Thus, it is timely to examine the role that public policy has played, is playing, and likely will play in efforts to improve teaching and in fashioning an appropriate balance between teaching and research activities. The effort devoted to teaching, by institutions and individuals, must compete with other demands; the assumption here is that greater attention paid to either teaching *or* research has consequences for the other, although that relationship is complex (Finkelstein, 1984, pp. 120–127; Webster, 1985, pp. 60–62; Finkelstein, 1995, pp. 33–47). It should also be understood that institutional missions differ greatly and, accordingly, public policy's impact will differ in regard to teaching-centered or research-oriented campuses and all intermediate models.

In seeking an answer to the question about the impact of public policies on teaching, this chapter first attempts to place in wider perspective— comparative and historical—the use of public policy in the United States to shape postsecondary education. It then describes some of the intended and unintended consequences for teaching and suggests lessons about the use of public policy to motivate teachers and, more generally, to influence the teaching process. In the main, this chapter argues that public policy can be employed both to promote effective teaching and (more likely in practice) to establish expectations that may well prove to be counterproductive as the heretofore mainly oblique nature of public policy's impact on teaching shifts to a more direct and potentially powerful relationship.

Cross-national and Historical Perspectives

To understand better how public policy currently engages higher education in the United States, it will be useful to view the American experience in both the broader context of other nations' experiences and to touch on the historical evolution of government's role in the United States as it affects higher education. The cross-national vantage point will help to underscore the uniqueness of the American experience; the historical lens will afford some sense, however abbreviated, of possibilities for and limitations of the policy process.

United States in Cross-national Perspective

Public policy and higher education are intimately connected in every nation. In almost all, the national government greatly affects most elements of how higher education is organized, whom it serves, what it provides, and so on.[2] A country's principal instrumentalities for addressing such fundamental issues as scope, access, finance, and quality almost invariably entail a national-level education ministry, whose mission may be relatively narrow or extensive, perhaps encompassing science policy and "culture," perhaps not. Many nations have created as well a national academy with authority over advanced research institutes that often functionally exist well apart from universities and frequently are in tense competition with them for ever scarce resources.

The variations are endless, but the authority of government, whether in market, blended, or command economies, is always present and often dominant. In only a few nations is there a robust private/independent university sector that is buffered (in varying degrees) from the dictates of the state. The United States presents an extreme example; half the institutions of higher education (albeit only a fifth of the students) exist in this nongovernmental sector. Only a few other countries—Japan and the Philippines among them—host significant private sectors to complement the public sector. In most nations, though, all higher education institutions are provided for by the state; thus it is not surprising that in the United Kingdom and Australia much ado has been made of recent efforts to launch in each a single private university. Interestingly, in some nations a private university may thrive in a state-dominated setting—as illustrated perhaps most graphically by the Roman Catholic University in Lublin, which outlived socialist Poland.

Many nations are organized in tiered, federal systems whereby governmental authority is apportioned between national and subnational levels; the venues for policy making for higher education thereby are diffused. The United States again constitutes an extreme case. Perhaps only Canada offers an example of less national-level authority for purposes of generating education policy; there the provincial governments reign supreme, and Ottawa is not a significant "player" in setting higher education policy. In many countries, different sectors—for instance, universities, teacher training colleges, technical institutes—are overseen by different national agencies.

In short, each nation's way of formulating higher education policy is idiosyncratic. In the sea of examples, the United States stands apart: parallel public and private domains *and* a public sector that is radically decentralized to fifty polities. The venues of decisive action are many, the intergovernmental crosscurrents strong. Though centrifugal and centripetal forces are ever in tension, the former have always prevailed. The American legacy is thus an astonishingly diverse array of institutions—unapproached in the number and heterogeneity of institutions, less susceptible to the prescriptions of any one governmental entity.

Through the Lens of History

Viewed historically, public policy has had little *direct* effect on teaching. This absence of a substantial direct impact can be distinguished from and contrasted with the *indirect* but nonetheless profound ways in which public policy shapes the teaching environment. This occurs as an unintended by-product of policies not devised specifically for the purpose of affecting teaching as such.

Federal Initiatives

The starting point for this analysis is the federal government.[3] Its role in shaping American higher education has been far less pervasive than that of the states. It is noteworthy, for instance, that the United States did not establish a ministry/cabinet-level education department until 1980. It was approved by only the narrowest of margins in Congress, reflecting widespread reluctance within the electorate and among their political representatives to entrust a greater education role to the central government. And, indeed, the newly elected president, upon taking office the following year, set about, in accordance with his campaign pledge, to disestablish the embryonic Department of Education. Although President Reagan was thwarted in that pursuit, the decades-long wait to found a freestanding education department speaks volumes of the ambivalence with which many view an enhanced federal presence in education.

Even so, the federal government has substantially influenced the overall direction and culture of higher education. Cited below are four conspicuous examples of how higher education has been significantly altered by federal-level initiatives, each of which has modified in important ways how higher education is conducted and each of which has permeated the culture and values within colleges and universities. Each development, that is to say, has shaped in substantial ways the environment in which postsecondary teaching takes place.

The National Land-Grant Act of 1862 (the First Morrill Act).   This landmark legislation sought to stimulate the creation and growth of colleges that would respond to more practical needs; the main effects were to prompt a redirection in the curriculum which in turn succeeded in attracting students whose interests were more pragmatic than had been characterized with preceding generations of students.

The Serviceman's Readjustment Act of 1944 (the "GI Bill").   This legislation facilitated veterans' access to colleges and universities. It changed forever the prevailing mind-set about who could truly benefit from "higher learning" and simultaneously set a precedent for federal intervention to stimulate access.

Federal Student Assistance.   Since passage of the Higher Education Act of 1965, billions of federal dollars have been channeled annually to millions of students via a host of federal student financial aid programs. Two major emendations occurred during the ensuing decade and a half.

The Education Amendments of 1972 were crucial. Congress, overriding vigorous opposition on the part of much of the higher education establishment, decided to funnel most of its student aid *through* the students themselves (rather than allocating lump sums to institutions for them to award) (Gladieux & Wolanin, 1976). This strategic decision had the profound effect of making federal student aid essentially portable and thereby empowering students, as consumers, to decide—by "voting with their feet"—where to spend the federal aid dollars they had qualified to receive. The age of student consumerism had begun in earnest: more powerful than a locomotive; more influential, in subtle but more far-reaching ways, than had been the student demonstrations circa 1964–70 in transforming higher education (Riesman, 1980).

The second milestone event in the chronicle of federally funded student financial aid was a shift in emphasis embodied in the 1980 higher education amendments, namely, the Middle Income Student Assistance Act (MISAA). As the costs of attending college escalated in real terms, political pressure to spread federal largesse more widely in order to provide relief for middle-income families proved to be irresistible. One consequence was to create millions of stakeholder families who were not only consumers (like their lower-income predecessors) but also likely to be experienced and more sophisticated in their demands that higher education respond to their educational expectations. This development undoubtedly had the effect of prompting more attention to teaching and, more generally, to undergraduate education.

The Federal Research Agenda.   Meanwhile, the federal government has been pouring billions of dollars into university-based research and development projects to advance a long list of national interests. The use of universities as instruments to pursue national objectives has had the effect of providing an enormous boost to the research domain on many campuses and to the values associated with it. In other words, federally targeted priorities fuel an enormous amount of campus academic activity. The Manhattan Project during the Second World War, the creation of the National Science Foundation (1950), the National Institutes of Health, and extensive research programs sponsored by innumerable departments and agencies—such as Defense, Energy, Agriculture, Space and Aeronautics—are federal initiatives that infuse campus research activity with money (even riches) and thereby confer both status and a large degree of autonomy on vast portions of the campus research enterprise. Extramural support serves, too, to "liberate" many faculty members, chiefly scientists, from the burdens of teaching.

Although the catalogue of federal programs that provide an impetus to research could be extended at great length, it must be recognized that *some* federal monies do purport to advance teaching effectiveness at the postsecondary level. Thus, in recent years the U.S. Department of Education (the Office of Education within the Department of Health, Education, and Welfare prior to 1979) has funneled money to campuses for *research* on teaching (most manifest at present through the National Center for Postsecondary Teaching, Learning, and Assessment and for five years prior to 1992 through the National Center for Research to Improve Postsecondary Teaching and Learning). In addition, the federal Fund for the Improvement of Postsecondary Education (FIPSE) for two decades has *directly* supported activities that emphasize and demonstrate effective college-level teaching, albeit with modest levels of support. Other examples could be cited, but the fact is that federal programs that directly seek to promote effective teaching in postsecondary institutions are tiny compared with the massive influence that federal research and development dollars have had in reshaping—some would contend badly skewing—campus priorities.

In all, the federal government's impact on higher education is at once sweeping and, despite the influences described above, circumscribed. Its effects on the balance between teaching and research, have, I would argue, distinctly favored research over teaching, even after making allowances for the impetus to robust consumerism wrought by student financial aid policies. This result has not been the consequence of a purposeful strategy intended to rearrange campus priorities in favor of research. Moreover, those initiatives that are intended to enrich teaching per se are few and not very impressive when viewed in the larger context. Rather, the dominant effect results from the federal government's having found higher education to be an eager instrument to accomplish particular kinds of research—meaning primarily "big science."

The Role of the States

From the earliest days of the Republic, various states (and the colonies before them) attempted to influence the conduct of higher education, sometimes in ham-handed fashion. Most notorious—and most consequential for higher education—was the action taken by the New Hampshire legislature in 1816. Expressing its strong disapproval of Dartmouth College, the legislature canceled the college's charter (which it had received from King George III in 1769) and formed a governing board to displace the college's in order to compel the college to serve more fully New Hampshire's citizens. In 1819 the U.S. Supreme Court held (in *Dartmouth College v. Woodward*) that New Hampshire had violated the U.S. Constitution by abrogating its obligation to abide by the original charter. Although the case was decided on grounds that were not specific to higher education, the outcome was hugely important, for it served to demarcate the boundaries, previously fuzzy indeed, between "public" and "private" higher education and thereby to stimulate the growth of both sectors. More to the immediate point, the legislature's intervention illustrated an appetite among the states—sometimes moderate, sometimes more ravenous—to shape what colleges do.

Another example surfaced a few years later when Connecticut's legislature voiced its displeasure with Yale's curriculum, which it perceived to be impractical and unprogressive. The legislature's criticism prompted Yale's president Jeremiah Day (along with a senior colleague) to author the famous Yale Report of 1828—probably the most influential defense of the classical liberal arts curriculum formulated during the nineteenth century (Rudolph, 1977). It was not the response the legislators had hoped for, but the college now lay beyond the decisive grasp of the legislature. Over the ensuing decades the instances are endless of state governments' efforts, often successful, to bend state colleges to policy makers' conceptions of the public interest.

As noted, in the radically decentralized system (or perhaps more accurately, nonsystem) of American higher education, the states are the primary patrons (and prescribers) of higher education. Of course, private sector support is crucial, too; it is in fact indispensable for the half of all colleges and universities that are "independent" (and often church related). Moreover, during the past two decades, as state budgets have been squeezed, contributions from the private sector increasingly have augmented the resources of public sector colleges and universities as well. (Private sector support, delivered primarily through the philanthropy of foundations, corporations, and individuals, is itself heavily influenced by *public* policy, most especially by federal and state tax policies. But that is another story.)

When the phenomenon of public policy's impact is viewed over time and in terms of its scope and relevance, it is indisputable that public policy shapes and reshapes what higher education does, in ways both blunt and subtle, purposeful and inadvertent. We turn now from public policy's broader reach to a closer focus on teaching.

Public Policy, Teaching, and the Current Environment

In seeking to understand how public policy currently influences the conduct of teaching, it will be useful to consider a number of disparate factors. Some, like the assessment movement, have as a central goal to stimulate more effective teaching. Others, like the public policies that shape academic labor market dynamics, are much more remote in intentionality but nevertheless have important—even salient—effects on the environment for teaching. While the relationship of some of the factors discussed below and in the subsequent section has only an indirect, even tenuous connection to the motivation to teach, it is useful to reflect on how each influences (or will influence) the climate in which teaching takes place.

The Assessment Movement

Generalizations about state-level activity in higher education are always difficult, given the often dramatic variations among the states. Nonetheless, for nearly a decade widespread political concerns at the state level have fueled a powerful assessment movement, that is, the establishment of mandated academic performance standards. Though couched in less threatening language, many state-level initiatives appear to be intended to make higher education an offer it dare not refuse: improve the quality of undergraduate education and demonstrate that quality has improved—or else. As colorfully described by one observer, "The 'put the money on the stump and trust me' era is gone forever" (McManis, 1988).

Complex and powerful, the assessment movement in postsecondary education began to assume significant proportions in the mid-1980s.[4] The movement's impetus flows from two distinct but intertwined objectives: to promote quality (which, as a practical matter, has meant improving undergraduate education), and to assure accountability, that is, to insist that educational effectiveness—meaning results—be demonstrated to those who pay the bills. In the public sector, the payer of bills in large measure is the states, and that helps to account for closer scrutiny of higher education by state policy makers in recent years. Prime movers have been a handful of state legislatures and governors. The latter, through the National Governors' Association and its Task Force on College Quality, have been instrumental in pushing the assessment agenda both wider and deeper.

The combination of very tight budget conditions and heightened demand for quality—meaning, in effect, enhanced attention to undergraduate teaching and its outcomes—may be having a significant effect on faculty work. At a minimum, an adverse impact on faculty morale seems clear. As state after state presses to determine workload measures and how much time faculty members actually spend in contact with undergraduates, the pressure mounts on faculty members to increase the time they devote to teaching. This is so despite workload data trends—albeit hardly conclusive—which show that faculty, generally speaking, are working longer hours and in fact have *not* been reducing their attention to teaching (Mingle, 1993). Yet the amount of time faculty at doctoral-level institutions spend with undergraduates is modest, a plump target-of-opportunity for reformers and state-level budgeteers. However, it should be obvious that obliging faculty members to be responsible for larger numbers of students does not necessarily translate into more effective teaching. Indeed, expanded teaching loads may save money but at the expense of teaching effectiveness.

Other state-driven strategies that have consequences for teaching include efforts to mandate changes in staffing patterns. For instance, California and Minnesota, among other states, have sought to roll back the proportion of faculty who are part-timers. But such requirements may run up against financial realities that prevent replacing inexpensive part-timers with full-time staff. Moreover, such efforts, whatever their long-range merits, will displace many highly effective part-time teachers in favor of "regular" faculty who in more than a few instances may be both less motivated to teach and less effective at it (Gappa & Leslie, 1993). Another example: Reacting to constituents' complaints, lawmakers in some states—Illinois among them—have enacted policies to require that graduate teaching assistants demonstrate proficiency in English before being allowed to instruct undergraduates.

Potentially more potent are statewide efforts to dedicate some portion of budgetary support for those campuses that can demonstrate quality and value added in undergraduate education. Tennessee has been the pioneer, initiating its "performance funding" program in 1979. No state has followed Tennessee's example exactly, and it is said that in Tennessee, as elsewhere, the budget crunch has squeezed out much of the monetary reward to high-performing campuses. Budgetary shortfalls may constitute only a temporary setback for proponents of performance funding. But with more budgetary slack, the Tennessee strategy may gain widespread acceptance— a development that would provide potentially powerful incentives for campuses to bolster teaching-related activities.

Professional Development

The extent to which institutions support faculty development programs is likely to have a direct and salutary effect on teaching. State-level appropriations do make some difference here, either directly or indirectly, by providing support for, say, teaching-learning centers, or days funded for professional development for faculty (such as "reflex days" at California's community colleges), or sabbatical leave programs. In a few instances a statewide faculty development "agency" is supported mainly by state funds. Perhaps the leading example is the New Jersey Institute for Collegiate Teaching and Learning. Established in 1989 by the New Jersey Department of Higher Education, the institute, which draws much of its financial support from nonstate sources, orchestrates an array of faculty development activities for public and independent institutions.

Other programs provide important opportunities for professional development but do not focus mainly on pedagogical issues. Summer institutes sponsored by, for instance, the National Endowment for the Humanities or the National Science Foundation are examples. Another related activity is the Fulbright Scholar Program, administered by the federally funded Council for International Exchange of Scholars, through which some thirty thousand American scholars since 1947 have lectured and conducted research in other countries.

Faculty development programs thus have considerable potential for enhancing effective teaching. They frequently are not accorded a high priority on campuses and tend to suffer financially when institutional budgets are under duress (Schuster, Wheeler, & Assoc., 1990). Nevertheless, public funding of such programs is an obvious lever to effect improvements in teaching.

The Role of Accreditation

The accreditation process—focusing, for present purposes, on the regional associations that accredit entire institutions rather than on the specialized accrediting groups that address specific (mainly professional) fields of study—has contributed to the momentum that is reinforcing teaching. It is debatable whether accrediting agencies should be considered to be engaged in "public policy." Strictly speaking, of course, "voluntary" accreditors are not government agencies. Nonetheless, accreditation is a prerequisite for institutions to qualify for some highly consequential government programs, particularly federal student aid programs, upon which numerous colleges have grown heavily dependent and without which many would collapse virtually overnight. Given the nature of the accreditation system and its interaction with public policy, the accreditation process might well be regarded as "quasi-governmental." However one conceptualizes the current model, accreditation should be understood in relation to the larger picture.

Viewed in perspective, the impact of regional accreditation on teaching becomes more distinct. Hand in glove with the surge of interest in assessment, accreditors increasingly have pressed institutions to provide evidence of results, outcomes, value added—in other words, to demonstrate (however imprecisely) the near-term *consequences* of the educational process. Put another way, the overlay of accreditation has contributed to the exogenous pressures on campuses to upgrade the attention they pay to teaching and to undergraduate education. This is because more effective teaching, in contrast to faculty research activities, is widely perceived to be the means through which improved outcome measures can be achieved. (Although undergraduates are sometimes collaborators with faculty on research projects, and such activities are thought to constitute excellent learning opportunities, this mode of teaching-learning at most institutions is uncommon.)

The dissolution in 1993 of the national-level (but nongovernmental) Council on Postsecondary Accreditation (COPA) has left a vacuum in the world of accreditation. And mounting criticism of regional accreditation associations seems to have put traditional accreditation increasingly on the defensive. Various strategies are surfacing for rethinking and reorganizing accreditation. Among them is a preference on the part of some research-oriented universities to insist that their priorities be accorded more respect in the accreditation process, possibly via a different accreditation mechanism. If such a differentiation comes to pass, the current pressures on research-intensive campuses to promote more effective teaching may abate somewhat. For the moment, accreditation appears to be, as the expression goes, "in play."

Research as Teaching

The juxtaposition of teaching and research, so commonly suggested, is an oversimplification. For one thing, research activity is often coupled with teaching. At the level of doctoral studies, the supervision of student-conducted research entails an indispensable form of teaching (Clark, 1995). Moreover, a wealth of literature attests to the effectiveness of teaching-learning that occurs when undergraduates collaborate with faculty on research projects. Thus public policy's impact on how teaching-cum-research is conducted is pertinent.

As previously noted, public funds direct and sustain a great deal of research—and thereby facilitate a great deal of high-level teaching. But it is perhaps most relevant to note here the extent to which public policy regulates and limits—in the public interest—the processes and even the scope of research (Hartle, 1994). Examples are numerous, but it must suffice here to identify several. These include, for instance, restrictions on the use of laboratory animals, on the handling and disposal of hazardous materials, proscriptions on some forms of "genetic engineering," and protection of human subjects protocols. Each restraint serves important social policy aims, but each affects the research process and in so doing shapes the teaching component of research.

The Academic Labor Market

Conditions in the academic marketplace heavily influence many aspects of how higher education is conducted; the effects are often subtle but nonetheless real. In very simplified terms, if faculty members are in short supply, they will be able on the whole to exert more leverage vis-à-vis their employers (or potential employers), resulting in a so-called seller's market. But if a surplus of would-be academics obtains (that is, in a buyer's market), the greater power to dictate what faculty members do will lie with employing institutions. Thus, a hard-to-hire faculty member in, say, finance, is likely to be able to fashion an appointment that provides more opportunities for research and less of a teaching load—or, of course, the other way around. Or a professor in the humanities, where surplus talent still abounds, may be more vulnerable to institutional priorities.

This is relevant because public policy influences the academic marketplace in many ways. Public policy can readily increase the demand for faculty by expanding access (and thereby enrollments) or can boost the supply of faculty by financing doctoral programs and fellowships. Market conditions significantly influence compensation, too, and compensation in turn has some relationship to the quality of persons attracted to and retained in academic careers. These are but a few of the more obvious ways in which public policy directly impacts on the academic marketplace, which in turn permeates the environment for teaching.

To be sure, the overall effects are difficult to gauge. The causal connection is certainly indirect, but the environment in which teaching takes place is nonetheless molded by marketplace dynamics. If faculty are in abundance, they are more apt to have to do the institution's bidding rather than having wide latitude to pursue their own agendas. This probably means, under prevailing conditions, that more faculty are expected to do more teaching. It is when faculty are dear that they are more apt to do what they prefer. Survey evidence makes clear that more faculty members would prefer to teach than to be held to expectations of publishing. But many faculty members are strongly committed to research, as demonstrated by various faculty surveys; this would presumably lead to less teaching by faculty in some types of institutions. This in turn suggests that in a strong seller's market, likely to emerge in the years ahead, faculty will tend to gravitate to more research at the expense of teaching. And, if economic and political conditions will have led to a significant increase in normal teaching loads, it seems probable that many faculty members, given a choice, would seek some relief via lighter teaching loads (Astin, Korn, & Dey, 1991, pp. 10–13, tables 4, 5; Dey, Ramirez, Korn, & Astin, 1993, pp. 7–12, tables 4, 7; Carnegie Foundation, pp. 41–42, table 30, chart 11; NCES, 1990, pp. 48–51, tables 4.4–4.7).[5]

Public Policy and the Future Environment for Teaching

Two recent developments may have far-reaching effects on teaching. The first is a concrete event: a recently promulgated federal law. The second is a swarm of activities with no end in view.

State Postsecondary Review Entities

A potentially important development at the federal level has emerged which conceivably could have a more profound effect on the domain of teaching activity than any previous federal initiative. This is the authorization in the 1992 amendments to the Higher Education Act of 1965 of the new State Postsecondary Review Program. Established in Part H (Program Integrity) of the legislation, this measure requires each state to establish a state review entity (in the parlance of the federal legislation, a "State Postsecondary Review Entity"—with the happy acronym of SPRE!). The inspiration for the SPRE concept was to provide a means to deal with abuses of student financial aid programs. The idea was to counteract high levels of loan defaults by providing the federal government with a basis for disqualifying an offending institution (often vocationally-oriented proprietary schools with high student loan default rates) from eligibility to receive student aid funds. Other institutional conditions—such as an institution that derives two-thirds of its general expenditures from student aid funds—are identified which would automatically trigger a state-level SPRE review. Now that proposed federal regulations for governing SPREs have been published,[6] some observers are fearful that the SPREs may take on significant evaluative roles with respect to more traditional institutions (Hartle, 1994).

It remains to be seen whether the federal government in conjunction with the SPREs ultimately will be drawn deeply into areas previously reserved for regional accreditation bodies; for now, Congress has decided not to appropriate funds for SPREs. Nevertheless, language that introduced the proposed rules is bluntly critical of "some accrediting agencies [that] have not taken sufficient care to ensure the quality of the education or training provided by the institutions or programs they accredit."[7] Thus the possibility clearly exists of deeper federal involvement. Meanwhile, momentum for greater state oversight continues to build. The results could entail complex trade-offs: greater emphasis on teaching and the measurement of outcomes accompanied by a significant weakening of institutional autonomy and the role of traditional accreditation.

Information Technology and Distance Learning

Higher education, it is perhaps trite to observe, stands at the brink of a technological revolution that is likely to change in dramatic ways how postsecondary teaching and learning will occur in the foreseeable future. Some predict a wholesale transformation; Peter Drucker, for instance, recently suggested that "it is a safe prediction that in the next 50 years schools and universities will change more and more drastically than they have since they assumed their present form more than 300 years ago when they organized themselves around the printed book" (1992, p. 97).

As new modes for accessing a worldwide network of information are developed at a remarkable pace, including interactive technologies, an astonishing array of possibilities for enhancing teaching and learning are being created. And, as the need grows to accommodate increasing numbers of students with limited institutional resources, resort to the new technologies becomes irresistible. How students will be taught and, indeed, who teaches them are yet to be determined.

In this process public policy initiatives are destined to play an important, perhaps crucial, role in shaping education methodologies. Of course, how teaching is done has been affected over the years by public policies that regulate communications technologies. Examples include the uses of radio and television, although each has had much less of an impact on teaching in postsecondary settings than was commonly assumed when they emerged.

One example of public policy's current role in fashioning future pedagogies is instructive. In 1989 the California legislature, aware of the rising tide of California students and the demand for "lifelong learning," enacted a measure that called for the development of a master plan for educational technology.[8] A commission issued such a plan (Calif. Planning Commission, 1992), entitled the "California Master Plan for Educational Technology"; it addresses many aspects of how a network should be designed to facilitate the delivery of instruction. It will fall to public policy makers to provide the resources to implement the master plan or variations on it.

The sprawling 350,000-student California State University system, meanwhile, is anticipating an increase of 140,000 to 170,000 students between 1992 and 2005; its current estimates contemplate that "over 50,000 such students will have to be accommodated through means other than enrollment on the existing twenty campuses—i.e., once their facility ceilings have been reached" (Commission on Learning Resources, 1992; Academic Communications Network Committee, 1994).

It is within the framework of technological systems instigated and shaped in part by public policy that postsecondary institutions—such as the CSU system—are now scrambling to engage the future. It is a future that will feature exciting new modes of teaching but will entail complex trade-offs as conventional classroom methods and face-to-face instruction give way, to a greater or lesser degree, to new strategies.

Thus public policy may have a greater role to play in a related, technologically driven arena: the likely emergence of many new and sophisticated providers of education and training. As capabilities for accessing information soar, as interactive modalities further develop, and as deregulation of telecommunications continues, the environment grows ever more attractive for nontraditional providers to engage in "teaching" activities (writ large) in competition with traditional postsecondary institutions. It is easy to anticipate parallel providers that, in seeking out market niches, will challenge conventional institutions across a broader spectrum of subjects and programs than currently exists. The tricky challenge to public policy makers and accreditors alike will be to ensure that services of questionable or of manifestly substandard quality—especially those of providers who seek to confer academic degrees—are not endorsed, explicitly or implicitly, as constituting adequate higher education.

Public Policy and the Motivation to Teach

The discussion of ways in which public policy intersects with teaching leads to several summary observations. First, public policy powerfully shapes colleges and universities. This applies with special force, of course, to public sector institutions whose lifeblood is state appropriations and, to a lesser degree, federal funding. Similarly, public policy exerts a strong influence on private higher education. Though not as extensive, the impact on private colleges and universities occurs in three ways particularly: federal student financial aid (without which many institutions could not survive, so dependent are they on the tuition revenue they receive via federal programs); research support (vital to the research-oriented institutions); and the attendant regulations that require recipient institutions to abide by a lengthy array of social policy requirements, ranging from the conduct of labor-management relations to occupational safety and health rules to complex legal standards for retirement programs and pension plans.

Second, not much of the vast repertoire of public policy directly affects how *teaching* is conducted. There are some examples such as a state's line item appropriations that sustain a teaching-learning center or federal funds that support teaching-related projects (FIPSE, noted previously, comes most readily to mind). More ambitious undertakings, like Tennessee's performance contracting approach, have immense potential for pressuring institutions to improve teaching effectiveness. But thus far, perhaps slowed by economic conditions, that strategy has not yet achieved widespread acceptance. However, those activities that purposefully seek to enhance effective teaching are small, even minuscule, viewed in comparison with the huge sums of public monies that each year pour into higher education from federal, state, and, for some institutions, local sources.

Third, the milieu in which postsecondary teaching takes place is pervasively affected by public policies that *indirectly* shape all aspects of teaching: who gets to teach (and the terms and conditions of their employment), what they teach, who they teach, what other pursuits—most often research—are rewarded and thereby compete for the loyalty of instructional staff. It is well to attempt to discern the many ways in which such activities have an impact on teaching, however unintentionally. It is quite another matter to attempt to modify those large-scale forces for the purpose of ratcheting up the quality of teaching itself. It is the old story of using a blunderbuss to eliminate a pesky mosquito: much unintended collateral damage is likely to result.

Fourth, in the same way that public policies both directly and indirectly affect teaching, they have an effect on the motivation to teach. With few exceptions, this dynamic takes the form of attempting to stimulate the motivation to teach by extrinsic means; that is, the motivation presumably is a function of *institutional* priorities that are responsive (in one degree or another) to the press of public policies—policies that compel an escalation of institutional efforts to enhance teaching. But the desire to teach well has long been closely associated with intrinsic rather than extrinsic motivations (Bess, 1977, 1982). Put in other words, public policy seems destined to be a crude and inefficient instrument for increasing the motivation to teach through positive encouragement. Public policy's natural bent with respect to teaching, regrettably, has been long on sticks and depressingly short on carrots. It need not be that way; more creative positive reinforcements are plausible. One can imagine enlightened federal and state governments committed to a policy, "Let a thousand FIPSEs bloom!" Reality, however, barely concedes space for one badly undernourished FIPSE. In the current economic and political climate, the valence of public policy incentives is negative.

Fifth, private sources of financial support, removed from much of the hurly-burly of the political process (except perhaps for tax legislation), have been highly instrumental in supporting programs that promote the development of faculty as teachers, at public and private institutions alike. The Kellogg Foundation and Lilly Endowment, to name just two, have decades-long records of facilitating activities that enhance teaching.[9]

Coda

Writing a century and a half ago, the renowned British historian and Whig politician Thomas Babington Macauley (1854, pp. 436–437) succinctly identified a fundamental tension in governing democratic societies: "I hardly know which is the greater pest to society, a paternal government . . . which intrudes itself into every part of human life, and which thinks it can do everything for everybody better than anybody can do anything for himself, or a careless, lounging government, which suffers grievances, such as it could at once remove, to grow and multiply, and which to all complaint and remonstrance has only one answer: 'We must let things take their course; we must let things find their own level.'"

Depending on one's philosophical and political leanings, one may be drawn to a more (or less) assertive role for government in the ordering and oversight of higher education. A more disengaged governmental role—letting matters "seek their own level" with modest expectations for accountability—arguably has not served well the proponents of effective teaching in some postsecondary settings. But the prospect of government attempting to shape directly how teaching is done surely presents a more chilling contingency.

In the final analysis, the campaign for more effective teaching and enhanced quality in undergraduate education should not lead, except incidentally, to the mechanisms of public policy. That quest must rely on the wisdom, resourcefulness, and motivation of campus-bound faculty and administrators who are committed to the goals of developing conditions in which effective teaching can thrive. Higher education's neglect of teaching has prompted an erosion of credibility and sometimes harsh responses. Higher education's recommitment to teaching can help to provide a measure of relief from public policy makers' growing penchant to manage the assessment movement. The stakes are considerable.

Notes

1. The scope of this chapter does not extend, except in passing, to the *political processes* that give rise to public policy for higher education and its implementation.

2. The most helpful overview of national-level organizational variations is Clark (1983). See especially chap. 4, "Authority," pp. 107–134. For a cross-national perspective of governmental policy making for higher education, see Cerych (1984).

3. The texture of federal policy making in higher education is best captured in Gladieux and Wolanin's (1976) excellent case study of the passage of the Education Amendments of 1972. See also Radin and Hawley (1988) and Schuster (1982).

4. For a helpful cross-national discussion of recent assessment-related activities in higher education, see Craft (1992).

5. Recent survey data on faculty preferences are relevant but do not entirely dispose of the issue.

6. *Federal Register,* 34 CFR Part 667, pp. 3604–3623. January 24, 1994.

7. Ibid., p. 3604.

8. AB 1470 ("Farr, Morgan, Quackenbush Technology Act"), 1989, enacted as Sec. 51872 of the California Education Code. S 1510 ("Morgan-Farr-Quackenbush Educational Technology Act"), 1992.

9. One outstanding example is described by Austin (1992).

References

Academic Communications Network Committee. (1994). *Leveraging the future: The telecommunications plan for the CSU.* Seal Beach, CA: California State University.

Astin, A. W., Korn, W. S., & Dey, E. L. (1991). *The American college teacher: National norms for the 1989–1990 HERI faculty survey.* Los Angeles: Higher Education Research Institute, University of California, Los Angeles.

Austin, A. E. (1992). Supporting the professor as teacher: The Lilly Teaching Fellows Program. *Review of Higher Education, 16*(1), 85–106.

Bess, J. L. (1977). The motivation to teach. *Journal of Higher Education, 48,* 243–258.

Bess, J. L. (Ed.). (1982). *Motivating professors to teach effectively.* New Directions for Teaching and Learning 10. San Francisco: Jossey-Bass.

California Planning Commission for Educational Technology. (1992). California Master Plan for Educational Technology.

Carnegie Foundation for the Advancement of Teaching. (1989). *The condition of the professoriate: Attitudes and trends, 1989.* Princeton: Carnegie Foundation for the Advancement of Teaching.

Cerych, L. (1984). The policy perspective. In B. R. Clark (Ed.), *Perspectives on higher education: Eight disciplinary and comparative views.* Berkeley: University of California Press.

Clark, B. R. (1983). *The higher education system: Academic organization in cross-national perspective.* Berkeley: University of California Press.

Clark, B. R. (1995). *Places of inquiry: Research and advanced education in modern universities.* Berkeley: University of California Press.

Commission on Learning Resources and Instructional Technology. (1992). *Project Delta: Planning phase.* Seal Beach, CA: California State University.

Craft, A. (Ed.). (1992). *Quality assurance in higher education.* London: Falmer Press.

Dey, E. L., Ramirez, C. E., Korn, W. S., & Astin, A. W. (1993). *The American college teacher: National norms for the 1992–1993 HERI faculty survey.* Los Angeles: Higher Education Research Institute, UCLA.

Drucker, P. F. (1992). The new society of organizations. *Harvard Business Review, 70*(5), 95–104.

Finkelstein, M. J. (1984). *The American academic profession: A synthesis of social scientific inquiry since World War II.* Columbus: Ohio State University Press.

Finkelstein, M. J. (1995). College faculty as teachers. In *NEA 1995 almanac of higher education* (pp. 33–47). Washington, DC: National Education Association.

Gappa, J., & Leslie, D. (1993). *The invisible faculty: Improving the status of part-timers in higher education.* San Francisco: Jossey-Bass.

Gladieux, L. E., & Wolanin, T. R. (1976). *Congress and the colleges: The national politics of higher education.* Lexington, MA: D. C. Heath.

Hartle, T. W. (1994). Will increased regulation threaten the academy's independence? *Change, 75*(1), 53–56.

Macauley, T. B. (1854). *Speeches.* London: Longman, Brown, Green, and Longman's.

McManis, M. (1988, Jan. 15). In *Capital Ideas,* National Governors' Association, 2.

Mingle, J. R. (1993). Faculty work and the costs/quality/access collision. *AAHE Bulletin, 45*(7), 3–6, 13.

National Center for Education Statistics [NCES]. (1990). *Faculty in higher education institutions, 1988.* National Survey of Postsecondary Faculty (NSOPF-88; NCES 90-365). Washington, DC: U.S. Department of Education.

Radin, B. A., & Hawley, W. D. (1988). *The politics of federal reorganization: Creating the U.S. Department of Education*. New York: Pergamon Press.

Riesman, D. (1980). *On higher education: The academic enterprise in an era of rising student consumerism*. San Francisco: Jossey-Bass.

Rudolph, F. (1977). *Curriculum: A history of the American undergraduate course of study since 1636*. San Francisco: Jossey-Bass.

Schuster, J. H. (1982). Out of the frying pan: The politics of education in a new era. *Phi Delta Kappan, 63*(9), 583–591.

Schuster, J. H., Wheeler, D. W., & Associates. (1990). *Enhancing faculty careers: Strategies for development and renewal*. San Francisco: Jossey-Bass.

Webster, D. S. (1985). Does research productivity enhance teaching? *Educational Record, 66*(4), 60–62.

19 The Politics of Motivation: A Comparative Perspective

MARTIN TROW

Since World War II the central problem for higher education in most Western industrial societies has been how to transform the small elite university systems of the nineteenth century and first half of the twentieth into the systems of mass higher education required to meet the growing demands both for wider access from segments of their societies and for more highly trained and educated workers from their labor markets. The pressures for expansion have varied in intensity among the major European countries, as have the responses to that demand by European governments. (The United States, for various historical reasons, is a marked exception here.) But on the whole, it is fair to say that the United Kingdom has moved more slowly than most modern societies toward mass higher education; it is only in the past few years that it has started firmly down that path. Moreover, it has done so not by allowing its universities to grow greatly in size, or by creating permanent parallel nonuniversity systems, but by promoting to full university status first the university colleges, then the regional colleges (some first to colleges of advanced technology [CATS] and then to universities); still other regional colleges have recently (1991) be-

The author would like to thank Professors Oliver Fulton and Tony Becher, and the Suntory/Toyota Centre for Economics and Related Disciplines and the Department of Sociology, London School of Economics, for their help and support during the preparation of this chapter.

come universities after a delay of a quarter of a century as polytechnics. That pattern of expansion poses special problems for the research universities in the emerging system of mass higher education, as we will see.

Over the past ten or twelve years British higher education has undergone a more profound reorientation than any other system in industrial societies. One aspect of that revolution has been the emergence of *managerialism* in the governance and direction of British universities. I suggest that managerialism as understood by central government in Britain is a substitute for a relationship of trust between government and universities, trust in the ability of the institutions of higher education to govern themselves. The chosen managerial mechanisms in the United Kingdom currently are assessments of the "quality" of the teaching and research done in universities, carried out by committees and individuals appointed by the central funding agency and linked directly to funding. It is not difficult to see that the character and criteria of these assessments will have great influence on the direction and work of the universities and departments being assessed. I want to raise the question of how effective this policy is and is likely to be, and what consequences for the life of British higher education seem to follow from it. It may be that other countries, and not least my own, have something to learn from the British experience.

The Concept of "Managerialism"

What do we mean by *managerialism*? It is not just a concern for the effective management of specific institutions in specific situations. The "ism" points to an ideology, to a faith or belief in the truth of a set of ideas that are independent of specific situations. Managerialism as applied to the institutions of British higher education takes two distinct forms, a soft and a hard concept. The soft concept sees managerial effectiveness as an important element in the provision of higher education of high quality at lowest cost; it is focused around the idea of improving the "efficiency" of the existing institutions. The hard conception elevates institutional and system management to a dominant position in higher education; its advocates argue that higher education must be reshaped and reformed by the introduction of management systems that then become a continuing force ensuring the steady improvement in the provision of higher education. In this conception management would provide this continuing improvement in quality and efficiency (i.e., cost) through the establishment of criteria and mechanisms for the continual assessment of the outcomes of educational activities, and the consequent reward and punishment of institutions and primary units of education (mostly departments) through formulas linking these assessments to funding.[1]

Those who hold the soft conception of managerialism—on the whole senior administrators and some academics in the universities themselves—are critical of at least some of the norms and attitudes that have marked British universities and academics in the past: their complacency and conservatism, their administrative inefficiency, their indifference to establishing links with industry and commerce or to broadening access to larger sectors of the population. Nevertheless, the "soft" managerialists still see higher education as an autonomous activity, governed by its own norms and traditions, with a more effective and rationalized management still serving functions defined by the academic community itself. By contrast, those holding the hard conception of managerialism, people on the whole in government and business rather than in the universities themselves, have no such trust in the wisdom of the academic community and are resolved to reshape and redirect the activities of that community through funding formulas and other mechanisms of accountability imposed from outside the academic community, management mechanisms created and largely shaped for application to large commercial enterprises. Business models are central to the hard conception of managerialism; when it is applied to higher education, as the current government does, the commitment is to transform universities into organizations similar enough to ordinary commercial firms so that they can be assessed and managed in roughly similar ways.

This hard concept of managerialism is currently the dominant force reshaping British higher education day by day and week by week. Its two characteristics of greatest interest to the present analysis are (1) the withdrawal of trust by government in the academic community and its capacity to assess critically its own activities and improve them; and (2) its need to find or create a "bottom line" that performs the function of a profit and loss sheet for commercial business. This "bottom line," if it could be found or created, would allow top managers in government departments and funding agencies to identify and assess the strengths and weaknesses of an enterprise (a university), its strong and weak units, and serve as an analytic tool for the continual improvement of the product and the lowering of unit costs.[2]

In brief, then, the withdrawal of trust in its universities by the British government has forced it to create bureaucratic machinery and formulas to steer and manage the universities from outside the system. In the absence of an effective competitive market, effectively precluded by government policies, bureaucratic institutions and their mechanisms are the alternative to a relationship of trust between state and universities. The bureaucratic agencies then create criteria of performance, and rules for reporting and accountability necessary for the assessment of the system and its primary units (i.e., academic departments), and for the application of the formulas linking assessed "quality" and funding. These links of assessment to funding are intended to ensure the automatic improvement of the efficiency and effectiveness of the higher education industry. In British higher education policy, external assessment linked to funding is thus a substitute not only for trust but also for the effective competitive market that is the chief control of both quality and cost in commercial enterprises.

Here I want to raise three questions:

1. Why was it that the government led by Margaret Thatcher which came to power in 1979 and its successor led by John Major withdrew trust from the universities and carried out such radical reforms in their organization and funding?
2. What are some of the consequences of this withdrawal of trust for the universities?
3. What are some of the assumptions underlying current central government policy in the United Kingdom, and how do those assumptions accord with the realities of academic life, particularly the realities of teaching and research?

These are broad questions, and I could not possibly answer them adequately here. I can only point in the directions in which answers might be found.

British Higher Education before the Thatcher Government

With the election of the government headed by Margaret Thatcher in 1979, the attitudes and policies of the British government toward the country's institutions of higher education changed dramatically and profoundly as compared with the policies of previous governments. Before World War II, British universities, taken all in all, received about a third of their operating expenses from central government, raising the rest from tuition payments, from local governmental subsidies, and, especially important for Oxford and Cambridge, from endowments old and new. After World War II, the spirit of democratization, the expansion of the welfare state under both Labour and Conservative governments, and the growing belief that

national strength and prosperity depended in part on an educated workforce led the state to take a more active role in the expansion and support
of the universities and of other institutions of higher education, some of
which became universities in the 1960s and others of which became polytechnics in the seventies and universities in the nineties. By 1951–52 the
state was providing roughly three-quarters of the universities' income and
had assumed the bulk of student fees and student support grants. By 1970
that proportion had grown to nearly 90 percent.

During this period, that is, from 1945 to 1981, the central institution for
funding the universities was the University Grants Committee (UGC), created in 1919 precisely to serve as the buffer between the universities, "autonomous" in intellectual matters under the royal charters, and the state,
which provided a substantial part of their support. And the UGC continued to serve this function during a period of substantial growth in British
higher education. Although the overall size and shape of the "system" was
determined by central government—for example, the decision to elevate
the Colleges of Advanced Technology to university status in 1963, and the
parallel decision to create a group of "new universities" during the period
1958–63—still, central government did not intervene in the internal life of
the universities it helped to create and pay for. In both parties and all governments it was accepted that British universities were among the finest in
the world, and as a unique system of elite institutions of higher education
they were perhaps preeminent. Knowledgeable foreign observers of the
British universities before the Thatcher era broadly agreed on three major
points: (1) they were unexcelled as teaching institutions at the first-degree
level; (2) they were distinguished research institutions, whose provisions
for systematic graduate instruction varied among disciplines but were
gradually improving; but (3) the society had not found a fully satisfactory
way to provide mass higher education with broad access alongside the
highly selective elite universities, though the creation and encouragement
of the polytechnics was a major step in that direction if their tendencies toward institutional drift could be constrained through the binary system.

The years leading up to the Thatcher victory saw British governments
struggling with the mounting costs of the university system while dealing
with an economy that had never fully recovered from the war, or perhaps
from the two wars. Nevertheless, while previous governments had asked,
rather politely, whether the universities could not find ways of providing
more education for less money, the universities continued to submit budgets through the UGC which reflected per capita cost levels matched only
by the most affluent private liberal arts colleges and universities in the

United States, cost levels that were reflected in average student/staff ratios of about 8:1 across the board.

The Thatcher Revolution

The government led by Margaret Thatcher which came to power in 1979 broke in fundamental ways with its predecessors in its relations with the universities as in other areas of public life—though it took some time for the universities to understand the depth of the change. Mrs. Thatcher and her ministers of education had a fundamentally different view of the nature of the universities than their own leaders and a quite different conception of their future. Their views, as they evolved over the next decade, can be summarized thus:

1. British universities are backward, conservative, self-serving institutions and are in part responsible for Britain's poor performance in the international competition for markets. In brief, they, along with the trades unions, the state-owned industries, and the professions generally, are among the established institutions that impede Britain's economic progress.
2. British universities, like other established institutions, are incapable of reform from within but must be forced to reshape their roles, missions, and functions.
3. Initially, the transformation of British higher education was to be accomplished by radically cutting their budgets, forcing them to seek new funds from sources outside government. That in turn would require them to become more efficient administratively and would require a measure of rationalization of their internal operations to be achieved by pressure from the (then) Department of Education and Science, with the help and advice of lay and business groups. These views, largely an expression of the soft or weak version of managerialism mentioned above, were captured in the Jarratt Report of 1985.[3]
4. Progressively declining support from central government would also make the universities more responsive to the real requirements of "the market," and most especially of business and industry, which employ their graduates.
5. Although in the long run one could hope that better internal management and the sharp disciplines of "the market" and its climate of competition would force the universities to become both more efficient and more "relevant," in the short and medium term central government

would still be supplying a substantial part of both operating and capital costs of the universities. That insulation from market forces, required by the traditions of British higher education and the practical impossibilities of cutting them loose overnight, meant that central government would have to administer its support grants in ways that encouraged the continuing reform of the universities and did not provide subsidies for a return to the bad old ways.

6. Therefore (and here emerges the hard version of managerialism), continuing support by central government of the universities would have to be accompanied by policies and regulations that would prod the universities to greater efficiency and relevance.

Among the policies guided by these views were:

1. the abolition of the UGC and its replacement by "Funding Councils," initially separate for the universities and the polytechnics but then combined when the polytechnics were granted university status in 1992. The new Higher Education Funding Councils (HEFCs)[4] are not intended like the UGC serve as a buffer between government and the universities, to protect the autonomy and independence of the universities from government and political pressure. On the contrary, and quite explicitly, they are an arm of government, an instrument for the implementation of government policy on universities which, in government's view, are by their nature and traditions recalcitrant and tend to defend their own parochial interests against the national interest as defined by the government of the day.

2. the separation of funding for teaching and research and the institution of separate assessments by committees of academics appointed by the Higher Education Funding Council for England (HEFCE) of each set of activities at the departmental level. These separate assessments, of teaching and research, linked to funding, are intended to introduce a measure of competitiveness into university life thought to have been absent during the UGC regime of assured block grants. They would thus function, especially in the context of level or reduced funding, as a kind of quasi market, with the inherent disciplines of market processes on the economy and efficiency of the producing units. But it is a peculiar market, a firmly rigged market. It leaves central government and its officials (rather than the student "consumers") to decide both on the quality of university activities and on the criteria by which those judgments are made. Moreover, government sets the prices of places, subject

by subject, for fully funded students, and also decides on that year's fees. The elevation of the polytechnics more than doubled the number of suppliers but reduced the number of price setters in the market effectively to one—very convenient for the buyer. What we have is the rhetoric of "the market," coupled with a substantial increase in the power of the external assessing and funding agencies, marking a real shift in power in the world of British higher education.

Other changes introduced by the Thatcher/Major governments—for example, the abolition of tenure in academic appointments—are aspects of the new relation between government and the universities, part of the effort to transform the universities into something more like commercial enterprises. However, they lie outside the scope of this chapter.

External Assessments of Research and Teaching Tied to Funding

British universities currently get their support grants from central government through what is called a "dual system" of funding research and teaching separately, as if they were distinct activities. That is a system that could only have been invented by nonacademics. People who actually teach and do research in universities know how deeply research interests, and even more, research perspectives, are brought into teaching and how much of the teaching of postgraduate students and increasingly of undergraduates is done through participating in their research and drawing them into one's own. The sharp separation of funding for teaching and research in the provision of general support for departments and universities is simply at odds with the realities of academic life. And the further that policy retreats from the realities for which it is designed, the more distorted must be its effects.

Setting this important issue aside, however, there remain the policies themselves: the separate assessments of the research and teaching activities of academics in English universities, in ways designed to determine how much money their departments and, in the aggregate, their universities will be given annually by central government. It is important to stress that what is being assessed are not individuals or universities but departments. The allocations resulting from these assessments are made known to the departments that have been assessed, which of course strengthens their claim on those allocations to the detriment of the authority of the vice-chancellor and the integrity of the university. The effects, of course, are variable among the universities.

However, if the assessment of the research qualities of whole departments rather than individual scholars or proposals raises a host of difficulties and unanticipated outcomes, the external assessment of the quality of a department's teaching probably rests on a basic misconception of what teaching is about. The assumptions of managerialism have come to dominate discussions about teaching. Some English academics remark that they need to be reminded about the actual nature of what they do, even if that is at odds with the assumptions of the assessments. The fundamental problem of trying to assess teaching lies in the assumption that it is one kind of activity, and excellence in it one kind of excellence. But teaching involves at least two parties, teachers and the taught. The quality of teaching is not a quality of a teacher but of a relationship, aspects of which are defined by the character, talents, and motivations of the learners. Teaching is not an action but a transaction, not an outcome but a process, not a performance but an emotional and intellectual connection between teacher and learner. Therefore, it cannot be assessed as an attribute or skill of a teacher or a department, independent of the learners who have their own characteristics that affect whether and how much they learn (about what) from a particular teacher and, indeed, how much he or she learns from them. That also means, among other things, that "teaching" cannot be assessed along any single dimension of "quality," nor can it be assessed at all without deep knowledge of its setting, of the styles and orientations of the teachers, of the character and diversity of the students, and of its long-term effects, effects that may be very different from what students report about teaching as they experience it.

In fact, the quality of teaching, which surely means an assessment of its effects on students, can hardly be "assessed" at all in the short term. What can be assessed is not "teaching but the absence of teaching, as when people do not meet their classes or substitute such things as political or religious views and doctrines for teaching. We can and should pay attention to how much teaching people do, both formally and informally, whether they actually get to their meetings with students sober and on time, read and respond to their written work, and the like. We can also expect and require that teachers in their formal relationships with students confine their teaching to their areas of professional competence—and need not approve teachers who exploit their privileged positions and the vulnerability of their students in the service of some sectarian positions or political or social doctrine. Moreover, we can be responsive to students' complaints about teachers who verbally abuse them, express racial or gender prejudice, or simply treat them disrespectfully. We can demand of university lecturers professional responsibility toward their jobs and a humane nonexploitative relationship with their students. But beyond that, we must depend on our appointment procedures to ensure that teachers know their subjects and are competent to transmit knowledge, or broaden perspectives, or stimulate curiosity, or raise ambitions, or prepare students to be able to learn throughout their lifetimes, or achieve some of the many other things that teachers accomplish through their relationships with students. And we need strong, clear internal procedures of review of the crucial processes and relationships to ensure that the standards that the university sets for itself are being met—and if not, why not.

All this means that almost everything in a university depends on the inner motivations of teachers—their sense of pride, their intellectual involvement with their subjects, their professional commitments to the role of teacher, their love of students or of learning—these and others are among the forces that lead teachers to bring their full resources to the teaching relationships. And these motivations of academics are usually quite independent of unpredictable external assessments and the remote incentives and punishments that can be attached to them.

However, the government's withdrawal of trust in the universities means that it was not prepared to accept the "inner motivations of teachers" as an adequate basis for motivating and directing their behavior. That is precisely the basis on which all professions, not least the academic profession, have claimed a measure of autonomy over their spheres of competence. But if, as I believe, the Thatcher/Major governments were deeply dissatisfied with the performance of British universities, then justifications by academics of the autonomy and self-direction of academics and their institutions by reference to the primacy of inner "professional" norms and motivations were seen by government as merely the familiar rhetoric that justified the self-serving and unsatisfactory performance of those institutions in the past.

But if it cannot trust the inner motivations of scholars, scientists, and professionals (and they are not all exactly the same, though similar in springing from inner values), how can government shape the behaviors of academics and thus of their institutions? One way, and the first employed, was simply to cut the budgets for the universities drastically. That certainly got the attention of the academics and affected their behavior even without directly influencing their inner motivations. As student/staff ratios roughly doubled over the decade and a half 1980–95, activities and relationships that were possible at the beginning of that period became less easy or impossible; class sizes grew, tutorials were phased out, and behaviors of academics and institutions were affected in other ways that are less obvious. No one, to my knowledge, has "assessed" the impact of the changing ratio of students to staff in British universities over that period, nor is the question often asked. The only aspect of university life which seems to be immune to "assessment" is the quality and wisdom of central government policy toward higher education.

It is not enough, however, to cut budgets. So long as academics have substantial control over their own time, they may or may not actually work harder, more efficiently, and more effectively, as government thinks they should. In the government's view, the way to get more efficient and effective behavior out of employees is to generate a competitive environment for the academics and then begin to tie rewards to more effective performance on the job. Or put differently, it is to replace what it sees as inadequate and self-serving inner motivations with a system of externally provided incentives and penalties keyed to approved performance. This linkage of performance to external rewards cannot exist side by side with the older structure of internal motivations, which to the government was indifferent to (the government's conception of) the public interest but was keyed rather to the special interests of the academic guild and its institutions and prejudices. So the problem presented itself: how to replace one structure of motivations which was rooted in the traditional patterns of academic life by a different structure of motivations, one whose source and model was the competitive world of private enterprise. This problem, articulated the more clearly the longer the government remained in office, led to the emergence of the two forms of managerialism to which I referred earlier. The soft and hard forms of managerialism correspond roughly to two phases of the managerial revolution in British higher education; the first developed within the universities under the pressures of coping with the huge budget cuts of the early eighties, and the second developed, after the demise of the UGC, around the central government funding agency, now the HEFC(E), aiming at introducing businesslike attitudes toward work and performance into the universities, changing their functions as it changes the motivations of their employees, not merely introducing more efficient rationalized structures of management as in the first phase.

The new philosophers of higher education in and around government were faced with a number of problems. One, obviously, was the deeply entrenched attitudes and arrangements within universities which were based on quite different norms and values and indeed held the norms and values of business in some contempt, at least as they were applied to the universities. These traditional academic norms and values were much more deeply embedded in the "older" universities; indeed, there is a clear, if not perfect, relationship between how deeply embedded those traditional notions of institutional governance are and how old a particular university is. But those traditional values of autonomy were on the whole less firmly embedded in the polytechnics, which had always had less autonomy and were, so to speak, used to substantial influence from local authorities, local industry, and, later on, the Council for National Academic Awards (CNAA). Putting the polys on a "businesslike basis" would have seemed to politicians and civil servants an easier and more realistic mission than accomplishing the same transformation in the universities. And the notion of keeping the polys a separate sector, more responsive to political and external direction, must have seemed attractive to some observers in and around government.

Despite these and other advantages, the political costs of maintaining the binary system would have been high. First, there was the steady pressure from poly directors and councils themselves: Having phased out the CNAA oversight, the polys were giving degrees and even doing research. How, then, could they be denied the title and status of "university?" But if "universities," then how could they be distinguished from all other universities; would that not be precisely the invidious distinction among institutions on status (ultimately class-linked) grounds to which British education has been subjected since its origins? Not only would abolishing the binary line appeal to the polys, and even to many university academics, guilty about their status and privileges in relation to the polys. For the government it would have had another substantial effect to recommend it: Ending the binary system would permit the application of many of the governing structures and mechanisms developed in connection with the polys to the old universities as well and thus, so to speak, help bring them to heel. Our study suggests that is what is happening now. There is a strange irony here: As the polytechnics emerged from the tutelage of the CNAA, they enjoyed a brief period of academic autonomy, only to lose it as they became universities and again found their work being assessed by agencies of central government.

The Search for a "Bottom Line"

Where does assessment come into this? One problem in patterning universities on the model of private business and industry is that the latter have a fairly simple bottom line of productivity and profitability, a bottom line that allows all observers to see how a concern is meeting its competitive environment. But British universities in the past have not had to compete for resources, nor do they have any very clear or obvious bottom line that government can use in assessing the institutions' performance. The extraordinary focus in government policy on "quality" in higher education—in a system in which it has not in this century been problematic and in which no responsible observer saw major problems—is part of the government's search for a bottom line, a way of assessing individual and group performance in the absence of the ability to assess a university's "success" or "profitability."

If market mechanisms and indicators in higher education are weak, or were made to be weak, that has made it all the more necessary to find some way of developing indicators of desired performance. Of these there were only two the government could imagine: One was the amount (and quality) of research academics and their departments and institutions would produce; the other was the amount and quality of their "teaching." The assessment of "research" by government has been going on since 1988, and it is having a variety of effects on the behaviors of academics in both the old and the new universities, as we have suggested above.

However, the government is currently also introducing a "bottom line" into the teaching work of academics and will try to assess and reward it as it does research. As I have suggested, I do not believe teaching can be assessed and rewarded by external agencies in any way that actually links rewards to "excellence" in teaching. Of course, a system linking assessments of "teaching" to rewards can be invented and put into operation. But it requires efforts to shift British academics from the internal motivations associated with professional work—intrinsic work norms and the desire for a good reputation among one's peers—to the external motivations that these managers believe are characteristic of private business and industry: the rewards of departmental and institutional grants for superior teaching which are deployed by the funding agency. Although the assessment of teaching in the universities by the funding agency is still new and changing, it is perhaps not too soon to see this as the next step of a systematic effort to make universities into "knowledge shops" run in businesslike ways, without all the traditional norms and values that (in the view of government) have crippled British higher education and reduced its contribution to national economic development.

This effort by central government requires—indeed, it assumes—the subordination of inner motivations to external incentives linked to these assessments. It can also be seen as requiring the deprofessionalization of the academic workforce, their transformation into middle managers or skilled craftsmen, interested in promotion and better pay as rewards for better performance as determined by external assessors against yardsticks supplied by government agencies. It also means that these skilled workers are producing and delivering a more or less standardized product that is subject, as in other industries, to control by management of costs and quality. That process of deprofessionalization is already under way as a natural and inevitable consequence of the withdrawal of trust by government in the universities and their guilds of academics.

For example, in the assessment of teaching by the funding councils, a central criterion, as one senior official in a funding council recently put it, is whether the teacher "delivers the course the customer (i.e., the student) expected to get." In this conception of the academic's role, the teacher produces a product that the customer buys, and the customer expects to get what he or she paid for. And that is a reasonably accurate (if partial) description of some parts of higher education: the straightforward transmission of skills and knowledge, in which students and teachers share a notion of what skills and knowledge are involved in the transaction. Even so, a good deal more happens in those relationships than is described by that transaction, much of it not part of the students' expectations when they enter the course. But more strikingly, there is no provision in this conception of "teaching to expectations" for the possibility that the teacher does not want to meet the students' expectations but wants rather to modify those expectations, and more broadly, to modify (and enlarge) the student's mind, character, and sensibility. That is what many British academics think they are doing or are trying to do; and there is much evidence to suggest that they are remarkably successful, certainly as successful as any group of academics in the world. Nor will they easily surrender those conceptions of teaching, embedded as they are in the norms of the university and the habits of academics, in response to the quite different assumptions of the external assessment exercises.

If British academics do not easily surrender their own notions of what teaching is about, how will they cope with the pressures of these assessments and their ambiguous criteria? That is what our study is about. We already have heard of various coping mechanisms by the university officers under conditions of high uncertainty; these are variously referred to as "games" and "scams" and involve the creative reporting of numbers and events, all wrapped in what is hoped is persuasive rhetoric that bears a somewhat loose relation to reality. But however "successful" these coping mechanisms, aimed primarily at gaining a workable grant, or at least reducing threatened cuts, one should not imagine that the assessments have little effect. Perhaps their effects are achieved most powerfully through their criteria, which, however resented, come over time to be internalized, and through the values implicit in the language in which discussions of teaching and learning are carried on in official papers.

Diversity and a Typology of Orientations to Teaching

Let us look briefly at the nature of teaching in universities, to see whether it is reasonable to expect committees of the funding council to be able to assess the teaching performance of academic staff and departments in ways that will allow government rationally to link institutional funding to the quality of teaching.

We can see some of the difficulties more clearly if we consider just one way of characterizing teachers by reference to their relationships with students, that is, by looking at four familiar but distinguishable patterns of teaching styles. Let us look at the four styles generated by the cross-tabulation of two simple dimensions of teachers' orientations toward teaching. One dimension distinguishes the orientation of teachers primarily toward their students or toward their subjects. The other dimension distinguishes between teachers who are oriented more toward the transmission of knowledge or toward the creation of knowledge. These two dimensions then define four familiar types of orientations of academics toward teaching:

	Orientation toward:	
	Subject	*Student*
Orientation toward:		
Transmitting knowledge	I	II
Creating knowledge	III	IV

Type I reflects a traditional teacher-student relationship: "I know my subject, and I will teach you about it." The subject, an academic discipline or the explicit aspects of a profession, is what competent scholars and scientists have said and learned about the substance of the field, about its "theories" and its methodologies. The assumption is that the student is motivated to learn, and the teacher's task is to provide expert guidance about what is of greatest importance in the literature and to help the student to learn how to read it.

Type II is a more "modern" or "progressive" orientation toward teaching, since it no longer assumes a high measure of motivation on the part of the student and accepts that a considerable part of the teacher's job is to motivate the student to learn. This may require "nontraditional" forms of instruction, most commonly finding a way to involve the students' own experience in the subject so as to make them see the relevance of it for their own lives and future. This orientation is a natural concomitant of the growth of broader access and mass higher education. It emerged earlier among teachers in the primary and secondary schools (and even earlier in the schools and departments of education) with the lengthening of the school leaving age and the growth in the population of reluctant and resistant students. This perspective lies at the heart of the Copernican revolution in education[5] which transformed American pedagogy in the schools as far back as the turn of the century. Its late arrival in British higher education reflects that society's long resistance to the incorporation of institutions of mass higher education into full university status. That has now happened, and we will be seeing the characteristics of Type II teaching gradually emerge as the criteria of "quality" in teaching employed by the new teaching assessment bodies.

Types III and IV, which center teaching around the creation of knowledge, are the natural orientations of research scholars and scientists who specialize in teaching postgraduate students: They are the orientations of people who see existing knowledge primarily as a way of gaining knowledge—the knowledge one needs to have in order to advance it. For such teachers the transmission of knowledge is, so to speak, a by-product of learning how to create it. But the lines are not clear. In the great research universities in both the United Kingdom and the United States, research scholars and scientists also teach undergraduates. Such research-oriented academics often cannot change their perspectives on their subjects just because their students are undergraduates, and they teach the latter as if they were graduate students, though with lower expectations about the undergraduates' performance or their contributions to knowledge. Such teachers assume a measure of motivation to learn whether it is there or not; "if they aren't motivated they shouldn't be here." That perspective is assailed as "elitist" by supporters of mass higher education, who know that whatever its other virtues, it brings larger numbers of more weakly motivated students into higher education.

These two different orientations (Types III and IV) are typically assumed by research scholars depending on how far advanced their research students are in their preparation for research. Research scholars and scientists teaching students in the first year or so of their graduate studies may well stress the nature of knowledge in their subject, assuming, as they might well do with postgraduate students, that they are motivated to learn (Type III). The other orientation (Type IV) is assumed by teachers (usually graduate advisors and mentors) who may try to learn the unique qualities of an advanced research student's mind and talents and shape their relationship increasingly more in response to each student's interests and qualities than merely to the subject alone.

Matters are a little different when these orientations are held by teachers of undergraduates. In the United States, teaching undergraduates through direct exposure to research is sometimes decried as at variance with the nature of liberal education and the gaining of a broad sense of the map of knowledge. Education oriented around research is inherently specialized, since academic research and the advance of knowledge is specialized. And research scholars are sometimes unable to drop their intense orientation toward creating knowledge as they face a classroom of undergraduates. But there is evidence that involving students directly in the research activities of their teachers has great potential for motivating them to want to learn, as they see at first hand the intrinsic rewards of the pursuit of knowledge as well as some of the disciplines associated with it. The broad success of the Undergraduate Research Opportunities Program at the Massachusetts Institute of Technology, which involves a very large proportion of MIT undergraduates in live, ongoing research under the direction of a research scientist at some point during their studies, attests to that. But MIT students can be assumed to be highly motivated; similar programs at the University of California and Stanford have had marked success with minority students from educationally weak backgrounds that required that their motivation be engendered rather than assumed before their real education could begin.

There are several points to be made about this typology of orientations toward teaching. First, it is a typology of orientations and not of people; individuals may have different orientations when facing different kinds of students—for example, graduates and undergraduates. Second, teachers may combine some of these kinds of orientations in their teaching—for example, a teacher intensely interested in creating knowledge may do it in part through a focus on where the frontiers of knowledge are and how the specific student can be brought there (III and IV). Or a bookish teacher, focused on his subject and rather insensitive or uninterested in variations among his students, may discuss the field in his lectures and seminars in terms of both how knowledge in the field is understood and organized by the discipline and how that area of knowledge is currently being advanced through research (I and III).

Third, teachers change over time; their orientations toward their fields and toward their students may also change and move from box to box.

Fourth, and important for my argument, all of these orientations can be found in our lecture halls and seminar rooms currently. Moreover, the diversity of orientations reflects the growing diversity of student interests, talents, and ambitions. All this means that there is no single dimension along which teaching can be assessed as "unsatisfactory" to "excellent." Put differently, a university will have, and indeed will want to have, people with all these kinds of orientations to teaching—teachers more concerned with their subject than with their students, teachers more concerned with creating knowledge than in transmitting it, and the other kinds too. And they are present, though not in the same distributions everywhere, in almost every kind of college and university. In the old polytechnics there are more transmitters than creators; in some fields teachers are more likely to be focused on the student than on the subject. But all these kinds of teachers are there in their variety resisting all efforts to assess them as if teaching were a performance, the performance of a skill that can be assessed and graded. As we who have taught and done research know, teaching and learning are not like that, not like that at all.

On the Long Delay of Effects

There are other forces besides the diversity of teacher-learner relationships which defeat efforts at assessment. One of these is the difficulty of knowing what the effects of teaching will be on the student over his or her lifetime. All of us have had the experience of reassessing our experience in college or university during the course of our lives, reflecting on how empty or ephemeral were some courses of study, how enduring in their influence on our thinking and feeling were others. And how different those later assessments are in many cases from the feelings we had about those teachers and their courses or seminars when we experienced them, in most cases before we were twenty-five years old.

Evidence for this beyond the anecdotal is provided in a study by Katherine Trow, who interviewed a group of forty graduates who had gone through a particular course of study at the University of California at Berkeley twenty to twenty-five years earlier.[6] Almost uniformly these people in their forties reported that they had been influenced during their lives after they left the university by their experience of that particular course of study and reading. But while the experience had this continuing influence, it also underwent a reassessment by the students, one that is not yet finished.

One former student, now a businessman, describes the effects for him of that particular program of study as "an intellectual net that has stretched over time." Another graduate, now a lawyer, observed, "As I've grown older, the impact sort of accumulated. . . . I remember somebody saying in 1967 or 1968 that 'you won't know about the truth of what we're saying, you're just children now.' And of course we were. But what's happened for me is that the longer I've lived with these books . . . the more I see [their relevance] in my life, and also in terms of my overview of history and culture and the present." And he goes on to say what we all know but cannot measure: "As you get older, you just know more, and you live more, and you have suffered more losses, and you have more sense of the complexity of the world and then you start to see. . . . You read a poem of Yeats when you are fifteen or sixteen or seventeen, and you read a poem of Yeats now and . . . you can have it now; you couldn't have it then." We cannot disentangle the impact of what that man read at Berkeley twenty-five years ago, or of the peculiar talents of his teachers, from what he has become since, or from all his life experience. But he has come to "have more sense of the complexity of the world" and grapples with it as his teachers twenty-five years ago hoped he would. What he read was at least in part what they put in his way—and they put those readings and ideas in his way in such a fashion that he did not discard them but is still living and struggling with them a quarter of a century later. My point is not to praise a liberal education, however much it needs praising. My point is that whatever is happening in a relationship between a student and her teachers (and other students and the broader academic environment), assessment teams cannot measure those effects while the students are still, in a sense, children, and not even very precisely later on, when the effects of education are mixed with all the experiences of life. The measurement of the effects of education in the short term may be crucial to the "bottom line," but it is an illusion.

Conclusion

In my critical discussion of trends in central government policy toward higher education in the United Kingdom, it should be clear that I believe that a university should be continually engaged in critical reviews of its own activities and departments. I have pointed to the great danger that the criteria of "success" or "quality" adopted in external "quality assessments" or reviews tend be chosen with an eye to the possibilities of the quantitative measurement of "quality," since those measures seem to be more "objective," are more easily accepted outside the institution, and are part of the ethos of managerialism. The paradoxical result may well be that vigorous efforts by agencies of central government to assess the quality of university work lead to its decline, as more and more energy is spent on bureaucratic reports[7] and as university activities themselves begin to adapt to the simplifying tendencies of the quantification of outputs. Our research suggests that departments and individuals shape their activities to what "counts" in the assessments, to the impoverishment of the life of the university, which is always more complex and varied than assessments of "outputs" can capture.

The only effective defense by the university against this tendency is to create procedures for review and maintenance of the quality of teaching and research which are firmly rooted in the intellectual life of the institution and its academic departments and members. And that in turn calls for a process of continual assessment through procedures and committees that work with departments and not against them, which try to understand the university and its departments qualitatively as well as quantitatively, and which coordinate its internal assessments in ways that are in the service of its intellectual life. The members of such committees, most of whom should be drawn from units outside the departments under review, must learn enough about those departments and programs to be able to recommend directions of development and corrective action, not merely give them scores. And those recommendations to senior academic officers should have consequences for the internal allocation of the university's resources.

In the United Kingdom, the greatly strengthened administrative leadership of universities which has grown out of the movement I have called "soft managerialism" is the best defense of university autonomy, and in current circumstances nearly its only defense. Our study shows us how effectively administrators, especially the professional managerial staff, defend their universities in a game whose rules are invented by others and are constantly changing. But the continuing decline of the unit of resource widens the gulf between administration and the academic staff. There are under the best of circumstances inevitable tensions between administrators and academics, arising out of their different values and interests. In most universities that is a healthy tension—between spontaneity and predictability, creativity and accountability, centrifugal and centripetal forces. But it makes all the difference to the life of the institution whether the administrators who "manage" the university and take responsibility for the whole of it are inside or outside it.

In criticizing the current trend toward the external assessments of educational quality, and in seeing them as more the product of an ideology of managerialism than as a way of improving the quality of education, I do not mean to suggest that the quality of higher education cannot or should not be improved. Indeed, a strong case can be made that higher education, both in teaching and research, is facing a grave crisis, for some aspects of which we academics must be held responsible. And teachers can be helped to be more effective, whatever their orientations toward teaching, whatever their talents and temperaments, as many successful programs of staff development attest.

However, some of the fundamental problems currently facing the academic world are only partly of our making and not wholly in our power to correct. I need only refer to the collapse of consensus about the nature of the cultural disciplines, and the loss of confidence that any scholarship affords any authority to assert anything. The deconstructionists continue to threaten to saw off the limb on which they are sitting. Even in fields not so devastated, the extreme specialization of studies arising out of the explosion of knowledge atomizes the curriculum and undermines any coherence in higher education. The incoherence of undergraduate studies in the United States results also from the modularization of courses and the freedom students have to elect among these modules in their accumulation of credits toward their degree, where again we were pioneers. And British universities move rapidly (if variably) toward modularization. Modularization gives students the freedom to drop in and out of universities and to move from subject to subject and from institution to institution over their whole lives, banking their unit credits in academic transcripts. How admirable (and indeed necessary) are these mechanisms of mass higher education, how wonderfully responsive to the diversity of student talents and preferences and to societal needs—yet with what consequences for the character of higher education?

Beyond this, what is happening to our students and to their inclination and capacity to study what we present to them as worthy of study? We slowly begin to recognize the effects of thousands of hours of television and computer games on young minds, not just on the minds of school dropouts but also on the minds of our students. A recent commentator suggests that "the problem here is the emergence of widespread aliteracy— a growth in the number of people who, although they can read, do not see reading as a pleasurable activity." And he notes that "in 1976 in Britain, 83 per cent of those between the age of 15 and 24 regularly read a daily paper, but by 1992 this had fallen to 59 per cent."[8] And this was happening as the proportion of youth staying on through upper secondary school and entering universities was growing rapidly.

These great problems facing academic, indeed intellectual, life—profound failures of nerve in some fields of inquiry, the explosive growth, transformation, and atomization of knowledge in others, the impact of mass culture on mass higher education—these and similar problems fall quite outside the "assessment of teaching" as the Higher Education Funding Council (England) imagines it. Managerialism, at least in its hard version, may allow governments to imagine that they control the uncontrollable. But for academics it is at best an irrelevance and a distraction from the daily business of teaching and learning and at worst a serious threat to already vulnerable institutions. Once again, it may be that the major task facing British higher education is to educate its masters.

Notes

1. The government's White Paper *Higher Education: A New Framework* (1991) is a document of hard managerialism: a brief collection of assertions and instructions to the academic community, wholly without argument or evidence for the policies it sets forth. (Indeed, on first reading it appears to be the executive summary of a longer paper that provides the evidence, argument, and context for the policies, but there is no such evidence or argument.) Its character can be suggested by the fact that this authoritative document speaks of a 50 percent growth in enrollments in British universities by the year 2000 and devotes no fewer than twenty-eight numbered paragraphs to the issue of "quality assurance," while saying nothing about capital investment in laboratories, libraries, classrooms, or equipment during this anticipated growth. (See Trow, "Thoughts on the White Paper of 1991," *Higher Education Quarterly,* 46(3), 213–226.)

If the White Paper of 1991 is a statement of hard managerialism, the Jarratt Report (see n. 3 below) was for British higher education the defining document of soft managerialism, a reaction by academic and professional administrators to the deep cuts in university funding of the early 1980s. It called for the strengthening and rationalizing of university administration, a goal that was substantially achieved by the time the White Paper of 1991 appeared.

2. Another illustration of "hard managerialism," as well as an indication of the government's lack of trust in the academic community, can be seen in the chief consultative document commissioned by the HEFCE on "possible ways for institutions to account for the use of research funds allocated to them by the Funding Council." The report was prepared by a firm of accountants and business consultants and written by men none of whom was an academic. Moreover, the study was "overseen" by a "Steering Group" of sixteen persons, all of them civil servants or university administrators, no single one of whom was currently engaged in either research or teaching. A more dramatic statement of attitudes toward the academic community that actually does the research the document is discussing could hardly be imagined. This lack of trust is visible also in the document's recommendations, one of which is that a detailed record of time spent on each of six types of activities be kept and reported by each academic researcher and linked to funding. (*Research Accountability,* Coopers and Lybrand, for the Higher Education Funding Council for England, n.d. but 1992.)

3. Committee of Vice Chancellors and Principals, "Report of the Steering Committee for Efficiency Studies in Universities" (the Jarratt Report), March 1985.

4. There are separate funding councils for England, Scotland, and Wales. They follow broadly similar policies but with some differences in implementation. In this chapter I am speaking chiefly of the funding council for England, which governs the bulk of British higher education.

5. This refers to the replacement of the subject by the student at the center of the universe of teaching. The metaphor is found in the seminal writings of Lawrence Cremin. See Cremin, "The Revolution in American Secondary Education, 1893–1918," *Teachers College Record,* 56(6) (1955), 303.

6. Katherine Trow, "The Experimental College Program at Berkeley: Some of Its Long Term Effects and Implications for Educational Practice," Council for the Renewal of Undergraduate Education, Stockholm, 1992.

7. The costs of substitution of bureaucratic management for trust are high but rarely assessed. For example, Janet Landa has noted that "the existence of trust economizes on transaction costs." "Culture and Entrepreneurship in Less-Developed Countries: Ethnic Trading Networks as Economic Organizations," in Birgitte Berger (Ed.), *The culture of entrepreneurship* (San Francisco: ICS, 1991), pp. 53–72. Conversely, the absence of trust greatly increases transaction costs. But these transaction and opportunity costs, in time, money, or other things are not done, are mostly hidden and not included in government's estimations of institutional efficiency or effectiveness.

8. Richard Woods, "No quick cure for newspapers suffering from poor circulation," *Independent,* August 4, 1993, p. 17.

VI   Summary

20 Fostering Faculty Motivation to Teach: Approaches to Faculty Development

ROBERT J. MENGES

All organizations profit from attention to the well-being and productivity of their employees. For colleges and universities, this means supporting the development of faculty and the quality of their teaching, since teaching is the activity that consumes the greatest amount of faculty time and energy.

Policies and practices for faculty development are rarely guided by knowledge about motivation for teaching, such as the knowledge presented in this book. In the present chapter, I hold up common faculty development activities for examination in light of our knowledge about motivation. My purpose is to differentiate faculty development activities that foster the motivation to teach from those that may actually depress or destroy such motivation.

Three Perspectives on Faculty Development

Views on faculty development differ significantly depending on whether one takes the perspective of the organization, the perspective of the professional development program, or the perspective of faculty themselves.

The Organization's Perspective: Human Resources Management

From an organizational perspective, faculty development is likely to be viewed as human resources management. This term began appearing in the literature during the 1950s and has come to refer to "the people side of organizations" (Walters, 1985, p. 3). The "human element" in organizations is acknowledged by Tracey to include "people as individuals and groups, their recruitment, selection, assignment, motivation, compensation, utilization, services, training, development, promotion, termination, and retirement" (Tracey, 1991, p. 159).

When considering human resources management, colleges and universities, like other educational organizations, should be seen as providers of services rather than as producers of goods. Two of the differences between service-oriented and goods-oriented organizations are especially significant for faculty development (Schneider & Bowen, 1992). First, services, in comparison with goods, are intangible. What students take from our courses and curricula and what faculty take from professional development activities resist objectification. Our usual measures of knowledge and skills, for example, are only proxy indicators of our broad goals. Second, in the service orientation consumers are active participants in production and delivery. Thus, learning and teaching are linked together as inseparable components of the teaching-learning process. The consummation of education requires that learners interact with teachers or at least with environments and materials prepared by teachers.

Because outcomes are intangible and because participation is so important, any intervention must focus on the *process* of education, not just on its products. In particular, we can examine the experiences of participants (faculty and students) for clues to the nature of the organization's climate. When these experiences are positive, a teaching-supportive climate may be inferred.

In short, from the organization's perspective, the task of faculty development is to manage human resources in ways that create and maintain a climate consistent with the organization's mission, that is, a climate that emphasizes the quality of teaching and learning.

The Teaching Center Perspective: Professional Development

Those who work in college and university centers for faculty development and teaching improvement commonly refer to their work as professional development. These persons constitute their own profession with distinctive publications, conferences, and organizations (Menges & Mathis, 1988).

Faculty development first gained recognition in the *Encyclopedia of Educational Research* through an article in the fifth edition (1982). Mathis characterized the objective of faculty development as "maintaining and improving the professional competence of the individual faculty member within the context of the many roles the faculty member has in fulfilling his or her obligations to a specific institution" (Mathis, 1982, p. 646). The breadth of faculty development is shown, for example, in the variety of articles published in *To Improve the Academy,* the annual publication of the professional association for faculty developers. Articles span instructional development, organizational development, and personal development, but what typically receives most attention is development as teachers.

In a model intended for planning and assessing faculty development efforts, Menges and Brinko (1990) offered a three-dimensional approach. One dimension of the model is temporal, referring to career stage or amount of experience. It ranges from trainees (graduate students) to emeritus professors. The second dimension delineates the roles that faculty fill, namely, instructional, scholarly/creative, service, and personal, since faculty development activities should specify which role or roles they are addressing. The third dimension deals with the organizational level at which faculty development activities are targeted, ranging from the individual faculty member through particular units in the organization to the academic profession and the nonacademic community.

Such models help to identify purposes and participants for faculty development programs, but they do not directly address motivational issues. Nor do they deal with nonfaculty constituencies for whom professional development programs are sometimes designed, that is, nonacademic staff, administrators (especially Chairs), and students.

The Faculty Perspective: Coping and Growth

Faculty themselves are likely to take a pragmatic view of professional development. Faculty work carries multiple demands, it requires a large repertoire of skills, and it must respond to varied constituencies including students, colleagues (both on campus and in the discipline beyond one's own campus), administrators, and segments of the general public (Sorcinelli & Austin, 1992; Finkelstein & LaCelle-Peterson, 1993).

From the faculty perspective, "faculty development" should enable professors to cope more effectively with daily demands at work, to protect significant time and energy for life beyond work, and to grow personally and professionally in ways that enhance feelings of intellectual excitement, accomplishment, and esteem. This is no less true when the focus is on teaching than when the focus is on other aspects of academic work.

The balance between faculty development in the service of the institution and faculty development in the service of individual faculty is delicate. The most common teaching improvement activities are likely to treat faculty as a group; these include orientation programs for new faculty, workshops, and feedback from standardized course evaluations. In the group setting, issues of individual motivation may well be ignored. As I have written elsewhere (Menges, 1991, 1994), faculty development too often makes faculty the *objects* of activities conducted by others, so that faculty themselves are limited to roles of trainee, recipient, and client. Attention to motivation helps to focus on the faculty perspective, that is, on how faculty experience the stresses, satisfactions, and efficiencies of work life.

These perspectives—the human resources perspective, the professional development perspective, and the faculty's own perspective—can be discerned in the responsibilities of three groups. Senior administrators articulate the organization's mission and determine human resources management policies; they establish the framework, set the climate, and underwrite costs of faculty development activities. Faculty development specialists design and deliver the services. Faculty are the intended beneficiaries. Yet these responsibilities are not as discrete as they may seem. As I argue below, benefits are enhanced when faculty themselves assume some responsibility for shaping and implementing activities aimed at enhancing motivation to teach.

Axioms for the Design, Delivery, and Evaluation of Faculty Development Programs

Previous chapters make various claims about circumstances that foster faculty motivation to teach. Here I list axioms based on theories presented in those chapters which I believe are relevant to designing, delivering, and evaluating faculty development programs. Later I use these axioms as a framework to examine commonly offered programs and services. Some of the axioms deal with characteristics of faculty development programs in general, some deal with more discrete program activities, and some deal with issues or criteria for evaluating program success.

Axioms to Guide Program Design

The following axioms speak to general issues of designing faculty development programs:

- Any program aimed at fostering faculty motivation to teach should (a) make desired values salient, (b) provide choice and minimize control, (c) acknowledge faculty feelings and perspectives, (d) convey appreciation and positive feedback (Chap. 4 in this volume).

- Programs should encourage faculty goals that are consistent with the organization's climate (Chap. 7 in this volume).
- Programs should be designed tightly around teaching as the formal institutional goal and should control sufficient resources to reinforce the appropriate teaching climate (Chap. 10 in this volume).
- Staff of faculty development programs should show their own enjoyment of learning (Chap. 5 in this volume).
- Programs should be designed to serve as models for vicarious learning, and program components (time, space, staff) should be organized so that they evoke in participants the intended feelings and behaviors (Chap. 6 in this volume).
- Program staff should (a) work with faculty as they set goals for their development using feedback as appropriate, and (b) praise faculty upon achieving their goals (Chap. 8 in this volume).

Axioms to Guide Program Delivery

The following axioms speak to delivering specific activities that compose faculty development programs:

- Development activities for faculty should (a) have clear goals and provide immediate feedback, (b) carefully balance challenges with the skills they require, (c) become increasingly challenging as skills increase, and (d) encourage concentration and avoid distractions (Chap. 5 in this volume).
- Communications should pair positive stimuli with desired outcomes, and reinforcers should be contingent upon performing desired behaviors (Chap. 6 in this volume).
- Training should be provided to help faculty reach short-term, realistic goals (Chap. 7 in this volume).
- Activities should introduce faculty to new working groups, for example, cross-department groups, and to new sources of feedback about teaching and learning (Chap. 10 in this volume).
- Activities should legitimize the helping role of peers and students and strive for "mutual intersubjectivity" (Chap. 3 in this volume).
- When dealing with systems for evaluating and assessing teaching and learning, activities should (a) emphasize multiple sources of evaluative information and ways of blending information from different sources and (b) examine information about individuals in light of institutional standards (Chap. 14 in this volume).

Axioms to Guide Program Evaluation

The following axioms speak to the evaluation of faculty development programs:

- While participating in program activities, faculty should report (a) that they felt absorbed and involved such that they lost track of the passage of time, (b) that they found the activities satisfying in themselves, and (c) that, as a result of their participation, they became aware of an expanded sense of self (Chap. 5 in this volume).
- At immediate and follow-up evaluations, faculty should report (a) that their behaviors have changed as intended with regard to targeted goals and (b) that their perceptions of organizational climate have changed in the direction of the formally stated climate (Chap. 6 in this volume).
- As a result of participating in program activities, faculty should report that they felt increased autonomy, competence, and connectedness with others (Chap. 4 in this volume).
- After participating in program activities, faculty should report (a) increased belief that their efforts will lead to success and (b) increased belief that success will lead to the larger positive outcomes they seek (Chap. 7 in this volume).
- After participating in program activities, faculty should report (a) high levels of personal commitment to their goals and (b) success in achieving their goals. Further, when goals set by individuals are compared with the organization's normative goals, the former goals should be higher (Chap. 8 in this volume).
- After participating in program activities, faculty should report that better information is available to them to serve as feedback about teaching and learning (Chap. 10 in this volume).
- In commenting on the assessment and evaluation system, faculty should report that they regard the system as personally useful (Chap. 14 in this volume).
- Outside evaluators should be engaged for formative and summative program assessment (Chap. 10 in this volume).

Constructive Critiques of Three Programs

According to published reviews of campus-based faculty development programs (Levinson-Rose & Menges, 1981; Weimer & Lenze, 1991; Angelo, 1989), the following activities are most common: workshops and seminars (including orientation programs for new faculty), individual consultation, financial grants and awards (for instructional improvement projects and for recognizing exemplary teaching), resource materials (such as books, newsletters, and videos), and colleagues helping colleagues (including mentoring and coaching).

To illustrate how such activities can be illuminated in light of the axioms presented above, I have composed scenarios describing programs of several types: (a) a faculty orientation and workshop program, (b) an instructional consultation program, and (c) a program of teaching awards. (None of these describes a real program, although I know each feature to have occurred on one campus or another.) After the scenario, I suggest how the program may foster motivation to teach as well as how it may fail to do so. Improvements are suggested in light of motivational theories.

An Orientation Program for New Faculty at a Comprehensive University

All new tenure-track hires at this comprehensive university are informed that the first duty under their new contract is attending a two-day welcoming orientation. The program is planned jointly by the university teaching center and the office of the academic vice president. Scheduled just before classes begin, the orientation is intended to expose faculty to the culture and values of the institution, to introduce them to key administrators and to one another, and to improve their teaching skills.

All of the new hires attend at least some of the orientation sessions, although as it turns out, several are briefly absent while they complete arrangements for their families' housing and for their children's schooling.

The first session includes briefings about payroll and benefits, parking, student services, campus safety, and so on. Faculty ask only a few questions after these presentations but say that they appreciate hearing from administrators with whom they will work in the future. They also say that they expect the speakers' handouts to prove useful. The morning session ends early because the academic vice president, attending to other pressing business, has rescheduled for the next day.

Lunch is organized around faculty "reference groups," cross-department groups intended to remain intact for the rest of the orientation and to reconvene at a follow-up meeting later in the term. During the afternoon, faculty tour the teaching center and the library for presentations about instructional services and facilities. Also on the tour are campus museums and the football stadium, where new artificial turf has recently been installed. Especially impressive, faculty say, are the library demonstrations of multimedia interactive technologies.

Day two, devoted to teaching, begins with remarks by each member of the faculty development staff. The teaching center director emphasizes the university's commitment to teaching, quoting from the mission statement in the faculty handbook. A panel of senior faculty, all of whom have been recognized as outstanding teachers, describe the successes and failures they experienced while developing their own teaching approaches. Panelists join the reference groups for what turn out so be lively debates about instructional approaches that are most appropriate for particular disciplines.

The academic vice president's rescheduled remarks are delivered at lunch and stress the importance of high-quality teaching for retaining students. In closing, the academic vice president admonishes faculty not to postpone starting a program of productive scholarship, since research and scholarship increase the vitality of teaching and, furthermore, scholarly productivity is essential when faculty are reviewed for contract renewal and promotion.

The afternoon begins with questions from several new faculty about resources for supporting research and scholarship. The faculty development director explains who in the administration is in charge of those resources and agrees to plan a workshop on the topic at the earliest available time, which turns out to be early in the spring semester. Several hours are then devoted to microteaching exercises as faculty teach something from their specialty to others in the reference group. Each demonstration is designed to illustrate a particular teaching skill, assigned by the group's facilitator, who is a member of the teaching center staff. These skills include explaining clearly, constructing provocative examples, asking questions that call for complex thinking, providing immediate feedback, and so forth. There is much good-natured joking as faculty review the microteaching videotapes and discuss what they might have done differently.

At the end of the afternoon, follow-up sessions are announced. A workshop on learning styles is offered a month later by the director of student services and features techniques for diagnosing student learning styles. The second planned event is a lunch reunion of faculty reference groups where faculty seem eager to describe the joys and frustrations of their first semester.

Surveys returned by participants evaluate all events positively. Faculty say they appreciated the contacts made at the orientation and feel they gained valuable information about resources of the institution. A minority criticizes the practicality of the learning styles session, although the ideas were provocative. Reference group reunions helped faculty cope with their anxieties, since, under the daily deadlines of teaching, most had not yet begun a research pro-

gram. They felt less guilty when they learned that others were having the same difficulties.

This orientation program deserves much praise. It occurred early, precisely when faculty want to meet administrators in the university and need to gain confidence as they develop teaching plans. The teaching center had high visibility in conducting the workshop. Reference groups helped faculty connect with other new faculty. Rapport was good at all of the events, and participants' evaluations were generally positive.

Microteaching was a vivid demonstration of active learning with immediate feedback and used content from the professor's own area of expertise. Disciplinary content always plays a major role when faculty recall teaching experiences that they find especially memorable (Froh, Menges, & Walker, 1993). Part of what defines memorable (motivating) teaching experiences is the teacher's sense of mastering something in the discipline at a deeper level. Microteaching is an appropriate vehicle for keeping teaching improvement activities centered in the discipline.

Despite these strengths, axioms derived from motivation research and theory reveal that the program has many shortcomings. First, scheduling the orientation when faculty are busy settling in and requiring that they attend probably reduced faculty feelings of control and autonomy.

Second, the content of the orientation conveyed mixed messages about organizational mission and climate. The director's emphasis on teaching was undercut by the academic vice president's emphasis on scholarship. In continuing to be faithful to the mission of teaching, the director had difficulty responding to faculty concerns about support for scholarship.

Third, the orientation format conveyed a motivationally dysfunctional message about responsibility and authority. The format implied that administrators, staff, and senior faculty are the experts from whom new faculty receive information and direction, implying that faculty have little to offer at such an occasion. In fact, many new faculty do have interesting and relevant professional backgrounds, but no attempt was made to capitalize on their skills and experience. Further, students were nowhere in evidence during the program.

Finally, activities were group based, and there was no opportunity to diagnose the needs and interests of individuals. Faculty did not specify their own goals and monitor progress on achieving those goals.

In summary, the faculty perspective was ill served (a) by the timing of the orientation, (b) by the mixed messages regarding the importance of teaching, (c) by the program's reliance on presentations by experts, and (d) by failure to specify individual goals that faculty could pursue during orientation and follow-up activities.

If an orientation program more consistently embodied axioms for fostering motivation to teach, what might it be like?

1. Persons who plan the program should agree on the particular characteristics of institutional mission and culture they wish to convey. The messages and activities of the orientation should then be framed to reflect those characteristics consistently. The teaching center should command sufficient resources to help faculty pursue the mission as articulated (Chap. 10 in this volume).

2. Faculty should be part of the planning group, even if that delays the orientation for a week or two. They can suggest varied activities so that participants have meaningful choices. New faculty should participate as panelists and facilitators, consistent with their previous experience. Staff should acknowledge the feelings and reactions that faculty express, modifying schedule and topics if necessary (Chap. 4 in this volume).

3. Participants should be encouraged to develop individual goals and to participate in activities that further those goals. Staff should assist faculty in choosing goals, should check to see that goals are congruent with the institution's mission, and should praise faculty for making progress toward attaining the goals rather than reinforcing them for merely attending the meetings (Chaps. 6, 7, and 8 in this volume). This requires extended interaction between staff and individual faculty, including follow-up contacts.

4. Teaching center staff and senior faculty, in their leadership roles, should eschew the stance of expert in favor of joining with faculty as learners (Chap. 5 in this volume).

5. Evaluations of the program should include surveys and perhaps interviews (preferably conducted by someone not directly involved in the program) both immediately and several months after its conclusion. Interviews should probe the extent to which faculty attained their individual goals (Chap. 8 in this volume), their absorption and satisfaction with the tasks they performed (Chap. 5 in this volume), and their perceived increases in autonomy, competence, and connectedness with others (Chap. 4 in this volume).

A Program in Instructional Consultation at a Liberal Arts College

Faculty at this liberal arts college have been concerned that student evaluations of their teaching were being used arbitrarily in personnel reviews. Further, they found that student evaluations were rarely helpful for improving teaching. Consequently, faculty voted to endorse a uniform procedure for course evaluations and to recommend an instructional consultation program. Students in all courses complete the same ten-item survey. For those items, norms are constructed so that courses of similar types may be compared. Results go to department Chairs, deans, and personnel review committees as well as to the teacher. Other items chosen by the teacher can be added to the set of ten; results for added items are reported only to the teacher.

Consultants are available to meet with professors who wish to discuss their course evaluations. As part of this program, the campus teaching center trains faculty as peer consultants. During consultations, which occur as early as feasible after the course ends, the consultant interprets ratings in light of the relevant norms. For items on which student ratings and norms are discrepant, the consultant provides teaching tips that might improve future ratings. Teachers are invited to check back in subsequent semesters for further consultation.

Many faculty have agreed to participate in the program, and they evaluate the consultations as interesting and useful. Few faculty, however, take advantage of follow-up appointments. Chairs, deans, and personnel committee members indicate that they have become more satisfied with the quality of evidence about teaching effectiveness available to them.

Among the positive features of this program is the way it reinforces the value of teaching and the need for adequate evidence about teaching effectiveness. The program cultivates collegial relationships by using peers as consultants. Confidentiality is maintained because the consultation itself is private and results are returned only to the teacher.

More problematic are the program's dual purposes: to improve the college's personnel review system and to enhance teaching. That the former is better served than the latter seems apparent. Consultants discuss evaluation results in relation to the "received wisdom" of campus norms. Suggestions are offered for the purpose of improving evaluations relative to other faculty rather than to one's own goals. The quality of information for personnel review has improved, but interest in follow-up consultations has declined.

Chairs, deans, and personnel committees regard the evaluation information with greater confidence, and that is a plus. The danger is that they will focus on student ratings as the *only* measure of teaching effectiveness. In short, the program appears to be more successful in meeting institutional goals than in serving the needs of individual faculty.

How could this program incorporate principles of motivation so that the faculty perspective is reflected more faithfully?

1. Consultations might begin with the consultant and professor jointly selecting goals for change and improvement. The consultant would probe the teacher's rationale for particular goals and discuss how much change the teacher regards as realistic. They could then choose pertinent survey items and other sources of information such as a class visit and interviews with students (Chaps. 4 and 8 in this volume). Once data have been collected, comparisons would be made not only with campus norms, a procedure that may foster damaging competition, but also with the teacher's own previous and desired levels of performance (Chap. 14 in this volume). In addition, the teacher might visit classes of colleagues who have been successful in reaching similar goals, or might read published reports about how others have pursued such goals (Chap. 6 in this volume). Goals and criteria for success thus emerge from ongoing dialogue rather than merely being accepted as inherent in the institution's hierarchy (Chap. 3 in this volume).

2. The consultation relationship should be extended over time. Once goals have been set, the first step is to attempt small changes. Assessment should be immediate, early in the term rather than only at the term's end (Rando & Lenze, 1994). As skills increase, goals should be made more challenging (Chap. 5 in this volume). Praise and other rewards should be contingent on evidence of improvement rather than merely on participation (Chaps. 6 and 8 in this volume). This requires a series of interactions between the teacher and the consultant, perhaps extending over several terms. Once the teacher has mastered skills of self-evaluation, need for the consultant will be reduced or eliminated.

3. When the program is evaluated, faculty should be asked about sources of information about teaching which are available to them and how the quality and utility of that information compares with what was available a year earlier (Chap. 10 in this volume). Faculty should also be asked to rate the usefulness of the information (a) for individual purposes and (b) for institutional purposes (Chap. 14 in this volume).

A Teaching Awards Program at a Research University

Rising tuition costs and decreasing external support for research prompt the president of this flagship state university to reaffirm its commitment to teaching. The president has raised funds for the purpose of endowing university teaching excellence Chairs to which faculty are appointed for three-year terms. The appointment includes a salary supplement during those years and a stipend that supports teaching innovations. Other cash awards go to outstanding teachers in each school of the university. All in all, approximately twenty awards are funded by the president each year.

Nominations for the awards, including self-nominations, are forwarded by deans to a selection committee. The committee reviews portfolios that include whatever evidence faculty choose to submit in support of the quality of their teaching. Letters conveying decisions of the selection committee praise the excellence of all nominees, even those who are not successful.

Although information about the number and characteristics of nominees is not made public, competition is regarded as keen. Nevertheless, the number of nominations seems to be declining, and several unsuccessful nominees have raised questions about procedures and criteria. They suspect gender and racial bias in the selection process, and they note that the majority of winners come from a minority of faculty who teach exceptionally large classes. Worrying that the presence of these awards may reduce funds intended to reward teaching through the usual merit review system, these faculty have requested data about the proportion of salary increment money which is awarded for teaching effectiveness.

In several departments, faculty make it known that concerns about the fairness of the awards and the considerable effort needed to prepare a portfolio have persuaded them not to apply. They will invest their energies in directions other than the teaching award program.

Programs that feature awards for excellent teachers, like this one, have much to recommend them. Awards and their attendant publicity convey to faculty and to the general public that the university values teaching. Awards in this program are significant, both in monetary value and in recognition from peers and administrators. Applicants have a good deal of discretion over how they will construct portfolios. The teaching center affirms its role on behalf of teaching by offering assistance as they design their portfolios.

There are also problems. The fairness of the program cannot be demonstrated, given the confidentiality under which it operates. Faculty are suspicious that it drains resources that might be used to reward teaching in other ways, such as increases to base salary.

Imagine a professor considering applying and pondering the likelihood of success. "Do I have what it takes to win? The application process requires a great deal of work; there are only a few awards, and it appears that certain kinds of faculty are favored over others. My own chances of winning are difficult to calculate, but they do not look promising. Even if I do win, I am unsure that my career will benefit in the long run. It might be better to invest this time and energy in another publication or grant application. I know that success in research leads to a permanent increase in salary rather than a one-year supplement, and research would impress my promotion committee more than a teaching award is likely to do. Also, my mobility would improve more if I add to my national prestige as a scholar than if I increase my local reputation as a teacher."

This program also conveys the message that, although some teachers deserve special recognition, most do not. The program promotes competition rather than collaboration, and that is likely to be contrary to other values that administrators seek to reinforce. Involvement of the teaching center is also problematic. Its reputation may be tarnished by association with a program in which faculty are losing confidence.

To improve the program's effectiveness in motivating faculty, special attention should be given to expectancy theory.

1. Steps should be taken to strengthen professors' beliefs that the effort of applying is likely to result in success, that is, in gaining an award (the first tenet of expectancy theory). Faculty could calculate their chances more confidently if they had information about selection procedures and criteria and about the characteristics of previous applicants and winners. Feedback should be given to unsuccessful applicants about the strengths and weaknesses of their portfolios (Chaps. 4 and 7 in this volume). To reduce the effort required in applying, the competition might be held in stages, each of which would require more information. Only a few of the most likely winners would then be required to develop a full portfolio (Centra, 1996).

2. The number and type of awards might be modified. Perhaps there should be more award categories, based on styles of teaching, types of courses, career stages, and so forth. Applications might be solicited from groups of faculty rather than only from individuals. As a result, individuals are likely to look more favorably upon their chances of receiving an award.

3. The other tenet of expectancy theory requires strengthened belief that an accomplishment (award) is instrumental for attaining the individual's larger objectives. Workshops might explore other possible outcomes of applying for or winning an award. For example, preparing the portfolio requires a good deal of reflection about teaching, and that process might prompt changes that in turn lead to more effective teaching. Second, the portfolio might be used to strengthen materials submitted during annual merit reviews. Third, if outside referees are part of the award selection process, one's national reputation and potential mobility might be enhanced. How important do potential applicants regard each of these outcomes? (Chap. 7 in this volume).

4. Evaluation of the awards program should assess faculty beliefs about the probability of immediate success, that is, of receiving an award, and beliefs about how success would affect long-term career objectives. Follow-up assessments should demonstrate that submitting an application, even if unsuccessful, has led to improved teaching. Finally, the quality of teaching by those who do receive awards should be monitored in order to demonstrate that awards serve as incentives for improvement, not just as recognition of past achievements (Menges, 1996).

Summary Guidelines for Faculty Development Programs

These scenarios and theories suggest characteristics of faculty development programs which are most likely to foster motivation to teach. In conclusion, here are four guidelines I find most compelling.

1. Collaboration. Senior administrators, faculty development professionals, and faculty themselves should collaborate in efforts to foster motivation to teach. None of these parties benefit unless all benefit.
2. Consistent priorities. Clear positions about the value of teaching in the organization should be articulated. All parties should express these positions consistently through written and oral communications as well as through formal programs.
3. Faculty involvement. Faculty must be the shapers of programs, not just the objects of program activities. Programs reflect the faculty perspective when they attend to faculty beliefs, perceptions, and goals.
4. Individualized, multistage activities. Programs should include opportunities for participating faculty to set individual goals, to monitor progress on their goals, and to experience positive consequences upon

attaining their goals. Single events should be avoided in favor of well-integrated activities that include cycles of goal setting, instruction, practice, and feedback.

Attention to axioms from theories and research on motivation make faculty development more difficult in some respects; subtle features of programs and activities must be examined in ways they would otherwise not have been examined. Such careful examination can lead, however, to programs that have far more positive effects on motivation to teach.

References

Angelo, T. A. (1989). Faculty development *for* learning: The promise of classroom research. In Susan Kahn (Ed.), *To improve the academy* (Vol. 8, pp. 37–60). Stillwater, OK: New Forums Press.

Centra, J. A. (1996). Identifying exemplary teachers: Evidence from colleagues, administrators, and alumni. In M. Svinicki & R. J. Menges (Eds.), *Honoring exemplary teaching*. New Directions for Teaching and Learning. San Francisco: Jossey-Bass.

Finkelstein, M. J., & LaCelle-Peterson, M. W. (Eds.). (1993). *Developing senior faculty as teachers*. New Directions for Teaching and Learning 55. San Francisco: Jossey-Bass.

Froh, R., Menges, R. J., & Walker, C. J. (1993). Revitalizing faculty work through intrinsic rewards. In R. M. Diamond & B. E. Adam (Eds.), *Recognizing faculty work: Reward systems for the year 2000* (pp. 87–95). New Directions for Higher Education 81. San Francisco: Jossey-Bass.

Levinson-Rose, J., & Menges, R. J. (1981). Improving college teaching: A critical review of research. *Review of Educational Research, 51,* 403–434.

Mathis, B. C. (1982). Faculty development. In Harold E. Mitzel (Ed.), *Encyclopedia of Educational Research* (5th ed., pp. 646–655). New York: Free Press.

Menges, R. J. (1991). The real world of teaching improvement: A faculty perspective. In M. Theall & J. Franklin (Eds.), *Effective practices for improving teaching* (pp. 21–37). New Directions for Teaching and Learning 48. San Francisco: Jossey-Bass.

Menges, R. J. (1994). Promoting inquiry into one's own teaching. In K. R. Howey & N. L. Zimpher (Eds.), *Informing faculty development for teacher education* (pp. 51–97). Norwood, NJ: Ablex.

Menges, R. J. (1996). Awards to individuals: A critique of teaching award programs. In M. Svinicki & R. J. Menges (Eds.), *Honoring exemplary teaching*. New Directions for Teaching and Learning. San Francisco: Jossey-Bass.

Menges, R. J., & Brinko, K. T. (1990). A three-dimensional model for planning and assessing faculty development efforts. *Journal of Staff, Program, and Organizational Development, 8,* 133–142.

Menges, R. J., & Mathis, B. C. (1988). *Key resources on teaching, learning, curriculum, and faculty development*. San Francisco: Jossey-Bass.

Rando, W. C., & Lenze, L. F. (1994). *Learning from students: Early term student feedback in higher education*. State College, PA: National Center on Postsecondary Teaching, Learning, and Assessment.

Schneider, B., & Bowen, D. E. (1992). Personnel/human resources management in the service sector. *Research in Personnel and Human Resources Management, 10,* 1–30.

Sorcinelli, M. D., & Austin, A. E. (Eds.). (1992). *Developing new and junior faculty.* New Directions for Teaching and Learning 50. San Francisco: Jossey-Bass.

Tracey, W. R. (1991). *The human resources glossary.* New York: AMACOM—American Management Association.

Walters, R. W. (1985). HRM in perspective. In W. R. Tracey (Ed.), *Human resources management and development handbook* (pp. 3–11). New York: AMACOM—American Management Association.

Weimer, M., & Lenze, L. F. (1991). Instructional interventions: A review of the literature on efforts to improve instruction. In J. C. Smart (Ed.), *Higher education: Handbook of theory and research* (Vol. 7, pp. 294–333). New York: Agathon Press.

21 The Motivation to Teach: Perennial Conundrums

JAMES L. BESS

Motivating faculty to teach in colleges and universities ought not to be a problem. After all, people who choose the academic life are professionals pursuing a high-status career with plentiful opportunities for reward and satisfaction, both internal and external. Yet, with respect to teaching, the perennial lament is that many faculty are frustrated with it, drawn by other incentives away from it, and not sufficiently induced to put effort and time into the activity to perform at high standards (cf. Boyer, 1987; Clark, 1987). Why this is the case has intrigued scholars, worried administrators, and disenchanted faculty themselves. In the chapters preceding this one, a rich and extensive variety of new tools for unraveling these conundrums has been presented. Given the complexity of the subjects and diversity of perspectives, a succinct summary is not possible. There are, however, a number of recurrent themes in the chapters that can usefully be reviewed and integrated here. In this final chapter, therefore, the central issues and perspectives about teaching motivation are recapitulated and some fresh messages presented.

Background

There is abundant evidence that faculty in American higher education are much the same as they have always been and at the same time very different. New generations of students and faculty in a new external social and cultural environment have enacted campuses that are distinctly different from the past in values, expectations, issues, and problems. Nevertheless, the basic form, structure, and goals of higher education remain the same. As institutions with somewhat self-contained aggregates of workers (individuals) linked by their common aim of helping their constituents determine and understand what is going on around and within themselves, colleges and universities constitute one of the primary modern intellectual and psychosocial agoras for collective and individual human growth and development. They also serve the larger society in a variety of ways—in knowledge production and transformation, education and training for the economy, and socialization for citizenship.

Why Study Motivation to Teach?

The need for new insights into faculty motivation seems particularly critical at this time. An increasing number of external constituents are voicing their disappointments with the return on their financial and emotional investments in the education of young people and, by association, with those presumably responsible for that education. Among these constituents are parents, state and local funding agencies, employers, and students themselves. Although these concerned groups have always been capable of expressing their displeasure, their separate rising and waning fortunes over the years reduced the collective impact of their negative evaluations of higher education. In the face of flush public budgets or good employment opportunities, or surplus students, some voices of protest became temporarily muted.

In recent years, however, all of the waves of discontent of these various dissatisfied constituents have crested at the same time, with the result a significant pressure to refocus institutional goals and to redirect faculty energies. As is usually the case, the external impetus to change disturbs the status quo, commands examination of traditional repertoires, insists on new thinking, and impels the creation of new agendas (cf. Becher & Kogan, 1980). Stung and stirred by the now open and apparently widespread criticism, many faculty across the country have confessed to some unhappiness with their work priorities and output. A good number ascribe the cause of their dissatisfaction to imbalances in the external (read "institutional") reward structure, where good research seems more worthy than good teaching (Edgerton, 1993). Others, according to some observers (Boyer, 1990), *inherently* prefer teaching rather than research[1] but have not learned how to access the joys and satisfactions of the former (Bess, 1977).

The worries about and explanations of motivation fall into the two or three categories that social scientists frequently use to describe most human behavior—the idiographic and nomothetic and their interaction effects.[2] The chapters in this book follow this conceptualization. The explanations begin at the central psychological core of individuality, move to the more immediate setting for teaching, and then consider the more distant social influences outside the institution. The material below similarly springs from these fundamental dimensions, though in reverse order. As will be seen, the essential argument to be made is that external normative constraints impede the generation of a local professional culture that supports teaching, that the structure of work in academia ensures the perpetuation of this nonsupportive culture, and that the image of the work lifestyle emanating from the culture and organizational structure attracts recruits to the profession who are not likely to seek or find satisfactions in teaching, thus impeding changes in both structure and culture.

Culture and the Motivation to Teach

The motivational states of all workers, including faculty, are importantly affected by unexamined assumptions that are embedded in culturally generated values. Conceptualizations of motivation in different societies are quite different (cf. Hofstede, 1980). For example, we have common Eurocentric notions of what work means, what we should "get out" of it, how "satisfied" we should be, and whom to blame if we do not derive sufficient rewards from it. We usually compare our own lot with others', and these comparisons very often determine not only the state of our mental well-being but also the effort we are willing to devote to various tasks (Adams, 1963; Huseman, Hatfield, & Miles, 1987). In other countries or even in certain Western settings, the strength of these assumptions is constrained, indeed, generated by indigenous organizational design, work processes, and commitment (cf. Marx in Bottomore & Rubel, 1964). In Japan, for example, motivation and satisfaction stem more from achievement of group than individual goals, work is organized collaboratively, and socialization and norms support both organizational practices and personal satisfactions.

So also with respect to the organization and execution of teaching in American colleges and universities, cultural expectations inhere. Most faculty have become socialized prior to their initial jobs to believe in and expect others to provide acceptable supportive work environments. They anticipate experiencing positive personal feelings associated with their very individualized effort and achievement in a highly competitive system, which is perceived as legitimate. These value premises and associated work arrangements and interaction patterns thus heavily influence the ways faculty come to feel about themselves as "successful" teachers, how they go about trying to find fulfillment through their teaching, and how they respond to frustrations and failures in their teaching. Indeed, expectations of success are often gender and ethnically grounded, thus additionally constraining the perception of opportunities for fulfillment—males, for example, frequently failing to be sensitive to or trained in female ways of looking for and finding/feeling evidence of teaching success.

The Faculty Role

Faculty in higher education are immersed in an organizational setting that is at once a bureaucracy and a polity, oftentimes somewhat anomalously both anarchic and strongly normed. Influences and obligations from beyond the boundaries of the organization with which faculty are titularly affiliated both help to define the role and its performance and to complicate it (Bess, 1992). Within the institution, the faculty are assigned roles that are connected loosely in institutional substructures organized mostly by knowledge boundaries. The individuals who occupy roles as faculty members in higher education bring with them to the work setting both cognitive and professional patterns of thought and habitual behaviors that they have acquired in the course of their role preparation and the idiosyncratic needs and personalities that define them as individuals.

Faculty are both line professionals and middle managers in this changing but not changing organizational system. Their line roles, teaching and research, are carried out through the modulation of knowledge signals they transmit to their constituencies. Teaching and research require interaction with realms of knowledge, the transformation of that knowledge for later use by others, the delivery of the knowledge, and the evaluation of the effectiveness of the knowledge transfer (Bess, 1994). Faculty research and teaching roles are directed at the integration of new knowledge into their clients' extant knowledge structures and thus necessitate an awareness of both cognitive and affective states of readiness among receivers, whether that readiness rests in professional colleagues or in students. In the latter case, students' psychosocial conditions are not only intimately related to receptivity to knowledge but are themselves, from a liberal education perspective, an important and equal object of instruction. Indeed, as Parsons and Platt (1973, pp. 193 ff.) note, faculty should, but usually do not, "lend affect" to students so that the latter can become attached to the cultural consequences of the knowledge they receive. For a variety of reasons, however, faculty give primary allegiance to "cognitive rationality," leaving to others (now an enormous student affairs administration and students themselves) the tasks of psychosocial student development. This bias toward rationality further inures faculty to the nuances of teaching and predisposes them to seek satisfactions largely through cognitive feedback.

Most faculty, in other words, are involved largely in decisions about how to establish an efficient articulation between themselves as knowledge holders and producers and others as potential knowledge users. They are also involved, though less purposefully, with manifesting a relationship between themselves and others which is mutually satisfying, which provides opportunities for growth, satisfaction, and joy.

There are a number of interfaces between faculty and two sets of significant others: (1) the relatively more sophisticated users of research productivity (the public consumers of information for a variety of purposes, utilitarian or consummatory); and (2) the relatively naive users (students). Of these two interfaces across which faculty operate, the first—primarily between faculty and other scholars—is impersonal and largely cognitive/rational. The primary media of this interface are print and increasingly (though still exiguously) electronic forms. The second interface—between faculty and students—is both cognitive/rational and affective, linking faculty with students in their cognitive and psychosocial naiveté. The media of this interface are also print and, to an increasing extent, electronic forms (e.g., E-mail) but also face-to-face interactions. The motivation of faculty to cross these interfaces involves preferences *both* for interaction with the recipients of the knowledge transfer and for the particular media that must be employed. For some faculty, interaction with certain recipients is not of interest. For some faculty also, the media are unfamiliar, cumbersome, and poorly organized, further confusing the teaching enterprise and confounding the opportunities for positive motivation. Reaching across the interfaces to a foreign public via a varied set of media is difficult and confusing.

Faculty also tend to view the world as sequential, logical, and meaningful. As postmodernists now frequently remind us (cf. Tierney, 1993), however, the apparent continuities in paradigmatic and would-be paradigmatic disciplines may not mirror the reality of life. Further, as Harland Bloland (1994) tells us, the hallowed traditions of merit, community, and institutional autonomy have slippery meanings in the postmodern modes of thought (cf. Bergquist, 1993). These more traditional biases of faculty may result in behaviors that are quite inappropriate to the subtleties of the highly differentiated clientele faculty serve in their teaching roles. For example, for those faculty seeking meaning and satisfaction primarily in the "logical" consequences that they believe should follow from their teaching efforts, alternative evidence of "success" (itself a modernist word) in their encounters with students and their efforts may not even be observed or may be deemed irrelevant to their ideologies and associated perceptual screens. The result for these faculty, who are still in the large majority, is an undermining of the likelihood of sustained motivation to teach.

Is it any wonder, then, that the motivational complexities of faculty are manifold, mysterious, and cryptic? The meanings and weights of the multiple influences on faculty behavior and thought must be teased out with a variety of subtle tools of analysis. One hopes that the earlier chapters in this book have contributed to understanding these puzzlements.

Educational Goals and the Organization of Teaching

Faculty usually make unquestioned assumptions about the goals of education and of their own pedagogical efforts. Hence, concerning teaching, they have expectations of what should be its visible outcomes and how it should be conducted. For example, most faculty tend to believe that acquisition by students of subject matter content is the telling cue to the faculty member's success. They believe also that integration of subject matters across different disciplines in a liberal education is not their responsibility. It is the student's. The latter must integrate the disparate ideas garnered from different courses. In effect, colleges and universities "employ" students (without salary) to be their own teachers,[3] partly because the predominant organizational model of teaching is one of a dispersed, factory-like attachment of knowledge components to students' intellectual chassis as they proceed through their undergraduate years. But (to abuse the metaphor somewhat) the students must themselves, without guidance, decide how the biology steering wheel is connected to the philosophy front wheels and the sociology brakes.[4] In the parlance of organizational design, faculty are in a "pooled" relationship to one another and to the composite product they produce (Thompson, 1967). The assumption is that faculty need not interact in order for the institution to accomplish its goals successfully. Such assumptions, of course, predispose faculty to seek satisfactions in teaching through isolated experiences rather than through collegial collaboration. The isolation of the teaching-learning task design fits their dispositions, moreover, since it matches the pattern of behavior they found in their successful undergraduate and graduate years, when long, hard solitary study meant sacrificing social satisfactions.

The Relation of Organizational Structure to Values

As organizational workers, faculty make commitments to produce that are sustained on the basis of inducements that the organization offers (Barnard, 1966). Their motivational states are thus a function of organizational conditions that can vary and are therefore subject to manipulation. Organizational structures, like the structural elements of society, inexorably give rise to values and beliefs that rationalize and support those structures. In a reflection of some historical materialism, the quintessential formal organizational structure for academic work in higher education—the department—was firmly and almost inextricably confirmed in its present form in the late nineteenth century (cf. McHenry, 1977). Originally a locus for organizing liberal arts studies for eighteen- to twenty-year-olds (or younger), the department began to change its focus and objectives by the end of this period. With the requirement that like-minded faculty be able to converse easily for the purpose of producing warrantable *new* knowledge to be fed into the emerging American industrial revolution, the research role was grafted onto the extant departmental structure, the result of which was flowering of the research graft and the allocation to the teaching stock of a pedestrian supporting role. With the addition of research and associated external professional societies that support publications circumscribed by disciplines, the departmental form of organization now largely serves research needs. Since research is conducted primarily in universities, and since these universities produce the scholar-teachers for the world of higher education, the departmental form of organization extends to the nonuniversity—that is, B.A. and A.A. institutions—as well. The values of research, then, dominate higher education at least partly because the research-focused structure of higher education generates them. In point of fact the very design of the craft of research generates a set of values, attitudes, expectations, and confirming behaviors that predispose faculty members to be motivated in various degrees toward that enterprise and to give minimal obeisance to other "non-valued" work (cf. Bensman & Lilienfeld, 1973; Clark, 1984).

Our expectations of people in work settings are determined by our perspectives on how people should and do become "engaged" with a variety of elements in work environments—for example, with "data, people, and things" at work (cf. U.S. Employment Service, 1986). That is, faculty arrive on their jobs anticipating a mix of task-related stimuli, with regard to each of which they look for some reaction, both behaviorally and intrinsically. They are conditioned not only by their prior socialization but also by biogenetic impulses that impel them to seek out stimuli that they have found rewarding.

The aggregation of faculty into subject matter departments, in other words, fits a need for communication among faculty engaged in subject-related research rather than a need to deliver services to students. Changing faculty motivation to teach, therefore, will require a fundamental change in the structure of the modes of interaction required for teaching. This in turn involves some reconceptualization by faculty of the meaning of liberal education and the organizational requirements for achieving it. Importantly, accompanying this shift in understanding will be the recognition that it is unreasonable to expect that the same faculty can both teach and conduct research using a *common* organizational structure. Different kinds of faculty and different structures for teaching and research are needed. This will in turn demand a change in professional preparation.

Is Teaching a "Profession"?

Given the nature of the selection, training, and evaluation processes for faculty in higher education, there is some considerable question whether teaching in colleges and universities is currently a "profession" (a subject of long-standing debate). The extensive literature on professionalism is in general agreement about what constitutes a profession. As characterized by Pavalko (1971), there are seven dimensions that distinguish an occupation from a profession: a body of knowledge and techniques developed by and honed by members of the profession, relevance to social welfare, an extensive training period, altruistic motivation, a commitment to a "calling," the existence of a community, and a code of ethics. There is some doubt, however, that "teaching" possesses many or even any of these. Yet faculty are expected to be motivated *as professionals* in their capacities as teachers. Just as the structure of research generates work values and orientations for faculty that compromise their commitment to teaching, so also the absence of professionalism in the teaching domain predisposes faculty to treat it as an occupation of lower status. Thus, in addition to changing the internal structure of colleges and universities to reflect teaching needs, the degree requirements for becoming and remaining a teacher must be significantly revised, as must the patterns of socialization during graduate study. As more faculty as teaching professionals are turned out of graduate schools, there will emerge a significant externally supportive complex of professional bodies. Currently, formal groups of faculty who are committed to teaching are still inchoate and are attached to larger professional associations dominated by research agendas and goals (e.g., the American Sociological Association and the Academy of Management). The circulations of journals dedicated to teaching in different disciplines are typically in the low hundreds and are addressed not so much to faculty as teachers as to faculty as scholars of teaching.

The most profound difficulty in professionalizing teaching in higher education is that most of the rewards of teaching are intrinsic while a significant amount of the rewards of research are extrinsic—for example, recognition of colleagues. In societies in which the status of occupations and the achievements within them are hierarchically organized, it is difficult for individuals to be content with intrinsic satisfactions alone. National prestige as a published scholar is accorded much higher status (by most, though obviously not all) than being a great teacher in one's own eyes and perhaps those of one's students and campus colleagues. It becomes, therefore, most important to identify as potential faculty individuals who are willing to take on this less socially rewarded role and who are likely to find satisfaction in it.

Idiocentric Approaches to Understanding Faculty Motivation to Teach

There are *some* internal organizational environmental conditions that can affect all faculty, in terms of both their intrinsic and extrinsic motivational "potential" (cf. Oldham & Kulik, 1984; Kulik, 1989). As Hackman and Oldham (1976) note, different individuals vary in the extent of their "growth need strength"—their desire for personal development. The conditions of work thus affect some individuals more than others, and different kinds of organizational levers, including leadership, are needed to deal with these differences.

It is likely, however, that most faculty have chosen their careers in anticipation of the opportunity to conduct research and to write about it. Those who persist through the rigors of the route to the Ph.D. are dedicated. They are driven by their image of the professorial life, however distorted that image may be. Their initial understanding of what it means to be a faculty member, originating in late undergraduate college years, is sustained and deepened by professionalizing and socializing contact with faculty mentors, who have been similarly trained (Bess, 1978). Faced with the demand to be effective in an occupation for which they are ill prepared and presented with quite different demands from their expectations, new faculty quickly become disenchanted and resort to "defensive" teaching (Boice, 1991).

Explanations of poor teaching include not only lack of ability but also, as Walker and Symons point out in Chapter 1 of this volume, low perceived self-efficacy (Bandura, 1993). Bandura explains that

> people who have a low sense of efficacy in a given domain shy away from difficult tasks, which they perceive as personal threats. They have low aspirations and weak commitment to the goals they choose to pursue. They maintain a self-diagnostic focus rather than concentrate on how to perform successfully. When faced with difficult tasks, they dwell on their personal deficiencies, on the obstacles they will encounter, and on all kinds of adverse outcomes.

There are four experiential ingredients that contribute to self-efficacy: enactive mastery or personal achievements, vicarious experience via modeling, verbal persuasion, and psychological threat (Bandura, 1982; cf. Gist & Mitchell, 1992). Most faculty choose their careers because they are confirmed successful student academics who see their futures in terms of the models of professors whose own success has been manifested in the research/publication tradition. Their self-efficacy has been developed through scholarship and writing as undergraduates and graduate students. Because of this career selection process, the pressures, frustrations, and challenges of teaching often force a decline in faculty feelings of self-efficacy in the teaching domain.

It is reasonable to believe, consequently, that not a few faculty come to accept unconsciously their lack of ability to teach well. In many ways, their condition is one of "learned helplessness" (Peterson & Seligman, 1993; Seligman, 1975). Their expectancies (in the language of expectancy theory) are more or less permanently low. They have come to believe that they cannot teach well. To avoid depression and feelings of guilt and shame, they seek self-esteem and enhancement in other, more rewarding activities, especially those for which they have already demonstrated some competence—research. They choose less ambitious teaching goals, work less diligently toward them, and achieve less (cf. Collins, 1992), or they find the necessity to elevate their self-esteem by placing themselves in positions of superiority vis-à-vis their teaching charges. In a larger sense, as David

McClelland (1967; McClelland & Winter, 1969) points out, "nPower" people—those seeking to dominate others—are "more likely to have glamorous lives" (Lemann, 1994) than "nAchievement" people—those seeking to find the most efficient means to accomplish tangible results. That is, power is exhilarating, according to McClelland, whereas incremental achievement is merely satisfying.[5]

Who are the faculty in American higher education? The pedestrian publisher who plots and plods? Or the risk taker who, as Lemann (1994) notes, would rather bet on a single number than on red or black? It is entirely possible that most faculty are nAchievers who aspire to be powerful, ever hoping that the most recently published article will miraculously be recognized as the definitive or breakthrough statement.

The route to power, however, appears to them not through teaching—especially to students whose slower, incremental learning abilities often reveal to professionally untrained faculty only barely perceptible growth. It is not surprising then that teaching for them is less than exhilarating. As noted earlier, what is needed, consequently, is the identification of faculty—through recruitment and judicious selection and encouragement of extant faculty—who seek the adventure of nAchievement through teaching. *They* see their own success in terms of students. They see the nuances of student learning, however slow, not as an opportunity for them to exert power or to dominate but as achievement of worthy goals, intelligently and imaginatively set.

Change Modes—Idiographic and Nomothetic

In the literature on organizational change, two camps are joined in a continuing controversy. One argues that structural change must precede attempts to change individuals, the other that individual and collective attitudes and values must first be addressed before change can take place. Between these two sectors a third, the sociotechnical (Cherns, 1987; Pava, 1986), recognizes the necessity to take both into account. The design of work must identify individual and social needs as well as institutional requirements for productivity. A social-psychological perspective (Sherif, 1979) is essential.

How, then, can at least some scholar-teachers be changed into teacher-scholars? How can a frustrated teacher be changed into a motivated teacher? How transform a confused teacher into one with purpose? And how identify and recruit persons whose personality dynamics strongly predispose them to seek the rewards of teaching rather than research? The point of these questions is to illustrate that there is no one institutional answer to the improvement of teaching motivation. There are as many answers as faculty members, but parsimony and the need for efficiency demand some generalized action. It should be clear from the arguments above that fundamental changes in the design of universities is a sine qua non of better motivation to teach. Organizing the university for teaching (as well as research in comprehensive colleges and universities) will create a market for individuals psychologically oriented toward that career, and it will create a work environment whose norms place high value on achievement in teaching. Such an organizational configuration may also educe the formation of professional societies that give external recognition to teaching, at least partly mitigating the apparent motivational shortfall of *only* self- or local approbation. Opportunities for intrinsic satisfaction from work are more likely to result from the matching of personal psyches and organizational and professional conditions that are supportive of strong effort and commitment. This "fit" between individual and organization has long been seen as an essential prerequisite to high-quality performance (Lofquist & Dawis, 1969; Edwards, 1991).[6]

Conclusion

In the discussion of motivation, as many of the chapters in this book reported, the question of the source of control over behavior is pervasive. Harking back to fundamental philosophical conundrums as well as to continuing contemporary debates in psychology and organizational theory about the balance of personal and social influences on behavior, the motivational literature provides no unambiguous guidance that usefully informs the practice of improving faculty motivation. In eclectic fashion, the chapters in this book avoid a conflict over the "truth" and seek instead to provide multiple possible explanations. The basic assumption of the book is that academic leaders can utilize many approaches and can have an effect on motivation. The levers they may use are both external and internal, with the former orchestrated to act on the latter in most cases, though depending on specifics, some motivators are explicitly external. The arenas of influence begin far outside with the general public, include professional associations, graduate programs, the academic marketplace, the college culture, and the departmental environment, and move to and inside the individual.

In the final analysis, the improvement of faculty motivation to teach depends on how faculty make sense of their work environments. Karl Weick

(1993) reports: "Commitment focuses sense making on three things: an action, a socially acceptable justification for that action, and the potential of subsequent activities to validate the justification. Thus commitment is an outcome of improvised design that facilitates interpretation."

Faculty must be helped to see that their involvement in teaching makes sense to them in terms of the perpetuation or accentuation of their conception of themselves as autonomous, effective human service professionals engaged in a task that provides and promises to continue to provide sustained good feelings. The structure of the environment in which faculty work must be matched to the needs of a new breed of professional teachers who see teaching as their central life interest.

How to break into the mutually reinforcing hold that culture, structure, and personality have on the traditional faculty member's orientation to teaching calls for an answer with which change agents in all environments continually struggle. There is hope and promise for the future, for teaching is, after all, a potential source of answers to life's most profound questions: who am I, how am I connected to others, how can and do my interactions with others provide sustenance and quality to my intellectual and emotional life? When faculty come to see teaching as providing answers to these conundrums, they will be motivated to teach well—and to like it.

Notes

1. Such reports must be viewed with caution, of course, as "below average" faculty in research productivity are discouraged by the current highly competitive research environment and the associated winner-loser, zero-sum status and reward hierarchy that follows from it. More on this later.

2. For a systematic discussion of extant theories on situational and dispositional explanations of behavior, see the collection of articles on this subject edited by Mitchell and James (1989).

3. Under different circumstances and with proper guidance, such self-directed integration could be an excellent learning/growing experience; but that is not the situation at present.

4. The particular disciplines or vehicle parts are irrelevant to the metaphor.

5. Although Judith Glazer (Chap. 3 in this volume) concludes that McClelland's theory ignores women's achievement motives, here we argue only that research-oriented faculty—of which the vast majority of faculty, male *and* female, are (Boyer's findings to the contrary notwithstanding)—when frustrated in their research achievement will employ their excessive power motives in the classroom.

6. For those who would argue that such specialization of function carries with it the danger of a return to the scientific management theories of Frederick Taylor, it is important to remember that "professions" are controlled by their members, not by management. For others who worry that the separation of teaching and research will vitiate

the innovativeness of teaching, the expanded definition of teaching to include curricular research, but not necessarily publication, will still be necessary (cf. Parsons & Platt, 1973, p. 141, on the "necessity" for specialization in academia).

References

Adams, J. S. (1963). Toward an understanding of inequity. *Journal of Abnormal and Social Psychology, 67,* 422–436.

Bandura, A. (1982). Self-efficacy mechanisms in human agency. *American Psychologist, 37,* 122–147.

Bandura, A. (1993). Perceived self-efficacy in cognitive development and functioning. *Educational Psychologist, 28*(2), 117–148.

Barnard, C. I. (1966). *The functions of the executive.* Cambridge: Harvard University Press.

Becher, T., & Kogan, M. (1980). *Process and structure in higher education.* London: Heinemann.

Bensman, J., & Lilienfeld, R. (1973). *Craft and consciousness: Occupational technique and the development of world images.* New York: Wiley.

Bergquist, W. (1993). *The postmodern organization: Mastering the art of irreversible change.* San Francisco: Jossey-Bass.

Bess, J. L. (1977). The motivation to teach. *Journal of Higher Education, 48,* 243–258.

Bess, J. L. (1978). Anticipatory socialization of graduate students. *Research in Higher Education, 8,* 289–317.

Bess, J. L. (1990). College teachers, miscast professionals. *Change, 22*(3), 18–22.

Bess, J. L. (1992). Collegiality: Toward a clarification of meaning and function. In J. C. Smart (Ed.), *Higher education: Handbook of theory and research* (Vol. 6, pp. 1–36). New York: Agathon Press.

Bess, J. L. (1993). Sow's ears and silk purses: Can teachers be made if they're not born to the task? In M. Weimer (Ed.), *Faculty as teachers: Taking stock of what we know* (pp. 21–24). University Park, PA: National Center on Postsecondary Teaching, Learning, and Assessment.

Bess, J. L. (1994, April). Tasks of teaching and teams of teachers: Disaggregating the role and linking the specialists. Paper presented at the annual meeting of the American Educational Association, New Orleans.

Bloland, H. (1994, April). Postmodernism and higher education. Unpublished paper, Winter Park, FL.

Boice, R. (1991). New faculty as teachers. *Journal of Higher Education, 62,* 150–173.

Bottomore, T. B., & Rubel, M. (Eds.). (1964). *Karl Marx: Selected writings in sociology and social philosophy.* New York: McGraw-Hill.

Boyer, E. L. (1987). *College: The undergraduate experience in America.* New York: Harper & Row.

Boyer, E. L. (1990). *Scholarship reconsidered: Priorities of the professoriate.* Princeton: Carnegie Foundation for the Advancement of Teaching.

Cherns, A. (1987). Principles of sociotechnical design revisited. *Human Relations, 40*(3), 153–162.

Clark, B. R. (1984). The organizational conception. In B. R. Clark (Ed.), *Perspectives on higher education: Eight disciplinary and comparative views* (pp. 106–131). Berkeley: University of California Press.

Clark, B. R. (1987). *The academic life*. Princeton: Carnegie Foundation for the Advancement of Teaching.

Collins, J. L. (1992, March). Self-efficacy and ability in achievement behavior. Paper presented at the annual meeting of the American Educational Research Association, New York.

Edgerton, R. (1993). The reexamination of faculty priorities. *Change, 25*(4), 10–25.

Edwards, J. R. (1991). Person-job fit: A conceptual integration, literature review, and methodological critique. *International Review of Industrial and Organizational Psychology, 6*, 283–357.

Gist, M. E., & Mitchell, T. R. (1992). Self-efficacy: A theoretical analysis of its determinants and malleability. *Academy of Management Review, 17*(2), 183–211.

Hackman, J. R., & Oldham, G. R. (1976). Motivation through the design of work: Test of a theory. *Organizational Behavior and Human Performance, 16*, 270–279.

Hofstede, G. H. (1980). *Culture's consequences: International differences in work-related values*. Beverly Hills: Sage.

Huseman, R. C., Hatfield, J. D., & Miles, E. A. (1987). A new perspective on equity theory: The equity sensitivity construct. *Academy of Management Review, 12*, 222–234.

Kulik, C. T. (1989). The effects of job categorization on judgments of the motivating potential of jobs. *Administrative Science Quarterly, 34*(1), 68–90.

Lemann, N. (1994, February). Is there a science of success? *Atlantic Monthly*, 83–98.

Lofquist, L., & Dawis, R. (1969). *Adjustment to work: A psychological view of man's problems in a work-oriented society*. Englewood Cliffs, NJ: Prentice-Hall.

McClelland, D. C. (1967). *The achieving society*. New York: Van Nostrand.

McClelland, D. C., & Winter, D. G. (1969). *Motivating economic achievement*. New York: Free Press.

McHenry, D. E., & Associates. (1977). *Academic departments: Problems, variations, and alternatives*. San Francisco: Jossey-Bass.

Mitchell, T. R., & James, L. R. (1989a). Situational versus dispositional factors—competing explanations of behavior—conclusions and future directions. *Academy of Management Review, 14*(3), 401–407.

Mitchell, T. R., & James, L. R. (1989b). Theory development forum—situational versus dispositional factors—competing explanations of behavior—introduction and background. *Academy of Management Review, 14*(3), 330–332.

Oldham, G., & Kulik, C. T. (1984). Motivation enhancement through work redesign. In J. L. Bess (Ed.), *College and university organization: Insights from the behavioral sciences* (pp. 85–104). New York: New York University Press.

Parsons, T., & Platt, G. M. (1973). *The American university*. Cambridge: Harvard University Press.

Pava, C. (1986). Redesigning sociotechnical systems design: Concepts and methods for the 1990's. *Journal of Applied Behavioral Science, 22*, 201–221.

Pavalko, R. M. (1971). *Sociology of occupations and professions*. Itasca, IL: F. E. Peacock.

Peterson, C., & Seligman, M. E. P. (1993). *Learned helplessness: A theory for the age of personal control*. New York: Oxford University Press.

Seligman, M. E. P. (1975). *Helplessness: On depression, development, and death*. San Francisco: W. W. Freeman.

Sherif, C. W. (1979). Social values, attitudes, and involvement of the self. In Monte M. Page (Ed.), *Nebraska symposium on motivation* (Vol. 27, pp. 1–64). Lincoln: University of Nebraska Press.

Thompson, J. D. (1967). *Organizations in action*. New York: McGraw-Hill.

Tierney, W. G. (1993). *Building communities of difference: Higher education in the twenty-first century.* Westport, CT: Bergin & Garvey.

United States Employment Service. (1986). *Dictionary of occupational titles* (4th ed.). Washington, DC: U.S. Department of Labor.

Weick, K. E. (1993). Organizational redesign as improvisation. In G. P. Huber & W. H. Glick (Eds.), *Organizational change and redesign: Ideas and insights for improving performance* (pp. 346–379). New York: Oxford University Press.

Contributors

Max Bazerman is the J. Jay Gerber Professor of Dispute Resolution and Organizations at the J. L. Kellogg Graduate School of Management, Northwestern University, Evanston, Illinois.

James L. Bess is professor of higher education, Department of Administration, Leadership, and Technology, School of Education, New York University.

Janice M. Beyer is the Rebecca L. Gale Regents Professor in Business in the Management Department, Graduate School of Business, and professor of sociology, at the University of Texas, Austin.

Robert T. Blackburn is professor of higher education at the Center for the Study of Higher Education, University of Michigan, Ann Arbor.

Mihaly Csikszentmihalyi is professor of human development in the Department of Psychology and Education at the University of Chicago.

Soosan Daghighi is assistant dean, executive programs, at the Faculty of Management, University of Toronto.

Edward L. Deci is professor of psychology, University of Rochester, Rochester, New York.

Diane M. Dunlap is Dean of the Graduate School, Hamline University, St. Paul, Minnesota.

Martin Finkelstein is director, New Jersey Institute for Collegiate Teaching and Learning, Seton Hall University, South Orange, New Jersey.

Dorothy E. Finnegan is assistant professor of higher education, The College of William and Mary, Williamsburg, Virginia.

Judith S. Glazer is professor, Department of Curriculum and Instruction, School of Education, Long Island University, Brookville, New York.

Douglas T. Hall is professor, Organizational Behavior, and director of the Executive Development Roundtable, School of Management, Boston University.

J. G. Hunt is the Paul Whitfield Horn Professor of Management, College of Business Administration, Texas Tech University, Lubbock.

Tim Kasser is in the Department of Psychology, Knox College, Galesburg, Illinois.

Gary P. Latham is the Secretary of State Professor of Organizational Effectiveness in the Faculty of Management, University of Toronto.

Edwin A. Locke is in the College of Business and Management, University of Maryland, College Park.

Wilbert J. McKeachie is professor of psychology and research scientist at the Center for Research on Learning and Teaching, University of Michigan, Ann Arbor.

Robert J. Menges is professor of education and social policy and director of the Center for the Teaching Professions, Northwestern University, Evanston, Illinois.

Richard T. Mowday is the Gerald B. Bashaw Professor of Management and Associate Dean, Lundquist College of Business, University of Oregon.

Sang H. Nam is assistant professor of management, Faculty of Business, University of Victoria, British Columbia, Canada.

Walter R. Nord is professor of management at the College of Business Administration, University of South Florida, Tampa, Florida.

Violina P. Rindova is in the Leonard N. Stern School of Business, New York University.

Arja Ropo is associate professor of management in the School of Business Administration, University of Tampere, Tampere, Finland.

Richard M. Ryan is professor of psychology, University of Rochester, Rochester, New York.

Jack H. Schuster is professor of education and public policy, Center for Educational Studies, the Claremont Graduate School, Claremont, California.

Daryl G. Smith is professor of education and psychology, Center for Educational Studies, the Claremont Graduate School, Claremont, California.

Joseph Stetar is associate professor of education, Seton Hall University, South Orange, New Jersey.

Stephen A. Stumpf is dean of the College of Business and Graduate Studies, and director of the Center for Leadership, at The University of Tampa, Tampa, Florida.

Cynthia Symons is assistant professor of psychology, Houghton College, Houghton, New York.

Martin Trow is professor in the Graduate School of Public Policy, University of California, Berkeley.

Charles J. Walker is professor in the Department of Psychology, Saint Bonaventure University, St. Bonaventure, New York.

Name Index

Subject Index

abilities, 27, 225–26, 228–29. *See also* competence; self-efficacy

academic culture. *See* organizational culture

academic labor market, 337–39, 373–74; career stages, 339; class distinctions, 352–53; demographic variables, 340–43; ethnic bias, 348–50; gender bias, 348–52; internal markets, 344–47; market equity, 348, 354–55; mobility, 346; supply and demand, 340–42

accountability, 338, 369–71, 425. *See also* performance review; teaching evaluation

accreditation, 371–72

achievement, 27, 42–46, 49–51

acquired needs theory, 6, 39, 42–45, 146–47, 230, 434, 436

administrators, 66–67, 219, 421. *See also* faculty-administrator conflict

affiliation, 42–46, 49–51

alienation from work, 73–75

assessment, 33, 268, 369, 390. *See also* accountability; accreditation

attributional theory, 147

autonomy, 59, 61–63, 65–67, 177, 306

autotelic learning, 85

behaviorism, 101–2

behavior modification, 5–6; administrative control, 94–95; change rate, 95; ecological design, 99; inappropriate rewards, 105–6; institutional decentralization, 94–95; modeling (vicarious learning), 99–100, 433; operant conditioning, 100–106; performance review, 101, 103, 105; positive reinforcement, 101–2, 117–18; respondent conditioning, 97–99; response repertoire, 106; shaping, 106

British education. *See* Great Britain

campus climate, 97, 252–55, 309

capabilities: individual, 27, 225–26, 228–29; organizational, 225–26, 229–30, 239–40

career stages, faculty, 28–33, 186–87, 304, 314–16; choice of career, 28–29; direct evidence for, 316–17; indirect evidence for, 317–19; labor market, 339; mature years, 32–33; midcareer, 31–32; motivational changes, 321; nontenured years, 29–31, 118; promotions, 155

Carnegie-Mellon University, 181–82

ceremonies, 98–99

challenge-skills balance, 27, 84, 209

Cinderella complex, 43

Civil Rights Act of 1964, 349

classroom: climate, 252–53, 259–60; control, 84–85; distractions, 84, 212; structure, 86–87, 97, 99

class size, 263

Library of Congress Cataloging-in-Publication Data

Teaching well and liking it : motivating faculty to teach effectively / edited by James L. Bess.
    p.   cm.
Includes bibliographical references and index.
ISBN 0-8018-5364-8 (hc : alk. paper)
   1. College teaching—United States.   2. Motivation in education—United States.
3. College teachers—Job satisfaction—United States.   4. Universities and colleges—United
States—Sociological aspects.   I. Bess, James L.
LB2331.T4246   1997
378.1'25—dc20   96-12049